PART-TIME TRAVEL AGENT

PART-TIME
TRAVEL AGENT

How To Cash In On The Exciting NEW World Of Travel Marketing

Kelly Monaghan

PART-TIME TRAVEL AGENT
How To Cash In On The Exciting
NEW World Of Travel Marketing

First printing July 1994

For information contact
The Intrepid Traveler
P.O. Box 438
New York, NY 10034

ISBN 0-9627892-4-0
LOC 93-081280

Publisher's Cataloguing in Publication Data
Prepared by Sanford Berman, Head Cataloger, Hennepin County Library, Minnetonka, MN.

Monaghan, Kelly
Part-time travel agent: how to cash in on the exciting NEW world of travel marketing.
New York: The Intrepid Traveler, copyright 1994.
PARTIAL CONTENTS: How you can become a travel agent — today! —Fine art of
selling travel. —Resource section. Guide to travel suppliers. On-line services. Travel industry organizations & associations. Travel schools. Further reading.
1. Travel agents — Vocational guidance. 2. Travel agencies — Management. 3. Travel
— Information services — Directories. 4. Travel schools — Directories. 5. Selling — Travel.
6. Tourist trade — Directories. 7. Tourist trade — Vocational guidance. 8. Home businesses
— Management. 9. Part-time self-employment. I. Intrepid Traveler. II. Title. III. Title: World
of travel marketing. IV. Title: Travel marketing. V. Title: New world of travel marketing.
910.068

Acknowledgements

A book like this doesn't just happen. I have relied on the goodwill and patience of numerous people both in and out of the travel industry. Thanks to readers Max Bowermeister of Travel Vistas and Doug Payette of Leisure Resource for reading early drafts and keeping me honest. A tip of the hat is also due to Sanford Berman, who was kind enough to provide CIP data for the book. Thanks, too, to my editor and wife Sally Scanlon for creating style and consistency where none had existed.

A special note of thanks is due Captain Bill Miller, CTC, who graciously agreed to pore over several versions of a very large manuscript in various stages of completion. His insight, advice, and his cheerful encouragement were of inestimable help.

Table Of Contents

Introduction

Travel! Adventure! Romance!

The three seem to go together naturally, don't they? So is it any wonder that thousands and thousands of people (maybe you?) dream of escaping from their humdrum lives to a new lifestyle that will let them sail the seven seas, climb the highest mountains, explore the four corners of the earth? A career that will actually let them get paid for doing something they love?

Of course there are any number of careers that involve travel on a regular basis. The military ("Join the Navy and see the world!"), the airlines, diplomacy, import/export, international trade, cruise ships — all these jobs involve travel. And chances are, if you're reading this book, you've dreamed of having one of those jobs at some point in your life. Unfortunately, most people never get past the dreaming stage. After all, deciding that what you *really* want to do is be a jet pilot or the captain of the *Love Boat* is one thing. Doing it is something else again. Not just anyone can be a jet pilot. Or a ship's captain. Or a diplomat. There's a lot of specialized (and expensive) training involved. Age can also be a factor. After all, not too many forty-year-olds are accepted in the Army. Not too many twenty-year-olds are appointed ambassador.

Another problem with many of the more traditional travel-oriented careers is that the job, not you, determines where you travel. The military officer goes where the government decides (and often finds people shooting at him when he gets there). The airline pilot shuttles back and forth endlessly between City A and City B. The career foreign service officer develops an expertise in Latin America and never sees the Far East.

Small wonder, then, that many people see the travel agency business as an inviting alternative. I sure did! Travel agents get to really *see* the world, I thought. They can travel where they want, when they want, and they get all sorts of great discounts when they do! What a great job! But then the doubts started creeping in: It's a whole new career. It requires all sorts of specialized training. It means a major commitment to opening an office, investing in fancy computer equipment, managing a staff. Ugh.

For a while, it seemed like just another dream deferred. But through a combination of perseverance and plain good luck, I stumbled on a way of getting into the travel agency business on my own terms. A way in which I could tailor the travel industry to me rather than the other way around. This book is about what I discovered.

These aren't precisely "secrets," but I've learned that very few people are aware of how easy it is to get into the travel game, on your own terms, in your own time, at your own level of commitment.

Do you just want to go on the occasional tour with a bunch of your friends or fellow club members? There's a way to do that!

Do you want to send your teenager on a "Grand Tour" of Europe for free? There's a way to do that!

Do you want to be a travel agent but avoid getting bogged down in fighting for the lowest airfare in a crazy fare-war atmosphere? There's a way to do that!

Are you interested in dealing in luxury cruises and nothing but luxury cruises? There's a way to do that!

Are you looking for a part-time job that will cover the mortgage or pay the private school tuition or allow you to stay home with the kids? There's a way to do that!

Would you like to make your entire living in the travel industry? There's a way to do that!

Do you just want to "try it on for size" before making a firm decision on whether selling travel is right for you? There's a way to do that!

Would you like to take your time learning the travel business, never exceeding your comfort level? There's a way to do that!

Would you be interested in making a nice income just by showing other people and businesses how to save money on travel? There's a way to do that!

Do you have zero interest in selling travel but still wouldn't mind saving a couple of hundred dollars every time you and your spouse take a vacation? There's a way to do that, too!

The new world of travel

Today it is possible to get involved in the travel industry almost instantaneously, with little or no experience or training, and start learning the business through actual hands-on experience in selling travel. By the time you finish this book, you will have all the information you need to begin a money-making part-time (or full-time!) travel career just by sharing the fun and excitement of travel with your friends and neighbors. I'll even tell you how to become affiliated with a multi-million dollar travel agency, immediately, and at absolutely no cost to you other than the price of a first-class stamp.

Here are just some of the ways you can participate in the exciting and lucrative world of travel as a part-time tour organizer or travel agent. One or more of these options is bound to be right for you.

- *Organize an educational tour.* Many tour operators who target their tours to the educational market are eager to find people like you who will round up a group of school kids for a foreign tour. In exchange for your efforts (and assuming you bring in enough business) you will receive a free trip for yourself and perhaps a cash payment to help defray additional expenses. You can often get a free trip by signing up as few as six kids.

- *Take your club on a tour.* If you belong to a group — a bridge club, the Kiwanis, the Podunk Marching and Chowder Society — you can organize a tour. Most of the time you will be dealing through a travel agent, less frequently directly with a tour operator. In exchange for bringing in a group of people, you (and the other folks on the tour) will receive a cheaper rate. In addition, as the organizer you may be in line for a "tour conductor" slot; in other words your friends not only pay less but you go along for free.

- *Take a cruise.* Many cruise lines offer programs similar to those offered by the educational tour operators — bring in enough couples and you cruise for free.

- *Become a "finder" for a travel agency.* Many travel agents will give you a finder's fee just for bringing in business. In this arrangement, you do none of the work of helping the customer decide which tour or cruise to take nor do you make the bookings. The travel agent does all that. You just get the customer through the door. But make no mistake, that is a valuable service and the travel agent will pay you a small cut of the commission. Typically you will get 20% of the commission (roughly 2% of the cost of the trip).

- *Become an outside sales representative for a travel agency.* This is the core relationship in the part-time travel business. I believe that after you read this book and realize how easy it is to become an outside rep and how many advantages this relationship offers you will become one as soon as possible. In this arrangement, you not only find the customer but you handle all the details of the booking as well. Because only certified travel agencies can purchase travel products and get the commission, you will have to hand the booking over to the agency. The agency just does the paperwork. In exchange for your doing most of the work, the agency will split the commission with you. A typical split is 50/50, but I'll show you how you can get even more!

These opportunities exist because of some very simple and easy-to-understand facts of economic life. Travel suppliers (tour operators, wholesalers, cruise lines) want to sell more of their "product." Travel agencies, which act as go-betweens for the travel suppliers, want to bring in more customers. There are a number of ways to do this: by offering a better

11

product, by providing better service, by creating better advertising, or by finding new and better ways to market their products and services. It is this last category — marketing — that has created some very attractive opportunities for folks like you and me.

Every travel product, from the cheapest airline ticket to the most luxurious round-the-world cruise, must be sold. That requires salespeople, and everyone in the business has them. The airlines have their reservationists, travel agencies have their sub-agents. At some point, everyone selling travel asks themselves some variation of the following question: "If I'm selling one million worth of product with 10 salespeople, why couldn't I sell two million with 20?" It's not that simple of course. Many things have to be taken into consideration when increasing your sales force: demand (doubling the number of airline reservationists will not double the numbers of calls coming in), overhead, salaries and benefits, training, and on and on. Still, the marketer can't shake the idea. "If I had more people selling for me, I'd bring in more money."

What, then, if they could bring in additional salespeople at no cost whatsoever? In fact, what if they could actually get people to pay them for the privilege of selling for them? What if they set it up so that these new salespeople would only get paid for the business they brought in? What if they "paid" these salespeople in free travel or through a discount instead of cash? The idea proved so attractive that more and more travel suppliers began experimenting with some variation on the theme. Cruise lines offered free berths to people who could sign up a bunch of friends to take a cruise. Tour operators who wanted to reach the multi-billion-dollar educational market made teachers their "sales force," offering free trips and cash stipends. Travel agents began to experiment with outside sales representatives — freelance, independent agents who sell tickets, tours, and cruises to their own customers and let the agency do the ticketing in exchange for a split of the commission.

Over the last decade or so, a number of social, business and economic trends have given this trend a push:

- ▪ ***Multi-level marketing or MLM.*** The success of Amway and similar companies gave the concept of multi-level marketing a new respectability. This is a marketing strategy in which a company relies on an ever-growing army of independent, part-time salespeople to distribute its products. Each individual may sell only a very small amount, perhaps just enough to keep themselves and their friends happy, but in the process, the company itself reaps substantial rewards. MLM programs are structured in such a way that ambitious reps can do very well indeed, while less ambitious folks can still contribute to the bottom line of the parent company. Many companies in the travel industry are finding ways to adapt MLM techniques to their businesses.

- ▪ ***The rise of the entrepreneur.*** More and more people are deciding that the "traditional" career model just doesn't work for them. Instead of sticking with the same company for 30 or 40 years, they are opting out of the corporate world to start their own businesses. For many of these people, the size of the business or the money to be made is less important than the freedom they will have to set their own pace and be their own boss.

- **The returning homemaker.** Today this is less of a trend than an accomplished fact of our economic life. Beginning in the '70s, rampant inflation made the traditional one-paycheck family more and more a thing of the past. Millions of women "returned" to the job market for that second paycheck. Many of them found they lacked the skills demanded by a more complex and technological workplace than the one they left to get married. Today's young mothers often count themselves lucky if they can afford a few months at home with their young ones before getting back to a full-time job. Many of these women (and some "house husbands," too) would give their eye teeth for a money-making part-time career that would allow them time with the kids.

- **The second-job syndrome.** After the two-paycheck family has come the two and a half-paycheck family. More and more family units are taking on part-time jobs. Sometimes it is a simple matter of economic necessity. In other cases, people are "test-driving" new careers or seeing if they might want to ditch their regular job and start their own business. Still others have heeded the advice of financial gurus and turned an avocation into a sideline business to gain not just the extra income but the tax advantages of running a small business.

- **Downsizing.** As more and more companies lay off more and more employees, more and more people are scrambling for another job — a job that's often not there. Many people are realizing that if they are going to find a job, they're going to have to create it for themselves. Indeed, some states are responding to this new reality by instituting programs that help the newly unemployed set themselves up in business.

- **Computerization.** The rise of the small, affordable, personal computer has made part-time business more attractive to many people. The efficiency offered by automation means that business opportunities that might have been seen as too time-consuming a few years ago are now seen as something that need take up only a few hours a week. Travel agencies, using the same cheap computers, linked together in a network, have the computer power to maintain and track fairly large numbers of outside reps. Whereas ten years ago having an outside sales force might have seemed like an organizational nightmare, today it's more likely to be seen as a piece of cake.

- **Franchising.** Over the last decade or so, franchising has boomed. Many of the entrepreneurs who start their own businesses do so under the comforting umbrella of a franchise. And the travel industry has not been overlooked. If you have the money, you can buy into your own travel agency. If you don't have the money, you can accomplish much the same end by becoming an outside sales rep. Think about it: You operate on your own (just like a franchise), have your own customers (just like a franchise), run your own business affairs (just like a franchise), but you still have an association with a larger entity that provides you with services (just like a franchise). And just as the franchisee pays a franchise fee, the outside sales rep for a travel agency splits the commission with the agency. Of course, legally speaking being a franchisee and being an outside sales rep are two different things. Still, the two arrangements have much the same practical effect. More and more travel agencies are applying the franchise metaphor when they consider adding an outside sales operation and are, consequently, becoming more open to the idea of having independent reps bring them business.

The end result is that, today, becoming a player in the multi-billion dollar world of travel has never been easier — if you know how to go about it.

The 'traditional' career paths

Of course, if you're the traditional type, you can always go out and start your own travel agency. These are the storefront travel boutiques that you see as you drive through your town. These are the places that are listed in the Yellow Pages under "Travel Agencies." People start agencies all the time. But they are usually not rank beginners. They are usually people who have been working in the travel industry for some time, who know the ropes and figure they can make it on their own. Sometimes they start an agency from scratch. Sometimes they hook up with one of the growing number of franchise operations to get a head start. In any event, they put up quite a bit of their own money — $50,000 or more in most cases.

Like most small businesses, travel agencies have a high mortality rate. It's a competitive business that sometimes operates on distressingly low margins. When you factor in the high cost of overhead and payroll, it can be easy to lose money. Many would-be entrepreneurs find it's just not worth it and shut their doors in a year or two.

Another option is to get a job at a travel agency or a corporate travel office. You can always go to a travel school (some reputable ones are listed in the *Resource Section* in the back of this book) to get the minimum qualifications needed to land an entry-level job in an agency. For most people, this is the only option. Travel agencies like to hire people who already know how to use the CRS (computer reservation system) they use to ticket flights, and this is precisely what the travel schools teach.

There are a number of drawbacks to this option, however:

- ***There is a great deal of competition for jobs.*** Look at the want ads. Over and over, you'll see they specify "two years SABRE experience" or "5+ years agency experience." That puts beginners at a distinct disadvantage. Most agencies have enough to do to make ends meet without worrying about bringing you up to speed.

- ***Entry-level pay is low.*** The typical starting salary in a small agency is $10,000 to $12,000. Of course, there is always the chance for advancement and many people in the industry make a good living. The median income for a travel agent is $15,000 a year and some people make more than $30,000.

- ***The work is far from glamorous.*** Most entry-level agency employees spend their day at computer terminals handling the nitty-gritty details of booking and ticketing. There is often little chance to meet with customers and share your excitement for the open road.

- ***The work is reactive rather than proactive.*** In the typical agency, the customer comes to you. As an entry-level employee you have little opportunity to develop new business. Moreover, it is the customer, not you, who determines the kind of travel products you wind up selling.

- ***The turnover is high.*** Many people find after a few months that agency work is a lot harder and lot less glamorous than they thought. You might be one of them. Even if you stick it out, you may find a constant stream of new faces at the office.

- ***The payoffs are down the road.*** Of course, as an agency employee, you are eligible for the benefits that come with being in the travel business (see *Chapter 12: Straight Talk About Travel Industry Benefits*), but in most agencies you will have to pay six months, a year, or more of dues before you get to take advantage of them. Also, many opportunities for free and reduced-cost travel are tied to agency volume. If your agency isn't big enough, or is having a bad year, your travel benefits may suffer accordingly.

- ***Travel time is limited.*** Even when new or low-level travel agency employees can qualify for free or low-cost travel, the time to take advantage of these deals is limited. Most employees get two weeks vacation, just as they would at a "regular" job.

This brief discussion is meant to be realistic rather than discouraging. Many people thrive in the agency atmosphere, have a lot of fun, sell a lot of vacations, have exciting careers, and become very successful. If you decide to go the traditional route, I would like to think that this book will prove helpful to you as you begin your climb up the career ladder. However, the main purpose of this book is not to tell you how to have a traditional career in the travel agency business. And if I have concentrated perhaps a little too much on the downside of the traditional path it's just to point up the positive aspects of becoming a part-time travel agent.

One size does not *fit all*

One of the most attractive aspects of the new travel marketing landscape is that it is very definitely not a one-size fits all proposition. You can design your own part-time travel career to suit your interests, your schedule, your working style and preferences, and your monetary goals. You can plan to work one hour a week or 80. You can plan to save money on just your own travel. Or you can plan to make money on the travel of a small circle of friends, or the travel of everyone in your neighborhood, town, county, or region. You can plan to earn pin money in your part-time travel business or you can set your sights on an annual income of over $50,000. It's all doable and it's all up to you!

- **Become a part-time specialist.** Suppose you love taking cruises, you do it once a year, and have cruised with several different lines. You are a natural to sell the joys and benefits of cruising to others. And if you want to specialize just in cruises — no short-haul airline tickets, no European tours — you should be able to find a travel agency that will be more than happy to handle all the cruise business you can bring in. Or perhaps you are lucky enough to be Irish and you know the "auld sod" like the back of your hand. You may want to specialize in travel to Ireland. You can use your special knowledge of the destination to add value to your services. You may even want to lead some special interest tours yourself, all the while earning a commission on every person you book.

- **Be a generalist.** You may decide that offering to book all types of travel for a select clientele will work best for you. If you know you can get a circle of family, friends, and neighbors to turn their travel needs over to you, you can get into the business quickly. There are some disadvantages to this arrangement which I will get into later, but it has the advantage of giving you a clear handle on your business. In other words, once you learn that Aunt Matilda spends $1,500 a year on travel, you can look forward to getting a steady cut of that sum.

- **Become a multi-level marketer.** Just as some travel agents will pay you a finder's fee to bring in a customer, some agencies that have growing outside sales forces will pay you a fee for recruiting a new salesperson for them. A typical arrangement is that you'll receive one half of one percent (.005%) of the new outside rep's gross bookings for the first two years he or she is on the roster. If the rep you bring on board generates only $5,000 in bookings per year, you'll receive $50 over that two-year period. Not a great deal of money, perhaps, but not bad pay for a referral that will take you less than half an hour to make. Later in this book, I'll show you how.

- ■ *Be a full-time part-time rep.* Although the emphasis of this book is on selling travel as a part-time avocation, there's no law that says that you cannot spend every waking hour building your own, highly profitable travel business. It's pretty easy to earn a 7% commission; if you sell the right products, you can make 10% or 12% or 15%. In a few rare instances you can make over 20% commission on some sales. Sometimes when you earn a free trip as a reward for your sales efforts, you have the option of taking that trip yourself — or selling it at full price and pocketing the entire fare! There are outside sales reps today who earn over $50,000 a year selling travel. Why not join them? If you have the drive and the commitment, there's no reason you can't.
- ■ *Be a by-the-hour travel consultant.* Most people involved in selling travel are compensated by commissions. But I know some enterprising souls who, in addition to receiving a commission as outside reps, charge their clients an hourly fee for helping them plan their vacations! If you have special expertise, in-depth knowledge of specific destinations, or provide special services like driving your clients to the airport, you may be able to charge up to $100 an hour for your services. This is a high-end strategy that requires special skill (and perhaps a bit of chutzpah), but it can be done.

Introduction

Is it for you?

Who should get into the part-time travel agent game? Now that I've been in it myself for a while and know how easy it is to get started, to make sales, to make bookings, and to make money, my answer is simple and straightforward: *Everyone!* After all, even if all you want to do is save money on your own travel for business and pleasure, the information in this book will enable you to save many times the purchase price. If you're not convinced by now, I would like to think that by the time you have finished this book you will be. In fact, you may even find you're so excited by the possibilities that you'll start your part-time travel agent career rolling *before* you've finished the book!

In the meantime, however, consider these good solid reasons for joining the thousands of people who are having fun and making money in the part-time travel lifestyle:

- ■ *Are you a traveler?* If you love travel yourself, you have already mastered a major challenge for anyone in sales — you know your product. It is now a relatively simple matter to translate the knowledge and enthusiasm you already possess into powerful sales presentations that will bring you your first bookings and steady repeat business. In addition, you'll start saving money on your own travel instantly.

- ***Are you looking for a low-investment part-time business?*** Look no further. As I've already said, and will explain in detail later, you can become a part-time travel agent today. And your initial investment can be absolutely zero (okay, maybe you'll use a stamp or two and make a few phone calls). I made my first several bookings with no business card, no stationery, no nothing!

- ***Do you need a flexible schedule?*** Here's a business that allows you to set your own hours like few others. You can chat with folks at work or call them at home at night. Work full-time one week and scale back the next. Whatever schedule works best for you, you can design a travel business to accommodate it.

- ***Are you a teacher?*** Many opportunities in the part-time travel field are aimed specifically at teachers. Moreover, teachers have more free time than many other professionals — free time that can be both a boon and a curse. As a part-time travel agent you can use your free time to sell travel *and* take advantage of it too!

- ***Do you have a built-in audience?*** Teachers do. They can reach their students and their students' parents. But other professions also offer their practitioners access to large groups of people — ministers, accountants, salespeople, the list goes on. All of these people come in contact with many people in the course of their work, people who are often prime prospects for a part-time travel business.

- ***Do you belong to a club or organization?*** Clubs and other affinity groups represent superb opportunities to make major sales. If you get ten people in your club to go on a cruise with their spouses, that's a $30,000 to $40,000 sale.

- ***Are you a small businessperson?*** If so, why not make travel an add-on to your existing product line? Everyone who comes into your shop can learn about the travel opportunities you have to offer. If you send catalogs or brochures to your customers on a regular basis you have already paid for the postage to send them a flyer about a great bargain on an upcoming tour or cruise. Or why not offer discounted travel to your employees as an extra benefit? You'll forego some or all of the commission, but the goodwill you generate will be hard to beat.

- ***Do you travel on business?*** Many people, myself included, often travel on business, pay their own way, and then get reimbursed by their employer or client. As a part-time travel agent, you can earn a commission on every bit of that travel. If you own your own business and spend a considerable amount of money on travel, then the prospect of saving 5% to 7% on your travel expenditures should make your bottom line sit up and take notice.

- *Are you in sales?* If you are, you've probably already thought of a dozen ways you can prosper in this sideline. Your existing sales skills will fit perfectly in the part-time travel business and you no doubt already have a large and ever-growing pool of prospects.

- *Are you retired?* Perfect. Not only do you now have the time to devote to learning about travel, but you are an integral part of the largest and fastest growing market for leisure travel. You can make a handsome part-time income, and enjoy some wonderful fringe benefits, just by specializing in the travel interests and needs of folks just like you.

- *Are you home with the kids?* Here's a way to make a bit of extra money at the same time you're burping and diapering. Much of your business with customers can be conducted on the phone; your friends probably won't mind if you're bouncing junior on your knee while you talk to them. You can use baby's nap time to get on the phone and call the travel suppliers. It's a perfect scenario for the homemaker or house-husband.

What's the catch?

If this is all sounding too good to be true, I know exactly how you feel. I felt the same way. In fact, I still feel that way. Part of me keeps wondering when I'll find "the catch." So far there doesn't seem to be one. But if I've pumped you up *too* much so far, perhaps it's time to bring you down to earth a bit.

If there is a catch to the part-time travel game, it's letting your goals outstrip your gumption. Another way of saying that is you've got to determine, first, what you want out of your part-time travel business and, second, if you have what it takes in terms of skills, time, commitment, and whatever to get it. For me the goals were pretty simple. I wanted a way to make something I loved — travel — more a part of my daily life. I'm not looking to make selling travel my sole means of making a living (I'm not going to be one of those $50,000 a year outside reps). I am looking to stretch my travel budget, to get more mileage out of my travel dollar. And I am looking to supplement my income by sharing the joys of travel with others. In both those areas I am succeeding to my satisfaction. So I am happy and feel my part-time travel business is on an even keel.

To help you guide your own thinking as you read through this book, let me share some thoughts that may help you put all this in perspective:

- *This is no get-rich-quick scheme.* Those who make large sums of money selling travel work very hard and earn every penny. How much money a person makes and how hard they have to work to make it, varies from person to person. Some people have more time to devote to their travel business than others. Some have more drive and determination than others. Some folks are natural salespeople; others will have to work harder to hone their skills. It may sound like a cliché, but how much money you make is up to you. I certainly can't predict how much you'll make, but I can almost guarantee you that if you think you can make a small fortune working just a half hour a day while watching television, you'll be disappointed.

- *It's a business.* The statistics tell us that the majority of new businesses fail in a year or two. There's no reason to expect that your part-time travel business may not meet the same fate. The difference is, of course, that you (presumably) won't expect your travel-related income to support you and your family. It's quite possible to use the strategies in this book knowing you'll earn just a few hundred dollars a year. If that's fine for you, then everything's okay. Of course, you can also seek to make selling travel a money-maker. And that's fine, too.

- *It's a service business.* Whatever else you are selling, you are selling customer satisfaction. If you have never worked in a setting in which you had to "please the public," you may be surprised at how much people will expect from you and how readily they'll blame you for things over which you have no control. Believe me, if the toilet in the luxury hotel in Nairobi backs up and overflows, it's your fault!

- *Things go wrong.* Most people who go into business have at least some bad experiences. I certainly can't guarantee that you won't have some of your own. You may just accept problems as a natural part of life. I think that's a healthy attitude. On the other hand, you may decide that the kinds of problems that tend to come up in this business aren't worth whatever you're getting out of it. So be it. Later in the book, I'll talk about some of the things that can go amiss and some ways you can protect yourself.

- *It involves selling.* No matter how glamorous travel may be, to make money at it you have to sell. That means looking for new customers, finding out about what their travel needs are, presenting them with attractive options, answering their questions, dealing with their objections, and, above all, asking them to part with their hard earned money. I happen to have a background in sales and marketing. In fact, over the years I have trained hundreds of salespeople in a variety of industries. I know from experience that selling is a skill and that like any skill it can be learned. I also know from experience that not everyone is cut out for selling. It's not so much that they *can't*, it's just that, for whatever reason, they find out they don't enjoy it that much. You may be one of those people.

Above all, there are no guarantees. Like I said, I enjoy earning at least part of my living by sharing with people the joys of travel. One way I do that is by writing books. In my first book, *The Insiders Guide To Air Courier Bargains*, I shared with people the secrets I had learned about saving hundreds of dollars by flying as an air courier. Lots of people do it. I do it all the time. Lots of people who read the book are now doing it too. But there was no way I could guarantee my readers that they would be able to go exactly where they wanted to go, precisely when they wanted to go there, for the absurdly low price they wanted to pay. Some people who read the book got free flights to Tokyo, while others, I'm sure, are still looking for their first freebie.

It's the same with this book. In it I will share with you what I've learned about the fun, the excitement, and the money making possibilities I have discovered in the part-time travel game. I will introduce you to some opportunities that I have taken advantage of that I think might work to your advantage as well. So far, it's working out well for me. But I have no guarantee that it will continue to work out as well as it has so far. Nor can I guarantee your success. The suggestions I make in this book are made in good faith, but I can assume neither liability nor responsibility for anything that might go amiss by following them.

How this book is organized

First of all, I have written this book with several assumptions in mind about you, the reader. I have assumed that . . .

1. You have relatively little experience in the travel industry, except as a consumer.
2. You have little or no background in selling.
3. You are primarily interested in a lifestyle in which selling travel products is a part-time avocation instead of a full-time job.

If any or all of these assumptions doesn't fit your profile, you should have no difficulty making the necessary adjustments as you read the book. Even if you have been working for a travel agency for five years, my guess is you will learn some new things from this book and, perhaps, decide to make some changes in the way you manage your career.

The book is organized in three main sections:

Part I: How You Can Become A Travel Agent — TODAY! In this section, I will lay out the opportunities that exist to get involved in organizing and selling travel on either a part-time or full-time basis. This information will allow you to construct your travel business on your own terms. Like I said, this is definitely not a one size fits all proposition.

I'll also show you how to get started in your new part-time travel business on a level at which you are most comfortable and point out some of the pitfalls as well as the pleasures of this exciting new lifestyle.

Part II: The Fine Art Of Selling Travel. Next, I'll show you how to translate your enthusiasm for this new lifestyle into actual sales, and put real cash in your pocket. You'll learn how to locate your very first customers, get to know their travel needs and preferences, use powerful benefits to sell high-ticket tours and cruises, and ask for their business with pride and confidence. This is a complete mini-training program in the classic core selling skills. It is patterned after sales training programs I created for some of America's most successful selling organizations.

Part III: Resource Section. Here you will find annotated lists of books, magazines, educational institutions, industry organizations, professional associations, and other resources you can turn to for more information. Every organization, association, or book mentioned in *Parts I* and *II* is included in the *Resource Section*.

How You Can Become A Travel Agent — TODAY!

Chapter One:
Becoming A Tour Organizer

Want to take a four-week, grand tour of Europe — absolutely free? All you have to do is take six paying teenagers with you.

I have found no quicker way to qualify for free travel than becoming an educational tour organizer. In this highly competitive market, tour operators are more than happy to give you a completely free trip just for signing up as few as six people to take a very moderately priced package tour. One even lets first-time organizers travel free with just five paying. Sign up more than six and you can put money in your pocket. One of the best parts about getting into the travel game this way is that you don't have to be affiliated with a travel agency to do it.

Touring with teens

Educational tours are designed for and marketed primarily to high school students, although as one executive of a large educational tour operator told me, "about thirty percent of the people who take these tours are adults who like to travel on programs that provide them with some learning activities or cultural enrichment activities." These aren't classroom tours, he was quick to point out, "but learning on the ground, as it were, in the course of travel."

Generally speaking, here's how the system works. Educational tour operators solicit high school teachers through direct mail campaigns to become recruiters for their tour programs. "Ask any high school teacher," says one educational tour insider, "and they'll tell you they have to shovel out their mail cubby, they get so much stuff from outfits like us."

These programs appeal primarily to teachers of languages or the humanities for whom foreign travel is a natural add-on or extension to their classroom activities. The teacher browses through the thick, glossy catalogs the tour operators send and selects an itinerary that appeals in terms of geography, emphasis, length, and cost. The teacher then contacts the tour organizer to discuss dates. If the teacher shows the potential to recruit a large enough group, the tour operator may tentatively block out a tour just for that school; otherwise, the tour operator may suggest putting two school groups together on the same tour. Generally, there is some negotiation over dates and the composition of the tour, but the tour operators try to do everything they can to accommodate the teacher's preferences.

"It's like putting together the pieces of a puzzle," says Charlotte Dietz, Vice President of the American Council of International Studies (ACIS), a major educational tour operator. "We have an operations team working out of what we call a 'structure.' We'll have groups from all over the United States picking the same trip. 'Showtime In London' may have a group of 20 that wants to go on the 17th of April and 45 that want to go on the 18th of April and six that want to go on the 16th of April. That's when we begin to pull the puzzle together. At certain times of the year, where there are strict vacation breaks, we guarantee people that we will not move them more than a certain number of days. In general though, it's dependent on what the demand is, what the air is [i.e., the availability of space on the airlines], what the vacation schedules are; but we maintain high standards in terms of guaranteeing people that they will be able to leave pretty much when they want to."

Once dates have been agreed upon, the teacher, after clearing it with the school, begins to promote the tour to students and their parents, all with the help of marketing materials and how-to guidebooks provided by the tour operators.

To make the tours more attractive to the target audience, they are priced very reasonably. The tour operators can keep the costs down since teenagers can be lodged three to four in a hotel room — something the average adult tourist usually will not tolerate — and because youths qualify for lower admission charges to many sights and attractions. The tours can be made even more attractive to parents (who, naturally, will be footing the bill) by getting participating students to raise some of the money to cover their costs. Tour operators will even help out with fund raising suggestions.

Since teachers are the primary sales force for these tours, the tour operators have made a wise decision to support them with first-rate backup materials. They provide teachers with appropriate color posters to stick up on the school bulletin boards and there are plenty of brochures for the individual tours that teachers can pass along to parents. Most operators in the educational field also provide their teacher-recruiters with detailed instructions on how to market their tours in the school. One operator developed a "Ten-Day Plan" to guide participating teachers through the process in a structured fashion. ACIS issues a "Teacher Enrollment Handbook." Some tour operators even provide toll-free help lines for teachers with questions.

Once the teacher has signed up six kids to take the trip, he or she is qualified to go on the trip free, to serve as the "teacher-counselor." This 6 to 1 ratio is known in the business as the "prorate": one free berth for every six people signed on. After the six-person minimum has been met, the teacher-recruiter begins to earn a "cash stipend" for each additional person recruited. In effect, it's a commission on sales. The amount of the stipend depends on the price of the tour. For example, on a tour priced at $1,600, the teacher might receive a stipend of $150 for each additional person on the tour. If the teacher signs up ten people, the stipend is $600 (4 times $150). Once 12 students have been recruited, the teacher-recruiter becomes eligible for another free berth and many spouses go along on this basis. Or the teacher can elect to take the stipend instead. The teacher who is lucky (or ambitious) enough to sign up 20 participants gets a stipend of $2,100 — in addition to the free trip, of course.

All in all, this is one of the best deals going in the travel business. Consider what the teacher is getting on this $1,600 tour. First there's the free trip for signing up six paying customers. That's the equivalent of a 16.6% commission! After that, the $150 stipend for each additional traveler is the equivalent of a commission of a little over 9%. Not too shabby for what can be a fairly easy sell to a captive audience.

Putting together a school tour

One of the things that makes putting together a school tour fairly easy is the assistance which the tour companies provide in abundance. First, there are the glossy brochures. Printed in full color on thick, shiny stock and professionally designed, they lend instant credibility to your marketing efforts. There are also beautiful posters for school bulletin boards and even videos of the countries to be visited. The last are almost guaranteed to whet the appetites of both students and parents. But perhaps most important of all, the educational tour companies are eager to help you become an accomplished salesperson.

Most tour operators provide short but savvy "manuals" to help would-be teacher-counselors map out an effective marketing program to make their recruiting efforts a success. The advice ranges from the fairly obvious ("Start early!") to the canny ("Do not raise this subject [medical emergencies] yourself as it may make the parents unnecessarily nervous.").

Despite the long lead time — getting the ball rolling in the first week of school is none too early for a Spring trip — the recruitment process can take remarkably little of the teacher's time, as one operator's "Ten-Day Plan" would seem to suggest. In outline, here's how they suggested a teacher proceed, step-by-step, over a period of about a month or two:

Day 1: Order all the material you'll need.

Day 2: Make a general announcement of both the trip and a student meeting in school. Discuss it in class, and hand out catalogues, itineraries, and other particulars.

Day 3: Continue to promote the student meeting. Put up posters, and spread the word among your fellow teachers,

Day 4: Keep up the promotion with more bulletin board announcements, classroom previews, and handouts. Make sure everything's set for the meeting.

Day 5: Hold the student meeting. Prime students to pitch the trip to their parents and get them to attend a parent-student meeting about the trip.

Day 6: Follow up with the kids about the parent-student meeting and mail out personal invitations to each parent.

Day 7: Continue to promote the parent-student meeting and get the meeting set up.

Day 8: Hold the parent-student meeting at which you attempt to gather as many signed applications as possible.

Day 9: Send in the applications you have gathered so far while continuing to push for new sign-ups. Review your progress and consult with the tour operator on next steps and additional tactics.

Day 10: Conduct another parent-student meeting and continue to request sign-ups.

There are even suggested agendas for both the student meeting and the parent-student meeting, sample letters to parents, and tips and pointers to guide you through each step of the process. Sounds simple, doesn't it?

Well, it is on the face of it. But the tour operators recognize that nothing is ever *that* simple. So there are alternate tactics and backup techniques. One operator suggests casting a wider net to include students from other schools, even adults. The *ACIS Teacher Enrollment Handbook* offers ten ideas for how the class can raise funds to underwrite its trip and another brochure lists a dozen outfits that you can turn to for fund-raising ideas and products. There are sample press releases, should you decide to spread the word through the local press. ACIS provides the prospective teacher-counselor with answers to the most commonly asked questions and suggestions for how to deal with parents' concerns. Other companies serving the educational tour market provide similar kinds of materials.

It is hard to imagine a teacher reading through this material and not becoming enthused both about the prospect of free travel on a fun-filled student tour and his or her ability to put together a group and make the fantasy a reality.

It's not just for teachers

High school teachers may be very familiar with the world of educational tour operators. But most people — teachers included — don't know that you don't have to be a teacher to take advantage of the fabulous opportunities offered by the tour organizations. Anyone with the time, energy, and imagination to go after this very lucrative market can participate.

Of course, there will be some people who will have greater access to this market than others. The principal's secretary, school board members, even the school custodian have firsthand contact with their target market. Clergy and community workers who deal with youths are other likely candidates to become "teacher-counselors." If you are the parent of a high-school student, you have a natural entree to the school administration and may even have a copy of a school directory giving the names and addresses of every parent with a child in the school. But even if you have no "in" whatsoever with your local high school, there is nothing to prevent you from promoting tours to this market — as long as you have the permission of the school authorities.

There is also no rule that says you have to restrict your marketing efforts to one school. If there are three high schools within striking distance of your home, you can promote the tour in all three, thus significantly increasing the chances that you will qualify for the free teacher-counselor slot. Obviously, you would not want to mix apples and oranges in this case — mixing freshmen from School A with seniors from School B on the same tour could very well lead to friction and complaints. With a little common sense and a modicum of effort and imagination, however, there's no reason you can't earn one or two free vacations each year by serving the teen educational market.

These tours are conducted year-round, not just during school holidays. Of course, teachers have the inside track on leading tours during the school year since they are in a better position than you or I to negotiate with the administration to take the kids away from their regular classes for a week or two in Europe. Fortunately, there's a way around this limitation because the tour operators are just as happy to arrange a tour for adults as they are for teens! In fact, as I noted earlier, fully 30% of those who take these tours are grown-ups. So if you feel more comfortable putting together a tour for your bridge club than for the local high school, go right ahead.

In principle, organizing an educational tour for adults is no different than organizing one for a school group. However, there are a number of points worth bearing in mind:

- ■ **Tours conducted for adults will be slightly more expensive** than those for the kids. That's due mostly to a daily surcharge for putting the adults in double rooms rather than triples or quads. Typically the daily add-on is about $10, hardly a princely sum.
- ■ **These tours are designed for a younger audience,** with an emphasis on learning — so if your adult group wants to tour the red light district of Amsterdam or the casinos of London, these tours will definitely not be for them. Still, there is a large adult audience for this kind of "cultural enrichment" experience.
- ■ **These are not luxury tours.** One way the tour operators keep the costs down is to book the less fancy hotels, often ones which are not centrally located. So don't expect the decor of the rooms or the quality of the meals to be the same as those you might have had on your last European tour; that tour was specifically designed for an older, more affluent consumer. You can negotiate with the tour operator for a better class of hotel at a higher rate, of course. Still, these tours offer great value. As long as the group knows what to expect, there should be few problems.

If you'd like to take things a step further, organizations like ACIS will work with you to design a custom tour to fit the needs and preferences of

your group. You simply sketch out the sort of thing you have in mind and the tour operator will research and price the itinerary. They will also determine the prorate for the custom tour and then set you loose to promote it. Needless to say, you will have to persuade an educational tour operator that you have a reasonable chance of success in promoting such a customized tour before they will take your proposal seriously.

College tours

If the idea of touring Europe with a gaggle of high school students doesn't appeal, perhaps a week in the sun-drenched fleshpots of Florida or Cancun is more your cup of tea. Or maybe your tastes run more to a week on the slopes with the party-hearty crowd. If so you may be cut out for the college tour market.

This market operates in almost precisely the same fashion as the educational tour market just described. There are, however, some important differences: The target audience is a bit older, a bit rowdier. The prorate is higher, usually one for 15 or 20. The emphasis is on fun and not on (gasp, shudder) educational values. The destinations are almost exclusively resort-area hotels that do not mind being overrun by hordes of college students on Spring or Winter Break. In other words, these are not properties in the luxury or first-class categories. The tours are also not "tours" in the sense that the word is used in the high school market, but "packages," involving just the basics — airfare, transfers, and room. Meals are seldom included, although on ski trips, lift tickets are invariably part of the package.

My personal feeling (and I'm willing to admit that I might be wrong) is that this market offers far fewer cross-over marketing possibilities than the educational tour market. Older travelers are far more likely to opt for a European tour of museums and historical sites than a week or two on a beer-can-strewn beach surrounded by collegians in full hormonal cry. Younger, but post-college vacationers can probably find much the same atmosphere in the better equipped singles resorts which cater to them.

In fact, this market is so specific that I would go so far as to say that it works best for college students — as both tour organizers and participants. Still, that's a huge market and this niche offers students an excellent way to get their feet wet and gain some experience and credibility in the travel industry.

That was the case with Ted Amenta who put together ski trips as a student at the University of Connecticut. Today, his company Rainbow Travel does the same thing, finding other college kids to put the groups together. Ted finds college students a good market. "For one thing, college students like to travel in groups," he explains. "They take their whole dorm floor, fraternity, club, or whatever, and they'll all go to the same place at the same time. So they're a good target. Groups are easier to deal with than individuals."

Ted's terms, which are pretty standard for this market, go something like this: The would-be campus tour organizer picks a specific trip he's interested in promoting. Ted overprints a standard tour flyer with the organizer's name and phone number and gives him a supply (tour organizers are overwhelmingly male in the college market). It's the organizer's responsibility to distribute the flyers and promote the trip on campus. The organizer is also responsible for collecting deposits and final payments, For every 15 trips sold, Ted provides the organizer with one free trip. "If the person decides they don't want to go on the trip, that they'd just rather have a check, I can do that, too," Ted points out. If the organizer cannot sell enough slots to qualify for a free trip, he receives a 5% commission on what he has sold. That commission can be received in cash or applied to the cost of his trip.

Most college tour organizers opt for the trip rather than the cash. Indeed, it's the lure of earning their passage that draws them to the proposition in the first place. Ted's own experience as a college tour organizer also illustrates another, creative, aspect of this type of arrangement. Since Ted and his friends were putting together ski trips, they had high visibility in the college ski market. As students, they also had the right to sell products directly to students on campus. They formed strategic alliances with ski equipment vendors in the area and conducted ski sales in the dorms along the lines of a Tupperware party. The result was that they were able to earn a modest commission and get all their own ski equipment and clothing at wholesale prices. "We probably took $500 to $1,000 cash between us," he recalls, "but basically we just took trips and whatever other fringe benefits we could get."

Another way for college students to take advantage of the opportunities in this market is to serve as a tour liaison. After you've organized and taken a few trips, your experience becomes valuable to the tour company and you can propose yourself as a tour staffer. This means that you accompany the tour and serve as an on-location troubleshooter — track down lost luggage, deal with the hotel on behalf of the group, and so forth. Compensation varies but includes, at a minimum, free travel and lodging.

Despite my misgivings, Ted feels the college trip market can have appeal beyond the campus. "We've had older travelers in the past. There'd be a group of about half a dozen guys around thirty to forty. They bring their wives and go on a trip with us because we have good prices. We tell them upfront that they're going on a basic, college tour, but we don't exclude anybody."

Organize a cruise

Perhaps the idea of a museum-hopping tour of Europe or a hectic week on the ski slopes of the Rockies doesn't appeal to you. Perhaps your tastes incline more to leisure and luxury — long, lavish meals, high-rolling casino gambling, and a night club or two. Well look no further. The cruise industry has your ticket. Better yet, you can cruise the Seven Seas for free in much the same way you can tour Europe — just by convincing a few like-minded people that your idea of a great vacation is just what they're looking for.

Like their counterparts in the educational and college tour markets, cruise lines are more than happy to have people like you and me supplementing their own sales and marketing efforts. You can put your energy and imagination to work organizing a cruise group just as you would an educational tour. However, there are a number of factors that set the cruise industry's free travel apart from the opportunities we have been discussing thus far.

The price of admission is a bit higher, for one thing. That is, you have to recruit more people before you can sail for free. Captain Bill Miller, CTC (Certified Travel Counselor), is a travel agent and an expert in the cruise business. In his book, *The Insider's Guide To Cruise Discounts*, Bill explains it this way:

> "Most cruise lines give one free cruise fare for every 15 fares sold in group space. This free fare is referred to as a Tour Conductor Pass. The tour conductor fare provides free passage for the group's leader.
>
> If you have enough people, your mate will also sail for free. This is how the cruise lines usually figure a group's tour conductor policy:
>
> > 1 for 15 means the 16th person sails for free.
> > 2 for 30 means the 31st and 32nd passengers sail free.
> > 3 for 45 means the 46th, 47th, and 48th passengers go free!
>
> Note: 3rd and 4th passengers in a quad cabin are not usually counted towards a tour conductor pass.
>
> Port tax is not included. Everyone must pay this."

Roughly speaking, this is about two and a half times the number of spaces you have to sell to earn free travel with an educational tour. On the other hand, most cruise bookings are for couples, so you're making roughly the same number of *sales*.

Secondly, the fares you will be promoting to your friends and neighbors when you organize a cruise group are different from the ones you would be quoted if you called up the cruise lines or a travel agent to book passage for yourself and your spouse. You will be promoting "group fares." Group fares represent discounts granted in recognition of the work you are doing in bringing business to the cruise line. Group fares need to be "negotiated" with the cruise line and that is one reason for the third major difference in dealing with the cruise industry —

You must coordinate your cruise-group organizing with a recognized travel agency. Cruise lines depend heavily on travel agents to book their cruises. That is why they are not about to alienate this important constituency by letting you and me steal the travel agent's business. If you approach the cruise line directly, they will tell you to deal through an agent. They might even be able to direct you to an agent in your area. Usually, however, you will have to find one yourself.

Here are Bill Miller's suggestions:

"If you're ambitious and ready to organize a group, you'll need to find a good travel agent. You need an agent who will teach you good skills. The agent must be someone who you will feel comfortable working with. Visit the travel agencies in your area. Ask them how they work with group leaders and outside salespeople.

Travel agents welcome potential group leaders, but past experience has made them careful. Until you prove yourself, they will probably have a 'show me what you can do' attitude. New group leaders with limited experience are rewarded with a tour conductor pass."

It may be that, as a newcomer, you will have to settle for the tour conductor pass alone. (It is roughly equivalent to a 6.6% commission on the 15 fares you have to sell to qualify.) On the other hand, there may very well be a travel agency in your area willing to give you a piece of the commission as well. The travel agency is being rewarded by the cruise line with a commission of 10% or more for all the business you are bringing in. It never hurts to ask for a share of that income. Of course, once you prove your ability to bring in a group, you should *demand* a split of the commission for any future groups. (By the time you finish reading this book, you will know how to get not only the tour conductor pass but 50% or more of the commission as well, your first time out. But for now, let's assume that you're a complete beginner with no inside knowledge of how the travel business works.)

Some novice tour organizers see cruise groups as a way of making extra money, regardless of the deal they cut with the travel agent. It is theoretically possible for you, as the cruise organizer, to quote your potential customers a price that, while lower than the advertised individual fare, is higher than the group fare available through the travel agent. You would collect the higher sum from your customers, pay the travel agent the lower sum, and pocket the difference. That's in theory. As a practical matter, there are any number of problems with this approach. First, the travel agent almost certainly won't stand for it, and if you try to go behind the agent's back, you run the risk of alienating the agent, the cruise line, and your customers. Also, cruise passengers have a wonderful way of finding out how much other passengers paid for their berths. Once they figure out they've "been had," you can forget about any repeat business from them. And repeat business, as we shall see, is one of the major reasons for selling cruises. There are plenty of ways to prosper by organizing cruises without trying to get clever and make a few extra bucks in this fashion.

Another word of caution. Cruises may not be an option for college or high school groups. A number of cruise lines, reacting to damage caused on board and the complaints of other passengers, have banned high school and college groups from their ships. Teenagers on many lines will not be placed in a cabin without an adult chaperone. If you book such a group and the cruise line does not know high school or college kids are involved, your group may be denied boarding at the dock. This is not to say that you absolutely *can't* book youngsters on a cruise. Just make sure you are completely upfront about what you plan to do when you approach the cruise line. If there are any problems or special guidelines to follow, they'll tell you. If the cruise line says yes, get their agreement to accept your group in writing, just in case.

When you are organizing a cruise, the travel agent will (or should) provide the same backup and support functions that the educational tour operators do for their teacher-counselors. In other words, they should be able to provide you with brochures, even videotapes, about the cruise line and advise you on such matters as deadlines for deposits and the proper way to walk your prospective shipmates through the cruise line's brochures.

Now, of course, you have to get that group of people together so you can qualify for your free tour conductor pass. Here's how Bill Miller describes the process:

Organizing a group can be as simple as calling all your friends.

Call your friend Marge:

"Hello, Marge. You know how we had been talking about doing something special this year? Well, you won't believe what a terrific cruise deal I've come across. It's on that fabulous _____ , sailing from Miami, and we'll save tons of money off the regular rate!"

"You mean that cruise that's always on the TV advertisements?" says Marge.

"Yep, that's the one. A seven-night cruise to the Caribbean with everything included," you say.

"Just imagine all the food!" says Marge. "The midnight buffets and the impeccable service! I won't have to cook!"

"The guys can play golf on the islands. And with the 27% that we'll save off the cruise price we can do some great duty-free shopping in St. Thomas," you remind her.

"WOW! Sounds terrific," says Marge.

"It really is a fabulous deal, but to get these great rates we'll have to get at least seven couples to go," you tell her. "Besides, it's more fun to cruise with a bunch of friends. Remember when we all went on that day trip together?"

"Yeah, we'll have to let everybody know," says Marge. "This is gonna be great."

You have just planted the seed. Next, tell everyone you know about the terrific deal on the cruise. Invite them to join you. Tell your butcher, hairdresser, minister, the insurance man, dry cleaners, the people at the library. Tell the society column writer at the local paper. TELL EVERYONE!

The important thing to remember is that selling through a network of friends and acquaintances can be a pleasurable and relatively easy experience — especially when the "product" is something as exciting and glamorous as a luxury cruise.

Organize a tour group

If sailing the high seas in style doesn't particularly appeal to you, there's no reason why you can't apply the cruise organizer strategy we just discussed to a land-based tour. Pick a tour you'd like to take, find a travel agent to deal through, and put together a group. The end result is the same: in exchange for putting the group together, you travel free on a tour conductor pass.

One tour conductor pass for every 15 paying customers may be standard in the cruise industry, but in the world of tour operators, where there are many, many more players, the arrangements vary somewhat. Some tour organizers may offer more generous terms while others look for a bigger group from their tour conductors. For example, Bennet Tours, of New York, which runs fully escorted tours to Scandinavia, requires 20 paying customers before they issue a tour conductor pass, and then it applies only to the land portion of the tour. The airfare is your responsibility.

In a situation like this, you have an incentive to drive a somewhat harder bargain with the travel agent you book through. Bennet suggests that you should be able to find an agency that will be satisfied with just the commission on the airfare, leaving the commission on the land package (or a portion thereof) to you. Considering that the land portion of a Bennet tour can run from $1,600 to $3,000 per person and that they offer a sliding commission scale ranging from 10% to 17.5%, based on volume, this could be a very attractive proposition.

The major difference, then, between organizing a tour and organizing a cruise is that in the world of tours things are far less cut and dried. Be prepared to shop around for both the best tour conductor deal from the tour operators and the travel agent that will offer you the best working relationship.

There is another important way in which tour companies differ from cruise lines: some of them may be willing to help you cut out the middleman — the travel agent.

Whereas the cruise industry seems to have a solid allegiance to the agent community, a small but apparently growing number of tour operators and travel wholesalers are willing to deal with private individuals on a one-time, ad hoc basis. Finding out which ones will deal with you on these terms can take a little detective work. As one tour operator told me, "We don't like to advertise the fact that we deal with the general public because, if that ever got back to the travel agents, they would complain that we were stealing business from them." And rightly so!

Still the phenomenon exists, and if you are interested you can seek out amenable tour operators. Some tour operators will actually advertise their willingness to deal with you this way. Usually this means small ads either in magazines that reach a highly specialized audience or in the travel trade press. For example, there are tour operators specializing in pilgrimages and other religious-oriented travel that will offer programs similar to those offered in the high-school and college travel markets. The parallel is obvious: Here is a specialized product, directed at a well-defined market with obvious "decision-influencers" already in place — in this case, members of the clergy. What better person to convince the flock to travel to the River Jordan than the minister who will baptize them when they get there?

If you are interested in the more straightforward mainstream tours, however, you will probably find that the tour operators who sponsor them are generally unwilling to deal with individuals in this fashion. But there are exceptions and, if you are determined to find them, my guess is that you can.

There are a number of reasons you might be interested in dealing directly with a tour operator and avoiding a travel agent. Some of them are better reasons then others, and you will have to decide for yourself if they warrant searching out a direct relationship with a tour company.

- **The hassle factor.** One reason people give me for going direct is that they don't want to go to the trouble or hassle of finding an agent to deal through. This could be because of embarrassment, temperament, lack of experience, or just plain orneriness. To these people I say that it may be easier than they think to ally themselves with a bona-fide travel agency as an outside rep on a one-time basis. The tour operator may smooth the way for them, even refer the business to an agency in such a way that it's a "done deal." If it's still a problem for you, I will show you later how to form a relationship with an agency that will take you on as an outside rep sight unseen, so that you'll be able to deal with any tour operator you want in an open and above board manner, and you'll have the widest variety of tours to choose from. Not incidentally, you'll also be able to deal with only the best and most reliable tour operators — an important consideration, as we'll see later.
- **Commissions.** Another reason to deal directly is the lure of larger commissions, or at least commissions that don't have to be shared with an agent. I have nothing against making more money, but I would counsel caution. Some (but not all) tour operators who are willing to let you "play travel agent" like this, may be on shaky financial footing. Before you enter into a direct relationship with a tour operator, make sure you are comfortable with whatever additional risks may be involved. (Later, I'll tell you how to protect yourself against this kind of thing when dealing with travel suppliers.)
- **Control.** Of course, there are people who simply want to run their own show and would just as soon not involve a third party if it's not absolutely necessary. In my opinion, this will

work best for those of you who choose a tight focus for your travel selling activities. For example, if you were specializing in travel to one country or region, you might be able to find a tour operator or two with a similar specialty whom you could deal with direct. You would, in effect, be dealing with them just as if you were a "regular" travel agent, which in many important respects you would be.

- **Your experience.** Another factor that will (or should) influence your decision is your level of experience. Tour operators will be understandably reluctant to deal direct with an inexperienced tour conductor, especially if there is a risk of offending the agents who bring them the bulk of their business. So if you are new to the travel game and decide to go this route, make sure you are prepared to convince the tour operator that working with you will be to their benefit. Some tour operators are more sensitive to the possibility of angering travel agents than others, but any tour operator willing to take the risk of dealing with you directly will certainly take a very long and hard look at the likelihood of your actually producing a group before giving the green light to this kind of arrangement.

If you are more experienced in the travel business, and especially if you are concentrating your efforts in one particular area, then it makes more sense to seek out direct relationships. Moreover, tour operators will be more receptive to working with you once you can demonstrate a track record or a following. (A following is a group of people who book through you regularly.)

I mention all this for the sake of completeness. All things being equal, I recommend that beginners at tour organizing operate in the more traditional way — through an agent. As you gain experience, you will probably want to become a regular outside rep with that agency. You may even consider becoming one from the outset. As you gain some visibility in the industry, you will find more and more opportunities opening up for you. I have been approached by tour organizers and wholesalers who are eager to deal with me directly. As it happens, the agency with which I am associated as an outside rep has no problem with my cutting deals like this. I am a true independent contractor in this sense. I am free to deal with whomever I choose.

Caution: Before we continue, let me just point out that there is nothing illegal or unethical in dealing directly with a tour operator, as opposed to going through an agent. The decision is more a matter of practicalities. However, some states have so-called "travel promoter laws" which regulate the sale of travel products. Be aware that your exposure to these laws may be different when you are working as an outside rep for a travel agency than when you are dealing directly with the tour operator. Many of the business and legal details of these relationships will be dealt with elsewhere in this book. For now, make a note in the margin to check with your lawyer on this before making your decision.

The freelance tour organizer

If you've ever been on a "package tour" then you've purchased the "product" of a "tour operator." These companies research a number of destinations and then assemble a number of separate elements into a single product (or "package") with a single price. The most common elements that are combined into a tour include airfare, arrival and departure taxes, transportation from airport to hotel, hotel rooms, tour buses, tour guides, restaurant meals, and admissions to museums and tourist attractions. Each of these elements will require separate negotiations with different companies or government entities and, then, separate payments to all of these separate companies. Putting together a tour also requires a lot of careful planning and coordination. It's not all that different from plotting a military campaign — and the process is often compared to just that. Once all the pieces are in place, the tour operator "costs out" the separate elements of the package, adds something to cover his or her overhead and time, adds something more to provide a reasonable profit, and then presents you, the consumer, with a single all-inclusive price.

What you may not know is that there are people who, on a smaller scale, do exactly the same thing. Ted Amenta, who puts together ski trips aimed at the college market, is one of them. Pat Berthrong, former actress, mother of six, and registered nurse, is another. Pat lives in Colorado and puts together tours to Ireland, mostly, but she has taken people to Paris and Venice as well.

Pat's tours of Ireland are intimate, highly customized trips she leads herself. The intimacy is guaranteed by the ground rules under which she works. "So far, I've been restricting myself to the number of people I can fit in a mini-van," she says. "That's six people, including me." The customization comes about because of Pat's joy in travel and the special delight she takes in finding the out-of-the-way bed and breakfast or offering her guests the kind of special Irish experience that larger, more "professional" tours simply cannot match.

"I'll take people to the local Irish nights, or *coelis* as they're called," Pat explains. "Each community has one night a week where they have live music and dance. It's just for the local people and it's fun. It's great! But it's not a 'tourist' thing. To walk in with thirty or forty people off a big bus would be a little embarrassing."

Pat's method for putting together a tour involves both planning and promotion, but mostly planning. "I'll send out blurbs to people I think might be interested and I also get a lot of word of mouth. I even had one gal call me all the way from Houston, who wanted to be included! Then I start checking the airfares." She starts well in advance and keeps checking back, always looking for a better deal. "So I don't get myself in trouble, I estimate the airfare on the high side. Then, if I find a better deal, I take it. But I'm always sure I won't charge too little."

Pat arranges for the mini-bus rental and bed-and-breakfast (b&b) vouchers through the programs offered by Aer Lingus. The voucher system allows you to use coupons for a night's lodging at participating b&b's, and most b&b's participate. Pat takes it one step further. She writes ahead to the quaint little b&b's she knows to lock in reservations. She also writes ahead for listings of local activities, such as horse races, and plans her itinerary accordingly.

She hosts "Irish nights" to get people excited about joining her next trip. She has a collection of videos and books that she'll lend out to pique interest. "And I'm kind of a camera buff," she adds, "so I have a lot of really nice blowups of pictures I've taken."

One of the big drawing cards of her tours is their offbeat and eclectic mixture of experiences — from Dromoland Castle ("That's sort of a come-on, to spend one night in a castle. They like that idea.") to a stay in a thatched-roof cottage ("There's a peat fire and a girl brings a pie, or a tart as they call it, and fresh baked soda bread. It's totally different than what they would ordinarily get."). Because she deals with small groups, Pat is often able to accommodate requests and tailor the trip specifically to the interests of her guests.

All of this takes planning, organization, and more planning. Pat is the first to admit it's hard work. "I get a kick out of it though. I really enjoy doing it, otherwise I probably wouldn't be doing it. I love planning the itinerary and I love surprising them."

Finally, Pat takes out insurance to cover unforeseen eventualities ("It costs about $35"), adds up all the costs, divides by the number of guests, and then tacks on another $200 or so per person. She's careful to get a deposit ("about half") up front, just to make sure people are serious about taking the trip.

Has she made a lot of money? Pat laughs.

"It hasn't been a lot so far, just a little bit extra. But I get a kick out of going places and I love to see other people having a good time. It just tickles the daylights out of me. Basically, what I'm doing is taking a free vacation every year."

Becoming A
Tour Organizer

Chapter Two:

The Outside Sales Rep

In the last chapter, we talked about ways in which you can earn free travel and extra money without being a "travel agent" in any formal sense of the word. The strategies we discussed that involved working with a travel agency didn't require any formal relationship or long-term commitment. You could go on earning free vacations and a bit of extra money like that for many years. Many people do and are quite happy. If you are serious about selling travel and putting together groups as a regular part of your lifestyle, however, then sooner or later you will have to form an ongoing, more or less formal, relationship with an agency. In fact, if you have successfully put together a group and booked it through an agency, that agency may actively encourage you to do more of the same. They may even suggest that you become an outside rep without you asking about it.

In this chapter, then, we will discuss how to become an "official" outside sales representative of a bona fide travel agency.

Why become an outside rep?

First of all, let's talk about why it is necessary to form a relationship with a travel agency. Why not just go out and sell travel? Why not just deal directly with the suppliers?

As we noted in the last chapter, there are some limited ways in which you can do that. But when it comes to dealing with the scores of airlines that fly the world and the dozens of cruise lines that ply the seven seas, the picture becomes decidedly more complicated. And that is why travel agents exist in the first place.

The suppliers have a need to distribute their products to the broadest possible market. All of them do that directly. You can call up any airline, cruise line, hotel, or car rental agency and make your own arrangements. But few suppliers are satisfied with that level of business. Indeed, few suppliers could survive on just the business they generate through their own efforts.

Travel agencies, then, fill a valuable function for the suppliers by going out into the marketplace and promoting the suppliers' products to the general public. They also collect fares and other fees from the passengers they book. And they do all this for free! Free, that is, until they actually make a booking. Then they expect to get paid out of the money collected from the passenger; they expect a commission.

What seems on the face of it to be a very simple relationship between the travel agent and the supplier is actually very complex. There is, in fact, a whole branch of the law — agency law — that deals specifically and in excruciating detail with the issues and problems that arise out of this relationship.

The suppliers, on the one hand, want the agent to deal honorably and professionally with the traveling public. They don't want their products and services misrepresented. They also want to make sure that the money collected by the agent on their behalf is actually received by them. The agents for their part want to make sure that their commissions are disbursed in a timely and accurate fashion.

As agencies grow, they seek to differentiate themselves from other agencies by negotiating better commission deals with certain suppliers which then become "preferred suppliers." This adds another layer of complexity. Add to all this the sheer number of suppliers and travel agents and you begin to see why it was imperative that some order be imposed on the industry.

Over the years, the industry — suppliers and agents, sometimes working together, sometimes working at odds — have created a system (or more accurately a network of systems) that regulate the way business is done. The result is that most suppliers will not, indeed cannot, deal with just anyone who decides he's a "travel agent." A number of organizations have been created to serve as buffers and conduits between the suppliers and the travel agents. They help assure the suppliers that the agents they deal through meet minimum standards of professionalism and fiscal responsibility. The agents, on the other hand, receive some assurance that they will get paid for their efforts and that their role as middlemen will be recognized and promoted. And both parties are assured that there is a system in place to regulate their dealings with one another.

One result of the system that has developed over the years is that the major suppliers (the airlines mostly) will not deal with any agency that doesn't have an "appointment" with or is not "accredited" by the proper industry entity. I use the word "entity" because these groups include industry associations, independent for-profit companies, and some that seem to fall in between. The ways in which these entities interact and overlap can be maddeningly confusing. The terms used to refer to them are equally confusing. I will try to unravel some of this confusion.

The Airline Reporting Corporation (ARC)

The Airline Reporting Corporation, or ARC, is a company set up and owned by the members of the Air Transport Association, an industry group comprising the major domestic airlines. All airlines, domestic and international, can benefit from ARC's services. Very few opt out of the system.

That system is a highly complex and sophisticated banking operation called the Area Settlement Plan. It's not a bank in the sense of your neighborhood bank but a bank-like system that regulates the payments going from travel agents to airlines on the one hand (ticket payments) and from airlines to travel agents on the other (commission payments). ARC acts as a sort of independent middleman charged with the fiduciary responsibility of making sure that everyone in the travel product distribution system gets what's owed them. (I discuss a bit more about how the system works in *Chapter 11: Getting Serious*. For now, all we need to know is that ARC oversees the movement of the billions of dollars involved in buying and selling airline tickets. Although the focus is on airline tickets, payments for other products such as tours can also be funneled through the system.)

Only travel agents who participate in this system can legally sell airline tickets and collect a commission. To do that, a travel agency must request an appointment from ARC and meet its stringent eligibility requirements. Among the most important are:

- **Bonding.** To make sure the airlines are protected from default by the agency, ARC requires the posting of a bond, which can range anywhere from $10,000 to $60,000.
- **Commercial premises.** ARC requires that all travel agents have an office, in a commercially zoned building that is easily accessible to the public and has a sign out front. In other words, no working from home.

There are many other requirements, but those are the major ones for the purposes of our present discussion.

When an agency has been appointed by ARC it receives a unique eight-digit identification number, sometimes called "the ARC number," which is attached to all its transactions with ARC and separates its bookings from the bookings of all other travel agents.

The International Air Transport Association (IATA)

The International Air Transport Association, or IATA, is another industry association of airlines, this time international ones. It is the international equivalent of the Air Transport Association (ATA).

Among the important things that IATA does is to administer the system of codes that are used to identify the world's airports and airlines. New airlines and new airports apply to ATA or IATA to be issued a code. (An airline doesn't have to be a member of ATA or IATA to get one.) These codes are used in every computerized reservations system (CRS) and make the easy, electronic booking of airline tickets possible. IATA also administers the system whereby travel agencies are identified via the unique, eight-digit code mentioned above. The number ARC uses, then, is an IATA number. That is why the terms "ARC number" and "IATA number" are often used interchangeably. (I told you it gets confusing.)

And just as the Air Transport Association begat ARC, IATA begat IATAN.

The International Airline Travel Agents Network (IATAN)

The International Airline Travel Agent Network, or IATAN, is a wholly-owned subsidiary of IATA. Or, to be more precise and even more confusing, it is the "operating name" of something called the Passenger Network Services Corporation, which is a wholly-owned subsidiary of IATA. (Didn't I tell you it gets confusing?)

Although the acronyms IATA and IATAN stand for very different things, within the industry they tend to be used interchangeably. Only by careful examination of the context in which they are used (or by asking the person using them) can you know for sure which entity is being referred to. In fact, to many people in the industry, IATA and IATAN are the same thing. For most purposes that's close enough, whatever the legal distinctions might be. (I keep telling you it gets confusing.)

Like, ARC, IATAN also endorses or "appoints" travel agencies, but in a different sense and for different reasons. Like ARC, IATAN wants to maintain the financial integrity of the industry, so its appointed agencies must meet fairly strict financial standards (a $25,000 net worth and $20,000 in working capital). IATAN agencies must also operate commercial premises, like ARC agencies.

Unlike ARC, IATAN embodies a marketing component. Member agencies can display the IATAN logo on their stationery and in their windows. It's sort of a Good Housekeeping Seal of Approval for the travel agent industry. The idea is that IATAN membership serves as a sort of guarantee to the public that the agent is professional and reliable.

Another small but important function of IATAN, which has received a lot of industry attention recently, is that it can issue ID cards to agents who work at IATAN agencies. The card is not issued automatically and there is no requirement that all agents in IATAN agencies have the ID card. The ID card has become important, however, because more and more suppliers are announcing that they will accept the IATAN card, and only the IATAN card, as proof that an individual is a travel agent. (See *Chapter 12: Straight Talk On Travel Industry Benefits.*)

IATAN has no system to parallel ARC's Area Settlement Plan. IATAN-appointed agencies simply avail themselves of ARC's services to settle accounts with the airlines.

What about cruises?

The cruise industry does not have a system that parallels the ARC Area Settlement Plan or the ARC or IATA system of appointments. Since most cruise berths are booked and paid for well in advance and since fares and schedules don't change with anything like the frenzied pace seen in the airline industry, sorting out commissions is not such a problem. And if an agency is already appointed by ARC or IATAN, the cruise lines have a high level of assurance that it is reputable.

There are a growing number of "cruise-only" agencies which, as the name implies, specialize in selling cruises and nothing else. Most cruise-only agencies have a relationship with an ARC agency (the very outside sales relationship we will discuss in this chapter!) to take care of the odd airline ticket. But for the most part, they deal exclusively with cruises and directly with the cruise lines.

In theory, anyone can declare him- or herself a cruise-only agent and start dealing directly with the cruise lines. If you decide to go this route, be aware of two things. First, your exposure to your state's "travel promoter" laws (if they exist in your state) will be greater than if you were booking cruises through an ARC/IATA-appointed agency. (See *Chapter 11.*) Second, you will be well advised to turn to the cruise industry associations discussed below for assistance and advice. The cost is modest and the training you receive can make the difference between a successful cruise-only operation and an ignominious flop.

Cruise lines take agencies much more seriously if they belong to one or both of the following associations, neither of which has the power to "appoint" agents in the sense we've just been discussing:

- ***Cruise Lines International Association (CLIA).*** CLIA is a marketing association of cruise lines. Through aggressive advertising, it sells the concept of cruising to the public at large. It also offers educational seminars for agents designed to teach the skills and techniques needed to sell the cruise experience effectively. By taking CLIA courses, you can become an "accredited" CLIA agent. By joining CLIA, you can display the CLIA logo on windows and stationery and call yourself "a CLIA agency." However, you don't have to be a CLIA agency to sell the cruises of CLIA cruise lines and collect a commission. Cruise lines *prefer* agencies to be CLIA members, but they don't insist on it.
- ***National Association of Cruise-Only Agencies (NACOA).*** The name says it all. This organization is to cruise-only agencies what the American Society of Travel Agents (ASTA) is to full-service agencies — a trade association representing the interests of its member agencies. Among the services NACOA provides its members are help and guidance in becoming a cruise-only agency and introducing themselves to the cruise lines.

You don't have to belong to either of these groups to deal directly with the cruise lines, but it's a whole lot easier if you do. They can open the doors to the cruise lines for you and provide you with the training to become a truly professional cruise-only travel agent — all at moderate cost. Another benefit of CLIA membership is that member agents get a slightly better deal on the deeply discounted familiarization (or "fam") trips cruise lines offer travel agents than do agents from non-CLIA agencies.

However, becoming a cruise-only agent right out of the starting gate is not something I would recommend. Get some experience as an outside rep first. You can take advantage of CLIA training programs without becoming a member. Once you have a better handle on the industry, you can decide if you want to join CLIA and hang out the "cruise-only" agency sign.

What all this means to you

There's more to all this, but we've covered the main points. In summary then, there are two ways to be able to sell airline tickets and collect a commission: get an appointment from ARC or get one from IATAN. Some agencies are affiliated with both. Indeed, more and more ARC-only agencies are joining IATAN because of the ID card. But that's another story, which will be dealt with at some length in *Chapter 12*.

In addition to being able to deal with the airlines, appointment is crucial for dealing with many other suppliers as well. Because the ARC/IATA number system is so well established and so convenient many hotels and most car rental companies use the ARC/IATA number as a means of identifying to whom commissions are due and disbursing them. In short, no ARC/IATA number, no commission. And when dealing with cruise lines, it's simpler at the beginning to deal through an established agency with which the cruise line is familiar than to go it on your own.

Of course, there's nothing stopping you from going out and becoming a full-fledged travel agent with appointments from ARC and IATAN. That, however, is a time-consuming and expensive proposition. The bonding requirements alone are beyond the means of many would-be travel entrepreneurs. Then there's the need to have an office, with commercial zoning, with all the attendant overhead. The cost of entry is so high that many travel agencies that go this route simply can't make it and fold within a year or two.

And *that*, at long last, is why it makes sense to become an outside rep for an agency that does have all the necessary appointments. Once you've affiliated yourself with an agency, you can begin selling travel almost immediately and funnel the business which you generate through that agency, using their ARC/IATA number. You avoid all the major expenses — the bonding, the overhead — and, if you play your cards right, you still can keep the lion's share of the commission.

In this chapter, we will examine just how that's done.

A word about compensation

To the uninitiated, discussions about how outside travel agents are compensated can be confusing. So before we get in too deep, let's take a few minutes to explain the jargon.

Most often, an outside rep's compensation is expressed as a percentage of commissions. For example, an agency might tell you, "You'll get 50% of everything you book." That means that you'll receive 50% of the commission (usually 10%) payable from the supplier to the agency. For example, if the fare is $1,000, the commission is $100, and you get $50.

Sometimes, people will "simplify" things by saying, "You'll get 5% commission." That's because most of us have come to think of 10% as being the standard agency commission, and 50% of 10% is 5%. This works as a very rough rule of thumb, but it is misleading since 10% is not a universal commission rate. For example:

- Most car rental agencies pay just 5%.

- While domestic airfares tend to be commissionable at 10%, commissions on international airfares tend to be 11%.

- Frequent promotions by foreign airlines seeking to jump start capacity can result in commissions as high as 20% on some routes.

- Many of the lower hotel rates are not commissionable at all. Agencies will book their clients at the lowest rate as a service to their clients, not as a way of making money.

- Many travel products, cruises for example, have commissions of 12%, 13%, 15%, or even higher.

- Some agencies have "preferred vendor" relationships with various suppliers that entitle them to special commissions that can be 20% or even higher.

- Some agencies double as wholesalers for a handful of travel products. In these cases, they may give the rep who books one of these products the entire commission. So if the commission is 12%, you get it all. The agency makes its money from its markup on the supplier's price.

- Some agencies will pay the rep a percentage of the base commission and all overrides. An override is an extra sum (usually expressed as a percentage) paid by the supplier as an incentive when certain volume conditions have been met. So if a cruise line offers a 12% commission and a 2% override and the rep gets 50% of the commission, he or she would get 8% on this booking (half of 12% plus 2%).

So for the most accurate reckoning, figure your potential commissions on the actual percentage split rather than using a rule of thumb. If you are getting 70% of the commission (as I do), your cut on a 10% commission is 7%. It's 7.7% on an 11% commission, 8.4% on a 12% commission, 10.5% on a 15% commission, and so forth.

Of course, sometimes when an agency says "You'll get a 5% commission" they aren't simplifying things at all. They are saying that you will get 5% of the total sale no matter what the commission rate is. They will keep all overrides and anything over 10% for themselves.

There is some other industry jargon that might be confusing. Some agencies might tell you, for example, "We offer a 60/40 split." That means one party gets 60% of the commission and the other party gets 40%. Don't automatically assume that you'll get the 60% (or vice versa). Always qualify who gets what.

Another thing to bear in mind when figuring your potential commissions is that they are paid on the "base fare" not on the total price the client pays. Many of us tend to think of our airfare as the price we actually pay, forgetting that in the typical $512 domestic air ticket, there is $18 of tax and other fees which are not commissionable. It's a small difference (10% of $18 is only a $1.80, after all, and the rep would get only a portion of that if it were commissionable) but over time it adds up.

What is an outside rep?

Essentially an outside sales representative (or 'outside rep') for a travel agency is a person who brings business to the agency and is compensated for his or her efforts solely on a commission basis. That means that the outside rep is an "independent contractor" and not an employee of the agency, an important distinction for a number of reasons, as we shall see.

Not all outside reps are created equal. For one thing, some are compensated better than others. To some extent the amount of compensation an outside rep receives is determined by the marketplace. In other words, compensation is a matter of what the agency thinks is fair and what the outside rep can negotiate. When the agency and the rep reach an agreement on a commission split, that becomes the "market rate" in this particular situation. However, the "market rate," whatever it may be, is also affected to a very great extent by the amount of work the outside rep is expected to do in bringing in business. The extent of the outside rep's responsibilities enables us to make useful distinctions between types of outside reps.

For the sake of simplicity, we will concentrate on the two main categories: full-fledged outside reps and bird dogs.

Finders, steerers, bird dogs

One category of outside rep is the "bird dog." As the term implies, these are people who flush out or bring in the game for the hunter, in this case the travel agency. Once the quarry is safely in hand, their job is over. Bird dogs can bring in small accounts (friends and neighbors, for example) or they can land major corporate accounts which will book a considerable volume with the agency each year for as long as the agency has the account.

If you are planning on letting the agency do most of the work, you will be in the bird dog category. For example, your Aunt Martha wants to go visit her granddaughter in New York, leaving on May 5th and coming back on May 20th. You relay this information to your agency, which researches the airlines serving the route, finds the lowest fare, and so forth. You then get back to Aunt Martha to see if she's happy with the itinerary the agency suggests. Finally, you recontact the agency to firm things up and have them issue the tickets. Since the agency is doing the lion's share of the work here, you can't expect to receive much more than a 2% commission, if that. There are agencies that will give you a similar modest referral fee if all you do is bring Aunt Martha in to talk to one of their travel consultants.

You can ask around at local agencies to see how (or if) they work with outside people in cases like this. If you do, there are two basic rules of thumb: First, most agencies will be reluctant to even discuss the proposition. They will figure (all things being equal) that they have more to lose than gain by letting you go out and "play travel agent" in this fashion. You are an unknown quantity and they will be naturally concerned that you might damage their reputation in the community. Second, whatever compensation they offer will be a take it or leave it proposition. Don't expect to have much negotiating leeway in this kind of situation. And don't be too surprised to find that, while you may get a cut of the commission on aunt Martha's first trip, you are cut out of the subsequent business she brings to the agency directly.

Bird dogs may be the "lowest" category of outside reps in terms of compensation but, make no mistake, they can play a valuable role in building an agency's business. Which is not always to say that a given agency will understand or appreciate that fact. It may be that serving as a bird dog for a local agency is just fine for you and there is nothing wrong with that.

Strange as it may seem, you may find it more difficult to find a situation as a bird dog than as a full-fledged outside rep. If you do become a bird dog, your initial arrangement may be tentative and "unofficial." As you begin to build a track record, however, you will deserve a more formal understanding with the agency, preferably one that is in writing and spells out your mutual obligations. More on that issue later.

Bird-dogging major accounts

At the other end of the scale is the bird dog who brings in a corporate account which will book many thousands of dollars through the agency on an ongoing basis. Here the matter of compensation is more open to discussion and negotiation. Donald Davidoff, who coordinates outside salespeople for Belair Travel in Bowie, MD, considers two variables in setting compensation — how much work the rep will do after the account is landed and how big the account is.

At the first level is the outside rep who merely "refers" an account rather than actually "sells" it. In these situations, Davidoff feels an upfront "finder's fee" is appropriate. "The fee should relate to the expected volume of travel and be equal to about 10% of the expected commissions," he wrote in *Travel Trade* magazine. In this situation, it would be logical to expect the agency to be conservative in estimating the expected volume.

If the outside rep takes a more active role and actually "sells" the account, Davidoff is willing to up the ante. "If we do not expect them to have anything else to do with the account once it is sold, then we usually pay 20%-25% of the commissions for the first year," Davidoff said. "This applies to accounts under $500,000. For accounts between $500,000 and $1 million, the commission can be as low as 15%-20%. For accounts over $1 million, 10% is usually appropriate. These differences are not relevant to most agencies because 92% of agencies in the U.S. are under $5 million in volume. It is not advisable for them to take on any account over $500,000." Be aware that the figures Davidoff is using here are *gross* figures. On a $500,000 account the agency commission would be approximately $50,000 (10%). So the bird dog's 15% commission would be $7,500

Of course, you will not always simply walk away from an account you have brought to an agency. This would be especially true in the case of an account you were able to sell because of a close personal relationship with one of the principals. You might want to serve as the liaison with the account (the agency may even insist on it!). In this type of situation, you might handle the "macro" issues — Is the relationship working well? Are they happy with the service? Do they need any special travel-related computer reports? — while the agency handles the "micro" issues — sending the VP of Sales to Indianapolis for a two-day business trip, booking rooms at the local hotel for visiting executives, etc. "In these cases," Davidoff advises, "the salesperson should get 25% of the first year's commission and 10% of at least the second year's commission in consideration for the time and effort of staying in touch." Davidoff also recommends that agencies pay a smaller commission (5%) in the third year to encourage the outside rep to stay in touch with the account and to discourage him or her from jumping to another agency, looking for those bigger first-year commission-sharing arrangements.

Here's how the payout to you as an outside sales representative would work at Belair Travel for an account that brought in $100,000 in volume each year. If you referred the account, you would receive $1,000. If you sold the account but had no further client contact, you would receive $2,500. If you performed a liaison function with the account, you would receive $3,500 over the first two years and perhaps $500 for the third year and each year thereafter. Not a bad arrangement. By the way, Davidoff's article in *Travel Trade* was headlined "Outside Salespersons: Is Your Agency Paying Them Too Much?" That would seem to imply that some agencies pay their outside sales representatives more for bird-dogging than Davidoff recommends.

The arrangements at Davidoff's agency are only one way to go. Other agencies have other formulas. For example, I am associated with an agency that has a distinctly different approach to outside reps who bring in corporate accounts. For each corporate account an outside rep signs up, they pay one half of one percent (0.5%) of volume for the first three years, one third of one percent (0.33%) for the next two years, and one tenth of one percent (0.1%) for the next five years. This arrangement involves no further contact between the rep and the corporate client after the sale. For a $100,000 account, the payout over ten years would be $2,660.

One thing to note about referral arrangements like this is that they function like an annuity. Let's say, for the sake of discussion, that you are an outside rep for an agency that gives you 25% of commissions the first year, 10% the second year and 5% the third fourth and fifth years. If you sign up just one $100,000 account each year, your income would look like this:

Year One	$2,500
Year Two	$3,500
Year Three	$4,000
Year Four	$4,500
Year Five	$5,000

The outside sales representative

Unlike the bird dog, the "true" outside sales representative functions in very much the same way as the travel agents working inside, as employees of the travel agency. That is to say, the outside rep is intimately involved in talking with customers, making suggestions, researching destinations and prices, planning itineraries, contacting suppliers, even entering booking information into a CRS (computerized reservation system).

The major difference is that the outside rep tends to be proactive rather than reactive. Rather than sit and wait for business to come walking in the door (as inside reps often do) the outside rep is out in the community, beating the bushes, looking for new business. Most travel agencies recognize the importance of this kind of activity. Many encourage or require their inside people to generate a certain amount of new business. Some agencies have outside sales reps on staff, with the specific responsibility to be out attracting new clients, corporate accounts, and groups.

The attraction the independent outside rep has for the agency is the same attraction the agency has for the supplier — it's a means to extend the agency's marketing reach and the agency only has to pay based on the rep's productivity.

Part-time, full-time

The amount of time an outside rep puts into the selling of travel can run the gamut from virtually no time at all to a full-time occupation. There are some people who form an outside sales relationship with an agency just to book their own personal and business travel. They are, in effect, their only customer. Some agencies will welcome this kind of business, others will not. At the other extreme are individuals who are seeking to make their entire living, often a very good living, as outside reps. They do this by aggressively pursuing new business, especially group sales and corporate accounts, where truly impressive commissions are possible.

Another useful distinction that can be made among outside reps is the amount of work the agency must expend to service their customers. Remember that the main reason most people become outside reps to travel agencies is that the agency can do things that they cannot — generate airline tickets and collect commissions.

Most outside sales reps (as I am using the term here) do all the work up to the point of actually generating the ticket. Anything less would put them in the bird dog category. In other words, they talk to Aunt Martha about her travel plans, find the best fare, call the airlines, make the booking, get the seat assignments, and so forth. Then they have to get Aunt Martha's ticket. To do that, they have to call the agency, talk to someone on the inside, and relay all the information they've collected from the airline (date, flight numbers, fare, record locator number, and so on). The person on the inside has to enter that information into the computerized reservation system, locate the booking the outside rep has made, claim it for the agency, and print out the ticket. All that takes time and effort on the agency's part, which is one

reason the outside person is getting 50% of the commission instead of 60% or 70%. At least, that is what the agency would most likely say if challenged on this point.

There are some outside reps who have their own CRS in their home office. They can make airline, hotel, and car reservations directly on the system and tell the system to print out the required tickets and documents on the agency's printer. Some outside reps even have their own ticket printers, so the entire operation requires no intervention at all on the part of the agency.

In theory, the amount of compensation you can expect as an outside rep should fluctuate according to how much work you're doing. If you've been getting 50% of the commission for phoning in bookings, you should attempt to renegotiate terms when and if you automate.

The "Travel Consultant"

The term "travel consultant" seems to be the title of choice among people who set up as outside sales reps for travel agencies. It's what I have on my business card. But there is a gentleman I know who adds new dimensions to the term.

Based on his intimate knowledge of Europe, primarily Switzerland and France, he charges his clients $100 an hour to help them plan their vacations. His services involve a great deal of personal attention and consultation, direct negotiations with hotels and other suppliers on the continent, and specific recommendations about restaurants, routes, and sights to see. He even drives his clients to the airport and picks them up when they return.

Of course, he also funnels the airline bookings and other commissionable elements through a travel agency with which he has an affiliation and earns a commission as well. This strikes me as a high-end strategy that would work only when you have extremely specialized experience and access to an affluent client base. I certainly wouldn't have the nerve to try it. But it's something to bear in mind. Perhaps, some day, it could work for you.

How much can I make?

"Selling is the only job where you can give yourself a raise any time you want." Seasoned sales managers and sales motivators like to cite this old saying because it means that a salesperson's compensation is up to them. They're paid on commission and, if they want to earn more, all they have to do is sell more and their income will go up in proportion. That's true as far as it goes and there are many outside reps in the travel business who make very handsome incomes.

I certainly don't want to discourage your dreams of making a princely sum as a part-time travel agent. Nonetheless, experience shows that what *you* can make will be determined, to a very large extent, by two variables — your commission structure and the dollar volume you can realistically expect to generate in the course of the year.

Outside reps will receive anywhere from 10% of commissions to 80% of commissions, depending on which agency they affiliate with and what they do. Generally speaking, the more work the outside rep does, the better the commission split. If all you are doing is steering clients to a particular agency, you can't expect to make much more than 10% or 20% of the commission. At the other end of the spectrum are outside reps who do most or all of the work associated with a booking. That means they spend the time to find out what the client needs and wants; research the available products, fares, prices, and options; contact the suppliers to negotiate prices and terms; make the actual bookings with the various suppliers involved, which could mean an airline or two, a car rental firm, and several different hotels. At this point, they may phone or fax in certain information (on airlines, most likely) so the inside people at the agency can generate the tickets or vouchers. Some outside reps may even have access to the agency's CRS and do the ticketing themselves. These are the reps who get 50%, 70%, or 80% of the commission.

Everything is negotiable, of course, and the exact shape your outside rep career takes will depend on the deal you are offered (or negotiate) with an agency. However, here are some general guidelines: You will either be a "bird dog," referring business to an agency, or a full outside rep, with your own clients. A relationship that falls somewhere in between is possible, of course, but agencies and outside people seem to prefer to keep things simple — either the rep does a little work for a small fee or does most of the work for a larger fee.

If you want that larger fee, expect to find a relationship in which you will do all the client contact and then phone or fax in the exact booking information. The agency will expect you to do the work; they are looking for a situation in which their inside people will have to do nothing more than enter the information into the computer system to generate the ticket. The agency will (or should) respect your client list. That is, they will not call your clients directly to solicit their business and cut you out of the loop.

Establishing an outside sales relationship

Let's say you've decided that you want to set yourself up as an outside sales representative and begin selling travel to your friends and family. What next? Your challenge now is to find an agency that you will feel comfortable working with that will also feel comfortable working with you.

There are two basic ways to do that:

1. Find a travel agency in your community or, at least nearby, that will take you on as an outside rep, or

2. Turn to the growing number of agencies that are willing to let you become one of their outside reps regardless of your location, pretty much sight unseen, and usually for a fee. These outfits are sometimes referred to, derisively, as "instant agencies" by people in the travel in-

dustry, but I feel they occupy a valid niche in the distribution of travel products.

I took the second route. I found an out-of-state agency that charged no fee to let me become one of their outside reps. (They have since changed that policy and now charge a modest sign-up fee.)

Despite my own decision, I think that finding a local agency you can work with is the preferable choice. Why? First of all, I am assuming that you have little or no travel industry experience. Although many of the instant agencies offer training, most of it is geared to mastering the computerized reservations system they use. (There are exceptions, of course.) Also, I don't think there is any real substitute for a caring mentor who will take you under his or her wing, show you the ropes, and be available to answer your questions on a timely basis. Local agencies also have the advantage of being close by. That means you can service the client who needs tickets *now*! Because I receive my tickets through the mail, I cannot match this level of service.

In the next chapter, I'll tell you how to follow the "instant agent" route. For now, let's concentrate on selling your services to a local agency.

Finding an agency

There are no hard and fast rules about finding a local agency with which to work but here are some suggestions:

- *Your own travel agent.* Why not consider approaching Susan, the owner of the travel agency you have been dealing with for the past several years? If Susan sees you are serious about adopting this new lifestyle as a part-time travel agent, she will realize immediately that, unless she signs you on, she will lose your business and perhaps that of some of your friends who also use her agency. She may be willing to accommodate you on that basis alone. Or maybe you know someone who is a travel agent, even though you don't book through him. My first foray into the part-time travel trade was through an agency owner I met during a radio interview I was giving about one of my books. We struck up a conversation, one thing led to another, and I became an outside rep for her firm.
- *Referrals.* Ask your friends about the agencies they use. Do they like them? Why? How big are they? Do they have a lot of agents? Are they professional? Do they specialize in a certain type of travel? This could lead you to a very likely candidate.
- *The chains.* Chains of franchised travel agencies such as Travel Network in Englewood Cliffs, NJ, recognize the value of outside reps in the marketing mix of their franchisees and are willing to put interested reps together with local agencies. They will be able to tell you what their policies are and refer you to agencies in your area that might be amenable to taking you on.

- **The Yellow Pages.** Don't overlook the trusty Yellow Pages. If nothing else, they will tell you how many agencies are out there competing for the travel dollar in your local area. Display ads will give you some clues as to which are the bigger agencies and what types of travel they specialize in.
- **Do your research.** Try to find out as much as you can about the agencies in your area before seriously approaching any of them. Check the Better Business Bureau to see if there have been complaints lodged against any of them. Drive by to see what they look like — sleek and inviting or grungy and sad. Drop in to check them out by posing as a would-be tourist. Or send in a family member if you are concerned you might be recognized later. Try to get an idea of how many people are on staff. Count the number of CRSs on the desks. Check the decals in the window to find out which trade organizations they are affiliated with. Button-hole customers you see leaving the agency; ask them what they think about the service they receive there. Would they recommend the agency to their friends? Gradually, as you gather more and more information, some agencies will start looking better than others, and you can narrow your choices accordingly.

Selling yourself to an agency

The more you can offer an agency, the more your self-confidence and the better your bargaining position. The less you can offer an agency, the less your self-confidence and the poorer your bargaining position. Here are some of the things that an agency will (or should be) looking for in an outside rep. How many of them apply to you?

- **Travel industry experience.** If you've got it, great! If not, don't despair. And remember, if you were a secretary and had to make travel arrangements for your boss, you probably know more about the business than you think you do. Take careful stock of your past experience to determine just how much prior knowledge you *do* have.
- **Sales experience.** If you don't have a background in the travel agency business, the next best thing is sales experience. Sales, as I like to remind people, is the most transportable of skills. Any travel agency owner with half a brain should be able to recognize that having a proven track record as a salesperson gives you a tremendous leg up. So if you've been an outside sales representative for a distributor, a sales clerk at a department store, or a telemarketer you have something to offer.
- **A following.** This means you have a client base you can bring with you to the agency. Unless you've been working in a travel agency and are looking for a career change, that probably doesn't mean a Rolodex full of people you've been selling travel to. But it could mean the membership of a fraternal organi-

zation of which you are an officer. Or it could mean the local PTA in which you are active. Are there any groups to which you belong or in which you have some visibility? The agency will want to know about that.

- *Market knowledge.* Do you know Italy like the back of your hand? Have you been taking three cruises a year for the past three decades? Are you an avid skier who has schussed down every major slope in the world? If so, you have knowledge that might prove useful to the agency and help convince them that you can build a following. In fact, you may already *have* a following of fellow enthusiasts and not know it!
- *Enthusiasm.* Make no mistake, enthusiasm alone will not win the day, but it's certainly a valuable quality to have — especially if it's tempered by realism. If you are inexperienced in selling travel, the agency may be willing to overlook that if you can show them that you have what it takes to learn what you need to learn and make a success of it.

Chances are that, as a beginner, you will be entering a buyers' market. That is, you will be far more interested in working with the agency than the agency will be in working with you. That, in turn, means you will have to work a little harder to convince the agency owner that working with you as an outside rep makes good business and economic sense.

Also, be aware that your beginner's status puts you in a relatively weak position as far as negotiating an attractive commission split. As I've said earlier, 50/50 is fairly standard in this type of arrangement with a local agency, but don't be too surprised if you are offered less. All things being equal, I would counsel not accepting anything less than 50/50. After all, if push comes to shove, you can always sign up with an out-of-town agency that will take you as you are, get the experience, build a following, and cut a better deal with the local agency later. In the end, of course, it's your call and working with an agency that's half a block from your house, with an owner who will really teach you the business, may be worth the trade-off in terms of compensation.

Is this the agency for me?

Just because it may be a buyers' market doesn't mean you should sell yourself short. After all, if you're not happy in the relationship, it's unlikely to work out well for either party. So don't feel you have to settle for the first thing that comes along. Before you make any commitments, take some time to decide if working with this particular agency makes sense for you and what you want to accomplish in your new travel business. Here are some things you might want to consider.

- *Is it big enough?* If the agency is too small or too new, it might not be able to give you the kind of support you need. You might even find that after a while you know more than the people on the inside. Also, the larger the agency's volume, the more attractive its commission structure will be with certain "preferred" suppliers. That, in turn, will mean more money in your pocket.

- *What kind of travel does it sell?* It may be that you want to concentrate on selling cruises. It might make sense, then, for you to hook up with a cruise-only agency, or one that does a lot of cruise business. On the other hand, an agency that does primarily corporate work may see your interest in cruising as a welcome addition to its business. The important thing is that both you and the agency feel comfortable with the fit.
- *Do they already deal with outside reps?* If so, you may find the relationship smoother than if they do not.
- *What about preferred suppliers?* Check to see what consortiums the agency belongs to. Membership in these co-ops, as they're called, means that the agency gets higher commissions when dealing with supplier-members of the consortium. That, in turn, means a higher payback for you. Some arrangements, particularly those involving cruise lines, mean not only better commissions but lower fares (guaranteed group rates or GG fares) for your customers, making you more competitive in the marketplace.
- *What kind of support can you expect?* The more willing the agency is to train you, the better the deal. At a minimum, you should expect that someone will be available and willing to answer your questions about the mechanics of making bookings and negotiating the best deals with suppliers.

The Outside Sales Support Network (OSSN), an organization which provides guidance and support to outside sales representatives in the travel industry, goes so far as to suggest that you interview the agency owner to find out if this relationship makes sense for you. Among the questions they suggest you ask are:

- Do you have, *in writing*, an "Outside Sales Agent Procedure Manual," outlining the commission splits and what is expected in the relationship?
- Do you have, *in writing*, a list of preferred vendors and their override commissions?
- Are you a member of a consortium or franchise?
- What industry organizations does your agency belong to?
- Will I have an inside contact to work with?
- Do you have a contract for me to sign as an *Independent Contractor*? (By the way, OSSN is an *excellent* organization. You'll find their address in the *Resource Section*.)

That may seem a little daunting and don't feel too bad if you don't think you have the nerve to grill an agency owner on all those points. But the point is well-taken. This is a business proposition. As a businessperson, you should be looking out for your best interests.

Your status as an independent contractor

You may have noticed that OSSN urges its members to be sure they have a contractual agreement with the agency in which they are recognized as "independent contractors." In other words, they are self-employed persons and not employees of the agency. This is an important distinction come tax time because as a self-employed person you can deduct things that employees cannot. (See *Chapter 11*.)

Because our elected representatives in Congress can neither write a decent tax code nor live within their means, the Internal Revenue Service is put under considerable pressure to extract every nickel possible under the confusing terms of the existing tax laws. They do this by "interpreting" the law in the narrowest possible way and challenging any business practice that they think is intended as a ploy to avoid taxation.

In recent years, the IRS has been particularly nasty about Independent Contractors. The IRS feels that many companies are transforming employees into independent contractors as a way of avoiding payroll and Social Security taxes. And to give the devil his due, many companies have done exactly that. But there are many other companies — travel agencies among them — who use legitimate independent contractors for legitimate business purposes. Unfortunately, given the IRS's penchant for attacking first and asking questions later, many legitimate companies and legitimate contractors have been forced to justify their business arrangements to a suspicious IRS. This is not only upsetting and time-consuming, it is expensive. And there's always the possibility that, because the i's haven't been dotted or the t's crossed in precisely the right way, well-meaning companies and individuals may suffer.

Consequently, before you embark on this lifestyle, take a few minutes to learn how to protect yourself. True to form, the IRS doesn't make it easy. The IRS determines if an independent contractor really is an independent contractor by playing a game of twenty questions. In theory, the answers will determine if you are, in fact, an employee in independent contractor's clothing. Here they are, as listed by Chicago CPA Richard S. Meyer in *Travel Weekly*:

1. Does the agency "supervise and control" you?
2. Can the agency "hire and fire" you?
3. Are you paid a straight salary (as opposed to a straight commission) and reimbursed for expenses?
4. Does the agency provide you with training?
5. Do you work continually with the agency and do the same kind of things that agency employees do?
6. Does the agency set your work hours?
7. Does the agency supply you with tools and other equipment for you to do your job?
8. Do you work on the agency's premises and have no significant investment in your own work space?
9. Do you have to perform your work in a certain order determined by the agency?

10. Does the operation of your business depend on the delivery of certain services?
11. Does the travel industry usually use employees to do the kind of work you do?
12. Does the agency have the right to bring in others to complete work you've begun?
13. Does the agency require that services be performed by a specific person?
14. Does the agency intend to treat you as an employee?
15. Do you have to submit regular written or oral reports to the agency?
16. Is there no way you can incur a loss?
17. Does the agency require that you provide it with your services on an exclusive basis?
18. Are you required to follow instruction from the agency on when, where, and how to work?
19. Do you offer your services to others on a regular or consistent basis?
20. Can you quit without incurring any liability?

Just to make the game more interesting, the IRS doesn't tell how many of these questions must have the 'wrong' answer before you and the agency are in trouble. And it doesn't take too much analysis to see that several of these questions could very well have a 'wrong' answer, suggesting that you are more of an "employee" than you might think.

Even if the IRS decides your independent contractor status is kosher, your state's tax department might disagree. States have their own, albeit shorter, test for vetting independent contractors. Sometimes called the A-B-C test, it asks:

A. Is there sufficient lack of control over the worker?
B. Does the worker work outside the agency's place of business?
C. Does the worker have a separate, independent trade or profession? (Separate business cards and phone listings could meet this test.)

None of this is meant to scare you. After all, thousands of people have been operating as outside sales reps quite happily for many years and have never experienced any tax-related problems. However, the law is the law and we all have a responsibility to comply with both the letter and the spirit of the law. That is why having a carefully drafted agreement between yourself and the agency, spelling out the precise nature of your relationship, is so important.

Be forewarned, however, that just because you have signed a piece of paper calling you an independent contractor doesn't guarantee that the IRS will agree. *Always* consult with a qualified attorney and accountant before entering into any agreement that can have legal or tax consequences. And in business that means just about any agreement you can think of!

The contract

Here is *one* contract used by *one* agency to formalize its relationship with its outside sales reps. It is provided only as an example, for the purposes of discussion. There are many, many variations on this theme and the contract placed in front of you by a local agency may be radically different in form and content. So don't think that just because a clause is in this contract that it *must* be in all contracts. Let common sense — or better yet, your lawyer — be your guide. All that being said, the following agreement covers most of the bases.

AGREEMENT

THIS AGREEMENT is made this _____ day of _____, 199_ by and between _____ hereinafter referred to as the "Independent Agent", and [name of agency], a [name of state] Corporation located at [address] hereinafter referred to as "The Agency."

Witnesseth

Whereas, "The Agency" desires to expand its sales of airline tickets, cruises and related services and

Whereas, "The Agency" has the potential to carry out this expansion and

Whereas, "The Agency" wishes to benefit from the experience and efforts of the "Independent Agent" in these fields.

Whereas, The "Independent Agent" has agreed to use her ability, knowledge, experience and training to assist "The Agency" in the aforementioned expansion.

Now thereof [sic] the parties agree as follows:

I.   "Independent Agent" shall grant to the agency her <u>Full/Part</u> time assistance and best effort by,
A. Attending once per week an organizational meeting at a time to be designated at which time a report will be submitted by the "Independent Agent" on sales calls and results.
B. Calling upon, telephoning or otherwise contacting prospective clients for travel services to be obtained through the agency.
C. Diligently carrying out sales endeavors for at least _____ hours per week.
D. Diligently following up any lead provided by the agency.

II . "The Agency" will use it's best endeavors to assist in the training of the "Independent Agent" in the use of the reservation computer system and relevant travel information.

III. "The Agency" agrees to pay the "Independent Agent" the following fees:

_____ percent (%) of the commission payable on sales derived from sales leads resulting in the purchase of travel services from the agency.

Fees are payable on a monthly basis.

Refunded tickets will automatically constitute a debit to commission of amount originally received.

IV. The "Independent Agent" shall not contact existing clients of "The Agency."

V. "Independent Agent" shall not represent any other travel company while associated with "The Agency."

VI. This agreement is valid for a term of 90 days from its execution at which time it may be renegotiated at the sole discretion of "The Agency".

No travel concessions will be allowed to the "Independent Agent" under this agreement.

VII. Nothing in this agreement shall be deemed to grant any power to the "Independent Agent" to make any contract or commitment in the name of "The Agency" without the express prior written consent of "The Agency."

This agreement shall be construed in accordance with [state] Law and the venue for any disputes under this agreement would be in [county], [state].

This agreement has been signed in duplicate this ____ day of _____, 199__, in [county], [state].

[Signed by "Independent Agent" and "The Agency"]

Suppose this contract were placed in front of you. Let's analyze it to see what it can tell us about how this particular agency seeks to operate with you, its "Independent Agent." First of all the term "Independent Agent" itself is important. The agency envisions a relationship in which you are a separate and independent entity, not an employee. This is important for all the reasons we discussed above.

This agency uses (or intends to use) both full-time and part-time outside reps, as indicated in Paragraph I. That would seem to indicate that they are open to dealing with the home-based individual who is not going to make this (at least at the outset) a full-time job. Paragraph I-A asks that the outside rep have some accountability for his or her sales efforts. But this is actually a benefit for you as well as for the agency. With this clause, the agency is committing to sitting down with you once a week in a face-to-face setting. This will give you the opportunity to ask questions and get the guidance you need. Subparagraph

C once again indicates that not only is the agency willing to work with part-timers but with several categories of part-timers. The actual number of hours (5, 10, 12, or whatever) that goes into this blank space is, presumably, a matter of negotiation between you and the agency. Obviously each agency will have a minimum number of hours they expect you to put in each week, but that number will probably be slightly different from agency to agency.

Paragraph II commits the agency to train you, a good sign they are not going to let you sink before you can swim. If you were to sign this contract, you'd probably want to take the fullest possible advantage of this commitment.

Paragraph III illustrates another important point about the relationship between travel agencies and outside sales reps — the commission split is negotiable! If it weren't, the agency would have simply inserted its "standard" commission in this space. The number that goes into this space will be the percentage of a percentage. In other words if you are getting half of the agency commission, the number would be 50%, not 5%. Remember that the commission payable to the agency is not always 10%. This is a crucial point. Make sure you are absolutely clear on what the deal is. Consult with a lawyer before you sign.

So what should the number be? I know of outside reps who have worked full time for 35% of the commission. I myself have worked for 50% and 70% of the commission. I know of agencies that give 80% of the commission (one charges a "start-up fee" of several thousand dollars!). Fifty percent seems to be a rough industry standard, especially when you are dealing with a local agency like this. Like I say, it's negotiable. Obviously, the higher the number, the more attractive the contract will be to you. But just because the number is on the low side, doesn't necessarily mean you shouldn't accept. The training may be worth it. The experience may be worth it. If this is your only means of access to the travel game, it may be worth it. Remember, that as you gain experience and prove your worth, you can always renegotiate or take your skills and abilities elsewhere.

The other items in Paragraph III create certain liabilities for you, the independent agent. Make sure you understand what they are before you sign. At a minimum you should expect to keep excellent records so you'll know what's due you at the end of the month. Will the agency provide an itemized accounting with your check? The contract doesn't say. It may well be worth clarifying this and getting the arrangement in writing. Again, a good reason to have a lawyer advising you.

The same can be said about the clause about "refunded tickets." It would seem that the agency reserves the right to determine what should be charged against your commissions and under what circumstances. Refunded tickets involve fees which can sometimes be larger than the commission you earned. I would say that this item requires further clarification. But I hasten to add that I am not a lawyer and you should seek competent legal advice on this one.

The agency wants an exclusive relationship with you (Paragraph V). This may be just fine with you, but then again it may not. For example, what if you found a cruise-only agency in your area that was willing to give you a better cut of the commission on cruises? If you'd signed this contract, you (presumably) wouldn't be free to work with them. Also, this provision would seem to violate one of the IRS's standards for determining independent contractor status; so this is probably an issue you would want to discuss with your lawyer.

In the real world, most outside reps feel most comfortable working with one agency. For one thing, it's just a lot more convenient. However, there are reps who deal with several agencies, placing each booking with the agency that gives them the best deal. You'll have to decide how you're most comfortable working. As a practical matter, however, the new outside rep will be well-advised to establish and nurture a relationship with one agency.

Like any good contract, this one is stacked in favor of the party that drafted it — in this case the travel agency. Paragraph VI would seem to suggest that you are committed to them forever, while they can cut you loose after 90 days. "At the sole discretion of 'The Agency' " means they don't even have to give you a reason. "It's just not working out" will do just fine. Essentially, the agency is trying to protect itself here. If you turn out to be a pain in the neck who is a constant embarrassment to the agency because you alienate your customers, obviously the agency wants a quick and painless way out. Of course, the law and lawyers being what they are, nothing is ever cut and dried. The laws of the state will have something to say about how and under what conditions a contract can be terminated or enforced. Still, this is probably something you'd want to talk over with your lawyer before signing this agreement.

Unlike some of the "instant agent" operations which will try to lure you with the promise of cut-rate and free travel, this agency makes it clear you can expect no such deals (Paragraph VI). Again, the agency is trying to protect itself here. It doesn't want you to get on the phone and start lining up fam trips before the ink on the contract is dry. This clause also helps assure the agency that you are serious about selling travel and not just looking for a free ride. On the other hand, travel benefits are something that an agent earns and, if you earn them, there's no reason why you shouldn't get them. This is probably another area you might want to discuss with both your lawyer and the agency. (There is a much fuller discussion of travel benefits in *Chapter 12*).

Paragraph VII seeks to protect the agency from lawsuits brought by angry customers. My guess is that the agency would seek to construe the term "contract" here as broadly as possible. In other words, if you say to the customer, "Don't worry, the weather in Cancun will be perfect," that might be construed as a "contract" on your part guaranteeing perfect weather. If the customer then sues because a hurricane hit Cancun during his stay, the agency wants to be covered. Again, talk to your lawyer and make sure that you understand what is at stake before signing.

Several items in this contract seem to be at odds with the IRS test

The Outside Sales Rep

for independent contractors. How *much* of a problem that represents is hard to say. Again, you'd have to get a ruling from your lawyer.

To summarize, this contract is presented here as an isolated example and to generate some interesting discussion. It is not meant to be a recommendation of what *your* contract should look like. The OSSN can provide you with other sample contracts, which differ from this one. So can any good lawyer. As always, you should rely on the advice of a competent legal professional when forging any important business relationship.

Summary

The information presented in this chapter should help get you started in your search for and negotiations with a travel agency in your community with which you can work on an independent, outside sales basis. If the prospect of doing that seems too overwhelming, don't despair. In the next chapter, I'll show you how you can become an outside sales rep "instantly," without a protracted search or tricky negotiations.

But before moving on, let's summarize the pros and cons of taking these two, slightly different routes to the same destination:

The 'Pros' of aligning yourself with a local agency

- It's convenient. The agency is close at hand and you can get tickets quickly, if needed.
- It's cheap. It shouldn't cost you anything to become an outside rep for a local firm.
- Help is close at hand. Hopefully, the agency will be willing to answer questions and teach you what you need to know. You may even be able to go into the agency and get training on its computers!
- An agency with which you have close personal ties may be more willing to work with you on getting perks like free or low-cost travel than one that is far away, for which you are just a number.

The 'Cons' of aligning yourself with a local agency

- Your commission split may be just 50/50 or less.
- You may be limited, by the agency's size, in terms of overrides (extra commissions) and other perks.
- It can be time-consuming to find an agency that is willing to work with you.

The 'Pros' of becoming an "instant" agent

- You can do it quickly, with little or no screening.
- You can often get better prices and commissions because these agencies have high volume.
- You can often get an excellent commission split, as high as 80%.
- You can get started right away.

- You can use your tenure with an "instant agency" to build a track record you can use to sell yourself to a local agency.
- If you decide this lifestyle is not for you, it's easier to walk away from an instant agency than a local one, where you may feel you're "letting the team down."

The 'Cons' of becoming an "instant" agent

- It can be expensive (although it doesn't have to be).
- You'll be dealing by phone and mail. That can be slow (the mail) and costly (the phone). You almost certainly will not be able to handle requests for last-minute bookings.
- You may have to commit to an investment in computer equipment and software. It can take quite a while to earn enough in commissions to pay off that investment; so if you decide the travel game isn't for you, you could wind up in the hole.
- If you have a serious problem with one of these agencies, seeking remedy can be difficult. It's hard to sue an outfit half a continent away.
- Sometimes it's hard to get personal assistance when you have a question or a problem.
- Finally, there is always the danger of being ripped off. You may be lured by "agencies" that aren't really travel agencies or by actual travel agencies that simply don't deliver on their promises. There is a discussion on "instant agencies" and how to shop for one in the *Resource Section*.

The Outside Sales Rep

Chapter Three:
Become A Travel Agent — TODAY!

If you're the impatient type, the travel business has a deal for you! It is possible to become a travel agent for a multimillion-dollar travel agency virtually overnight, no questions asked.

I know because I did it myself.

As I mentioned before, a growing number of travel agencies are expanding their horizons by taking on outside sales representatives. Most of them charge a fee for allowing you to book travel through them and share the commission. When I became an "instant agent," the agency I hooked up with charged no fee whatsoever. That, alas, has changed. They are now charging a one-time, $50 sign-up fee — a lot more than nothing but still well below what most "instant agent" operations charge.

In theory, the travel agency makes its *real* money on the travel you book. The sign-up fee, or membership, or whatever they call it, is (again, in theory) merely to cover the cost of setting you up in their system, providing you with materials, training, and so forth. In practice, some agencies offering this opportunity charge such high start-up fees (up to $3,000) that I suspect they are seeking to profit on the sign-up fees alone. Assuming a 50/50 split with the agency and an average commission rate of 10%, you'd have to sell $60,000 in travel just to recoup your $3,000 investment! I strongly suspect that many people who go this route discover that the travel game is harder than they thought, become disillusioned, and quit. The agency, meanwhile, has their $3,000 and whatever it made on the travel the hapless, would-be agents managed to book.

But I digress. Once you pay your fee and get your "membership" in the mail, you are ready to start booking trips and earning commissions. Assuming you have gone into this new relationship with your eyes open and without any unrealistic expectations, this can be a very good deal indeed

In this chapter, I will tell you how I went about becoming an "instant agent." But before I do, I should remind you that my experience covers only one agency, and each agency operates just a bit differently. I am describing my experience for a number of reasons. First, it is *my* experience. It's a lot easier to describe things you've actually done (as I discovered in high school, bragging about my nonexistent success with women). Second, I hope that my experience will give you some feel for what it's like to become an "instant agent" and begin to learn the ropes of the travel business.

What I can't, and don't, pretend to do in this chapter is describe what *all* instant agent experiences will be like. Had I signed on with a different agency my experience, obviously, would have been quite different. It might have been better; it might have been worse. Nor am I suggesting that you should follow my lead. In the *Resource Section* of this book, I list many agencies offering to make you an outside sales representative; you will also find there a discussion on how to comparison shop for these opportunities. Do your own research. Make your own decisions.

Leisure Resource

Leisure Group Limited is a Connecticut corporation involved in a number of entrepreneurial travel businesses. They are tour operators and wholesalers, handling destinations as disparate as Slovenia, in the former Yugoslavia, and the tiny Turks and Caicos Islands of the Caribbean. Under the names Generic Travel & Tours and Ethnic Resource, they are airline ticket consolidators, buying space at rock-bottom wholesale prices and selling at deep discounts. One of their businesses is Leisure Resource.

Leisure Resource is a travel agency. Just like the travel agencies you see on Main Street in your home town. The major difference is that Leisure Resource is tweaking and expanding the usual system of distribution of travel products.

Rather than have an in-house staff of travel agents (they actually *do* have some) waiting for customers to walk in the door, as most travel agencies do, Leisure Resource sells travel through a nationwide network of outside sales representatives in the United States and Canada. They also have a few reps in Europe and Asia. These reps find the clients, book the travel, and funnel the ticketing chores through Leisure Resource's office. Leisure Resource issues the tickets or other travel documents, collects the commissions, if necessary, and then shares them 60/40 with the outside rep — that's 60% for the rep, 40% for Leisure Resource!

The best part is, they make it very easy for the prospective outside travel agent to get involved. All you have to do is fill out and sign a simple form. There's a one-time $50 sign-up fee, no monthly charges. Leisure Resource makes its money on its share of the commissions.

My biggest question when I joined was, "Why would they want to take a chance on an inexperienced, bumbling idiot like myself, going out and trying to sell travel?" As Bruce Reichert, Leisure Group's President, explained it to me with a smile, "There's no way you can hurt us. You can only help yourself." So far, that's proven to be true.

Here, based on my own experience, is how the Leisure Resource system works:

Signing up

The first step in becoming a Leisure Group Member (as their outside reps are called) is to request an application form. But before you go running off half-cocked, let me warn you: This application form is a *contract*. As such, it should be treated with care. Consult a competent professional before deciding that signing it and sending it in is in your best interests.

That having been said, the form lays out the simple and straightforward business proposition Leisure Group has for you:

- They are a fully appointed IATA travel agency. That means they have all the necessary appointments and certifications (ARC, IATA, CLIA) to sell airline tickets, tours, and cruises, and collect the commissions.
- In exchange for your sign-up fee, you will be able use their appointment when dealing with suppliers. In effect, when you call a supplier, it is just as if you were a full-time employee sitting in their office in Milford, CT.
- They will give you 60% of the commission on everything you book, subject to some exceptions and limitations, which I will explain shortly.
- There is a one-time $50 sign-up fee to become a Leisure Group Member. (This is what Leisure Resource calls their "Basic Program," which is best-suited to beginners. There are other, more elaborate programs, offering a higher commission split but requiring a larger investment. I will discuss them in a bit later in this chapter.)

And that, in a nutshell, is it! When they receive your application, they will send you a slim "manual" outlining their policies and procedures and assign you a "Leisure Group Member Number," which identifies you to their computer systems and which you will use in all your dealings with them. Once you have this material in hand, you are a travel agent.

Working with suppliers

Working with Leisure Resource is almost like having your own travel agency — almost. First of all, you operate under a business name of your own choosing. Leisure Group wants you to list a company name on your application. Although you could probably use your own name as a company name, you'll probably want to come up with a separate business identity, even if it is something like "Joe Smith Travel." I use "The Intrepid Traveler" which is also the name of my publishing company, so it's very convenient.

If you'd like, you can go down to Main Street, rent a storefront, and call it "Joe Smith Travel," just like a "real" travel agency. Some Leisure Group Members do just that. Most of those that do, however, are experienced travel agents. Most newcomers, like myself, operate out of their homes or out of existing business premises, their "travel agency" consisting just of a business card. All that Leisure Group asks is that somewhere on your business card it say, "A Leisure Resource Affiliate."

While you can call your new travel business anything you choose and present yourself to the world under that name, Leisure Resource is very particular that you represent yourself to suppliers (airlines, cruise lines, tour operators, hotels, etc.) as Leisure Resource and only as Leisure Resource. The reason is quite simple: you are using Leisure Resource's IATA number. It is that identity that allows you to function as a travel agent and collect your commission. Without it, things get hopelessly muddled.

As a Leisure Group Member, you quickly learn the answers to the following questions, when they are asked by a supplier:

- *What's your agency?* You say, "Leisure Resource."
- *What's your IATA number?* You give Leisure Resource's IATA number.
- *What's your name?* You give your last name only.
- *What's your address?* You give Leisure Resource's street address in Connecticut.
- *What's your phone number?* You give a *specific* Leisure Resource number in Connecticut.

Most suppliers you deal with will already have Leisure Resource in their computer databases. Most systems use the telephone number, since it is unique, to identify the agency. So if you give your own telephone number or a different Leisure Resource number (they have several), the supplier will not be able to locate Leisure Resource on its computer.

Leisure Resource insists that you use your last name only because, with well over a thousand outside reps, trying to sort them out and figure which Joe or Mary goes with a particular booking is nigh on impossible. This can feel a little awkward since most of the people you deal with on the suppliers' end will identify themselves only by their first names.

In theory, the supplier should never guess that you are an outside rep working from a phone on your dining room table in Peoria; they should think you are working at a desk in Milford, CT. If you think the airline will think it's strange that an agent in Milford is booking a flight from Peoria to San Francisco and back, don't worry. They won't.

In practice, some suppliers will come to know where you're really located. Usually this will mean tour operators or cruise lines that have to send brochures directly to you. That's fine, just so long as the all-important computer database has the correct information. When the question of where to send brochures comes up, I simply say, "I'm an outside rep. Can you send them to my home without messing up the computer records?" Some suppliers can do this. Others have a policy of sending brochures only to the home office. In that case, I have to pay the postage to have Leisure Resource forward them on to me.

Booking through Leisure Resource

As an outside rep, Leisure Resource expects you to do everything a "real" travel agent would do, short of entering the booking into the computerized reservation system (CRS) and printing out the ticket. (And, if you're experienced enough or ambitious enough, you can even do that!) The last thing Leisure Resource wants is for you to call them up and say, "Hi, my Aunt Martha wants to fly from Cleveland to Pittsburgh sometime next Monday morning. Whatcha got?" No. You are expected to make all the contact with the airline and make Aunt Martha's booking, gathering all the information Leisure Resource will need to generate the ticket. (I will discuss the process of contacting various types of suppliers and making bookings in *Chapters 6* through *10*.)

Once you have made the booking, the next step is to send the information in to the home office. There are a number of ways to do this:

- **Phone it in.** At this writing, Leisure Resource is still accepting bookings by phone, although they keep saying they will phase this out. They require you to use their local number, instead of an 800 number, which is meant to discourage the practice. If you do call in a booking, you are expected to have all the required information at your fingertips. Leisure Resource provides booking forms with their manual which make gathering and recording the necessary information a relatively foolproof process.
- **Fax it in.** This is preferred. It's faster, cheaper (because they have a toll-free fax number) and less likely to generate errors.
- **Use a CRS.** More advanced agents can link themselves to Leisure Resource through one of several computerized reservations systems. In this case, the booking is "queued" to the Leisure Resource computer and the ticket is generated automatically.
- **Mail it in.** If there's enough time before the booking deadline, you can mail in your booking.

In the case of an airline booking, Leisure Resource will print out the ticket and send it to you along with a check representing your share of the commission. If you want the ticket sent anywhere else but to your address or by any other means than regular mail, there is a charge, ranging from $1.00 to send a ticket regular mail to a different address (a client's, for example) to a whopping $50.00 for same day delivery. (Airborne priority overnight is $8.50.)

There are a number of variations on this theme. Some bookings don't involve tickets or other types of documentation and don't need to be sent in immediately. These include:

- Hotel reservations, when the client will pay on checkout.
- Car rentals, when the client will pay upon return of the car. Many foreign car rentals, however, require prepayment.
- Travel Insurance.

At Leisure Resource, bookings in these categories are handled differently. You simply keep track of the bookings you make (hotel, client name, date of arrival, etc.). Then, every two weeks or so, depending on the kind of volume you are doing, you send in a list of your recent bookings. Leisure Resource will then send you your share of the commission when they receive it from the supplier.

Your commission

As I mentioned earlier, Leisure Resource gives its outside reps in the Basic Program 60% of the commission due to Leisure Resource from the supplier. There are some exceptions to that, however:

- There is a $5.00 minimum fee per booking to Leisure Resource. When Leisure Resource's 40% share would be less than $5.00, they adjust your share accordingly. You have to be booking pretty cheap travel for this rule to kick in.
- When you book one of Leisure Group's wholesale products, you keep the whole commission, usually 10%.
- Any agent bonuses are yours to keep. Sometimes suppliers will have special deals to encourage you, the agent, to choose them rather than another supplier. For example, a Caribbean resort will offer a $50.00 incentive for every booking made within a certain time period. Usually, the booking agent fills out a coupon and sends it to the supplier. The bonus payment is then processed separately from the regular agency commission.
- Tour conductor passes. If you book a group large enough to qualify you for a tour conductor pass, it's yours to keep. You could also sell it, for full price.

In my experience, Leisure Resource pays promptly. In the case of airline tickets, that means that I receive my commission check in the same envelope with the ticket. For other kinds of bookings, I have to wait. For example, a car rental in Europe may have to be prepaid months prior to the trip, but I only get my commission some time after the client returns from the trip. That's because many suppliers don't pay commissions until after the travel is completed. The rule of thumb is: when Leisure Resource gets paid, so does the agent. My experience seems to bear this out. To my knowledge, I've never had a commission payment held up.

In many cases, you will collect your commission up front. When a client pays by check or cash, you simply deduct your share of the commission and forward the resulting "net" payment to Leisure Resource. When the client uses a credit card, you'll have to wait for your commission. You can consider asking your clients to pay by check or cash but, in my experience, people like to use their credit cards for the additional convenience and protection they provide.

Some suppliers (hotels, especially) have a way of being "forgetful" when it comes to paying commissions. Leisure Resource expects you to hound the supplier in cases like these. They will take their 40% cut when the payment comes in but will not help you dun the supplier.

Training

There is no training included in the basic sign-up fee. However, Leisure Resource has recently implemented an extensive optional training program which includes selling skills and geography in addition to CRS training (on Sabre). It's available through a network of community colleges around the country for about $900 or in a home-study version for about $250. Your other option is to learn as you go.

The manual you receive does have a lot of useful and helpful information, but it falls far short of answering all your questions. At least it fell far short of answering all mine. On the other hand, you don't have to be a rocket scientist to book travel. Like any business, it has its own jargon that may seem impenetrable and complicated at first. But gradually you catch on.

This book is, in part, a response to all the problems I had learning the ropes and getting to the point where I could deal confidently with suppliers without feeling awkward. There are a host of sources of information and support beyond this book, and I will point you towards those as well in the *Resource Section*. Suffice it to say that if you want to learn the ropes, you can. And you can do it faster than you think.

The "fine print" and other problems

Leisure Resource sees itself as providing you, the independent sales representative, with a service. It does not see itself as being responsible for your mistakes. That means, among other things, that . . .

- You accept full responsibility for all tickets and other travel documents you order through Leisure Resource. If you have Aunt Sadie's plane ticket sent to you via regular mail and the U.S. Post Office loses it, you're responsible for replacing that ticket.
- If you make a mistake in the booking and the ticket has to be reissued, you pay any additional costs or penalties. Likewise, if the client decides he wants to leave on Tuesday instead of Wednesday, Leisure Resource won't absorb the costs; that is a matter between you and your client.
- If a client's trip is canceled and the commission is recalled, you must assume responsibility and suffer the consequences.

All in all, these are not onerous conditions. But they can result in unexpected and annoying expense. I know, because it's happened to me.

Recruiting new members

Selling travel isn't the only way to make money as a Leisure Resource member. You can begin building a steady stream of passive income by recruiting new members for the Leisure Resource network of outside reps. It's not a multilevel marketing scheme in the Amway sense. Rather, you earn a modest referral fee based on the new member's productivity.

For every new member you bring on board, Leisure Resource will give you one half of one percent (0.5%) of the new member's commissionable bookings for the first two years of their membership. As Leisure Resource explains it, it's like changing the 60/40 commission split to 60/35/5 — 60% for the new member you signed up, 35% for Leisure Resource, and 5% for you. It's important to note that the referral fee comes out of Leisure Resource's share of the commission not out of the new member's.

If you sign up an experienced travel agent who has the potential to do a lot of business quickly, your potential share can be significant. If you sign up a beginner, your share will be negligible, since most people just starting out will take two years to learn the ropes and start becoming truly productive. Still, it has the potential of bringing in a nice bit of "extra" income.

One of the best ways to take advantage of this feature is to recruit a corporation to participate. Any company that spends more than $100,000 a year on travel is a prime candidate to become a Leisure Group member, just to book its own travel. This is a special version of Leisure Group membership in which the subscribing company actually has a CRS and a satellite printer, which can print out airline tickets on the spot. This program has a slightly different payout schedule, which was explained in some detail in the "Bird-dogging major accounts" section of *Chapter 2: The Outside Sales Rep.*

The trick is getting your cut. The Leisure Resource manual says, "We make payments upon your request in July and January." The key words here are "upon your request." I have found that, left to their own devices, the home office has a way of overlooking these payments. You can't assume they'll make them automatically. My experience is that it helps to know who you've signed up. Simply handing out application forms at the mall is not a good way to get rich. Many people will never sign up. Second, it helps to know if people you referred, and who *have* signed up, have been active. It's even better if you know how much they've booked. That way you can get in touch, provide Leisure Resource with some specifics, and nudge them to calculate and forward your share of the commission. Even after you've reminded them, however, you may find that they have "overlooked" some of the people you signed up.

Options for the experienced agent

If you devote yourself wholeheartedly to becoming an outside rep, you may find that eventually you will want to become a little more organized and professional about your business activities. Or, perhaps, you are already an experienced travel professional and are ready to branch out on your own, with your own storefront operation. If so, Leisure Resource is willing to help you grow.

- *Automation.* For about $275, Leisure Resource will supply you with the software for one of four commercial CRS systems — Commercial Sabre, Access (SystemOne), Worldspan, or Corporate Apollo. Hardware is your responsibility. Training, either at your site or at Leisure Resource's office, is also available for an additional fee, ranging from $300 to $1,250 depending on the system and location of the training. With reservation software, your commission split goes to 70/30.

- **The Mini-Branch and Branch programs.** For those who want to take the next step (or for those who may already be full-fledged travel professionals and are looking for a less costly way to open their own storefront agency), Leisure Resource offers two branch programs. Becoming a branch office requires that you meet certain ARC requirements, most noticeably having an actual "office" in a commercially zoned building, with a sign. You operate under your own name (as opposed to Leisure Resource's) and are required to carry errors and omissions insurance. You pay annual ARC fees ($425 first year, $250 a year thereafter) and have the option of joining IATA ($390 first year, $65 a year thereafter).

  Essentially the branch programs allow you to function as a completely separate travel agency except that Leisure Resource handles the cumbersome and time-consuming job of submitting regular reports to the Airlines Reporting Corporation (ARC). The main differences between the programs are the fees payable to Leisure Resource for handling the ARC reporting and the commission splits. In the Mini-Branch program, you pay $2,500 a year and collect 75% of the commission on all ARC documents. In the Full Branch program you pay an annual fee of $5,000 and collect 85% of the commission on ARC documents. You collect 100% of all other commissions. Your choice of program would depend on your projection of how much ARC business you would be doing annually.

The cost of these options strikes me as moderate, especially compared to what many other "instant agencies" charge. Moreover, they are options; many other instant agencies require a heavy up-front investment in hardware and software — before you know if that's really the route you want to go. Also, these options allow you to become, in effect, a travel agency without the onerous bonding expenses of going the more traditional route.

Summary

Leisure Resource may not be the ideal solution for you in your search for a way to get involved in the travel business. I have tried to be up-front about the drawbacks, both in this discussion and in the pros-and-cons summary in the last chapter. But I suspect it could work quite well for a good many people who pick up this book.

It's certainly working for me so far, although I am keeping my options open and will move to another agency if it appears to be in my best interests. That, after all, is part of what being an independent contractor is all about.

I should also point out that when I hooked up with Leisure Resource, they weren't charging a sign-up fee and they were offering a 70/30 split to all comers. They pulled back, they told me, because they were getting too many people who weren't taking it seriously. The $50 is supposed to take care of that.

Would I have signed up if the deal was what it is now ($50 and 60/40)? I'm not sure. If I could have negotiated a 60/40 split with a local agency, it would be a no-brainer — go with the local agency. But I think a beginner would be hard pressed to get that kind of a deal. Also, I might well have decided that writing a $50 check was a lot less painful than finding (and negotiating with) a local agency.

The major disadvantage I have discovered in working with Leisure Resource is distance. It simply takes time to deal with an agency that may be half a continent or more away from you. I have to wait for tickets and get very nervous when the mail is slow. Others might find the lack of training a drawback, although I must say I kind of enjoyed the challenge of learning on my own. My hope is that the information in this book will mean you won't have the same problems I did in learning the ropes.

In the end, you'll have to make your own decision — a local agency or an "instant agency" like Leisure Resource. I can't make that decision for you, but I've tried to help a bit by listing a number of "instant agent" opportunities in the *Resource Section*. Along with the list, I provide a detailed discussion of how to be an informed consumer when it comes to these opportunities.

Chapter Four:
Setting Up Your Travel Business

One of the best things about getting into the part-time travel game is that it's so easy to do. By now, you may have already hooked up with an agency in your home town or sent away to one of the "instant agencies" to become an outside rep. Another aspect about this lifestyle that really appeals to me is that it's so easy to "set up shop" and actually start selling travel. When I made my first sale and booked my first ticket, I had literally nothing to show that I was, in effect, a travel agent. No storefront with posters in the window and brochures in wall racks. No desks. No computerized reservations system. No fancy letterhead and envelopes with the name of my agency on them. Not even a business card! And the amazing thing is, I could have gone on operating that way indefinitely.

Most of you will want to get a *little* more formal and organized than that, however. In fact, if you want to go to the other extreme, it's possible to become virtually indistinguishable from a "real" travel agent. That is, you can have your very own storefront and the whole nine yards. My guess is that very few of you will want to go that far — at least not immediately.

This chapter, then, is intended to show how easy it is to become a part-time, and profitable, travel agent with very few of the trappings and very little of the overhead of most businesses. In *Chapter 11: Getting Serious*, I'll show you how your part-time travel agency can become more professional as your business and your ambitions grow.

Your first "office"

First of all, I'm going to assume that you'll be running your part-time travel business from your home. Most people in this lifestyle do. The good news is that you don't have to refinish the basement or clear out the attic to create an office for yourself. You really don't need a room for your office at all. Your "travel agency" can quite easily consist of a supply of business cards, an address book or Rolodex, and a telephone, preferably one with an answering machine attached. That's it! Oh, if you want to get fancy you can throw in some stationery, too, although I think you'll find you won't use it much.

Your business card doesn't have to be fancy, either. I got mine through an outfit called The Stationery House, (800) 638-3033, that charges $23.25 to print up 500 simple but classy engraved cards — the kind with raised printing. You might even be able to beat that price through a local printer. You may want to bill yourself simply as "Joe Smith, Travel Consultant," or you may want to create a catchy business name for your new enterprise. It's up to you.

While your business card doesn't *have* to be fancy, a snazzy card can't hurt. In fact, it can go a long way toward establishing your credibility and enhancing your image. For the cost, a professionally designed and printed business card can be your most effective advertising. When you hand your card to potential clients or to suppliers' reps you meet at industry functions, they will form their first impression of you and your business when they glance at your card. If you want to "splurge," splurge on your card.

You'll also need some way of keeping track of your growing list of customers. For starters, a cheap address book or Rolodex will do just fine. As you get more serious or busy, or both, you can expand your record-keeping system. I'll give you some ideas along that line a little later.

And, of course, you'll need a phone. It could be your existing home phone for now. As you get more customers, you may want to consider adding a separate line just for your travel business. It should have call-waiting and an answering machine so you don't miss any calls from would-be customers. If you have a dedicated line for your travel sideline, you'll probably want to have a "travel agency" message on it like, "Hi! You've reached Joe Smith, Travel Consultant." Your answering machine message can even do some advertising for you, alerting callers to special deals you may have found for tours or cruises.

And that's it! You're in business! The phone and the address book you probably already have. The business cards will have to be ordered. But remember, once you've got your outside rep status lined up, you're in business just as soon as you decide to be. Business cards or not.

Defining yourself

Probably the hardest part of setting yourself up as a part-time travel agent is deciding just what your business is all about. At first, you may think that you will be, indeed should be, just like any other travel agent in town. That's because you're familiar with the model of the "traditional" travel agency. Let's take a moment to examine that model and figure out why it is the way it is.

The "traditional" travel agency is a storefront operation. It's down there on Main Street, with maps and colorful posters in the windows and a few black-and white-flyers taped to the glass touting "super" deals to special destinations. Without having to say so in any concrete way, the traditional travel agency sends out a very clear message to anyone who walks by: "Here I am, ready to take on all comers! No matter where you want to go, no matter how you want to get there, no matter what you want to do, no matter how long or short your journey, I'm the one to see!"

That's quite a responsibility! If someone walks into this agency and says "I want to fly upstate and back," the travel agent isn't going to say, "Sorry, there's not enough money in that ticket to make it worth my while." If someone walks in and says, "I want to go trekking in Bhutan," the travel agent isn't going to say, "Gee, I don't even know where Bhutan is." Oh, the travel agent *could* turn away business; some no doubt do. But most simply can't.

Why? Because a traditional travel agency represents a large financial investment and involves considerable overhead. The agency needs to generate a lot of business every month before it can even begin to think about generating a profit. So there is tremendous financial and psychological pressure to snare every piece of business that walks in the door. Then, too, there is the matter of professional pride. By opening a storefront agency, the owner is saying that he or she is equally capable of serving the short-hop customer and the voyager to exotic locales. That's what being a full-service travel agent is all about!

While operating a traditional storefront agency has its rewards, it also has its problems and perils. Primary among them is, that by taking on all comers, the storefront agency inevitably winds up doing a major portion of its business in cheap airfare. There are a number of problems with this:

- Because the fares are low, so are the commissions.
- The fixed costs of processing tickets and reporting to ARC eat into those low commissions, and the rent and utilities still have to be paid
- Purchasers of cheap travel tend to shop around, cancel reservations, change dates, and so forth. Many agencies will absorb any reticketing costs rather than antagonize what they hope will be a regular customer.
- Airline price wars produce a flood of passengers who want their tickets rebooked at the new, lower fares. During the Great Fare War of 1992, thousands of travel agencies lost money on every single ticket they rebooked.
- The amount of money earned for the amount of time invested is often negligible when selling cheap travel. By the time a customer hems and haws about dates, has the agent check ten different carriers searching for a cheaper fare, books, changes his mind and alters the dates, the travel agent's $20 commission will seem paltry indeed. It can take the same amount of time to help a client select and book a cruise that will pay several hundred dollars in commissions.
- Even with international flights where the fares are higher and the commissions slightly bigger, the picture doesn't improve much. Unlike the domestic market, the international airfare market is characterized by heavy discounting through consolidators. Much of this consolidation is done to satisfy the demand from various ethnic communities traveling to "the Old Country." "Many companies in the ethnic markets are willing to work for five to fifteen dollars per ticket," warns one travel agent. "In all these markets, your client will have

checked with thirty agencies before they talked to you and will contact thirty more after you."

- Many industry observers point to the problems associated with selling cheap travel as the primary reason for the high mortality rate among traditional storefront travel agencies.

Avoiding the cheap-travel trap

One of the best things about being an outside sales rep is that you are not bound by the expectations and restrictions placed on a traditional travel agency. As an independent operator, you can avoid the cheap travel trap.

In practice, that's easier said than done, especially by the beginner who doesn't yet have a following or a readily defined area of specialization. When you're just starting out, most of your first prospects will be family, friends, and neighbors who will have a need precisely for the kind of cheap air transportation I've just been talking about. You also may find that some of your customers will "try you out" with a simple plane booking or two before they trust you with putting together that African safari. Finally, you'll probably find, just as I did, that it's hard to turn down the chance to make your first booking, even if your commission will only be $13.40.

Of course it's true that those $13.40 commissions have a way of adding up, and unless you make a hard and fast rule against booking *any* airfare-only trips, you'll find cheap travel accounting for some portion of your business. It doesn't have to be an annoying part of your business, either. For example, I have a number of friends who travel home to see the folks once or twice a year and, bless their hearts, they're more than happy to let me book their flights. It's a simple cut-and-dried proposition; since they've been flying the same route for years, they just tell me what airline, what time of day, and sometimes, even which flight number they want. It takes me no more than a few minutes to make the booking. Under those circumstances, the modest commissions I earn represent a good return on my investment of time and effort.

Of course, for some of you, appealing to the market for cheap travel may be your best shot at success. For example, if you already have a retail establishment, it's a simple matter to turn a corner of it over to your new travel business. Unless you make a clear-cut decision to specialize in, say, cruises, a retail-based operation will naturally attract the cheap-airfare consumer, and that can provide a very nice stream of income.

As you gain more firsthand experience with your new part-time travel agent business, you will have to make your own decision about cheap travel. My personal choice is that while I don't always turn it away, I don't actively solicit it either and am choosy about the requests to which I respond. The important point to remember here, however, is that there is a fundamental difference between you and the storefront agency. While they pretty well have to accept any and all business that walks through the door, you have the choice of going out into the community and seeking only the kind of business that you want — business that will offer a high payback for the time and effort you invest.

The advantages of specialization

The more you adopt an "all things to all people" stance in the marketplace, the more likely you are to fall into the cheap-travel trap. The best way to prevent that from happening is to define yourself as a "specialist." By doing so, you do not necessarily cut yourself off from all other areas of the travel business, but you do provide a focus — both for yourself and your clients. By specializing, you make it easier for yourself, since it takes less time to gain an in-depth knowledge about one destination or mode of travel than about dozens. At the same time, you provide your potential customer with a convenient way to remember you — "Oh, yes, she's the one who books all those wonderful cruises!"

Businesses of all kinds specialize, and even businesses which seem very specific indeed have further specialized within their own market niches. It's called "positioning" by the MBA marketing types and it works like this: Cadillac and Harley-Davidson both sell something that will get you from point A to point B. But the similarity ends there. Harley-Davidson specializes in motorcycles. But saying that doesn't mean to imply that a chopped hog from Harley and a rice-burner from Kawasaki are one and the same vehicle. That's because Harley-Davidson has "positioned " itself very precisely in the marketplace. Their products appeal to a different kind of person and for different reasons than do Kawasaki's sleek racing numbers.

The fascinating thing about positioning is that, whether you are aware of it or not, you will "position" yourself in your part-time travel business. Over time, the people who deal with you will develop a "picture" of your business in their minds, just as they have a picture in their minds about what Harley-Davidson represents to them. Since you're going to be positioned anyway, why not spend a little time thinking about it?

You may survey your available options and choose to specialize from the beginning of your travel selling career. Or you may begin to specialize gradually as you feel your way to your niche in the travel business. However you do it, the key to specialization is knowledge — you gain an in-depth familiarity with your area of specialization through a combination of study and experience. That means you become better equipped to advise your clients, offer them a wider range of options, alert them to great deals, or warn them of things to steer clear of. But specialization has another, equally important, benefit: You increase your earning power! That's because you work more efficiently. Someone who knows all the ins and outs of booking a scuba holiday will earn their $200 or $300 or $400 commission a lot faster than the person who is making this kind of booking for the first time.

There are any number of ways in which you can specialize:

By destination

Pat Berthrong, whom we met in *Chapter 1*, specializes in Ireland. Even though she sometimes ventures to other destinations in Europe, it is her firsthand knowledge of the Emerald Isle that enables her to differentiate herself from the major tour operators by providing the kind of very special, off-the-beaten path experiences that the majors just can't match.

I know of an outside rep for a New England agency whose speciality is European FITs (that stands for "Foreign Inclusive Tours") with an accent on budget travel. If that sounds like she's limiting herself, think again. Europe is a *huge* market for the vacation traveler and the choices are so mind-boggling that keeping on top of all the changes is more than a full-time job. In exchange for her efforts, she has made herself an expert in one of America's favorite vacation destinations — Europe — a destination which is a natural for many people in her area. She is also building, I am sure, a steady referral business.

Do you have a favorite destination? One you'd like to get to know better? One you love so much that every time you describe it, your friends start thinking, "Gee, maybe *I* should go there?" Then you may have found a profitable area of specialization. It's a lot easier to sell a destination you know and love than one you've only seen in travel brochures.

Of course, as a destination specialist you will have to make frequent trips to the area to check out the hotels, attractions, and tourist bureaus, to keep up-to-date on your market. It's a tough job, but someone has to do it.

By mode of travel

The most obvious example of this kind of specialization is the proliferation of cruise-only agencies. These are storefront operations which are just like any other travel agency office, except that all they sell are cruise vacations. There's no reason why you can't have the same kind of business, operating from your home.

Cruises have a lot going for them from the agent's point of view:

- *They are a relatively high-ticket item* (although they represent excellent value for the traveler). You should make several hundred dollars on every cruise booking you make.
- *They represent a well-defined, well-promoted market* — you have Kathie Lee on television selling for you!
- *They generate repeat business.* While a lot of people profess to *hate* cruises, the people who like them are very loyal. Eighty-five percent of people who take one cruise, take another, and that kind of repeat business is the key to a very profitable business.
- *The cruise lines help you sell them.* Cruise lines (at least the big ones) are very savvy marketers. They will provide you with all sorts of sales support, including video tapes to show to clients.

Cruises aren't the only way to specialize by mode of transportation. I know of a gentleman on Long Island who, as an outside rep and independent contractor, specializes in motorcoach tours, an extremely popular mode of leisure travel among seniors. Or you might be a person who just loves trains. Many train lovers will travel far and wide to recreate the kind of romantic journeys that are a thing of the past here in the States but can still be found in Europe (the Orient Express!), India, and Latin America.

By theme or activity

Another way to focus your travel marketing is by what your customers do when they get to wherever it is they are going. In this kind of specialization, the destination is almost secondary, it is the activity that takes priority. Here are some examples of specialization by activity:

- *Skiing.* Avid skiers get tired of skiing in the same old place. Once they get bored with Killington, they want to ski the Rockies and the Alps. If they're real fanatics, they'll head South of the Equator so they can ski in the summer. There is a burgeoning industry of ski-oriented tour operators to serve this market.

- *Golf.* Golfers are an easily identified and targeted group that can be lured with the prospect of playing PGA-rated courses in the Caribbean or the spectacular holes of Hawaii, or the legendary links of Scotland.

- *Scuba diving.* This is another activity that has spawned a mini-industry of specialty tours. Once people get hooked on diving in the Keys, they want to dive The Bahamas and explore the great reefs off Belize. Sooner or later they'll get a hankering to swim with the great whites of Australia's Great Barrier Reef.

- *"Alternative travel."* This is a catch-all phrase that is used to describe a grab-bag of vacation options that are outside the mainstream. That could mean a white-water rafting trip in Borneo, a three-week trek through the valleys of Nepal, or a month working on an archaeological dig in Israel. This is a small but growing segment of the travel market and, despite its countercultural tinge, it is definitely not cheap travel. There are good commissions to be made here.

- *Pilgrimages.* There are a limited number of destinations throughout the world (Lourdes, Fatima, Israel, Mecca, and others less well-known) that attract a steady stream of religious travelers. The consumers for this type of travel are also easily reached through religious organizations.

And these are only a few of the options. It seems that, today, there is a tour for every interest — tennis players, opera buffs, nudists, whatever, you can find a place to send them. The key to succeeding with this type of specialization is a sincere interest in and knowledge of the activity or theme involved. I should also point out that some areas of specialization might prove to be limiting. If you live in rural, heavily Mormon Utah, for example, you may find the market for pilgrimages to Catholic shrines quite tiny.

By market segment

Some travel agents concentrate quite profitably on certain types of customers rather than on destinations or activities. Usually, this means serving the special needs and interests of specific (and easily identified) segments of the population. Here are just a few examples of this type of specialization:

- **The disabled.** There is a growing market for travel and tours geared to the special needs of the disabled. As the options for leading a full and productive life have expanded for the disabled, so has their disposable income, and the disabled are just as keen to visit the great cities of Europe or ride on an elephant's back as anyone else. Many people are finding a profitable niche (and a lot of goodwill, too) by serving this market.

- **Recovering alcoholics.** These travelers also have special needs and tend to respond to the idea of traveling in groups. After all, it's easier to avoid temptation on a cruise if it's a "dry" cruise with other former tipplers. Many tours for this market include special support activities. Again, as with so many other special interest areas, there are a growing number of tour operators offering tours targeted to this market.

- **Religious groups** are another market with special, but often overlooked, needs. They may travel to Europe this year and Australia the next, but they will respond to the travel agent who appreciates that they are looking for an experience and an ambiance which jibes with their strongly held beliefs.

- **Budget, or mid-range, or luxury travelers.** People are also defined by the amount of money they can afford to spend on their travel. Depending on where you are located and the kind of access or exposure you have in your market, you may find it most profitable to pursue the budget traveler. Or you might find a better fit selling mid-range tours and cruises. Or you may be able to gain entree to the luxury market and sell up-scale vacations to the wealthy.

By payback

It may seem crass, but some agents like to go where the money is. We may be talking now more of a subspecialty than a specialty, or perhaps it's more accurately referred to as a marketing strategy. In either case, there are a number of ways in which the bottom line can determine where you focus your efforts.

The agency with which you affiliate as an outside rep will no doubt have a number of "preferred suppliers." These could be the members of a consortium to which the agency subscribes or suppliers with whom the agency has some sort of one-to-one relationship. The net result is the same: higher commissions. It makes perfect economic sense to concentrate on selling the tour products of these preferred suppliers. For example, I can book an air and hotel package to a Caribbean resort through one of my agency's preferred suppliers and earn 10.5% commission (that's my 70% of the 15% this supplier offers my agency). I could book *exactly the same* package through another tour operator and earn only 7% (70% of 10%).

If you examine the offerings of your agency's preferred suppliers, you may find that you will have a very nice "product line" to offer your customers. It will be rather like having a clothing store and choosing to carry only certain lines. The difference, of course, is that if your customer doesn't want what your preferred suppliers have to offer or if the preferred supplier offerings aren't right for your customer, you are free to sell them something more appropriate.

You may discover through experience that you can sell more of certain travel products more readily than others. That should tell you that you could increase your volume if you concentrated on those products. Higher volume, of course, means more money for you. Which products will turn out to be "winners" for you is impossible for me to predict. That will depend on a complex mix of your expertise and enthusiasm, the demographics of your market, and sheer luck. But once those winners emerge, you may want to consider the implications carefully to see if there's an opportunity you're missing.

Another way of letting the bottom line guide your business is to concentrate on the upper-income market segments. You could sell a wide variety of destinations and types of travel but specialize in luxury. Every doctor, lawyer, dentist, corporate VP, and stockbroker in your area takes vacations, and the vacations they take tend to be more glamorous than most. What's more, all the doctors, lawyers, dentists, and stockbrokers are listed in the Yellow Pages (the corporate types are harder to find), so they are an easily targeted audience.

By focusing on groups

No area of specialty offers a better promise of high payback than group travel. That means that instead of sending a couple on a trip, you send a dozen people, or 20, or 50 There are all sorts of groups that travel together — church groups, high-school reunion classes, college groups, fraternal organizations, the list goes on.

Here's where your commissions can be truly gratifying. If sending a couple to Europe nets you $400, imagine what sending 50 people there will pull in! It will likely be more than $400 times 25. Why? Because you'll undoubtedly get a better rate of commission for bringing in a large group.

Sometimes you can find groups that remain pretty constant from year to year. For example, one part-timer I know services a group of students and faculty from Indiana which comes to New York once a year for a week of theatergoing. Then there's a women's club here in New York that sponsors a trip to London just about every year. The faces change from year to year, but there's always a bunch of people traveling.

Groups like that can form a good base for your group business. But to really succeed, you'll have to beat the bushes for accounts. That can mean a slow and painstaking process of contacting potential groups, locating the right person to deal with, proposing some kind of group experience, and working closely with your inside contact to promote and market the idea to the membership.

Selling to groups is fundamentally different from the onesy-twosy kind of travel bookings that most part-time outside agents do. For one thing, you won't find 20 people walking up to you and saying, "Oh, you're a travel agent? We'd like to go on a safari." No, you have to go and seek them out. That makes selling group travel a very specific type of sale.

By focusing on corporate travel

"Corporate travel agencies" are a special niche in the travel industry. These are agencies which operate out of modest offices in high-rise buildings rather than from storefronts. They don't deal with the general public (for the most part). Companies are their clients, not individuals. They make their money by serving all the travel needs of a business — booking air and hotels and rental cars for the client company's personnel when they travel on business. They usually offer their client companies lower fares, in effect rebating a portion of their commission, hoping to make their money on the increased volume. This type of business is heavy on domestic air travel, demands an encyclopedic knowledge of fare structures, requires its practitioners to play the CRS like Horowitz played the piano, and is fiercely competitive.

I don't think most of the people who will read this book have a prayer of competing in this marketplace as part-time (or even full-time) outside reps. That doesn't mean you have to turn your back on corporate marketing completely, however. If you stumble onto a chance to "sell" a corporate account, pursue it. In *Chapter 2: The Outside Sales Rep*, I have described how you can make money by bringing a corporate customer to an agency that specializes in handling that kind of business.

Creating a mix of specialties

If you specialize at all, you will most likely wind up mixing and matching among these various alternatives. You might focus on budget travel to Latin America, thus specializing in both a destination and a market segment. Or if you specialize in activity-based travel, you may find yourself in the group business since birds of a feather, after all, flock together.

It is this tendency of people of like interests to flock together that produces another advantage of specializing — your customers are easier to reach. If you are selling luxury cruises, you can make some generalizations about your customer base — they are well-to-do, for example. It's relatively easy to figure out where the well-to-do live in your community. You also don't have to be a rocket scientist to figure out that doctors and lawyers tend to be more well-to-do than most. Or perhaps you may discover that your best customers are senior citizens. If so, you'll know that well-to-do seniors are people you want to contact.

Knowing all this, it is possible to get lists of these people's names and addresses. Doctors and lawyers are in the Yellow Pages, remember? And consumer mailing lists broken down by zip code are available as well, though often for a price. It is also a relatively easy matter to identify the upscale retirement communities within a 50-mile radius of your base of operation. Now you can begin a proactive campaign to drum up interest in your target market, instead of waiting for someone to come up to you at a cocktail party and say, "Gee, I'd sorta like to take a luxury cruise."

A final thought on specialization

There are some very sound financial and marketing reasons to specialize, but I would encourage you to think with your heart as well as your head. My experience has been that the people who succeed in their specialties have a certain affinity for what they are doing. Scuba divers book dive vacations, people who are seriously concerned about the needs of the disabled concentrate on that area, people who sell budget travel love to travel that way themselves.

You're probably reading these words because you love to travel. What are your favorite destinations? What do you like to do when you go on vacation? With which segments of your community do *you* have a particular connection or affinity? Consider these questions as you examine your options in the travel selling game. The answers may point you to a profitable and personally fulfilling definition of your travel business.

Of course, the chances are a lot of you won't specialize immediately or even anytime soon. And some of you may never get around to specializing at all. You might find that booking a cruise this week and then calling dozens of suppliers next week to nail down a specialty tour is part of the fun of the travel game. It's also generally true that the less travel you sell, the more difficult it is to specialize. That's because specializing implies marketing and if you're just going to book a few trips each month for close friends and family, then your business isn't developed enough to think about marketing. What's more, you're probably relying on walk-up business for the few bookings that come in — just like a storefront agency!

Still, you may find it worth your while to consider some of the options available to you for defining your travel business and positioning yourself in your market. By having an idea of what has worked for others, you can get a better sense of what might work best for you.

The next step: office machines

As I've noted, it's perfectly possible to start selling travel with little more than a fistful of business cards and a telephone. But after a while, as your business expands and you begin to see that you can make some significant income in this new lifestyle, you're probably going to want to add a few bells and whistles to your operation. The two big investments you will want to consider are a fax and a computer.

If you already have one or both of these wonderful devices, great! You're ahead of the game. If not, you'll want to proceed carefully and keep a close eye on the cost-benefit ratio of any investment you make. There is a bewildering array of choices out there, and so many variables to weigh in making a decision that the shopping process can quickly become a frustrating nightmare. One way to proceed is to buy a "Buying Guide" type of publication. These are magazine-format publications which list, describe, and rate the numerous machines on the market. Another way is to talk to "experts." I find this to be an arduous task since the experts tend to be passionate about the machines they have chosen (especially computers) and equally passionate against all others.

Here is a selection methodology which, while not particularly elegant, makes a lot of sense to me. Find someone who has a fax or a computer they like. Get them to tell you about it, how it works, how they use it in their business. Ask them what you'll be able to do with it. Tell them the sort of things you'll need it to do and ask them if it can do those things. Then get them to show you how the machine actually does those things. Most importantly, get a sense of whether or not you'll be able to call on them, once you have the machine, to ask for their help and suggestions. Shop around for the best price once you've settled on a brand and model.

This system probably works better with computers than with fax machines but it can be used for both. My theory is that while you might not wind up with the cheapest machine, the time you save shopping and dealing with problems and questions after the purchase will compensate for any extra cost.

I will not try to cover all your options here. That would take another whole book! But I will make some observations which, hopefully, will prove helpful as you set up your home travel agency.

Faxes

Fax (or "facsimile") machines translate images, such as a typed letter or an advertising flyer, into digital code which can be transmitted over telephone lines to another fax machine. The receiving machine decodes the message and creates a copy of the original image. There are a number of reasons you might find a fax machine useful in your business:

- ■ ***To communicate with your agency.*** Even if your agency is just across town, you may find the convenience of a fax worth the investment. Bookings and other messages have a way of getting garbled when they are transmitted over the phone . A fax can prevent that. A faxed message also creates a record of what was "said." In my case, it's virtually essential that I have this capability. The agency I deal with for most of my ticketing is in the next state. I can still phone in bookings (and run up a long-distance phone bill) but they keep saying that soon they will require all bookings to be faxed in. Fortunately, they provide a toll-free fax number.

- ■ ***To communicate with suppliers.*** When you're working on a booking with a short time fuse, it can be a tremendous help if the tour operator or other supplier can fax you information (price lists, terms and conditions, whole brochures). Getting brochures in the mail can take days, even weeks. A growing number of suppliers have "fax-back" service — you dial a toll-free number, punch in the code for the information you want (usually obtained from an advertisement), punch in your fax number, and the material is faxed to you immediately. Royal Caribbean cruise lines has a service called CruiseFax, which allows agencies to have the latest cruise discounts just minutes after Royal Caribbean decides to offer them.

- ***To communicate with customers.*** Sometimes you will need to obtain some form of credit card authorization from a client. He or she can photocopy their credit card, write on the photocopy the travel being booked and the costs (e.g. "2 tickets to California from Joe's Travel, $842"), sign the photocopy, and fax the resulting document to you. You can then present (or fax!) the fax you receive to your agency or a supplier as proof that this person did indeed authorize you to charge the travel to their account. Obviously, not all customers will be able to do this, but you'll be surprised at how many can; faxes and copy machines are common in most places of business these days. You also may find it convenient to fax confirmations to clients on bookings they've phoned in. In effect, you are saying, "Here's what you told me you wanted. You'd better call if it's not right." It's an extra safeguard which can prevent problems and ill-feeling later.

- ***To save time.*** No matter with whom you are communicating, situations will arise where time is of the essence. The ability to fax something in a matter of minutes can sometimes mean the difference between snaring a $350 commission or losing it! A perfect example occurred while I was working on this section. Because of a glitch in a booking, my agency needed to get my signature on a form that I had to return to them, so they could send it to the supplier, so my client wouldn't lose the booking. It all had to be done by the afternoon of the same day!

- ***To save money.*** In spite of the initial cost of fax machines and the on-going costs of phone lines and such, you may find that in some instances a fax will actually help you save money. One form of saving can be realized through increased efficiency. It takes less time to fax something than to find and address an envelope, put a stamp on it, and take it to the post office or mail box. That's time that can be better spent generating income for your travel business.

  Real savings start clicking in if you are doing a great deal of foreign business. Let's say you've become a destination specialist for France. Rather than telephone suppliers and run up gargantuan phone bills, you can fax them. Faxes seem to be ubiquitous in the French hospitality industry, with even the tiniest hotels and quaintest restaurants boasting their own fax machines. It can cost very little to send a terse fax requesting a reservation, and if you program the machine to send the fax late at night, you'll get the best possible rates. The reservation will be confirmed by return fax.

Fax machines cost anywhere from $250 to $1,500 or more. As a rough rule of thumb, figure you can get a fax machine that will please you most of the time for $500 or less. I say "most of the time" because it seems

*Setting Up
Your Travel
Business*

inevitable that once you've had a machine for a while you find yourself longing for a particular feature you could have had for a few dollars more. Here are just *some* of the major variables involved in choosing a fax machine:

- **Plain paper or thermal paper?** Thermal paper comes in long rolls, needs to be cut, feels greasy, smudges, cannot be recycled, and fades over time. Plain paper is . . . well, plain paper, just like you use in most copy machines. The type of paper a fax machine uses directly affects the cost: thermal paper is cheap, plain paper is pricey. If you want plain paper faxes, figure on paying a premium for a machine.

  My personal feeling is that aesthetics don't play much of a role in day-to-day travel-related faxing, so the cheaper thermal faxes work just fine. If you want to file some faxes for long-term reference, you can photocopy them onto plain paper for storage. One strategy, which I have adopted, is to get an inexpensive fax and an inexpensive personal copier. The total cost is still less than a lot of plain paper fax machines, and I get more functionality out of the deal since I can use the copier for occasional copying chores that I had to take to the local copy shop before.

- **How many phone lines?** The ideal situation is to have a separate, or "dedicated," phone line for your fax. However, if you want to save a few pennies, it's possible to have both a fax and a phone on the same line. Some faxes will automatically determine if an incoming call is a fax or voice communication and route the call accordingly; others require manual switching. Check out these features carefully to see how they work and how convenient their operation will be for you and the people who will be calling and faxing to you.

  Other than the cost of the machine itself, the cost of an additional phone line is the biggest financial consideration in adding a fax to your office. I bit the bullet and got a dedicated line. There's no reason why, if you're working from home, this cannot be a residential (as opposed to business) line. You only need a business line if you absolutely must have a Yellow Pages listing and (in my humble opinion) that's inappropriate for most part-time travel agents.

- **When do you fax?** Sometimes, you'll have to fax something right now, this very instant. But not all faxes are that crucial. Look for a fax machine that allows you to send a fax at a later time ("delayed transmission"). If you're using one phone line for voice and fax, you can schedule less important faxes for transmission after business hours, leaving your phone line free for business calls. If you're faxing long-distance, you can take advantage of low night-time rates. Another money-saver is a feature available on some machines that allows you to fax half-pages for short messages, saving on transmission time.

- **What about a fax/modem?** A *modem* is a device that allows data to be transmitted between computers over phone lines. A *fax/modem* is a modem that also allows computers and fax machines to communicate. In effect, you can turn your computer (assuming you have one) into a fax. I have this capability and can attest to its advantages and disadvantages. The main advantage is that letters, bookings, and so forth that I create directly on my computer can be faxed immediately. In other words, I don't have to print them out, go to the fax machine, and transmit them. There are, however, a number of disadvantages. I cannot fax existing printed matter that's not in my computer. For example, if I wanted to fill out a form and fax it, I couldn't. (Well, actually I *could*, but I'd have to scan it into the computer first, a slow, slow process and one that requires an additional piece of equipment.) The same goes for a magazine article or a flyer from a tour operator. Another problem is that, while I can receive faxes through the computer, printing them out is a slow process that prevents me from doing other work on the computer. I now use the fax/modem for outgoing, computer-generated communications and the separate fax machine for everything else.

Computers

If the choices confronting you with fax machines are bewildering, the choices in computers are downright nightmarish. I am not even going to begin to try to untangle this Gordian knot, but I will try to give you some pointers based on my own experience. Hopefully, they'll ease your way, if and when you decide to automate (as we computer types say!).

First of all, why get a computer at all? There are two main reasons. One has to do with running a business in general, the other is very specific to the travel business.

Getting your act together. Computers not only allow you to take care of the annoying details of your business and personal life in an efficient, organized, and speedy way, they can actually impose order where none existed before. My personal finances were the usual jumble of receipts in a shoe box before I got a computer program to track them. Now I can account for nearly every penny I spend. Come tax time, I touch a few keys and I'm ready to head off to my tax advisor.

Here are just two of the most obvious ways you can put a computer to use in your new part-time travel business (or any business, for that matter):

- **Tracking your customers.** At the simplest level this can mean having a computerized address book or Rolodex. In computer lingo, this is a "database." If you want to get more sophisticated, you can get programs that allow you to construct extensive and quite sophisticated databases. For example, later in this book I will give you a *Client Profile Form* that you can use to learn more about your clients' travel habits, patterns, likes, dislikes, and so forth. If you put the information from the profile form into a computer, you can have all this data at your fingertips instantly. If you find out about a great package for golfers, you can access your client database (there's that computer lingo again) and get a list of every customer you have who plays golf.

- *Doing mailings.* I hardly ever did promotional mailings before I was computerized. It was just too much of a hassle. Now I can generate mailing labels in a few minutes. I can also churn out hundreds of form letters, each personalized to a different recipient ("Dear Joe," . . . "Dear Martha," . . . and so forth). It's a tremendous advantage for the one-person business.

On-line reservations. The second main reason for getting a computer is that, once you've added a modem (a device that translates the information in one computer into a form that can be transmitted to another computer over ordinary telephone lines), you can gain access to a whole world of up-to-the-second travel information. If you've seen a travel agent working at a computer screen to book a ticket for you, you've seen a CRS (computerized reservation system) at work. The one the travel agent uses is designed for professionals and takes a fair amount of time to master. What you may not know is that modified versions of some of these CRSs are available to anyone with a computer and modem. Using them, you can gain access to much the same information that "professional" travel agents have. You can research airline fares, routings, and car rentals just like they can. It's even possible to use these pared-down reservations systems to make bookings for your clients and have the system alert your agency to print out the ticket!

You can gain access to these systems by joining an "on-line information service" such as CompuServe, Prodigy, GEnie, or America On-Line (see the *Resource Section* for more information). These services are sort of an electronic blend of public library and old-fashioned coffee shop. You dial into them through your computer modem. Once "inside" you can read through reams of information (encyclopedias, old issues of *The Wall Street Journal,* and many other options). If you see something you'd like to keep, you can "download" it — transfer it from their computer to yours via modem.

The two major reservations systems available through on-line services are EaasySabre, provided by Sabre, an operation of American Airlines, and Worldspan/Travelshopper, an operation of TWA, Northwest, and Delta airlines. I'll talk about how you can take advantage of them in *Chapter 6: Booking Airlines.*

Hanging out with fellow travelers. Electronic bulletin boards like Prodigy, CompuServe, and the others also let people with similar interests make contact and "chat" about subjects that interest them. Typically, the service will offer separate "forums" or "special interest groups" (SIGs) on a wide range of topics. CompuServe, for example, has a Travel Forum, which is further subdivided into a number of "sections." Services like this offer you, the part-time travel agent, a potential gold mine of information. Have a client who wants to go to Sri Lanka but you know nothing about it? You can "log onto" (enter) the Travel Forum and post a message like, "Does anyone have any suggestions for a vacation in Sri Lanka?" While there are no guarantees, you might get a lot of very good suggestions along with some warnings about places and properties to avoid.

A particularly interesting section of CompuServe's Travel Forum is called "The Biz," which is reserved for those actively participating in the travel industry as travel agents, suppliers, reservationists, tour guides, or whatever. You have to state your case to gain admission to this section (which you can do electronically), but it doesn't seem to be too difficult. I have found this to be an excellent source of advice and assistance when I find myself stumped by some supplier policy or booking procedure. Other on-line services have similar travel-related special interest groups.

These forums are not free. Typically, they charge a per-minute fee in addition to the service's "basic" charges. It is very easy to get so enthralled with exploring this world of special interests that, before you know it, you have run up a bill that would choke a horse. I know because I've done it. The people who run these forums for the on-line services — "'sysops" or "systems operators" as they are known — also have a way of keeping you talking. They'll post innocent messages like, "Gee, Suzie, that was an interesting point you raised. Why not tell us more?" Or they'll take exception to something you said or challenge your position. The result: more time on line and a higher bill. As with so much else in the world, "*Caveat emptor*!" ("Let the buyer beware!")

Being business-like

Since your part-time travel agency is a business, you'll probably want to conduct yourself in a business-like manner. To my mind, the most important element of professionalism is behavior, rather than degrees, licenses, or certificates. Still, the world at large, not to mention the representatives of your city and state governments, tend to pay attention to these little details. While it's perfectly possible to conduct your business affairs with just a business card and a ready smile, sooner or later you will want to "get your act together" and start acting like the bona fide business that you are. You should also be aware that your failure to dot all the "i's" and cross all the "t's" might expose you to some unpleasant legal consequences. Here are some thoughts along those lines:

- ■ *Fictitious name certificate.* It's called different things in different places, but the idea is quite simple. When a sole proprietor does business under a business name ("Acme Dry Cleaners," or "Hermione's House of Hair," or whatever), he or she will have to register that name with the local authorities. If you decide to do business under your own name (for example, "Joe Smith") and arrange to receive all checks under that name, you probably don't have to register. But if you decide to do business as "Joe's Wonderful World of Travel" you should register. This prevents the kind of misunderstandings that would arise if two people started doing business under the same name. It also provides a legal, public record that you, Joe Smith, do in fact have a business called "Joe's Wonderful World of Travel,"

To register your business name, go to the office of the County Clerk at your county court house. They'll be able to tell you what to do. Generally, all that's involved is checking the county records to make sure no one already has the business name you want to use, filling out a form, and paying a modest fee. (Unless, of course, you live in New York City where the fee is an outrageous $120!) In return, you get a certificate saying that you are now doing business under the name you've chosen.

- **_Business checking account._** One of the most important reasons for registering your business name at the county court house is that you will not be able to open a business checking account without the proper certificate. And you'll need a business account if you want to cash a check made out to the name of your travel business and not to you personally. Bank regulations are strict and your bank will balk at accepting a check made out to "Jane Jones Travel," even if your name is Jane Jones. Another reason for having a separate business account is to manage your money and segregate funds, something which may be required under your state's laws.

- **_State laws._** While all businesses must register their business names, some states require certain kinds of businesses to do more — to register and pay a licensing fee. Because of the proliferation of travel scams, some states have attempted to address the problem through so-called "travel promoter laws." My feeling is that some of these laws do more to inconvenience honest business people than they do to deter criminals. But the law, as you know, is the law. If your state does have a travel promoter law, you may be bound by its provisions. On the other hand, you may be exempt as the outside sales rep for a travel agency. State laws differ widely, so you should check to see what the ground rules are in your state. The fact of the matter is many outside reps, through ignorance or choice, operate without regard to local and state regulations. Most of those that do are, I would guess, well-meaning people trying to make an honest buck. Most of them experience no problems. But if you are in violation of the law, even if out of ignorance or on a mere "technicality," the consequences can be irritating at best and financially devastating at worst. Why take the risk? See a lawyer.

- **_Lawyers._** It used to be said that the only things that are certain are death and taxes. It's probably time to add lawyer's fees to the list. Even if it irks you to have to do it, consult with a competent professional early in your career as a part-time travel agent. If you're going to be signing a contract with an agency, you'll probably want to have that vetted anyway. So while you're in the lawyer's office, ask her about the points raised here. The guidance you get will be worth the price in peace of mind.

Help is at hand

This book will get you started in your new lifestyle as a part-time travel agent but it cannot answer all your questions and it certainly cannot provide all the reference material you will be needing in the months and years ahead. Sooner or later, you'll come across a question or encounter a problem that is beyond the scope of this book. So do yourself a favor; begin putting into place a support system that will fuel your professional growth. Here are some thoughts and suggestions:

Join a professional organization

All professions have organizations and associations that are dedicated to enhancing the professionalism of their members. The world of outside sales reps and part-time travel agents is no exception. I joined the Outside Sales Support Network (OSSN) very early in my career as a part-time agent and I haven't regretted it for a second. OSSN offers a number of benefits. Here is a sample:

- *A quarterly newsletter* filled with selling tips, news of interest to members of the outside sales confraternity, announcements of fam/seminars, and lists of agencies which actively support the concept of marketing through an outside sales force. If you've been having trouble finding an agency to hook up with (or are dissatisfied with the one you are hooked up with), this might be a good source of information.
- *Fam/seminars,* usually held aboard cruise ships, that provide on-going training to members in sales skills and industry knowledge. Because the cruise lines benefit by having travel agents familiarize themselves with their ships, the cost of these seminars is very modest, and there's plenty of shipboard time for relaxing and just plain having fun.
- *"The Official Outside Sales Travel Agent Manual,"* which covers some of the basics of the trade and is included in your first year's membership fee (currently $55). The section on part-time travel agents and the law is itself worth the cost of membership.
- *Errors and omissions insurance. Available to members at a modest cost,* this is a specialized form of business insurance that protects you in case a client sues alleging that they suffered because you screwed up in performing your professional duties as a travel agent.

- ■ *Reduced prices on industry publications and reference works.* For example, the *Official Hotel Guide*, a massive reference work with a cover price of $385 was recently available through OSSN for just $197.
- ■ *Networking and learning opportunities.* Most important of all, from my point of view, is that OSSN encourages members to get together at the local level for their mutual support. Typically, chapters meet once a month and there is a modest fee to cover the cost of renting the hall and/or providing dinner. The meetings usually feature a guest speaker from the industry — a representative from a hotel chain, a cruise line, or a travel insurance company, for example. Some meetings in the New York area have actually been held aboard cruise ships. The meetings are invariably interesting and filled with hints and tips that will make you more knowledgeable and help you to sell better. They are also a great way to get to know your fellow outside reps. The contacts and friendships that develop this way can be invaluable.

Another organization serving much the same needs as OSSN is the National Association of Commissioned Travel Agents (NACTA), which was formed in May of 1990. Like OSSN, NACTA has a newsletter, insurance offerings, and local chapter meetings. They also offer "the opportunity to work together on group tours that will guarantee you larger commissions." Since I am not a member, I cannot personally vouch for the organization; but it is worth checking out.

All things being equal, I would recommend that you join the group that offers regular chapter meetings close to where you live. You can find information on how to contact these, and other travel industry organizations, in the *Resource Section*.

Find a mentor

You may be able to find a mentor — someone who will take you under their wing and guide your professional development — at the agency with which you have affiliated as an outside rep. Or you may hit it off with a more experienced outside rep through an organization like OSSN and be able to turn to that person for advice. But no matter what the source, find a mentor if at all possible. Having a good mentor is a real gift, and most people will be flattered that you are seeking their expertise and will derive tremendous self-fulfillment by helping you up the ladder of success. But don't take advantage of their time or abuse their goodwill and, whenever possible, find a way to pay them back for their kindness.

Learn about your product

It's not too soon to begin collecting a reference library about the products you want to sell. Some of this material you will have to go out and buy. If you are specializing in a destination, for example, you will want to have a good collection of current guidebooks to the area. But much of the material you will need (or at least find *very* helpful) can be obtained for free.

Destination information can be obtained from the tourist bureaus that represent every U.S. state and most foreign countries. Don't overlook foreign tourist bureaus that serve a particular province or region. There is also a veritable mountain of brochures and other support material that can be gathered from tour operators, packagers, and other suppliers.

Rather than try to get *everything* available (an impossible task which, if you could achieve it, would force you to move out of your house because it would be filled with brochures) let me suggest a plan of attack. First, check with your agency to see which consortiums it belongs to. A consortium is a group of suppliers, usually tour operators or cruise lines, which offer higher commissions to agencies that commit to bringing them a certain volume of business. (I am making the assumption that the lion's share of your leisure travel will consist of tours and packages.) Your agency should be able to give you a list of the suppliers in the various consortiums, along with their toll-free telephone numbers. Call these suppliers and request their general brochures; once you have these in hand, you can then request more specific information as you need it. The idea is to build up an awareness of which products are available to you at the best commissions.

Of course, the preferred suppliers don't have all the tours. So do some investigating to find out which other tour operators cover your area of interest, and request information from them as well. You'll find telephone numbers for some major tour operators in the *Resource Section*.

Build a reference library

Any good professional has a reference library close at hand. No matter how good you are, you can't keep every little scrap of information in your head. In addition, to materials about specific destinations and the offerings of specific suppliers, here are some suggestions for your collection based on my personal experience. You'll find a far more complete listing of reference materials in the *Resource Section*.

- It's handy to have a one-stop reference that will provide you with definitions of industry terms and acronyms and guide you through the sometimes mysterious codes used to identify airports, airlines, car rental companies, and so forth, *The Intrepid Traveler's Complete Desk Reference*, which is available from The Intrepid Traveler, will fill the bill, but there are other sources on the market. They are listed in the *Resource Section*.
- *The Official Tour Directory* is a good (and moderately priced) source of information about suppliers. It is arranged geographically and by special interests. So if a client is interested in a dive vacation in Australia, this guide can tell you whom to call.
- One of the big hotel guides is also very handy. They're expensive but they cover a lot of territory. I find them useful be-

Setting Up Your Travel Business

cause many people are interested in a hotel package. That is, they want to fly somewhere and stay in one place for the length of their stay. With these guides you can find out which hotels offer what kind of packages (honeymoons, weekend getaways, all-inclusives, etc.). Then you can call wholesalers to see which ones can put together a hotel-airfare package for you.

- Subscribe to a few industry publications. If you can get some freebies through your agency, go for it. I get *Travel Weekly, Tour and Travel News*, *Travel Agent,* and *Jax Fax*, as well as a few others. These publications will not only begin to give you a feel for the business but also contain a great deal of information that is immediately useful (commission deals, new tour products, etc.). You can often pick up half-off subscription offers to some of these trade magazines from friends in the business who already subscribe. A list of industry trade publications will be found in the *Resource Section*.

- Build a clipping file, designed according to your needs. The trade publications regularly include supplements devoted to a particular destination. Hang on to them. The specific information will go out of date, but if a client asks about The Bahamas or tours to the Holy Land, these back-issue supplements will let you talk knowledgeably and tell you who to call.

Like I say, these are some suggestions. As your own travel business develops, use the *Resource Section* in this book and your own investigation to determine which reference materials you want to have on your shelf.

Go on-line

If you have a computer and a modem, and belong to one of the on-line information services mentioned earlier, you may have another source of help at your fingertips. The Biz section of CompuServe's Travel Forum is one such source of answers. If some procedure is puzzling you, or you don't know the meaning of some acronym you have come across, you can post a message there and, hopefully, receive an answer from a fellow agent.

Agents on The Biz swap recommendations about consolidator fares (some consolidators are members of the Forum), tour operators, and so forth. There are also on-going conversations about issues and events in the industry that you can browse through and read at your leisure. Even if you don't actively participate, you can learn a lot just be reading the posted messages.

Chapter Five:
Getting Started

Let's assume that you have now, through one means or another, become an outside sales representative for a travel agency. You are now, if not a full-fledged travel agent, at least a partly-fledged one. You can now sell travel to your friends, family, and neighbors. You are part of the huge and ever-growing travel industry.

First of all, congratulations! You're probably all fired up and rarin' to go. That's great. Your enthusiasm will stand you in good stead.

Second, be careful! You may have taken to heart my remarks in the last chapter about defining yourself. I certainly hope you did. But it is in the nature of things that, to begin with at least, you will wind up taking on all comers and fielding some requests that may puzzle you. Once you start spreading the word that you're in the travel business, your next door neighbor may say, "Gee, I have to go to Denver next week. Can you get me a ticket?" Your uncle might say, "Your Aunt and I want to take a cruise this winter. Which one should we take?" A coworker-worker might say, "I'd like to take that cross-country sleeper train I heard about. How much does that cost?"

In short, there's no way of predicting what your first booking will be. Also, as you get your bearings in your new line of business, there will be no clear pattern to your bookings. You'll probably find it hard to say, "Oh, I don't want to handle that sort of thing," or "Gosh, I don't know anything about cruises yet. Can you wait 'til next year?" No, chances are that, regardless of the request, you'll say "Sure, I'll check that out for you."

The situation is complicated by the fact that the agency you hooked up with most likely doesn't want to spend its time answering your "dumb" questions. They want bookings. Bookings with no mistakes, no problems.

You're pretty much on your own. And that can be a bit scary. I know because I've been there. I can't make you an expert in the next few pages, nor can I cover all the possible permutations and combinations. But I can pass along the basics and offer a few tips. This chapter and the ones that follow, then, are designed to help you make your first bookings with a modicum of self-confidence and a minimum of errors.

Travel products

Conveniently, perhaps inevitably, the travel industry can be divvied up into a fairly small number of "products." Airline tickets are one product, cruises are another.

Taking things a step further, it can be helpful to distinguish between "product lines" (airline tickets, for example) and the individual products available in each line. In other words, a coach seat on Continental and a first-class seat on British Airways are two different *products*, although they belong to the same *product line*. So, looked at from this perspective, knowing that your client wants an airline ticket does not immediately tell you which specific product will be right for her.

Generally speaking, though, once you know what the customer wants, you'll know immediately where to go to get it. As you gain more experience in and exposure to the travel business, you will become more and more comfortable dealing with these products, just as if they were nuts and bolts or cans of soup. You will also learn that, just as a steel bolt differs from a can of minestrone soup, each travel product is a separate entity, with its own jargon, booking procedures, and folkways.

Your clients will have a need for different travel products at different times. Often they will have a need for more than one travel product during a single trip. Which products they need will determine a number of things:

- *The supplier.* Different suppliers sell different things. You can't book a cruise from Avis. That may seem crushingly obvious, but it is an important distinction because it can determine . . .

- *Your access to the product.* There are some products you simply cannot sell unless you meet the right qualifications. For example, unless you are presently an accredited travel agency, an employee of such an agency, or an independent contractor for such an agency, you cannot sell Aunt Matilda an American Airlines ticket from New York to London and collect a commission. On the other hand, you might be able to find a consolidator who would sell you a ticket to London at a "net fare," which you could then sell to Aunt Matilda for whatever you thought she'd be willing to pay.

- *Your profit.* Some products pay higher commissions than others. Domestic air can pay 9% or 10%, international air 10% or 11%, cruises and tours anywhere from 10% to 15%, and some car rentals just 5%.

- *Your profitability.* It is a truism in the business that it takes just as much time to book a $5,000 tour as it does to book a $200 airline ticket. Obviously, the tour will make you more money than the ticket. (Of course, it probably will take you longer to *sell* the tour, but that's another consideration.) The point to be made here is that, as a businessperson, you will be concerned not just with how much money you make in a given transaction, but how much time and effort you have to expend to make it. You may make only $15 on a domestic airline ticket that takes you 20 minutes to book. But you may have to spend several hours to research rates, book, and confirm a luxury hotel room in Helsinki that nets you a $40 commission. It doesn't take long to figure out which one is more profitable.

- ■ **_The ease of booking._** A round-trip ticket from Omaha to Osaka is a pretty straightforward proposition. Once you know what you are doing, you should be able to research the possible fares pretty quickly. A tour of Japan, on the other hand, could mean days of research — checking your library, contacting many suppliers, and reviewing dozens of brochures and itineraries — before finding the right fit for your client. The ease of booking will also be determined by your familiarity with the product. If the bulk of your business is selling cruises, it will be correspondingly more difficult to fly a client to the middle of the Amazon jungle and help him hire a boat and a trusty Indian guide.

- ■ **_The language you speak._** By this I mean the special jargon that all industries use as a kind of shorthand to speed the flow of business or exclude outsiders or sometimes both. If cruises represent only 5% of your bookings, you will feel the same uncertainty every time you book one that you feel when you resurrect your high school Spanish on your occasional trips to South America.

  Note: The jargon I'm talking about here is the jargon used between you and the reservationist. *Never* use jargon when discussing travel with your clients. You'll just confuse them and damage your chances of making the sale and building an ongoing relationship.

Some general notes on bookings

Before we look at the individual travel products in detail, let's take a moment to review some general considerations that are common to booking *all* travel products. Every booking you make for a client can be seen as having several steps or stages:

Step One: Gathering information

Your first task is to gather *complete* information about what the client wants. This may seem obvious, but inexperienced travel agents often go off half-cocked.

For example, your good buddy Harold wants to fly to San Francisco on the 15th and return on the 28th. Terrific. Off you go to make the booking. But wait. Does Harold want to leave in the morning or the afternoon? Is he more concerned with schedule or price? Does he want to use a specific airline so he can boost his frequent flyer credits? Does he prefer a window or an aisle seat? And what's he going to do in San Francisco? Does he need a hotel reservation? A rental car? These are all things you need to know *before* you start the booking process.

Of course, the client might not have all the answers. That's fine, too. That's one of the reasons people use travel agents — to help them make choices. When the client doesn't know *exactly* what he or she wants, ask what the *parameters* are. In other words, how much leeway do you have to make decisions on the client's behalf without checking back with the client for permission?

The goal of this stage is to avoid having to call the client back to request more specific information. Not only is this not a very efficient use of your time, it doesn't do much to reassure your customers about your competence.

A word of warning, however: *Never* let your embarrassment stop you from calling the client when you have forgotten to get some crucial bit of information. Hopefully, the tips and techniques that I discuss below will help you avoid this unpleasantness, but mistakes do happen. Chalk it up to experience. Ultimately, the client will be more annoyed by a faulty booking than by your calling back for more information.

Step Two: Research

Your next job is to go out and see what's available and at what price. In some cases (like Harold's trip to San Francisco) this will be a pretty straightforward proposition. But what if Harold had asked you to look around for a vacation destination for him and his wife, "somewhere warm." Fulfilling that request will take a bit longer.

Again, your goal here is to get *complete* information to present to your client. If the client asks three questions that require you to say, "Gee, I'll have to check and get back to you," you probably haven't done your research properly. Obviously, you can't anticipate every question the client might ask, but you should be able to research the most obvious options. This requires doing a good job of gathering information about the client's parameters. ("What's your absolute upper limit on the cost?") It also means asking logical questions when doing your research. ("What's included in the honeymoon package and what's extra?")

Don't worry too much if you report your findings to the client and then find you have to go back and do more research. From a purely business standpoint, you might prefer not to have to do this, since the more time it takes to make a booking the less profitable it becomes. But often your research will open new possibilities the client hadn't considered before. And that's part of the service you provide.

Step Three: Making the sale

In all but the most straightforward of situations, you will have to get back to your client either to make sure that the arrangements you have made are satisfactory or to discuss the several options available and guide the client to a decision. This is what's meant by "making the sale." Of course, in many — even most — cases, you will have made reservations to lock in a fare or guarantee a berth, knowing that reservations can be changed or canceled.

We will discuss techniques you can use in making the sale in *Part II*. For now, just be aware that until the customer has agreed to your recommendations and given you the green light to proceed, the booking is not official (the "sale" has not been made). At a minimum, review verbally with the customer all the key elements of the booking (time, date, supplier, fares, etc., etc.). Make sure you have it right and the customer agrees that you have it right. You may also provide this information in written form.

Step Four: Making the booking

As we just saw, this step may have preceded Step Three or you may be carrying out these steps in tandem. However, it plays out, you have to actually make the booking with the supplier to make the client's trip happen.

Again, as a general note, your goal here is to have complete information to give the supplier. The specific information you need will depend on the product you're booking and the supplier with whom you are dealing. Here are some of the more frequently overlooked bits of information that can slow down the booking process for beginners:

- Credit card expiration dates.
- The name "as it appears" on the card. You may know the client as Ken Smith but his credit card might say John Kenneth Smith.
- The billing address for the card.
- The client's daytime (or other) phone number.
- Frequent flyer numbers. Also, client identification numbers for any number of "affinity programs" for hotels, car rentals, etc.
- Passport numbers.
- Special requests. For example, does your client require a special meal on the flight, or a wheelchair?
- Your agency's IATA number. This number identifies your agency and separates it from all other agencies. You probably won't make this mistake more than once. Keep the IATA number handy until you have it memorized. Stick it on your phone.
- Your agency's "official" phone number. Many suppliers identify agencies by their phone numbers, since they are unique. Some agencies have more then one phone number; make sure you know which one to give to suppliers. Again, this is one of those mistakes you probably won't make twice.

The specific steps you take to make bookings for different travel products will be discussed in the next five chapters.

Step Five: Confirming the booking with the client

Finally, you have to get back to the client and confirm the booking. To "confirm" the booking you have to verbally review with the client the key elements of the booking (date, time, supplier, cost, etc., etc.). You may also provide this information in written form. If this sounds familiar, you did much the same thing in Step Three.

This is partly a matter of professionalism and courtesy. It is also a safeguard. If you have made an error in the booking, better to find it out now than when the customer gets to the airport Tuesday and discovers the ticket is for a Wednesday flight.

The magic words

I know that some of you reading this will have a great deal of trepidation about presenting yourself as a travel agent for the first time. So before you pick up that phone to make your first booking let me share with you some "magic words" I discovered. They will go a long way to helping overcome any nervousness or uncertainty you may have. The magic words can vary from situation to situation, but they go something like this:

> *"I'm kinda new at this; so if you could sorta
> guide me through the process, I'd really
> appreciate it."*

Another variation might sound like this:

> *"I just started as an outside rep and I've
> never made one of these bookings; so forgive
> me if I sound a little hesitant."*

I suppose there are some sourpusses out there who won't respond to these magic words, but I have found the reservationists who work for the various suppliers to be a pretty nice bunch of people. For example, when I was just getting started, an airline reservationist helped me get a commission that I otherwise would have missed out on by patiently explaining the booking procedure for frequent flyer awards. Also, these people are very well trained by their companies. Most suppliers realize that the quality of service they provide to you, the travel agent, can mean the difference between getting a steady stream of business from you or having you cross them off your list.

So if you ever get the feeling that you have to "pretend" to be a travel agent, my advice to you is "just don't do it." 'Fess up that you're still learning and place yourself in the capable hands of the reservationists. Most likely, they will respond in a very positive and friendly way. Remember that these people get far more than their fair share of abuse from "know-it-all" travel agents. You can be the exception. My experience has been that if you are polite and friendly to them, reservationists will bend over backwards to help you out.

Summary

The number of travel products is truly mind-boggling. That is why it is comforting to know that virtually all bookings follow a certain structure or pattern, which recurs over and over. Until you get into the rhythm of it, you may want to check back to this chapter from time to time and review the general notes on bookings.

Yet in spite of the similarities among the booking processes for the various travel products, there are also some very important differences. In the following chapters, I will walk you through the specifics of making bookings for each of the major travel products:

- Airline tickets (*Chapter 6*).
- Hotels (*Chapter 7*).
- Rental cars (*Chapter 8*).
- Tours and packages (*Chapter 9*).
- Cruises (*Chapter 10*).

Chapter Six:
Booking Airlines

I'm starting off with airlines for two main reasons. First, airline bookings are the most complex and daunting for the brand-new part-time travel agent. And, second, my very strong hunch is that your very first booking is likely to be a domestic airline ticket.

Airline tickets are the throbbing heart of the travel agency business. It's no accident that one of the main things that distinguishes a "real" travel agency from all others is a computerized reservations system (CRS). And a CRS is all about booking and printing airline tickets. Oh sure, you can book many hotels, some tours, and most rent-a-cars with a CRS, but their primary function is to serve the airlines. It is the airlines, after all, that created, maintain, and sell the majority of today's CRS systems.

As I explained elsewhere, the selling of airline tickets involves huge amounts of money changing hands. It requires a large, expensive, and complex bureaucracy to make sure that all that money flows smoothly and winds up in the right hands. This is the primary reason that the cost of entry into the world of the "traditional" travel agency is so high.

Booking airline tickets is, as I mentioned, one of the most complicated and daunting jobs facing the part-time travel agent. There are a number of reasons for this:

- The number of choices (of airlines, fares, routings, schedules, and so forth) is huge. It can take a long time to sort through your available options.
- Doing it right requires access to one of the CRS systems. While there are a number of printed resources you can use, nothing beats a CRS for up-to-date information.
- There is virtually no way around the electronic infrastructure of the CRS systems. Sooner or later, the booking information has to be entered into a computer to generate the ticket. While you, the outside rep, may not do the actual entering, you will be expected to provide all (or most) of the information to be entered.
- Because computer systems are completely unforgiving, the

information you provide must be precise, accurate, and in the required format. So booking airline tickets requires a high degree of attention to detail.

Providing a complete course of instruction in how to handle airline bookings is well beyond the scope of this book. There are simply too many permutations and combinations. What I will provide is guidance that will get you started and help you avoid the most common mistakes. The good news is that, if you have ever booked an airline ticket for yourself, you will be able to book them for others. And if you ever get stuck, just remember the "magic words!"

Misteaks can kill you (how to avoid them)

Because they involve so many different elements, airline bookings are prone to errors. Making a mistake in a booking is not only embarrassing, it can cost you money. The best insurance against making costly errors is to have a system that lets you gather and transmit information completely and accurately. A good system will have checkpoints built into it to insure that information is checked and double-checked for accuracy.

Your campaign for accuracy begins the minute you get a request from a client. All too often, the beginner will gather incomplete information, discover the gaps when researching the booking, and have to get back to the client to fill in the holes. This kind of embarrassment is easy to avoid.

The *Client Request Form* on page 111 lets you capture the key information you need from your client to do your job quickly and efficiently. It is designed to be used with the client's initial request for any travel product — airline ticket, cruise, or tour. You can use it as is or adapt it to suit your preferences. Let's review it briefly as it pertains to airline travel.

The key things you need to know at this time are:

- *The passengers' names.* Don't laugh. You may know who the client is, but do you know the names of his wife and two kids who will also be going on the trip? The airline will want to know.
- *Destination.* This is pretty self-explanatory.
- *Dates and times.* This is not so self-explanatory. You not only need to know that the client wants to fly on the fifth, but you also need to know at what time she wants to go. She may want to get there for lunch or she may not want to leave until after work. Don't automatically assume that people will volunteer this information. Frequently, when they ask you to look into getting them a ticket to, say, San Francisco, leaving on the fifth and returning on the fourteenth, they are just shopping for fares. So it never occurs to them to mention that if they *do* go, they'll want the evening flight. Remember that *when* a flight leaves can affect the fare.
- *Client preferences.* Does the client have a preferred airline? Is he willing to trade convenience for a lower fare? How flexible are the dates? If business class is full, will she fly coach?

While it's not always necessary to have the following information, it's nice to know:

- **Frequent flyer numbers.** At this early stage, you may not need to know this information. Once you have settled on a particular itinerary, however, it's nice to be able to include the client's frequent flyer number with the booking. If the customer isn't a member of the airline's frequent flyer program, you can usually enroll them at the time of the booking.
- **Seating preference.** Window or aisle, smoking or non. It can make a difference to many clients.

Your goal in gathering this initial information is to have enough data to be able to research available flights and fares and make an actual reservation (to lock in specific flights, seats, and fares). This will not always be possible but it is the ideal.

Note: In *Chapter 16: Qualifying*, you will find a *Client Profile Form* on which you can begin to compile dossiers on your customers. You can use the form to record some of the information mentioned here. So for the next booking you won't have to ask again. This will not only make you more efficient but will enhance the client's opinion of your professionalism.

Researching available flights

Your next step is to find out what flights go where the customer wants to go, when the customer wants to go there, at the price the customer wants to pay. In most cases, it's safe to assume that the customer wants to fly at the lowest possible fare. Getting this information is the trickiest part of the whole process. As a beginner, you have several information sources available to you:

The airlines

There's no reason why you can't book flights for your customers the same way you would for yourself. Just pick up the phone, dial the 800 number of your favorite airline (or one that's likely to fly to your customer's destination) and inquire about flight availability and fares.

There are a number of problems with this approach, however:

- It's hit-or-miss. You're often not sure which airline flies where. Of course, they'll tell you if they can't help you out and often they will point you to the right airlines (if you ask).
- Fare comparison is difficult. You'll have to call several airlines and write down a lot of information.
- It's inefficient. Doing all this takes time, and time is money.

One way to save a bit of time is to get hold of the airlines' schedules. These are small booklets crammed with current flight departure and arrival times. They will tell you where the airline flies, but they won't help you with fares. (Text continues on page 112.)

Notes on the Client Request Form

The *Client Request Form* is designed to be used when you are first talking with a client and gathering basic information about his travel needs. It is designed primarily for air travel, but can be used to gather information about any form of travel.

Most of this form is self-explanatory. Here are some notes on items that may need clarification:

- **Date & Time.** Don't forget to find out *what time* the client wants to fly. Will he leave first thing in the morning or after work? Does she need to be at her destination by a certain time?

- **Special Instructions.** Note any special requests the client may have. Also, record any parameters the client has given you in making the booking. For example, "Schedule more important than price," or "will fly Delta if American is not available."

- **Age.** A passenger's age is important only when a child, youth, or senior fare is involved.

- **FF#s.** Frequent flyer numbers are useful to have because you can enter them into the record when making a booking with the airline.

- **Hotels/Rental cars.** Don't forget to ask the client about hotels and rental cars. These are easy add-on sales.

- **Other Information.** Use this space for notes on tours or cruises — or anything else that doesn't fit elsewhere. A discussion on the kind of information you will need to gather from tour and cruise customers will be found in *Chapters 9* and *10*.

- **Credit Card.** It's not always absolutely necessary to have this information now, but it can be helpful. For example, you will only be able to hold a hotel room for a client's late arrival by giving the reservationist a credit card number.

Client Request Form

Client: _____ Phone: _____

Address: _____

_____

Booking Information

Destination(s): _____ Preferred Airline(s): _____

_____ _____

Departure Date & Time: _____ Return Date & Time: _____

Preferences: ❑ Window   ❑ Aisle   ❑ Smoking   ❑ Spec. Meals _____
             ❑ First   ❑ Business ❑ Coach   ❑ Other _____

Special Instructions:

Passengers

Last Name	First Name	Age	FF#s

Hotels? Rental Cars?

Other Information

Payment Information

Credit Card #: _____ Exp.: _____

Name on Card: _____

Billing Address & Phone: _____

If you live in a smaller city, your local airport is probably served by just a handful of airlines. Most, if not all, of your customers will be leaving from this airport. It's a relatively simple matter to drive out to the airport, stroll by the ticket counters, and get copies of the schedules of all the carriers. This will tell you when you can get your client out of town, but it will not always tell you when you can get them to their final destination, especially if it is overseas. The airlines that serve your local airport will, of course, be able to book your customer to any destination. But they won't include the destination in their schedules if they don't fly there themselves.

If you live in a large metropolitan area, going to airports — or even airline ticket offices — to collect schedules is a whole lot less feasible. For one thing, it could mean several days of driving, parking fees, and trudging through terminals or office buildings to collect schedules from all the airlines that serve the area. Then, too, you would find that some of the ticket counters you visited (no matter at what airport or ticket office) would be out of current schedules. You could ask the reservationist at the 800 number to send you a schedule; but that could take weeks, if not months.

Just organizing and filing all this information would be a problem. But on top of everything else, airline schedules go out of date with stunning rapidity. Most of them are out of date in at least a few details before the ink is dry on the page.

So to sum up, if you live in a smaller market and your customer is making a simple journey — Knoxville to Chicago, Charleston to Denver, Baton Rouge to Cheyenne — it can be relatively easy to use the airlines' reservation systems as your informational resource. If you live in a large metropolitan area or if your customer has a complicated or foreign itinerary planned, this option is far from ideal. In either case, the worst part of it is, you'll never be sure you couldn't have cut a better fare deal elsewhere when you limit your research to phoning the airlines or checking their printed schedules.

The Official Airlines Guide (OAG)

A step up from the airlines' printed schedules and the goodwill of their reservationists is the *Official Airlines Guide,* invariably referred to by its initials, OAG. The OAG is not a single publication but a family of publications that come in different sizes, different versions, and different media — electronic as well as print. Some are targeted to the peripatetic businessperson while others are aimed at the travel agent market. Some versions will slip easily into a pocket, others are the size and weight of the telephone directory for a mid-sized city.

For our purposes, the most important versions are the *Desktop Flight Guides* which can best be described as computerized reservations systems in print. There are two "editions" — the North American Edition (which includes Canada, Mexico, and the Caribbean) and the Worldwide Edition. The Worldwide Edition is published 12 times a year and does not include fare information. The North American Edition, on the other hand, comes in four versions: biweekly with fares, biweekly without fares, monthly with fares, and monthly without fares. To be a full-service travel agent, you really need both editions.

Each issue of the *Desktop Flight Guide* contains vast amounts of information. The most important information is the schedules of all the airlines. It is possible, using this information, to construct an itinerary between any two points covered by that particular Edition. Depending on your location, it may be necessary to use both editions to construct an international trip. Each issue contains complete and easy-to-follow instructions on how to use the *Guide*. In addition, each issue contains an array of useful reference material, which we'll discuss a bit later.

All this information does not come cheap. A subscription to both the Worldwide Edition and the biweekly North American Edition with fares costs over $600 a year. Lay that out and in just two years you will have spent enough to have bought a computer and gained access to an on-line computer reservation system.

Of course, it's possible to get hold of a back issue of one or both of the Flight Guides. You might try begging one from a travel agency. Even better, try some corporate travel offices; they are big buyers of the OAG. The problem with using an old OAG, of course, is that the information changes rapidly. OAG estimates that there are an average of 170,000 changes in each monthly issue. Most of these are relatively minor schedule changes, but airlines also drop some routes entirely while adding others. Therefore, relying on outdated information can be a risky proposition.

Nonetheless, having an old issue of the OAG handy can be very helpful. It contains a lot of useful information that doesn't go out of date quite as quickly as airline flight schedules and fares. Among the tidbits in the OAG are:

- Airline codes, airport codes, and various airline abbreviations for things like Class of Service and Equipment. This information will come in handy when and if you start using on-line computerized reservations systems, which are discussed later in this chapter.
- Information on all the airlines' frequent flyer programs, including toll-free numbers to sign up your clients and a run-down on each plan's travel partners (hotels and car rental agencies that give mileage credits to the plan's participants).
- Information on "frequent lodger" programs at many hotel chains.
- Toll-free numbers for airlines and car rental agencies.
- Seating maps showing the exact configuration of seats on many airlines.
- Information on connecting times at airports, which lets you determine the amount of time your clients will need between flights to assure they'll be able to make their connections.
- Maps of major airports.

Finally, we should also mention the *OAG Electronic Edition Travel Service*. This is OAG's version of computerized reservations systems like

Apollo and Sabre, which are used by travel agencies. You can subscribe to the service and access it directly from your home computer at fairly stiff rates ($28.20 per hour during prime time and $10.20 per hour during non-prime time). The service is also available through on-line services like CompuServe, GEnie, Dow-Jones, and others. On CompuServe, as on many others, the service carries a premium charge. For contact information on OAG and on-line products and services, see the *Resource Section*.

Your home computer

As mentioned in *Chapter 4: Setting Up Your Travel Business,* most store-front travel agencies have computers sitting on their agents' desks which give them access to a computerized reservations system (CRS). There are several competing CRS systems, each owned and operated by a different airline or group of airlines. Despite their competition, all CRS systems give agents access to the same information about flights (with a few minor exceptions).

The terminals on the agents' desks are linked by phone to a massive computer database containing up-to-the-minute information on schedules and fares for virtually all the world's scheduled airlines. Using these terminals, the agents can tell you how to get from your home town to any other city in the world. Then they can make the booking electronically, guaranteeing you a seat. Finally, they can print out your ticket and hand it to you.

What you may not realize is that you can do the same things (save printing out the ticket) from almost any home computer provided you have a modem and subscribe to an on-line service (see *Chapter 4,* as well as the *Resource Section*, where you will find a discussion of the various services and the options they offer). I subscribe to CompuServe, the largest of the on-line services, which gives me access to both EaasySabre, a version of the Sabre system owned by American Airlines, and TravelShopper, a version of the Worldspan CRS which is jointly owned by Delta, TWA, and Northwest.

The best way to research fares and schedules

Of the three methods of research, I recommend the third — using your home computer to gain access to on-line information from the airlines' CRS systems. If you have a computer already, your start-up costs will be well under $100, the cost of the software and sign-up fee for the on-line service you choose. Research your options well, since your choice of on-line service will affect what's available to you. Prodigy, for example, offers only a stripped down version of EaasySabre, while CompuServe gives you access to Commercial Sabre and even allows you to switch to "expert mode" as your experience grows.

Another factor influencing your choice of on-line service will be which CRS system you will want to use. For the quick and easy method I will outline in a moment, you can use either EaasySabre or TravelShopper. However, you should be aware that both systems allow you to "queue" bookings to your travel agency. In other words, you can make the actual reservation on-line and then instruct the computer to transmit that booking electronically to the agency for which you are an outside rep, so that it can print out the ticket. However, this will only work if your agency is on the same system. EaasySabre can only queue bookings to a Sabre agency. TravelShopper can only queue bookings to a Worldspan agency. The sign-up and monthly fees assessed by several of the "instant agencies" you'll find listed in the *Resource Section* cover the costs of CRS software and on-line fees.

When you sign up for an on-line service on your own, you will pay a monthly user's fee. Payment schemes vary but usually involve some combination of "basic" services, which are available on an unlimited basis for a set fee, and "extended" services, for which you pay an additional per-minute fee. On CompuServe, the airline CRSs are part of the basic service (currently $8.95 a month). So if you are using the service just to gain access to the CRS, your on-going costs will be extremely modest.

If you don't have a computer, you'll have to get one if you want to do your research and bookings on-line. There's good news on this front. If you are planning to use the computer just to gain access to the CRS, you can make do quite nicely with an older IBM-compatible model that you can buy very cheaply. There is so much competition in the PC world that many older models have a very low "street value." You may even be able to get a free computer if you have a computer literate friend with an older model gathering dust in a closet.

Bear in mind, however, that a computer is fast becoming an indispensable element of any serious home business. As discussed in *Chapter 4*, it enables you to keep your records, balance your books, and stay in touch with the world outside. My recommendation would be to acquire the best computer system your funds will allow.

About EaasySabre (and TravelShopper)

The CRS with which I am most familiar is EaasySabre, which I use on CompuServe. I am less conversant with TravelShopper, although it operates in much the same way. Most of what I have to say about EaasySabre will have its counterpart in TravelShopper.

Once you have access to an on-line service that carries EaasySabre, you will have automatic access to EaasySabre itself. Please note that, while American Airlines provides EaasySabre to any on-line service that wants it, the service itself decides how it will look on screen.

EaasySabre lets you check the schedules of 650 international airlines and make reservations on 350 of them. You can also book with over 27,000 hotel and condo properties and rent cars from some 50 auto rental firms.

When you access EaasySabre for the first time you will be asked to "join." It's a free membership; they just like to know who you are. One of the benefits of "membership" is that you'll be sent the *EaasySabre Reference Guide*, a 20-page pamphlet containing some helpful hints for using the system. (You can request the guide before joining by writing to Sabre Travel Information Network, P.O. Box 619616, Mail Drop 3259, DFW Airport, TX 75261-9616. That way you can have it in hand when you log on for the first time.)

Worldspan says its TravelShopper is so easy it doesn't need a reference guide. They may be right. Both systems have "help desks" which can be reached through an 800 number. EaasySabre's number is constantly busy. TravelShopper's hardly ever is.

The *EaasySabre Reference Guide* contains some good information and will certainly get you started. It is by no means, however, a complete how-to for the system. Its name not withstanding, you will probably find that it's a bit hard to get the hang of EaasySabre unless you've had some prior CRS experience. While it is certainly easier than its professional counterpart, Sabre, which the travel agencies use, even the computer literate will need some experience to become comfortable with EaasySabre's menus and the procedures for researching and booking.

Once you're "in" EaasySabre, you will be presented with a series of menus — numbered lists of options for what to do next. Simply select the number of the option you want and type it in. It takes time (I sometimes call the system Slooow Sabre) but it gets you there. Once you become familiar with what you're looking for, you can start to use some shortcuts.

Systems like EaasySabre let you do a remarkable number of things. Among the things you can find out from EaasySabre are:

- Which airlines fly from Point A to Point B and when. When a trip involves changing planes, the system gives you all the details including flight numbers.
- Fares, round-trip and one-way, to all destinations. These fares are kept current by the computer system.
- The rules that govern fares. You will soon discover that there are a bewildering number of fares to any given destination. The system allows you to examine the "fine print."
- Which planes are used on which flights.
- The seating configuration on the flight you're interested in.
- The weather at the destination.

Once you have all the information you need to construct the itinerary, you can:

- Reserve airline tickets. These reservations will hold a seat, but they are not official until the ticket is purchased or until your agency tickets it.
- Reserve a rental car at the destination.
- Do the same for a hotel.
- You can even book some tours directly on the CRS.
- If you're affiliated with a Sabre agency, you can enter your agency's code into the system and the reservation will be transmitted electronically to your agency so they can generate the actual ticket on their printer.

Eventually, you will want to learn all the ins and outs of EaasySabre (or TravelShopper). You may even decide that you want to go the whole nine yards and queue your bookings to your agency's "pseudo city code." But when you're first getting started, you want to get the information you need fast, make the reservation, and get back to your client as quickly as possible.

The easy way to research fares & flights

Here is the lazy man's way to researching and booking a flight. It makes use of both the on-line CRS and the airlines' highly trained reservationists who are just a toll-free phone call away. It involves three simple steps:

- **Step One.** Find the cheapest fare. This information is available on the CRS.
- **Step Two.** Find out which airlines fly there at that fare. Also on the CRS.
- **Step Three.** Call the airline, double-check everything, and make the booking.

To illustrate the process, let's suppose you get a call from a friend who wants to fly from Charleston, SC, on Friday, October 22, to Kansas City, MO, and return on Monday, October 25. He wants to leave after work on Friday and get back sometime in the evening on Monday. He wants the cheapest fare and doesn't care which airline he flies on.

Here, step by step, is how you would go about researching that booking, via an on-line information service.

The EaasySabre version

Let's do it first on EaasySabre. You dial up CompuServe and access EaasySabre. You see this screen:

```
We must periodically request that you review EAASYSABRE terms and conditions
if you have not already done so. Before reviewing, we encourage current users
to sign on to EAASYSABRE so that we may note your having reviewed this
information and not require you to review it again each time you sign on.
New EAASYSABRE users should select option 2.
Please enter your AAdvantage Number.
Quick Path example:
ID,PASSWORD,NEW PASSWORD
Or select one of the following:
1  I have read and agree to the Terms and Conditions
2  Proceed to the Terms and Conditions
3  Exit EAASYSABRE
>
```

A couple of notes are in order here: You don't need an AAdvantage number to use EaasySabre, and I'll show you how Quick Path works a little later in the chapter.

At this point, you may want to activate the option in your software that will save your entire session on EaasySabre to a file, which you can call up later for review or print out for easier reference. You are an EaasySabre member, so you choose the fastest option, which is number 1. At the prompt (the little ">" symbol at the bottom of the screen), you type "1" and get to the following screen:

```
                        EAASYSABRE MAIN MENU
1 System Quick Tips                  6 Profile Review and Change
2 Travel Reservations and Information 7 Travelers Access
3 Weather Information                8 Official Recreation Guide
4 AAdvantage                         9 Sign Off
5 Application to use EAASYSABRE
To select one of the options above, enter the number:
** Quick Tip:  These system navigation commands are always available:
   /Help or  ? for assistance
   /Res  or /R to go to the Reservations Menu
   /Top  or /T to return to the Main Menu
   /Exit or /E to return to your System Operator

>
```

At this point, you begin **Step One**, taking advantage of some keyboard shortcuts, known as FastTracks and QuickPath, which is an abbreviated version of FastTracks. (It's not important that you understand quite what you're doing at this point. Just be assured that if you type the instructions given here, EaasySabre will give you the information you need to know.)

You type in the following at the > prompt:

/FARES,CHS,MCI,22OCT,ALL

This is an example of what EaasySabre calls Quick Path. The "/" simply tells the system to pay attention to and follow the instructions that follow. The instructions say, "Give me the fares (FARES) from Charleston (CHS) to Kansas City (MCI) on October 22 (22OCT) for all airlines (ALL)."

CHS and MCI are codes that identify the specific airports involved in this itinerary. The *EaasySabre Reference Guide* lists some of the commonly used airport codes. If you get stuck there is a way within EaasySabre to ask, for example, "What is the code for Cleveland?" Eventually, you will probably want to get a list of all the world's airport codes. Such a list can be found in *The Intrepid Traveler's Complete Desk Reference* (available for $14.95, plus $3.00 shipping and handling, from The Intrepid Traveler, P.O. Box 438, New York, NY 10034-0438); it will let you find out the code for Rome's Fiumicino airport (FCO) or determine where in the world HOM is (Homer, Alaska).

By typing /FARES,CHS,MCI,22OCT,ALL, you get:

```
        From: (CHS) CHARLESTON, SC          FRIDAY   OCT-22
          To: (MCI) KANSAS CITY, MO
All airlines - Regular and discount fares       Fares in: USD
_____

    One Way    Round Trip   Fare Code     Airline(s)
    _____    _____   _____     _____

1   347.00                  KE14NR        DL
2   347.00                  HE14NR        US
```

3 347.00	VE14NR	AA
4 347.00	QE14NQ	UA
5 347.00	BE14IP	CO
6 388.00	ME7NCNR	DL
7 388.00	ME7NR	DL

To view fare RULES, enter the line number of the desired fare, or

8 View MORE fares	11 View available FLIGHTS
9 CHANGE fare request	12 View fares for a SPECIFIC airline
10 View the FIRST fares display	13 View fares from HIGHEST to LOWEST

>

Since EaasySabre lists fares from lowest to highest, you now know that the cheapest fare from Charleston to Kansas City is $347.00. You also know that five airlines, Delta (DL), USAir (US), American (AA), United (UA), and Continental (CO) fly out of Charleston, and they are all matching each other on the fare.

By glancing at the fare code column for these fares, you learn a number of important things. The initial letters (K, H, V, Q, and B in this case) are standard codes that indicate a "special" or "bargain" fare. The initial code for standard coach is Y; for first-class, F; and so forth. The remaining letters are a sort of abbreviation that explains the specific fare. KE14NR, for example, tells you that this is an excursion fare (requiring a Saturday stay-over) that must be purchased at least 14 days in advance and is non-refundable. So you know from glancing at the codes that the fares you're most interested in are all non-refundable (once your client buys the ticket he's stuck with it) and that they require a 14-day advance purchase.

This screen also tells you that if there are fewer than 14 days before October 22 but more than seven, the lowest fare would be $388 (ME7NR, for example).

(By the way, a complete listing of all the codes and abbreviations used in EaasySabre and other computerized reservations systems will be found in *The Intrepid Traveler's Complete Desk Reference*; see above.)

If you were curious about the fare rules, you could select the line number of a fare (for example, "2") and type it in. You could then read the fine print on restrictions and conditions.

For now, you have the information you need to proceed to Step Two, which is to find which airline offers the most convenient schedule. So you type in:

/AIR,CHS,MCI,22OCT,6P,1

You are telling EaasySabre, "Give me the schedule (AIR) for flights from Charleston (CHS) to Kansas City (MCI) leaving on October 22 (22OCT) at about 6:00 p.m. (6P) for all airlines (1)." EaasySabre will reply:

FLIGHT AVAILABILITY

From: (CHS) CHARLESTON, SC
To: (MCI) KANSAS CITY, MO   FRIDAY   OCT-22

Flight	Leave	Arrive	Meal	Stop	Aircraft	OnTime	Classes of Service**
1 DL1055	CHS 505P	ATL 611P		0	M80	8	F Y B M H Q K L
DL1675	711P	MCI 810P	D	0	M80	7	F Y B M H Q K L
2 DL1191	CHS 655P	ATL 804P		0	757	8	F Y B M H Q K L
DL1479	859P	MCI 955P		0	M80	6	F Y B M H Q K L
3 US1272	CHS 430P	CLT 519P		0	734	9	F Y B H Q M K
US1249	600P	MCI 721P	D	0	733	5	Y B H M

To SELECT a flight, enter the line number, or

8 View MORE flights   11 View all FARES
9 CHANGE flight request   12 Translate CODES
10 View FIRST flight display   13 View LOWest one-way fares

** Quick Tip: Select your flight, then choose Bargain Finder when prompted and
    EAASYSABRE will select the class of service for the lowest available fare.

>

This screen tells you a number of important things. First, there is no non-stop flight. If there were, it would have been listed first. Second, there is no flight that doesn't involve changing planes; that, too, would have been listed first. Since EaasySabre tries to find the best flight first (in this case, the one leaving closest to 6:00 p.m.), you can tell that the Delta flight leaving at 6:55 is probably your client's best bet since it gives him a comfortable amount of time to get to the airport after work.

Each letter in the Classes of Service column refers to a different fare, each with its own conditions and restrictions. As you can see, any given flight has quite a number of different fares, far more than just "first class" (F) and "coach" (Y). All the other letters (B,M,H,Q,K,L) refer to various discount fares. In theory, the fact that they are listed here means that seats at the fares corresponding to these letters are still available as of the time you logged onto EaasySabre. Remember that the cheapest fare on Delta had a fare code that began with the letter "K"? This screen is telling you that the fare is still available.

If you wanted, you could continue in EaasySabre, checking other outbound flight options and picking flights for the return journey from Kansas City on the 25th. (You'd type "/AIR,MCI,CHS,25OCT,4P,1.") However, you decide that, since this is a pretty straightforward request, you have enough information. So you type:

/EXIT

This takes you out of EaasySabre. You then proceed to log off CompuServe to clear your phone line for Step **Three**, calling Delta's 800 number to speak with a reservationist, confirm the fare, inquire about the best return flights, and make the actual reservation.

The TravelShopper version

You can do much the same thing in TravelShopper. When you log on, you will be greeted by this screen:

```
***TRAVELSHOPPER*** MAIN MENU
Hello MR TRAVEL AGENT

What would you like?
  0 [P] Profile adds/changes - Frequent traveler program enrollment
  1 [A] Available Flights/Book Flights
  2 [F] Fares/Fare restrictions
  3  -  View/Change Previous Reservation
  4 [O] Other Services/Nice to Know Info
  5 [L] Low Fare Finder Description
  6 [C] CAR Availability/Information
  7 [H] HOTEL Availability/Information
   ** Help Desk 1-800-892-1011 **
[R]-Reserve Flight using code  [E]-Exit
Key [?] for system commands
>
```

The letters and symbols contained in the square brackets ([ ]) are TravelShopper's menu commends. You will type "F" at the prompt and get:

```
FARES/FARE RESTRICTIONS
Enter Departure City or Code.
Expert entry: bos;Chicago;Sep15;2;
>
```

TravelShopper will walk you through a booking step-by-step. But as the "Expert entry" line (above) shows, you can also use short cuts, much like EaasySabre's Quick Path. Notice that in TravelShopper you can use the actual city name if you don't know the code. Note, too, that you separate elements in the instructions with a semicolon (;) instead of a comma (,).

Since you know the codes, you type:

```
>CHS;MCI;OCT22;6;
```

This will produce the following screen:

```
What TYPE of Fares do you want to see?
 1-Normal & One Way Specials
 2-Normal, One Way And Round-Trip Specials
 3-Children (Age 2-11)
 4-Military, Government, VUSA, and Senior.
 5-BY BOOKING CLASS CODES - Enter "5" and the booking class code(s) desired.
   (Max. of 5 codes e.g.,  5f or 5c.y or 5f.c.y.b.m)
 >
```

(Note: VUSA in line 4, above, stands for "visit USA," a fare available only to travelers from outside the country.)

Type "2" and you will see:

Enter Airline Name or Code or key RETURN for all airlines.
>

Since you want information on all airlines, hit the return key. This will result in the following screen:

Fares shown LOWEST to HIGHEST
Fares for 22OCT - See Restrictions
From: CHARLESTON   SOUTH CAROLINA
     To: KANSAS CTY INTL KANSAS CITY MO

Fare #	Airline Code	OW Amount RT	Fare Code
1	CO	$347.00	BE14IP
2	UA	$347.00	QE14NQ
3	DL	$347.00	KE14NR
4	US	$347.00	HE14NR
5	AA	$347.00	VE14NR
6	DL	$388.00	ME7NCNR
7	CO	$388.00	KE7IP
8	UA	$388.00	HE7NCNQ

Key RETURN for higher fares
Key Fare Number to See Restrictions

[CH] -CHange Type of Fare or Airline   [A] -Available Flights
>

This information should be familiar. TravelShopper anticipates your next move and lets you see available flights simply by typing "A" at the prompt. You will then see:

22OCT/FRI   CHARLESTON to KANSAS CTY INTL
#	FLIGHT	LEAVE	ARRIVE	EQP	STOPS
1	DL1191	CHS- 655P	ATL- 804P	757	0
	Connecting at: ATLANTA				
	DL1479	ATL- 859P	MCI- 955P	M80	0
2	DL1055	CHS- 505P	ATL- 611P	M80	0
	Connecting at: ATLANTA				
	DL1675	ATL- 711P	MCI- 810P	M80	0
3	US1272	CHS- 430P	CLT- 519P	734	0
	Connecting at: CHARLOTTE				
	US1249	CLT- 600P	MCI- 721P	733	0
4	DL1055	CHS- 505P	ATL- 611P	M80	0

```
Connecting at: ATLANTA
NW 829  ATL- 720P  MEM-744P D95       0
Connecting at: MEMPHIS
NW1035  MEM- 830P MCI- 950P D95       0


Key Line # for Booking Details, or Key RETURN to see more


[RF]-Return Flights  [F]-Fares  [CH]-CHange Parameter
[SA]-Specific Airline available flights  [CC]-Connection City
>
```

TravelShopper has the advantage of spelling out the names of the cities in which your customer will have to change planes.

Checking back with your client

In the example given above, I assumed that this was a cut-and-dried situation, one in which the client would rely on you to make the best decision. Of course, you could always have stayed in EaasySabre (or TravelShopper) a bit longer, and examined all the available options, including return flights for the 25th. If you saved the session on your computer, you could then print it out and have all the information at your fingertips when you called your client to discuss the pros and cons of the various options and make a final decision on an itinerary.

In any event, it's a good idea to make a reservation with the airline *as soon as possible* for at least one itinerary. This will prevent the embarrassing situation of checking back with your client, and selling him on the flight you have chosen, only to find the flight sold out when you call the airline to make the actual booking. Remember that reservations can be canceled if need be. You cannot throw people off a fully booked flight.

In some cases, of course, there is not much point in making a reservation. If, for example, your client has just asked you to check fares for a trip that is under consideration but not definite, you might want to hold off for a while. People will not make a decision to take a trip simply because you made a reservation for them. As you gain experience with the industry and with your clients, you will be able to play this decision by ear.

As you gather information about your client's itinerary, whether you do it all at once on EaasySabre or do some of it on EaasySabre and some on the phone with the airline, start entering the information on the *Client Booking Form* (page 129). This document serves as your official record of the itinerary and can be used to transmit your booking to your agency for ticketing. Work in pencil, since the details may change as you research various options and check with the airline about seat availability.

Discipline yourself to use this form (or another like it that you develop yourself). Never keep your booking information on odd scraps of paper and the backs of envelopes. That is a surefire recipe for disaster. As you gain experience, you may want to add to (or subtract from) the items on the form to better reflect the way you do business with your agency.

When you call the client, review the following points:

- The dates and times of flights. If you have reserved or researched more than one possibility, you may want to include details like whether dinner is served. That may help the client choose among alternatives.
- The fare. If several people are going on the same trip, quote the fares individually and for the entire group. If there are several fares, explain the trade-offs. For example, a cheaper fare might mean more stops en route or a change of plane.
- If the fare is non-refundable (most seem to be these days), make sure you impress this fact upon the client. It is also a good idea to make a note on your *Client Booking Form* to the effect that you informed the client of this fact.
- If any charges or fees will result from changes to the ticket once booked, this, too, should be impressed upon the client.
- If a reservation has not been made, alert the client to the possibility that seats might not be available when you do try to book. Some fares are also not guaranteed until the ticket has been paid for.

If flights are not yet booked, make them as soon as possible after getting the client's okay. If you have booked several different itineraries, get on the phone and cancel the ones the client won't be using.

Making the booking

If you are working in EaasySabre or TravelShopper, it is possible to make the actual booking on-line and have it transmitted electronically to your agency. I consider that to be an "advanced" technique, however, so I will not presume to teach it here. Most beginners will find it far more reassuring to make the actual booking with a live human being at the airline's reservations desk. That way you *know* you've done it correctly because (assuming you give them the right information) the reservationist will not let you do it wrong.

Let's assume, for the sake of discussion, that you have fully researched the itinerary from Charleston to Kansas City and back for your client, have run it by him, gotten his okay, and are now ready to firm it up with Delta. Simply pick up the phone and dial Delta's toll-free reservations number. When the reservationist answers, identify yourself as a travel agent:

> *"Hi. This is Mary Jones. I'm a travel agent
> and I'd like to make a booking, please."*

Then, slowly and clearly, provide the reservationist with the following information:

- The passenger(s) name(s). You will also need to have handy the client's phone number for the airline's records.
- Class of service. You can say "coach" or "economy" but you

can be more accurate by specifying the fare code. There are several different "coach" fares and you're looking for the cheapest. You need only give the first letter of the code.

- The departing city and the destination. Be specific. If you say "Charleston," the reservationist might think you mean Charleston, West Virginia. If you say "New York," the reservationist won't know if you mean La Guardia Airport or JFK. You can avoid all confusion by using the three-letter airport codes.
- If there's a change of planes involved, as there is in our example, give the ultimate destination first. You can get specific about the exact flights once the reservationist has the information on his or her screen.
- The date of the outbound flight.
- The first flight number or the time of the flight. If there is a change of planes, you should have the second flight number handy as well, although you probably won't have to use it. The airline's reservation system will provide it to the reservationist automatically.
- The date of the return flight.
- Flight numbers (or times) for the returning flight or flights.

In my experience, some airlines prefer to get flight numbers, others prefer flight times. Flight numbers change while the time remains the same, or times change while the flight number remains the same. So it never hurts to check to make sure there hasn't been a change in either flight number or flight time that EaasySabre didn't have. If you have selected an outbound flight but not a return flight, the reservationist will help you make the best choice. The reservationist will enter all this information into the airline's computer system. This process is known as "building a record."

Make sure you get the names of *all* the passengers. It's easy to forget that you don't know the names of your friend Bill's two kids until you try to book flights for them. If there is the possibility of getting a reduced "youth" fare, usually on an international flight, you should have the ages of the kids as well.

Once the itinerary is set, the next item for discussion is the fare. If you know what the fare should be, it's a good idea to be proactive. Say something like, "I'm showing a fare of $387 in K class." If there is any problem or discrepancy, give the complete fare code and find out what the problem is. Sometimes, the reservationist will quote a higher fare and only "find" the right fare when you mention the code. You should be aware, however, that the cheapest fare is assigned only to a finite number of seats on the flight. Once they're booked, you may be stuck with a higher fare.

Next, get an assigned seat for your passenger and give the reservationist the client's frequent flyer number, if he has one. If he doesn't, you can enroll him in Delta's program right over the phone. It's a nice gesture and one which the client will appreciate.

Most airlines will also ask for a telephone number for the client in the city of departure. Some will want to have a contact number in the destination city as well; if you don't have one, simply say you don't know. You won't be marked down for it.

The reservationist will read back the details of the booking. Listen carefully and check the information against your written itinerary. Make sure they match.

In addition to the specifics of the itinerary, there are a number of other key bits of information you will want to get from the reservationist:

- Always make sure to ask for the "record locator number." This crucial bit of information is a random mix of numbers and letters (mostly letters) that forms a unique identifier for this particular booking. Record that number on your *Client Booking Form*.

- Ask about the ticketing deadline. This is especially important if the client hasn't yet made a definite decision about going.

- It is also a good idea to get the name of the agent who made the booking for you. Typically, they will give you their first name. Less frequently, the reservationist will give you their "sine" (pronounced "sign"), which is a two letter code that identifies the individual. Make a note of this on the *Client Booking Form*. This can come in handy later if there is any dispute about the booking.

Transmitting the booking

The final step in the booking process is to communicate all the information to your agency so that it can issue the ticket. If you have filled out a *Client Booking Form*, you have all the information you need, organized, and in one place. If you phone in the booking, just read off the information. You may want to develop your own version of the *Client Booking Form* so that you record the information in the order in which your agency prefers to have it read to them over the phone. Once you have read the information over the phone, ask the person at the agency to read the booking back to you to make sure nothing got lost or misunderstood in the transmission. Another option is to fax your completed booking form to the agency; this avoids the problem of missed signals altogether.

Once the agency has the information, it will go to its own CRS, locate the passenger record (via the record locator number), claim the booking as its own, and print out the actual tickets and boarding passes the passengers will present to the airline on boarding the plane.

The next step is to get the tickets to the clients. There are several ways to do this. Since how the ticket is delivered can affect your income, it's worth taking the time to examine the alternatives:

- ***You can pick up the tickets at the agency and hand deliver them.*** This is, far and away, the best alternative. Also, if you've hooked up with a local agency, it's easy. Make sure that, before you leave the agency, you double-check the ticket against your *Client Booking Form* to make sure everything is correct. If there are mistakes, this is the time to find out. If you faxed your booking in, and can prove that the mistake was made by the agency, you shouldn't be liable for the cost of fixing it.

- ***You can have the tickets mailed to you and then hand deliver them to the client.*** If you are dealing with an out-of-town agency, as I do, this is your best alternative. My agency picks up the cost of postage when they mail tickets and other travel documents to me. However, if the post office loses the tickets, the liability is mine and not the agency's. Again, as soon as the tickets arrive, check them for accuracy.

- ***You can have the tickets mailed directly from the agency to the client.*** This is a less attractive alternative since you can't check the accuracy of the tickets until the client receives them. (Unless, of course, you look them over in the agency before they are mailed.) However, if you, the agency, and the client are all in different cities, this may be your only alternative.

- ***You can arrange to have the ticket delivered to the client by any number of expedited delivery systems.*** These include Priority Mail, Express Mail, UPS, Federal Express (next day or second-day) and so forth. My agency will even arrange same-day delivery but at a staggering cost. Unfortunately, it will sometimes be necessary to resort to these forms of delivery.

Most agencies will deduct the cost of any form of expedited delivery from your share of commission. My agency even deducts $1.00 from my commission check when they send tickets via regular first-class mail directly to the client. The cost of overnight shipping can eat up a big chunk of your commission for a $200 flight. Make sure you are very clear on your agency's policies in this regard. Your agency may have printed up a schedule of charges for various delivery options. (Mine has.) If they haven't, ask them to provide one. Simply explain that you want to make sure you know the ground rules in order to avoid any future misunderstandings.

There are a number of ways to protect yourself (and your pocketbook) in these kinds of situations:

- Explain to the client that there will be an additional charge for expedited delivery and have the agency add the charge to the client's credit card. Obviously, you should check with the agency beforehand to make sure they can (and are willing to) do this.
- Collect the fare plus any additional shipping charges in cash.
- Finally, weigh the extra cost of shipping against the total commission and the circumstances. If the client is a regular, seldom requires expedited delivery, and has just booked a $6,000 trip, you might decide to absorb the charge for the Federal Express shipment as a cost of doing business.

Notes on the Client Booking Form

The *Client Booking Form* can be used to record an airline booking and transmit that booking to your agency for ticketing. It will also help you make sure you haven't overlooked anything. Of course, the agency through which you book may have its own form. If so, use it.

Most of this form is self-explanatory. Here are a few notes on items that may require clarification.

- **Reservationist.** While not absolutely necessary, it's a good idea to record the name of the reservationist with whom you made the booking, just in case some misunderstanding arises later about what you were or were not told.

- **Age.** A passenger's age is important only when a child, youth, or senior fare is involved.

- **Notes.** Note special meal requests or anything else you feel is worth recording.

- **Flight details.** Record in full the following: the date of the flight, the airline (use the code), the flight number, departure time (on the 24-hour clock), the departure city (or code), the destination city (or code), arrival time, and the assigned seat. Record each segment separately. In other words, if the passenger has to change planes in Chicago to reach Indianapolis, the entire journey will be recorded on two lines, one for each flight. It is always preferable to use the two- and three-digit codes for airlines and airports.

- **Class.** This is the airline's one-letter code for the fare attached to the booking. It is the first letter of the fare code. You might want to record the entire fare code in the "Notes" space.

- **Special Instructions.** These would be instructions to the ticketing agency. For example, "Send the ticket directly to the client, not to me."

- **Credit Card.** If the client pays by cash or check, you can simply check that space. If the payment is by credit card, there is a space for the client's signature. This allows the *Client Booking Form* to substitute for a credit card imprint. See *Chapter 11: Getting Serious* for more information on handling credit card payments.

- **Hotels/Rental Cars.** Use this space to record the key information about hotel and rental car bookings, including the confirmation number for the booking. This will allow your agency to identify your commission when it is paid by the supplier.

- **Booked By.** Include the information your agency will need to identify this booking as yours and get the commission payment to you.

Client Booking Form

Client: _____ Phone: _____

Address: _____
_____

Booking Information

Airline: _____ Record Locator: _____ Reservationist: _____

Passengers

Last Name	First Name	Age	Notes

Date	Air	Flt #	Dep	Fr	To	Arr	Seat	Class	Notes

Fare per person: _____ Total fare: _____

Date booked: _____ Booking Deadline: _____

Special Instructions:

Payment Information

Cash ___ Check ___ Credit Card #: _____ Exp.: _____

Name on card: _____

Billing Address & phone: _____

Cardholder Signature:

┌─ Hotels ──────────────────┐ ┌─ Rental Cars ──────────────┐
│   │ │   │
│   │ │   │
│   │ │   │
│   │ │   │
└────────────────────────────┘ └────────────────────────────┘

┌─ Booked By: ───┐
│   │
│   │
│   │
│   │
└───┘

The four traps of cheap fares

Unless your clients are unusually well-heeled, most of the bookings you make will be for the least expensive ticket available. There's nothing wrong with that — as long as you know the rules that apply to cheap fares and take care to abide by them. Watch out for these pitfalls:

1. The 24-hour rule

Most cheap fares you book with the airline must be ticketed within 24 hours of the booking or 7 or 14 days in advance of the flight date, whichever comes first. In other words, it may be 30 days before flight date and you may think you have plenty of time, when in fact you only have 24 hours to get that booking ticketed. "Ticketed" means having the ticket printed out by the machine at your agency. Most agencies will check the booking date to make sure the ticket complies with all the airline's rules before they generate the ticket. That's because the airlines are very fussy about making agencies stick to the rules. If the ticket is issued late, the airlines will charge the agency a penalty (a "debit memo") and the agency will pass that charge along to you.

Let's say you make a cheap-fare booking on Tuesday for a flight 20 days away. The first thing you should do is inform the client of the rule: "This booking has to be ticketed by tomorrow, Wednesday, at 3:00 p.m.; so let me know as soon as possible if you want the ticket issued." Let's say you did that but the client forgets to get back to you until Thursday morning. You have a number of alternatives:

- Call the airline and make a *new* booking for the same flight for the same client. Get the new booking ticketed immediately. Then cancel the old booking. But suppose there are no more seats available? Then you have to . . .
- Speak with the customer service representative at the airline reservation office and ask for a waiver. If you're lucky they'll grant one. Otherwise, you'll be forced to . . .
- Contact the sales office of the airline (the customer service rep who turned down your request for a waiver will be able to give you the number) and speak to the rep whose territory includes your agency. Ask him or her for a waiver. Again, you may get lucky and receive one. Otherwise, you will be reduced to . . .
- Calling your agency and begging for help and forgiveness. Sometimes the agency will be able to work around the problem by creating a hand-written ticket where the discrepancy in dates can be fudged. They almost certainly will charge you a fee for this service, but that can be preferable to picking up the difference between what you told the client the cheap fare would be and what a new ticket would actually cost.

In the worst case scenario, you will be forced to go back to your client and explain that because you didn't stay on top of their booking, they will either have to pay a much higher fare or forego the trip.

2. The "no guarantee" rule

No fare, cheap or otherwise, is guaranteed until it is ticketed. So even if your cheap fare doesn't have to be ticketed in 24 hours, waiting a week can have unfortunate consequences. Promotional fares expire, airlines decide it's time to boost fares, and so forth. You also can't rely on what the reservationist tells you. They may have the best intentions in the world, but they don't know what evil plans their superiors are hatching behind their backs.

So, regardless of what a reservationist tells you about fares and ticketing deadlines, the sooner you tell the agency to ticket the client, the better the odds of getting the quoted fare. Since most airlines have a habit of making fare changes in the dead of night, the fare you are quoted in the morning will probably still be good until the close of business.

3. The "non-refundable" rule

Many cheapie fares are non-refundable — period. This means it is important that you provide your clients with all the facts. Impress upon them the non-refundability of the tickets they are getting. Suggest that they consider taking out trip cancellation insurance, just in case. The higher the cost of the tickets, the more you should insist.

Most people are reasonable. But if someone gets stuck holding several thousand dollars of non-refundable tickets that they can't use, there may a strong temptation for them to decide that the travel agent didn't warn them and that, therefore, the travel agent should be sued. Some agencies go so far as to create a paper trail of what they have told the client. Some actually have clients sign a statement to the effect that they have been counseled to accept insurance and have declined.

4. The "exchangeability" rule

Most cheap fare tickets can be exchanged (for a flight on a different date, for example) for a fee of between $35 and $50. Unfortunately, the 24-hour rule takes effect again in these situations. And since the agency must have the old tickets in hand before new ones can be issued, the exchange will entail running up a bill with Federal Express. The client doesn't want to pay for any of that. Neither does your agency. Guess who pays?

Again, the key here is making the ground rules very clear to your clients. If you have told them, up front and explicitly, that any changes in the ticket will incur a fee, most people will realize their responsibility to pay it.

Getting paid

Commissions on airline tickets are calculated on the "base fare," that is, the fare *before* taxes are added. The fare quoted by the reservations systems is the fare *including* tax. The tax on domestic airline tickets is 10%, which in theory should make it easy to calculate the base fare. Unfortunately, some airports levy an additional "tax" or "passenger facility charge (PFC)" on every airline ticket. The airlines simply add the fee to the base fare and the tax and quote the resulting amount as the fare. So the effective tax can be higher than 10%. In addition, higher taxes apply to flights to Alaska and Hawaii. If you want to know for sure, you can ask the airline reservationist what the base fare is.

The rate of commission is set by the airline issuing the ticket. It can vary, but it is usually between 9% and 11%, with 10% being pretty standard. International flights, especially those on foreign flag carriers, have higher commissions. Recently, for example, the average domestic commission rate was 9.99%; the average international commission rate was 14.39%. In addition, there are sometimes special, usually time-limited, commission rates on certain routes. This information may be available from the reservationist.

Making sure that the airlines get paid for their tickets and that the travel agency receives its commission is the job of the Airlines Reporting Corporation (ARC). When the customer pays by cash or check, the agency deposits the payment in a special escrow account to which ARC has access. Credit card payments are processed through the issuing airline. Once a week, on Tuesday, the travel agency submits to ARC a report on all its airline business for the previous week (Monday through Sunday). Ten days after the Sunday on which the weekly reporting period ends, ARC reconciles its accounts with the agency. If the agency owes ARC money, ARC withdraws that sum from the escrow account. If ARC owes the agency money, it sends the agency a check through the mail.

The system is pretty efficient, so the odds of your agency not getting paid it's commission are slim. It also follows that the agency should have the commission for your booking in hand no later than about 20 days from the date of booking.

When you get *your* money is another matter. My current agency is very good about paying on airline commissions — the commission check arrives in the same envelope as the tickets, along with a computer-generated form explaining in exquisite detail what's what. That means they are paying me *before* they get paid. To my knowledge, no other agency operates this way. My previous agency was a small local agency; there I waited almost three months for payment with no explanation, when it finally came, of what it was for. Some agencies have arrangements whereby they will write you a check weekly or on, say, the fifteenth of each month covering all commissions generated during the previous week or month and also provide you with a detailed breakdown of what the check covers. Still other agencies have policies that they will pay the outside agent a commission only after the client has traveled. That means if you sell a ticket for use nine months in the future (a not too uncommon occurrence), you may have to wait almost a year for your share of the commission. In theory, this protects the agency against cancellations; in practice, it allows them to hold onto your money for an extended period of time.

In defense of the travel agency, it should be noted that most agencies operate on razor-thin profit margins. So there is a very strong incentive for them to hold onto money as long as possible and to weight the fiduciary relationship in their favor. That thought, however, will be of little comfort when you are steaming over a commission check that is long overdue.

Because of the vast disparity in payment arrangements, you should be very clear on precisely what an agency's policy is before you sign on. You also might want to make this an important item on your checklist as you do comparison shopping among agencies. Payment schedules might well become a point of negotiation between you and a local agency; the larger "instant agencies" have set policies, and it is unlikely that they will negotiate them on an individual basis. You should also bear in mind that, the more complicated the agency's payment system is, the more complex your own record-keeping will have to be, just to keep track of what is owed you.

Consolidators

If you are booking international travel for your clients you may want to consider the benefits (as well as the pitfalls) of using consolidators. In the simplest terms, a consolidator is someone who buys wholesale and sells below retail. In this case, the commodity being purchased is airplane seats. Consolidators "buy" large blocks of seats from the airlines at steep discounts. Then they turn around and sell those seats at a price that is well below the "face value" of a ticket but still high enough to earn them a profit. While some consolidator tickets are available for long-haul domestic flights (especially to Hawaii), this is primarily an international phenomenon. Competition is stiffer on international runs and some of the smaller foreign carriers are willing to be quite aggressive in their discount pricing to consolidators.

Why do the airlines sell them this space? For a variety of reasons. For one thing, the airlines reckon they will never sell all their seats at the prices they publish and with the restrictions they place on them. So they sell a portion of their seats to consolidators in the interests of having full, or at least fuller, flights. Selling to consolidators is also a good way for the airlines to raise much-needed cash — now, rather than later. In a sense, the airline is borrowing against its inventory of unsold seats. In exchange for getting paid for next month's flights today, the airline is willing to sell at a discount to the consolidator.

The basic attraction of a consolidator is price: Consolidator fares are (or should be!) lower than anything you can get directly from the airlines. I say "should be" because some surveys have revealed consolidators selling "discount" tickets at a higher price than the cheapest excursion fare. The old warning, "Buyer beware," applies in this area just as much as it does in others — and maybe more so. Some consolidators deal only with travel agents, while others sell only to the public, and still others sell to both. It might be reasonable to assume that consolidators that sell just to agents will have better prices than those that sell to the public; but even here you should comparison shop. Even if a consolidator sells directly to the public, you should be able to buy a ticket from that consolidator for a client and resell it at a higher rate, while still offering your client a good deal.

Another, less frequent, reason for using consolidators is availability. It may be that a consolidator has the only tickets left for a particular destination during a particular time frame. It is also unfortunately true that a consolidator cannot always get you tickets to where your customer wants to go, when she wants to go there.

Consolidators will quote you fares in one of two ways. Some consolidators quote "net" fares only. In this case you would mark up the cost of the ticket to your client. If the ticket cost, say, $700, you would write out a check for $700 to the consolidator, collect a check for, say, $800 from the client and bank the difference. The client, by the way, will not know what you paid for the ticket. Consolidator tickets are invariably handwritten on blank ticket stock; the space for the fare will contain only the notation, "Bulk," meaning the consolidator paid a bulk (i.e. discounted) rate for the ticket.

With net fares, you are free to charge your client whatever you feel is a fair price for both the ticket and your services in obtaining it. As a practical matter, however, you will probably not want to charge more than the lowest fare available directly from the airlines. That's just smart business. On the other hand, you might want to pass the ticket along at cost or at a very modest mark-up for a friend or family member.

Some consolidators, on the other hand, quote commissionable fares. That means that the quoted fare includes a commission for the agent and you will receive a check from the consolidator for your commission, just as you would if you were booking a "regular" ticket. Typical commissions are 10%. But commissions of 12% and 15% are not uncommon, and some consolidators advertise commissions of "up to 27%." Obviously, in these cases, the markup is fixed, unless you choose to rebate a portion of your commission to the client. You will also have to wait (in most cases) for your check and may have to remind "forgetful" consolidators that they owe you money.

Most consolidators prefer to operate on a "cash and carry" basis. They will probably accept your check but will not be too happy about credit cards. All things being equal, cash is probably the easiest way to deal with consolidators. As long as the consolidator is on the up and up, it's quick, it's clean, and it gets your money into the bank quickly.

Many clients, however, prefer to use credit cards. They are more convenient, and many people have learned that they can stop payment on a charge if they feel ripped off in any way. Many consolidators who quote net fares will work with you if your client wants to use plastic. You decide the price you want to charge for the ticket, then add a "service charge," typically 3%, to cover the consolidator's costs in processing the charge. Let's say the consolidator's net fare is $900. You decide to charge your client $1,000. With a 3% service charge, the total cost to the client would be $1,030, which would be the amount charged to his credit card. The consolidator would then give you a check for $100.

If, on the other hand, the consolidator won't accept plastic and the customer demands it, you may not be able to provide a consolidator ticket. The exception would be if you are running your travel agent business as an adjunct to an existing retail business which already has merchant status — that is, can accept credit cards. You would process the client's card through your existing business and write a check to the consolidator.

Consolidators are located all over the country. Most specialize to some extent; in other words, there are very few consolidators that can get you a ticket to *any* destination. Generally speaking, the location of a consolidator is not an impediment to doing business. You can live in New York and get tickets from a consolidator in Los Angeles. It's all handled on the phone and through the mail. For my part, I prefer to deal with consolidators whose offices I can get to in person. That way, at least, if something goes wrong, I have a desk I can pound on and demand satisfaction. Of course, I live in New York and many consolidators are close at hand. If you live in a smaller city you may have no choice but to deal with consolidators on a long-distance basis.

Most consolidator tickets are sold on a non-refundable, non-changeable basis; that's certainly true of the cheapest ones. In fact, most consolidator tickets lack many of the "extras" associated with "regular" airline tickets. Some tickets, for example, will not earn the customer frequent flyer miles. On the other hand, some consolidators will supply you with tickets that have all the usual bells and whistles. The trade-off, naturally, is money. The more options, the higher the price. It is important both for you to understand exactly what you are buying and for the client to understand what she is getting and giving up in this cut-rate ticket.

What's the best flight for the client?

The exact flight you eventually book for each individual client will depend on a number of interrelated variables. Some will be more important than others, depending on circumstances. It is your job as the client's agent to weigh the variables and guide the client to the best choice.

In the vast majority of cases, the price of the ticket will be the number one criterion when it comes to choosing straight air travel, especially when an international flight is involved. If you can find a consolidator ticket that's $50 less than anything a rival travel agent is quoting, you'll be a hero. This tendency towards penny-pinching holds true even among high rollers. Who wants to pay $6,000 for a first-class ticket when it can be had for $5,699?

However, other factors sometimes are as important as — even more important — than price. Of these, the airline is perhaps most important. Many people have been seduced by frequent flyer programs into putting all their travel eggs into one airborne basket. Other people have found the service and reliability of one airline to be superior to all others and will go out of their way to use it when at all possible. Some customers I've had have insisted on flying with a US carrier on their overseas flights.

Schedule can sometimes be an overriding factor. If the client can save three hours by paying a bit more or flying a different airline, he might opt to do just that.

Finally, we should note the role of commissions in selecting air travel for your clients. In the long-term, the best deal for the client will be the best deal for the travel agent: Satisfied customers keep coming back and every time they do, they generate another commission. Nevertheless, airlines compete for the agent's attention and one way in which they do that is by sweetening the commission structure. That can be tempting. If you know you can send a client to Tokyo on United for $1,000 at 11% commission or Japan Air Lines for $1,100 at a 30% commission, what would you do? (This example is fictitious but similar to ones that actually crop up.)

You might say that the best deal is on United and that you should book that flight. But consider this: You could rebate the customer $100 on the JAL fare, equaling the United fare, and still pocket a larger commission. Assuming a 50% split with the agency, the difference in commission would amount to $$110, so even with the $100 rebate, you'd make $10 more — $65 instead of $55. Many outside agents would not have a problem with that. On the other hand, an airline in bankruptcy was offering 12% commissions on domestic travel, partly to lure back agents who refused to book clients on a bankrupt carrier. (If the airline folded, their clients could be left stranded.) As it happened, this airline emerged from bankruptcy and no one was left holding the bag. But what would you have done in the meantime? Run the risk of stranding your clients for a few extra bucks?

Commissions can raise some tricky ethical conundrums. You should always safeguard the best interests of your customers. On the other hand, as a businessperson, you cannot be completely blind to legal opportunities to increase your margin. Weigh the alternatives and try to make an honorable decision.

Summary

As lengthy as this discussion has been, it has only scratched the considerable surface of the subject of airline ticketing. If you keep booking air travel you will eventually have to deal with "open jaw" tickets, circle trips, round-the-world fares, one-way fares, frequent flyer awards, ticket redemptions, and many other niceties that drive travel agents to distraction. Gradually, you will begin to understand why I went on and on in *Chapter 4* about avoiding the "cheap-travel trap."

The good news is that the reservationists at the airlines are there to help you. They have certainly been very kind to me. With a bit of luck, or through some smart shopping, you may also wind up working with an agency that will help you learn the ropes and take the time to coach you in the more advanced skills and techniques. The bibliographies in the *Resource Section* will point you towards books that can help fill in gaps in your knowledge. There's even a listing of ASTA travel schools should you feel the need for more formal training.

There's even more good news: Compared with booking airline tickets, booking the other travel products we will be discussing is a piece of cake!

Chapter Seven: Booking Hotels

Hotels and travel agents have a troubled history of working together. Unlike airlines, hotels were slow to appreciate the position of the agent in the travel industry. Many of them saw little point in offering a commission. Even those that did were haphazard about actually paying up. Some hotels had a habit of offering commissions only on their higher rates, then informing the arriving guest that a lower rate was available, thus finessing the agent out of the commission. As a result, many agents have looked on hotel bookings as a value-added service to their customers rather than as a source of income.

This has started to change. More and more hotels, independents as well as chains, are courting agents. Even the budget chain Motel 6 pays commissions on bookings. And collecting a commission has become a better bet. According to a survey by *Travel Weekly*, 79% of all hotel commissions owed to travel agencies are now being paid. Not a great record, perhaps, but a decided improvement.

In fact, hotels can be a very nice source of income, especially when your customers are heading for a resort, a romantic bed & breakfast mansion, or to a downtown hotel in a major city; in these situations, the per-night charge can be as high as $200. A five-day stay in one of these high-ticket establishments can be worth a hefty commission to the agent who books it.

Gathering information

While misteaks . . . I mean *mistakes* . . . are not as lethal in booking hotels as they are in booking airline tickets, they are still embarrassing at best. In the worst cases, they can lose you a good customer. So it is in everyone's best interests that you take the time to collect the right information from your client when the subject of booking a hotel comes up.

Usually, a hotel booking will be a model of simplicity. A single business traveler or a couple on vacation need a room for a night or two. Often they will even know precisely where they want to stay. Nothing could be simpler. But sometimes it gets more complex. Here is a checklist of the key information that can go into a hotel booking:

- **The dates of arrival and departure.** This is pretty self-explanatory.
- **The location of the hotel.** Don't laugh. The customer may be flying into New York City but need a hotel in Rye, or Stamford, or Montclair, or any of hundreds of other locations in the New York metropolitan area. Even in a smaller city, location can be an important factor. Always ask where the client will be in the city being visited and what she is going to be doing. This will help you pinpoint the hotel that will be most convenient for the client.
- **The number of rooms.** If there will be more than one, you will also want to know who's going to be in which room and who's going to be paying for each room. Don't automatically assume your client is picking up the entire tab for a multi-room booking.
- **The ages of any minor children.** This lets you shop for "kids-stay-free" specials and other discounts.
- **Room configurations.** First of all, will it be a double or single? Hotels charge different rates for the same room depending on the number of people in it. So ask your client if a spouse or companion will be along. (If you are also booking airline tickets, you may already have this information.) Beyond that, there are many possibilities in hotel rooms: double rooms with two double beds, double rooms with one king-sized bed, double rooms with an extra bed, and so forth. The makeup of the traveling party may dictate the room configuration needed. If your client likes a specific room configuration, note this as a client preference (see below).
- **Price range.** In general, people are not as price-sensitive when it comes to hotels as they are about airline fares. A businessperson may be meeting clients at her hotel or need a hotel within walking distance of his ultimate destination. Beyond that, marketing campaigns by the major hotel chains have educated people to expect a "comfortable night's stay" when they travel. Indeed, many travelers have come to look on their hotel as a way to pamper themselves on the road, perhaps to compensate for the sacrifice of being away from home and family.

  Of course, if you offer a client a choice of three hotels, at three different prices, she may choose the least expensive. But when she finds that the hall carpets are old and shabby, the room smells faintly of mildew, the mattress is soft and lumpy, and the bathroom faucet drip-drip-drips through the night, she won't blame herself for being cheap. No, she will blame you! So, you are better off finding out what general price range a client will accept. (You may have to educate people on this point; most people are horrified when told the cost of even a modest hotel room in places like New York City, for example.) Once you've determined the range, you will have some leeway in recommending an appropriate property.

- *Credit card information.* Typically, the client will pay for the hotel room with a credit card on departure. Hotel reservationists will frequently ask for a credit card number to "hold" the reservation. Be aware that this means that they will charge the room to the client's credit card even if the client doesn't show up! If you (and the client) want to book the room on this basis, you will need to know the client's name as it appears on the credit card, the number, expiration date, and (perhaps) the billing address and a telephone contact.

These points cover the basics. There are additional bits of information that you might need when making a specific reservation for a specific client. They will be discussed a bit later.

Research

Sometimes, clients will know exactly where they want to stay. In that case, your job is easy. Sometimes they will request a specific chain. Sometimes they will know generally where they need a hotel ("Near the airport."). Sometimes the customer will have no idea where the hotel should be, except, of course, that it should be somewhere in the metropolitan area to which they are traveling. In most cases, you will have to do at least some research to find an appropriate property for your client.

Here are some of the major sources of information; see the *Resource Section* for price and publisher information:

- *Official Hotel Guide* and *Hotel and Travel Index.* These two references, published annually and quarterly, respectively, by Reed Travel Group, are the industry standards. They are expensive but will make you feel like a pro. They contain very complete information on a wide range of hotel properties, including tidbits not readily available elsewhere, such as commission rates and the names of the computerized reservations systems through which a hotel's rooms can be booked. They also tell you how old the hotel is, an important bit of information that can warn you that one property may be less desirable than a brand-new property down the street.

You may want to hold off on making a major investment in reference works until you see how your business is developing. Fortunately, there are a number of lower-cost alternatives:

- *Hotel chain directories.* Every chain of hotels publishes a free directory of its properties. You can pick these up at the reservation desks of hotels in your area or as you travel. You can also request copies from the good folks at the hotels' toll-free reservations numbers. Be warned, however, that it can take as long as two months for a requested copy to show up in the mail.
  The chains' directories contain a wealth of useful information, including (in many cases) thumbnail maps of cities and

the neighborhoods around specific properties. Listings of individual properties invariably tell you what points of interest (tourist attractions, colleges, corporate headquarters, military bases, etc.) are close by and how far away they are. All of this can help you pinpoint the best hotels for your clients. The directories also provide a wealth of information about the chain's special programs for frequent lodgers, senior and weekend discounts, and so forth — information which may be of interest to you and your clients. While they seldom tell you how old a property is, they will point out the newer properties or ones that meet special standards of excellence. Building a reference library of hotel directories is a good idea, even if you have no immediate use for the information they contain.

- *AAA Tour Books.* Members of the American Automobile Association (AAA) can obtain free copies of *Tour Books* covering various regions of the country. These books have the advantage of giving you AAA's independent ratings of properties.

- *On-line services.* Limited information on hotels can be gathered through EaasySabre or TravelShopper on an on-line service such as CompuServe. Searching them can be a way of getting a rough overview of what's available in a specific area and what the range of prices is. You can also make reservations directly through these systems, but I wouldn't recommend it for the beginner.

  Here's how you'd access hotel information on EaasySabre. We'll use the Los Angeles area for our example. Type in "/HOT,LAX,20MAY,24MAY,2" to start. That's "/HOT," a code for "hotels," followed by the three-digit airport or city code, the date of arrival, the date of departure, and the number of people in the party. You can then browse through a listing of hotels. There is not a lot of detailed information on each property, but you can quickly find out the lowest available price and how far the property is from the airport.

  In addition to EaasySabre and TravelShopper, other hotel information sources, such as *OAG Travel Planner* may be available through the on-line services, most often for an additional fee over and above standard access charges. All in all, I prefer the more comprehensive print references. (For more on on-line services, see the *Resource Section.*)

- *The trade press.* The magazines that cover the travel industry offer a constant flow of new information about hotels. New properties, mergers and acquisitions, special programs or offers for travelers, special commission rates and incentive deals for travel agents, and so forth. You may want to glance through recent issues when researching a hotel for a client, just in case something pops out at you.

- *Hotel toll-free numbers.* If worse comes to worst, you can call the toll-free number of a hotel chain you know the client likes and ask what's available where the client is going. This is a last-ditch ploy, however, because it won't necessarily be the most convenient for the client or offer the most amenities for the price paid.

Keeping your hotel research collection up to date will be an ongoing chore. All guides to hotels go out of date, perhaps sooner than you imagine. That's one reason Reed brings out its *Hotel and Travel Index* quarterly. The chains may update their directories several times a year. The *AAA Tour Books* tell you when the information in them becomes obsolete.

What to look for

Once you have your reference materials, it's time to pick the right hotel or a suitable selection from which your client can choose. First you want to cover the basics: location, price, preference. In other words, you want a hotel that is convenient for the customer, is in a price range with which the customer is comfortable, and meets the customer's criteria (brand name, style, or whatever). There are some other things you will want to be looking for:

- *What's included?* Extra touches like complimentary cocktails, or free breakfasts, are not only nice to know about, they may help make up the customer's mind.
- *Special offers.* If you are calling the hotels, ask about any special offers they might have going at the time the client will be visiting. For example, hotels sometimes offer the third or fourth night free during special promotions.
- *Amenities.* What does the hotel have to offer besides a comfortable room? Extras like tennis courts or proximity to a shopping mall might be important to your client. You will want to be able to provide as much information as possible.
- *What's in it for you?* It's also appropriate to find out if the chain offers a competitive commission and, if so, if there are any special deals for you, the agent, available.

Factors influencing your choice

Unless the client makes a specific request, you have a fair amount of leeway in recommending hotel accommodations. This gives you more of a chance to make a choice and then "sell" it to your client than you have when booking airline tickets. You can make a case for a property that's slightly more expensive or one that provides you with some special payback, in the form of a higher commission or entry in a sweepstakes for example. It's the travel industry equivalent of the suit salesman selling the $500 wool suit with two pairs of pants. The important thing is that the client feels happy with the choice and doesn't feel he has been arm-twisted into paying too much money.

Client preferences

Never forget that your first duty is to the client, so client preferences are the most important factors in choosing a hotel. Among the things that may be important to your client are:

- **The hotel chain.** Travelers develop brand loyalties, and you should know those of your customers. Many hotels have "frequent lodger" programs which mimic the frequent flyer promotions of the airlines. It's a good idea to know to which programs your clients belong and make a note of their membership numbers on the *Client Profile Form* (see *Chapter 16: Qualifying*).
- **Frequent flyer programs.** Even if the client is not a member of a frequent lodger program, he or she is probably in one or more frequent flyer plans, the vast majority of which have tie-ins with hotels. Try to pick a hotel that will earn the client maximum mileage. This can be a powerful selling point.
- **Type of room.** This means configuration. Some clients prefer a king-sized bed and a non-smoking room. Others will insist they stay on the "concierge level" of a hotel, where they receive an extra level of service and amenities. A relatively new wrinkle in hotel marketing is the "green room." These are specially designated rooms that are "environmentally friendly" and feature special air filters, biodegradable soap, recycled paper products, and so forth. These may be attractive to some of your clients; they also are priced higher than other rooms, resulting in a slightly better payback for you!
- **Extras.** Today, many hotel properties come with a long list of amenities. Some of these may be important to your client. If your client wants or needs things like an on-premises health club, a pool, meeting rooms, fax service, a 24-hour restaurant on the premises, or any of the dozens of other things hotels are providing to lure guests, you, the travel agent, should know this.
- **Location.** This can sometimes be an overriding factor. And don't forget that a more expensive room in the right location can actually be less expensive if it saves the client the need of renting a car.

As I mentioned earlier, price tends to be less of an issue in choosing a hotel. That is not to say it can be completely overlooked. The cost of a hotel room tends to become important in relationship to the purpose of the trip. Someone traveling on business may want or need a flashy hotel in a good location. The same person traveling to visit family may only require the most basic motel room. This goes back to the most basic rule of booking travel: find out *why* your client is going.

Also, I don't want to convey the impression that you should attempt to book the client into the most expensive hotel room you think you can talk him into. Far from it. Within the price parameters the client has given you, or which you feel are appropriate, you should always strive to get the best deal possible. (See "Getting the best rate," below.)

Again, what's in it for you?

Hotel properties are constantly trying to attract your attention with special commission deals, spiffs, and contests. Sometimes making the "right" hotel booking can put an extra $50 in your pocket or give you a chance of winning a free vacation. There are two problems with this:

- First, if you are a small operation — and outside sales reps almost invariably are — you may find that a hotel's promotion never seems to coincide with your customers' travel plans, and
- Second, there's always the temptation that you will spend more time chasing a $50 bonus than doing the more important job of looking out for your clients' best interests.

Chances are, you will find the first more of a problem than the second. Still, as I've said before, you are a businessperson. It's only smart business to keep your eyes peeled for any opportunity to legally contribute to the bottom line. You will find a more complete discussion of commission deals, contests, and the issues they raise in *Chapter 11: Getting Serious*.

You should also bear in mind that, as your client list grows, these special hotel deals and offers will become more attractive. That's because you can market them proactively. For example, an all-inclusive Caribbean resort may offer a $100 bonus for every booking made during a certain three-month period. If you have a large and growing list of customers, you may be able to put together a special promotion, complete with brochures from the resort in question, and find several takers.

Otherwise, it's a matter of luck whether a client's trip to Seattle will coincide with a special commission deal being offered by a hotel there. It's not a bad idea when calling around to research hotels for a customer, to ask the reservationist if there are any special deals for agents being promoted at the moment. The reservationist should have this information.

Getting the best rate

Just as you want to get the best deal for your client, the reservationist wants to get the best deal for the hotel. Hotel rates are a bit more open to discussion than airline fares. Within broad limits, reservationists have the discretion to settle for any of a number of different rates for the same room. Typically, they will first quote the highest price for a given category of room, the so-called "rack rate." With a little prodding, you can often do better.

Let's say, for example, that your client wants to stay on the concierge level of a certain upscale hotel, a fairly expensive room. You notice in the chain's directory that this property is a mile away from a major corporation. You can ask for a corporate rate, mentioning the major company's name, and save your client $40. Whatever you "lose" in commission will be more than made up in goodwill and customer loyalty.

Here are some suggestions on bargaining for a better rate:

- ***Membership rates.*** Groups like the American Association of Retired Persons (AARP) and the American Automobile Association (AAA) have negotiated attractive rates for their members

at many hotels. Of course, it helps if your client is actually a member of one of these groups; often they will be asked to show a membership card at check-in to qualify for one of these rates.

- **Corporate rates.** Sometimes just asking, "Do you have a corporate rate?" will garner a lower rate. Other times you will have to pick a corporation. For example, you might say, as in the example above, "My client is with AT&T," if you knew there was an AT&T office nearby. These aren't policed as thoroughly as membership rates; the reservationist just needs some justification for offering the lower corporate rate.

- **Promotional rates.** If the rate is still too high ask if there are any "special promotional rates" available for the dates your client will be staying. Sometimes, the reservationist will "discover" a rate that she had overlooked before.

- **Quote a price.** Sometimes you can succeed by begging for a lower rate. You might try saying something like, "Gee, my client doesn't want to spend more than $79 a night but I'd like to put him into your hotel. Could you accommodate him at that rate?"

Be aware that some lower rates are not commissionable. The reservationist will sometimes use that as a subtle bargaining chip by saying something like, "We have a lower rate but there's no commission on that." So be careful about bargaining too hard, unless you are willing to forego a commission. Working on the theory that honesty is the best policy, you might try asking, "What's the lowest rate I can get and still get a commission?"

Making the sale

Ideally, the customer will leave the choice of hotel up to you. The customer knows you understand her needs and preferences, including the price range with which she's comfortable; so she trusts you to make the best decision. Arriving at this point usually requires developing a track record with the customer such that she will trust your judgment.

Sometimes a client's willingness to give you free reign will vary with circumstances. In many cases, however, customers will feel most comfortable when you offer a range of choices and let them make the final decision. Part of your job in researching the alternatives is to narrow the choice to those properties that best meet the customer's needs. You definitely *don't* want to get back to a customer and say, "I've come up with seventeen hotels in Centreville; let's go over them."

So as not to overwhelm the customer, be prepared to present just three choices, with two major contenders and a fallback. Of these, one should be *your* choice and should be presented first ("I would recommend . . ."). Be prepared to justify your choice with specifics. Always give the customer the option of choosing your primary recommendation before presenting the other choices.

Your second choice should be presented as an alternative. You can use phrases like, "A bit farther away, but slightly less expensive," or "If you'd like something a bit more luxurious," to highlight the tradeoffs you are presenting. A good travel agent will be able to discuss the pros and cons of the properties intelligently. Your recommendation will be more persuasive if you can point to your own experience of the hotel or that of another, satisfied, customer.

A much fuller discussion of the techniques of making the sale will be found in *Part II*. For now, the important things to remember are that you must get a clear go-ahead from the customer and make sure the customer understands all the key elements of the booking — price, frequent flyer points, the fact that the room will be held with his credit card, etc.

If none of the choices tickles the customer's fancy, you may have additional properties to recommend, or you may have to do some more research.

Making the booking

You may actually make the booking before you make the sale; you would do this to hold the room. Whenever you make the booking, do so in a methodical and professional manner. You want to make sure that nothing is left out that will inconvenience the client, embarrass you, or cost either of you money.

First, identify yourself as a travel agent. You might say:

*"Hello, this is Martha with Anytown Travel
Agency. I'd like to make reservations for a
client, please."*

This is the only way you will be able to collect your commission. At some point during the booking process, the reservationist should ask for your agency's IATA number, address, or some other identifier. Don't conclude the booking until you have given this information!

Information to give

You will want to provide the reservationist with the following:

- The date of arrival and the number of nights the party will stay. Hotel reservationists seem to prefer a number of nights rather than a date of departure.
- The number and configuration of room(s). For example, two doubles with king-sized beds.
- The name in which the reservation will be held. It is seldom necessary to provide the names of others in the party. If it is, the reservationist will tell you. The exception of course, would be if different people are paying for different rooms.
- Any client preferences. This would include things like "non-smoking room," "on the ground floor," "near the pool."
- The client's frequent lodger number or frequent flyer number, as appropriate.
- The client's approximate time of arrival if known. If it will be a late arrival, you will have to provide a credit card number to guarantee the reservation.

- The client's credit card information, if the booking is to be guaranteed.
- Flight arrival, if the hotel provides pickup or shuttle service from the airport.

Information to get

There is also some very important information you will want for your client and for your records on each booking you make:

- **Confirmation number.** Like the record locator number in an airline booking, this is a unique identifier for this booking. You will want to give this number to the client, just in case there is any misunderstanding at check-in.
- **The name of the reservationist.** It's also a good idea to ask for the name of the reservationist. If a problem arises later, it's good information to have. You don't have to make it sound like you're asking just to check up on the reservationist either. I do it like this:

> *"And your name is . . . ?"*
> *"Jim."*
> *"Well, thanks, Jim. You've been very helpful
> and I appreciate that."*

- **The rules of the booking.** Usually this means the time until which the reservation will be held without a credit card to guarantee it. But there may be other conditions that you and your client should know about. Make sure you relay the important information.
- **The hotel's local phone number.** This can come in handy in case the client is delayed.
- **Commission information.** Again, make sure that the reservationist has your IATA number. If he or she doesn't seem to know what you're talking about, ask about their commission structure and policies. If they don't seem to have one, you may want to think twice about steering business their way. You also might want to ask if there is any special commission incentive available. Sometimes, special commissions will only be given if you ask for them. If there is one, make a note of it and remember to tell your agency.

Of course, if you make two or more bookings to hold space, you should make sure to call back the "losing" hotels to cancel those bookings after the client has settled on the hotel he or she wants.

Relaying the booking

Your final task is to get back to your client, confirm that the reservation has been made, and provide the client with all the information about the booking he or she will need. That could include:

- The quoted rate.
- The confirmation number.
- Rules of the booking.
- Hotel phone number.
- Directions to the hotel or instructions on how to request airport pickup service.

Getting paid

Getting paid your hotel commissions is not as sure a bet as collecting on your airline bookings, alas. If you're interested in the odds, you have your best chance of collecting a commission (according to the *Travel Weekly* survey mentioned earlier) from a United States chain hotel (86%). International chains have the next best record (78%), followed by domestic independent hotels (69%) and foreign independents (60%).

Moreover, hotels typically don't begin to think about paying your commission until after the client leaves, sometimes 30 days after the client leaves. Since many trips are booked well in advance, this means not just a long wait for your commission but the possibility that commissions may be forgotten (by you, the hotel, or your agency) or otherwise fall through the cracks.

A complete discussion on making sure you get your commissions will be found in *Chapter 11*.

Foreign hotels

The discussion so far has assumed we were booking domestic hotels. The picture can change, however, when it comes to booking hotels overseas. First of all, it should be said that there are a great many hotels in far-flung parts of the globe that can be booked just like a Holiday Inn in the next state — through a toll-free number here in the States. These are, for the most part, hotels that are part of an American chain. Still, there are many hotels around the world which, for the time being at least, haven't been gobbled up by the major American chains. Here are some thoughts on booking them:

Hotel representatives

Foreign hotels are just as eager to market their services as anyone else. Many of them have turned to "hotel representatives" to make their properties more accessible to American travelers. A hotel representative, as the name implies, represents a foreign hotel chain, a number of foreign hotel chains, or a collection of independent foreign hotels here in the United States. Usually a hotel representative will deal with both travel agents and the general public.

The advantage of booking through hotel representatives is convenience. You call them up, (many have toll-free numbers), make your booking, and, down the road, collect your commission. The disadvantage, as I have found, is that their rates are much higher than those you can obtain directly from the property itself. I have found this true for hotels in Venezuela ($35 vs. $20) and the south of France ($240 vs. $170). Now, if your client doesn't mind paying these rates, I suppose that's fine. There are, however, other alternatives.

Booking direct

In these days of global communications, there is no reason you cannot make bookings directly with hotels in foreign countries. Many guidebooks list local phone numbers for the hotels they cover, and many hotels have faxes. Indeed, I was surprised when traveling through France how many small inns and quaint restaurants have fax machines.

I have found that the best way to book is by fax. You can call when your rates are lowest and not worry who will answer the phone. Language is less of a barrier; most hotels will have someone on staff who understands English or will be able to find someone who does. The hotel can confirm the reservation and provide information about any deposits that might be due by return fax. If the client's trip is far enough away, you could also do this by mail.

As for getting paid, you have two choices:

- Rely on the hotel to pay you. This is risky, and the hotel may not have the facilities to pay you in U.S. currency.
- Charge the client a booking fee to pay for your time and the cost of faxing overseas. Most clients will accept this, especially if you can point out to them that the cost of the hotel plus your fee is less than you were quoted by a hotel rep. In other cases, this will be the only way you *could* have made the booking.

Booking direct will probably be most attractive to outside reps who become destination specialists. They will gain an in-depth knowledge of the area, may have language skills, and may even be able to develop special relationships with unique and charming inns that will offer special value to their clients.

Voucher programs and packages

Mention should also be made of voucher programs, which allow the traveler to purchase a book of coupons that can then be redeemed at participating hotels or bed & breakfasts throughout a country or region. Ireland is one example of a country that has a well-established voucher program.

It also may be possible to get your client a "hotel package" through a tour operator. Typically this would involve a stay of several nights or a week at a set price. See *Chapter 9: Booking Tours And Packages* for more information on dealing with tour operators.

Chapter Eight:
Booking Rental Cars

Rental cars are a small, and therefore often overlooked, niche for the outside sales rep. Like hotels, they are something that travelers will often book for themselves prior to the trip or select upon arrival.

"Will you be needing a car?" is a question you should train yourself to ask your customers whenever you are making a reservation for airline tickets. Often they will not; relatives will be picking them up or they will be relying on shuttle buses and taxis while away. When customers do need a car at the destination, however, booking one for them is a relatively painless process that can result in a small but steady stream of additional income.

Small because car rentals are generally not a high-ticket item to begin with. In addition, most travelers are price conscious when renting, and car rental companies often offer lower commissions — or none at all! — on discounted rates. Steady because the major car rental companies have a good track record on paying commissions.

Gathering information

As with any travel booking, make sure you have a clear grasp of *why* the customer is traveling and what he or she plans to be doing on the trip. That knowledge can help you guide the customer to wise decisions in renting a car.

The key ingredients of a car rental are fairly straightforward:

- *Place, date, and time of pickup.* Typically, the customer will pick up the car at the airport upon arrival. Sometimes, the customer will want to pick up the car later in the trip, at a different location. Be alert to the possibility that the place and time the customer requests may not be optimal.
- *Place, date, and time of return.* Most car rental rates are based on the assumption that the car will be returned to the location at which it was picked up. Deviations from this rule can result in significantly higher base rates or the addition of a "drop-off fee." Some rental companies will allow a car that was picked up at the airport to be returned to a downtown location in the

area without penalty (or vice versa). Most will charge more when a car is rented in one city and returned in another.

- **Type of car.** The size and model of the car affect the rental rate. The standard categories are sub-compact, compact, mid-sized, and full-sized. There are any number of other options, from luxury cars, to RVs, to vans, to pickup trucks. Some companies even offer, in selected markets, "fantasy" cars like vintage Corvette convertibles or Rolls Royces.
- **Type of rental.** In other words, is it a daily or a weekly rental?

You may already know some of this information if you are making air arrangements as well. In addition to this basic information, there are some other things you will want to know about your client.

- **Brand preferences.** Many clients will have a preferred car rental company. This preference will be based on factors such as the customer's perception of the company's quality and reliability, frequent flyer mileage tie-ins, or even the car company's frequent-renter program (which offers various perks to members). You should, of course, familiarize yourself with this information and record membership numbers on the *Client Profile Form*.
- **Car preference.** Some people will insist on at least a mid-sized car. Others want nothing but the cheapest sub-compact. It's a good idea to ask what the customer wants you to do if the preferred car size is not available.
- **On-terminal or off.** Airports have a limited amount of space for car rental companies. Those that have counters and pickup points inside the terminal pay dearly for that privilege. The other companies are relegated to satellite locations, outside the terminal, reached by a free shuttle bus. Obviously, the on-terminal locations are more convenient and quicker for the traveler. Often (but not always) that will mean a higher rate.
- **Price.** If the customer has a preferred company and a preferred car type, then price becomes a non-issue in most cases. If price is a concern or becomes an issue, you will want to ask the customer how much convenience can be sacrificed in the interests of economy. Then you'll have to do some comparison shopping in your research phase.

Less frequently, you will need some additional information:

- **Additional drivers.** If more than one person will be driving the car, you will need to know their name(s).
- **Driving record.** Some of the major car rental companies are now doing routine checks of the driving records of all renters at pickup time. If the renter has any moving violations or too many points on their license, they can be denied a car. You may want to alert your clients to this new policy. If it is a problem, you may want to suggest alternatives — a different

driver in the same party or a different company that doesn't do such checks.

At this point, you should analyze the customer's request to see if you can make any money-saving recommendations. Many customers will "overbook" a rental car, thinking that their only option is to pick up and return the car at the airport. Consider this alternative scenario:

- Day One: The customer arrives at the airport and takes a shuttle bus to her hotel.
- Day Two: The customer picks up a rental car from a downtown location.
- Day Three: The customer returns the car to the same location.
- Day Four: The customer takes the shuttle bus back to the airport.

A four-day rental has become a two-day rental. Alternatively, the customer might pick up the car at the airport and return it downtown or vice versa.

Or a customer might want to use his preferred rental car company overseas, when a local firm might offer a much better rate. Or perhaps you are aware of a special promotional rate that might be attractive to your customer. Being aware of the possibilities, and being able to counsel your customers, will result in their loyalty and repeat business.

Research

If your customer is intensely loyal to a particular company, your job is easy. If not, things quickly become more complicated. Car rental rates are extremely competitive and volatile. Rates go up and down, policies change, promotional rates come and go. So if you are looking for the best deal, prepare yourself for some serious comparison shopping. For example, *Consumer Reports Travel Letter* researched the cost of one-way car rentals (i.e., when a car is rented in one city and dropped off in another). In one example cited, they surveyed five companies and found a $164 difference between the high- and low-cost companies. In another, they looked at eight companies and found a $264 gap between the high and low prices quoted.

Car rental information is available on EaasySabre (see above) and other CRSs. Typing, for example, "/CAR,SFO,2APR,4P,SFO,6APR,3P" will get you into the car rental area. The ingredients in the code, after "/CAR," are the airport or city at which the car will be picked up, the pickup date, the pickup time, the airport or city at which the car will be returned, the drop-off date, and the drop-off time. If you wanted a specific car company and knew its code, you would add that to the string. Without the car company code, EaasySabre will give you a menu that lets you pick the company whose rates you want to view.

Because of the many different types of cars and rates, the system cannot provide a side-by-side comparison of what the various companies are offering, as it does with airline fares. You will have to pull up informa-

tion on each company in which you are interested to find out car types, rates, and other information. Despite this inconvenience, EaasySabre does provide some useful information:

- It tells you which companies serve that particular airport or city.
- It tells you whether the company is on or off terminal. It also tells you if there are other local rental sites.
- Most useful, it tells you whether certain categories of car are still available or are sold out — a not too uncommon occurrence at holiday times.

Remember that you should be able to set your computer to "archive" or store the screens from your EaasySabre session for later reference or print out. With your comparative information in hand, you can then call the companies directly for more information and to make reservations.

Most beginners will find it easier to call the car rental companies directly to begin with. As a practical matter, that means limiting yourself to the major players in the field — Hertz, Avis, National, Budget, Alamo (in Florida), and perhaps one or two others. For one thing, your customers (unless they have expressed a different preference) will expect to rent from a major company and will question your selection of a lesser-known brand. Also, the major companies have the widest coverage of destinations. Finally, we should note that researching what *every* company has available takes time, especially over the phone; you have to decide whether the investment of time is worth the payback.

Of course, you can look at as many different companies as you choose. You might want to call around to some new companies just to familiarize yourself with them, learn what they have available, and get a feel for the kind of options that are out there.

Before you make your calls, create a simple grid or table on a piece of paper to record the information you collect from the various companies. This will make it easy to compare and will give you all the information you need when and if you go over alternatives with your client.

Factors influencing your choice

As with any booking, you will have to weigh a number of factors when considering car rental companies. Some of them may be at odds with others.

- *Client preference.* The customer is always right and should be booked with the company he or she prefers, unless availability is a problem. Or if price becomes an issue.
- *Price.* Price is usually expressed as a type of car rather than a dollar figure. Generally speaking, if a customer wants Avis, they will not be particularly concerned that an Avis compact car costs $5 more than one from Budget. On the other hand, if the customer is looking for the absolute lowest cost, don't assume that "big" companies with on-terminal locations will automatically be more expensive than "little" companies with off-terminal locations. Always check.

- ***Convenience.*** All things being equal, book your client with a car company that has on-terminal pickup. If their preferred company is off-terminal at a particular airport, see if they want to shift allegiances in the interests of convenience.
- ***What's in it for you?*** As with hotels, it can be hard to track special promotions, contests, commission rates, and so forth. But they exist with car rentals, just as they do with other travel products. If you have the leeway, you might want to steer your customers to rent with a company that will provide you with some advantage. As always, balance your self-interest against the client's best interests and make the right decision.

Making the sale

Most car rentals are straightforward enough that you should be able to discuss the client's needs and simply make the booking. The client will trust you to make the best decision based on his or her preferences. If you have to get back to the client to discuss alternatives, try to limit the variables as much as possible. In other words, the client can have car A with car company B for price C or car X with company Y for price Z. Once you introduce too many variables, the customer (and you) will become hopelessly confused and the discussion will wander around in circles. Present the customer with a clear choice; be able to discuss the pros and cons; then let the customer decide.

Making the booking

Whether you make several bookings ahead of time to hold the cars or wait until you and the client have reached agreement on the best alternative, follow these simple steps when you call the reservationist to book:

Information to give

First, tell the reservationist that you are a travel agent making a booking. Then, provide the basic booking information as outlined earlier:
- Place, date, and time of pickup.
- Place, date, and time of return.
- Type of car.
- Type of rental.

It's probably also a good idea to ask the reservationist if there are any special offers or promotions available that might give your client a better deal. Often car companies will have free upgrades or similar promotions going, but will only give them to you if you ask.

Make sure you provide the information that will assure your commission. That could include all or some of the following:
- Agency name, address, and phone number.
- Agency IATA number.
- Your name.

The key thing to get from the reservationist is the confirmation number for the booking. It's also a good idea to make a note of the reservationist's name, just in case. In addition, make sure to record anything the reservationist tells you that should be passed along to the customer.

Relaying the booking

When confirming the booking with the client, simply repeat the key booking information and the confirmation number. That's all the customer should need. Then be sure to cancel any extra bookings that you may have made to hold cars while the customer was deciding which company to use.

Foreign car rentals

Many of the companies that you deal with for domestic rentals have international operations that can provide your clients with cars in many foreign countries. These reservations can be researched and made exactly as you would a booking in the next state.

However, you should be aware that a better deal might be available from a company that specializes in overseas rentals. Firms like Kemwel and Auto Europe offer very attractive rates to the leisure traveler. Some of these rates require airline tie-ins; that is, the traveler must arrive on a certain airline to qualify for the rate.

Most domestic bookings are simply reservations — a car is held for the customer's arrival and the customer pays for the rental by presenting a credit card at the time of pickup. Many foreign bookings, however, require prepayment of some sort, especially the budget ones. These booking are treated more like a tour element (see *Chapter 9: Booking Tours & Packages*) than a domestic car rental. In these cases, the car company will provide your customer with a voucher that the customer will present upon arrival overseas. The traveler will also be required to present a credit card at that time to cover any additional or unforeseen expenses (and there always are some), along with a valid driver's license, passport, and visa, if one is required to enter the country.

Getting paid

Rental car commissions, like hotel commissions, are paid only after the trip has been completed. In the case of foreign car rentals, the commission payment is not due until 30 days after the car is returned. It may not be paid until some time after that.

Making sure you get what's coming to you will require careful record-keeping and persistent follow-through. A complete discussion of making sure you get your commissions will be found in *Chapter 11: Getting Serious*.

Chapter Nine:

Booking Tours & Packages

"Wouldn't you like to make $200 on every phone call?"

That's the come-on used by Travel Impressions, a tour wholesaler, in its trade advertising aimed at travel agents. $200, it turns out, is the average commission paid out on the tour products Travel Impressions offers. Of course, as an outside agent, you would only be in line for a portion of that $200 — $100, perhaps $120. Still not a bad payout for a single phone call.

That is why tours are so attractive to travel agents in general and why they should be especially attractive to you, the prospective part-time travel agent or outside agent. In addition to the high per-sale income that tours offer, there are a number of other attractions to this particular travel product:

- Tours are, almost by definition, largely a leisure product. That is, people take tours when they are going on vacation. Consequently, they are less price sensitive. Unlike the business traveler or the short-hop airline passenger, people shopping for tours are not looking for the absolute lowest price. They are looking for value within their budget. Most often, a good travel agent will be able to find out exactly what that budget is.
- Because tours combine a number of separate elements, much of the travel agent's work is already done. You have far fewer worries about messing up the airline reservations because the tour operator has taken care of them for you — unless, of course, the tour is land-only.

What is a "tour?"

For many of us, the word *tour* conjures up images of the "if-this-is-Tuesday-it-must-be-Belgium" type of experience. We picture harried tourists being shunted from place to place at a maddening pace, stuffed on buses, whisked past historical sights, rushed through museums, and dumped, exhausted, at the end of the day into hotels with mysterious plumbing fixtures. Some tours are like that, no doubt. But for the travel agent, the word *tour* has developed a much more generic meaning.

Some travel agents may quibble about definitions but, for all practical purposes, a "tour" is any combination of travel products that can be booked and sold as a single unit. Some operators use the word "package" to distinguish offerings that don't include the more "traditional" elements of a tour, such as group travel and a guide. In their parlance, airfare to London combined with four nights in a hotel and two theater tickets would be a package. Two weeks of sightseeing in England with a guide and group motorcoach travel from site to site would be a tour.

"Tour" or "package," the key point to remember is that a number of ingredients are bundled together and sold for a single price.

The power of the package

One reason that I put the discussion of tours and packages here, after airline tickets, hotels, and car rentals, was to make the following point: Packages, which are nothing more than a tour product, allow you to combine airfare, hotel, and rental car into one pre-priced product that is not only cheaper for your customer than the three elements booked separately but that pays you, the travel agent, a higher rate of commission. In fact, it is possible to book a package that saves your client money, while putting more money in your pocket than you'd have earned had you booked each element separately.

Even if you never become an outside travel agent, this single booking strategy can save you hundreds of dollars a year just on your own travel, both domestic and foreign.

Packages are an often overlooked option in domestic travel. For example, clients traveling to another city to attend a professional conference would typically think of getting an airline ticket and reserving a hotel room as two separate bookings. You might think that way, too. But put together a package for your clients, and you may be able to offer them the same air-hotel combination at a better price. Or, for only a bit more, you may be able to add a rental car to the package.

Domestic packages are not available everywhere. You will generally find them offered only to larger cities with a steady tourist trade — cities such as Boston, New York, Orlando, Miami, New Orleans, Las Vegas, Los Angeles, San Francisco, and Washington, DC. But packages are sometime available to smaller markets as well. Some tour wholesalers may even be able to create a package for you; just call them up, tell them what you're after, and ask what they can put together for you.

Overseas, you will find a package to just about any major destination, and quite a few minor ones as well. Even tour operators who advertise escorted, all-inclusive tours will often be able to provide you with just air, a car, and a hotel if that's what your client wants.

Packages can even be good products to sell to clients who insist, "We're not interested in a tour." Say, a couple wants to fly to Paris and explore the chateau country on their own. They are perfect candidates for a "fly-drive" package, combining air and a rental car. You can probably even find a package that has hotel vouchers thrown in, so your clients can pick hotels or b&b's along their route or choose alternate lodgings as the spirit moves them. Packages can offer such good value that clients like them even when they don't use all (or any) of their vouchers. It's also a lot easier to get your commission when you're working with one U.S.-based supplier rather than a string of foreign hotels. So, as you begin serving your new customers in your new travel agent business, keep in mind the power of the package to save your clients money while making money for you.

Gathering information

You will probably find that there are three kinds of tour customers:
- Those who know exactly what they want.
- Those who have no idea of what they want.
- Those who are somewhere in between.

Obviously, the first type of customer is easiest to serve. For the others you will have to do some careful probing about their expectations — what they like, dislike, and so forth. This is what is known as "qualifying the customer" and a complete discussion of the techniques you can use will be found in *Part II* of this book. For now, let's look at some of the more obvious things you will need to know:
- ***Who, what, where, when, and why?*** These questions provide the basics. Family or couple? What sort of things are they hoping to do? Where would they like to do them? When do they want to go? And, for all of the above, why? Often the "why" can be the key element in making the right choice. A couple looking to "get away from the kids" should not be steered toward Disney World!
- ***How?*** People looking into a tour-type vacation usually fly to the destination and then get around by rental car, escorted motorcoach, or local transportation. However, there are many vacationers who want a train experience. Others want to bike, pony trek, sail or hike. Still others want to cruise. Since cruises are a whole separate category of travel experience, we will discuss them in the next chapter.
- ***Budget.*** Try to get as specific information as possible about how much the customer is willing to or can spend. "We don't want to spend a lot of money," doesn't really give you what you need to go on. Some people will be very forthcoming. Others will hedge, perhaps worrying that you will try to sell them something 20% more expensive than the figure they provide. More suggestions on qualifying budget will be found in *Chapters 16: Qualifying* and *18: Handling Your Customers' Concerns* in *Part II* of this book.
- ***How do they prefer to pay?*** Payment terms can make a big difference to many clients. Some people simply won't book unless they can pay with a credit card. Others will pay more on a credit card than they would if they had to pay by check.

Since most tours require deposits (unless the departure date is very close), showing a willingness to work with the client to spread out payments can help you book more tour business. Even a deposit of as little as $10 is an important commitment from the customer. You may have a week or longer to get the rest of the deposit.

- ***Past experience and present expectations.*** A good benchmark for what people will like in the future is what they liked (or didn't like) in the past. Ask your clients about their past vacation experiences (especially ones similar to the one they are now planning). "What was your last trip to Hawaii like? Where did you stay? How did you like it?" Their comments will help you determine what to keep the same and what to change. Again, you will find a much lengthier discussion of this in *Part II*.

Research

Learning about tours and tour products is an on-going responsibility for the serious travel agent, part-time or no. You should begin your research even before you start working on your first tour booking. The research itself can be fun; it can also save you time when that first booking comes along. Just be aware that you will never be able to know everything there is to know about tours; there are just too many, and the players and particulars keep changing.

If you have decided to specialize in a destination, you are way ahead of the game. In that case, you actually may be able to know all there is to know, or at least come close to it.

Here are some research tools and strategies you may want to follow:

- ***The Official Tour Directory (OTD).*** In my humble opinion, this tool is indispensable. It is also relatively inexpensive as specialized travel industry reference books go. It is even possible to get discounts on it through organizations like OSSN. Another possibility is to scrounge an out-of-date-copy from a friendly travel agent.

  The OTD is like a Yellow Pages of the tour industry (and about the same size, too). Broken down by geographical areas served and cross-referenced by special interests, it lists hundreds and hundreds of tour operators who can get your clients where they want to go and give them the experiences they are looking for. One tour operator may be listed many times, once under each country or region to which they operate tours.

  The listings do not give detailed information about all the tours offered by each operator. Rather they give you the phone number (usually toll-free) to call for more information. Don't be shy. If something catches you eye, call and ask for a brochure. Advertising taken out by some of the companies listed provides more information, and some mega-companies actually arrange to have their brochures bound into the back of the directory. A free "Fax-It-To-Me" service lets you received faxed brochures almost instantly from some of the larger operators with ad listings.

Caution: The fact that a tour operator is listed in the OTD may tell you something about its seriousness as a travel provider, but it is not an absolute guarantee that the company is reliable or provides first-rate experiences to tourists.

- ***Your agency's preferred suppliers.*** Of special interest to you will be those tour operators listed in the OTD who are also preferred suppliers to your agency. There are a number of reasons for this. The most important, perhaps, is money. Your agency's preferred suppliers pay higher commissions, which presumably will be passed along to you. Another reason is that, by concentrating on selling the products of your agency's preferred suppliers, you will develop a growing familiarity with their offerings. That, in turn, will save you time (and therefore make you money) when it comes to doing research for your one-hundredth tour customer. (For more on preferred suppliers, see *Chapter 11: Getting Serious.*)

- ***The trade press.*** Another source of information about tours is the trade press. Even though the *Official Tour Directory* is published twice a year, it can never be completely up-to-date. Tour companies are constantly offering new tours, amending existing ones, and phasing out old ones. New tour companies come into being all the time. The trade press documents this constant parade of products.

  Some publications, like *Travel Weekly* and *Jax Fax*, conveniently divide their coverage into sections. That makes it easy to find information about specific destinations. Many publications, *Travel Weekly* and *Tour and Travel News* among them, regularly publish separate supplements that focus on a specific destination (Hawaii, Europe, Southeast Asia) or activity of special interest (skiing, golf, honeymoons).

  The trade press will also keep you posted on which tour operators are no longer in business or seem to be headed for the dustbin. While it may seem unfair, any indication in the trade press that a tour operator may be in trouble is sufficient reason to stop booking with them. (See the discussion on "protecting yourself" in *Chapter 11.*)

- ***Clipping files.*** It's a good idea to maintain a clipping file of destination and tour operator information that is of particular interest to you. This becomes a relatively easy task if you specialize in a destination or type of travel. If you are trying to be all things to all people, you may start to contemplate the benefits of specialization as your clipping file threatens to take over your house. I would especially recommend that you hold onto the special supplements covering destinations

and activities. These involve no clipping, usually provide a wealth of information on a number of suppliers, and are easy to store and refer to.

Other sources of clippings are travel magazines and the travel section of the Sunday paper. The articles in them invariably focus on the destinations themselves rather than on specific tour operators. But it is a simple matter, using the OTD, to locate an operator that offers tours to a destination mentioned in *Travel & Leisure*, say, or a wholesaler who can book your client into that luxurious hideaway mentioned in *Conde Nast Traveler*.

Brochures

If there's a tour, there's a brochure. In most cases, it will be difficult, if not impossible, to sell a customer on a tour without showing a brochure. This is not a problem. In fact, a good brochure can be an excellent sales tool for you. Sometimes, an attractive brochure will sell a tour even when the agent is a less-than-compelling salesperson. This means, of course, that you should plan on having the appropriate brochures when selling tours. Whether you have the right brochures on hand when you need them is another matter. Here are some thoughts on getting brochures:

- **Your agency.** If your agency is local, you may be able to go to their office and put your hands on the brochures you need.
- **Your own brochure collection.** If you have decided to specialize, it's a good idea to start amassing a collection of appropriate brochures, especially from your agency's preferred suppliers.
- **Tour companies.** You can request brochures from tour companies. This can raise a number of problems, however. Some tour companies will only send brochures to the agency itself. This will slow things up considerably if your agency is out of town. Also, your agency may charge you postage to forward the material. Mine does. Even when you can get the brochures sent directly to you, the wait can seem interminable. Tour companies vary widely in their responsiveness to requests for information. I've received brochures so long after requesting them that I've sometimes forgotten why I asked.
- **Fax.** As mentioned earlier, the *Official Tour Directory* lists companies that will fax information on certain tours. Sometimes you can call a tour company and get them to fax brochures to you. They aren't quite as effective as the real things when it comes to presenting the tour to the client but they are a lot better than nothing.
- **Other agencies.** If worst comes to worst, you can always go into another agency in town, pose as a tourist, and collect the brochures you need. The downside, of course, is that they will be stamped with the name of the agency from which you got them! Carefully apply a mailing label over the other agency's name and stamp on your own name.

- **Trade shows and seminars.** Suppliers are constantly exhibiting at trade shows and holding free seminars for the agency community. When you attend, come home with a bagful of brochures. For more on free seminars, see *Chapter 11.*
- **Other options.** If all else fails, you can use guidebooks, articles clipped from newspapers and travel magazines, even your own holiday snapshots as brochure substitutes. In fact, material like this can add extra punch to your presentation even when you have brochures.

Brochures are not just glossy sales aids. They contain crucial information about the terms and conditions of the tour. This is information you must have to do your job properly. It can be very dangerous to sell a tour without a brochure. So if you can't get the brochure itself, at least get the tour operator to fax you the terms and conditions and the pricing information.

Brochures can also help you pin down appropriate tours for customers who are indecisive or come to you with only a vague idea of what they want. After talking with them a bit, give them a bunch of brochures and say, "Here are some tours that might be right for you. Why don't you look them over. Then we can sit down and go over the ones that appeal to you."

When you are giving brochures to customers to take away with them, make sure that your name and phone number go with them. Most brochures have a blank space on the back page where the travel agency can print or stamp its name, address, and phone number. Staple your business card here. Or make up and use a rubber stamp.

What to look for

At first you will be matching up a client's stated desires with likely sources that can fulfill those desires. Let's say the client says, "I want to go somewhere warm and lie on a beach for a week," or "I'm attending a conference in Cannes and my wife and I would like to get a car and explore Provence." OTD and your agency's list of preferred suppliers will quickly tell you who does the Caribbean and who rents cars in Europe.

That could be quite a long list; so you will need more information to winnow out the most appropriate choices. Give some thought to the specific *type* of tour product your client is looking for. That will determine which operator you call. And, again, just because the client says, "We're not interested in a tour," doesn't mean that a tour operator isn't the best source to call. Remember the "power of the package."

- **Fully escorted tours.** Some travelers are most comfortable with the type of tour where they travel with a group, are met at the airport by someone who knows where they'll be staying and eating, and have a guide to shepherd them along at every stop of the journey. This is a huge market. If this is what your client is looking for, you will most likely be able to satisfy their needs through one or more of your preferred suppliers. Tours in this category are sort of like blue plate specials in a restaurant; the prices are very attractive but you can't make substitutions.

- **Customized tours.** Some companies specialize in putting together special tours that go beyond the blue plate special model of the fully escorted tour. If your client has specialized requests, you may have to deal with one of these companies. Chances are you will still be able to deal with a preferred supplier.

- **Specialized tours.** The more off-beat your clients' interests (birding in Borneo or hiking in the Hebrides), the more likely you will have to deal with a small, specialized tour operator. Ecotourism and "soft-adventure" traveling are perfect examples. Usually this means dealing with someone who is *not* a preferred supplier or a major operator.

- **Wholesalers.** Many of your agency's preferred suppliers are probably wholesalers as well as tour operators. It's a malleable distinction. It means that, in addition to offering fully escorted tours and standard packages, they can put together special combinations for your clients on an ad hoc basis. A good example would be when your client has heard from a friend that such-and-such a resort in Jamaica is a good place to stay. A Jamaican tour wholesaler will be able to put that resort together with an air ticket, and perhaps a rental car, and quote you a single price for the package.

Tours can be seen as representing an entire spectrum of travel experiences. At their simplest, tours may be an airline ticket and a single hotel. At the other extreme, they can be months-long journeys through several countries, involving planes, trains, motorcoaches, several guides, many hotels, and specialized activities. What you look for in a tour operator will change somewhat as you move along this spectrum.

Here is a list of criteria offered by one tour operator, Absolute Asia, in its advertising materials. While these points don't apply universally to all tour operators — and many of them don't apply at all to simpler types of tour products — they are a good place to start:

1. How much experience does the tour operator have in handling the destination to which clients are traveling?
2. Does the tour operator have its own offices in the destination?
3. Is the tour operator offering standard government-controlled tour packages (where applicable)?
4. Can the tour operator choose from a range of accommodations in given cities?
5. Are meals a al carte at local restaurants or are they set menus in hotels?
6. Will the tour group include only Americans, or will other nationalities be part of the group?
7. Can clients vary the itinerary as they travel?
8. Are departures set on fixed dates or is some flexibility allowed?
9. Has the tour organizer actually visited the destinations?

10. Can the tour operator handle all necessary arrangements including air ticketing, visas, and ground services in multi-destination trips?
11. Are air and visa services included in the advertised price?
12. Are prices subject to change, or are they guaranteed?
13. What background information can the operator provide concerning health, safety, and other practical matters?
14. Can the operator provide references from past clients?
15. Can the operator make special arrangements, such as overland crossings or visits to remote villages or archaeological sites?

The fine print

Somewhere on every brochure, often in teeny, tiny type, are the "Terms and Conditions" or "General Conditions" under which the tour operator sells the tours listed in the brochure. The customer will sometimes ignore this information. You never should. Before you recommend a tour to a client, read the terms and conditions and make sure you understand them, agree with them, and can justify them, if necessary, to the customer.

The Terms and Conditions can also serve as a helpful reminder to you about what's important. Among the things they cover are:

- *Deposits.* It's the rare tour that doesn't require them. Usually they are required within seven to ten business days of making the booking. You will also be told when final payment is due. It can range from 30 to 60 days prior to departure.
- *Late booking fees.* Because tours are generally planned well in advance, most tour operators penalize those who book shortly before departure.
- *Revisions/changes.* Tour operators don't like to make changes to bookings once they're made, so they'll often build in a penalty for doing so.
- *Cancellations/refunds.* Tour operators will refund money in the case of cancellations, but they don't like to do it. Therefore, they build in elaborate rules and restrictions concerning when and under what conditions refunds will be issued. Typically, there is a penalty for cancellations; that is, you don't get all the money back. Sometimes, the cancellation penalty is graduated; the closer the departure date, the less the client gets back. In either case, no money will be refunded after a certain point, sometimes as much as 30 days prior to departure.
- *Insurance.* Because of cancellation hassles, most companies will recommend that your client take out insurance. Very often they will follow up this suggestion with an offer to sell that insurance. This insurance may be commissionable to you, although the brochure (since it is intended for the client's eyes) probably won't say this.
- *Responsibility/liability.* This will probably be the longest section of fine print. Here the tour operator presents a long

litany of things that are beyond its control and for which it will accept no liability. These are things like airline delays, hotels going out of business, natural disasters, and international terrorism. Presumably they pay some lawyer a lot of money to draft these sections to protect themselves from lawsuits. Of course, if something goes wrong, some other lawyer will make a lot of money by suing them anyway. Go figure.

Form of payment

There is another aspect of the "fine print." It won't show up in the brochures, but it is very important for you to know. That is the form or forms of payment the tour operator will accept. The way in which the operator chooses to handle payment may affect your decision on whether to use them or not.

There are two basic ways a tour operator will accept payment:

- **Credit cards.** Most of the larger tour operators will accept credit cards. This makes it easy on everyone, and many customers prefer to use plastic because of the flexibility and protection the cards provide. You may have to time your booking carefully so that the charge shows up on next month's bill instead of this month's. That can mean instructing your agency not to submit the card before a certain date.

  All things being equal, you're better off if the customer uses a credit card. That way, if a problem develops with the supplier, the customer has some recourse — he can tell the credit card company he's disputing the charge. The argument becomes one between the customer and the supplier, not between the customer and you. *Chapter 11* offers important advice on dealing with credit cards.

- **Agency check.** This is a business check with the name of the agency on it. If you're an outside agent, that means the name of the agency through which you book and not your own business name. If you are dealing with the tour operator directly, it would be your business check. If you can collect a check from the customer, this arrangement sometimes (but not always) has the advantage of allowing you to deduct your commission up front and pay the tour operator a "net" amount. The trouble is, many customers don't want to pay by check and won't understand or particularly care about your problems in dealing with the tour operator. If this is going to become an issue, it's better to find it out during the research phase — before you get the customer all excited about taking the tour.

Some tour operators who prefer agency checks will accept credit cards for an additional charge intended to cover the fees the credit card company charges the tour operator. This, too, can cause problems with customers, who won't understand when their $1,000 tour costs $1,030.

You also may find that, for one reason or another, your agency doesn't like issuing agency checks. So even if your customer is willing to pay by check, you still have a problem. Check to make sure you know your agency's policy on this score before you find yourself in an embarrassing situation with your customer or the tour operator.

Factors influencing your choice

Unless the client has made a specific request for a tour operator (or unless you know that the client has had a bad experience with a particular tour operator), you have wide latitude in recommending the best tour product to meet your client's needs and desires.

Client preferences

First and foremost, of course, is giving the client what he or she wants. In other words, the tours you suggest should match *as precisely as possible* the list of wants and needs the client has given you. Getting the match right is a matter of getting to know your customers, asking them the right questions, and listening closely to their answers. Those skills will be discussed more completely in Part II of this book. However, we should note here that, in the area of client preferences, you will want to pay particular attention to:

- **Budget.** Ideally you will begin your research and selection phase knowing what the customer's budget is. (Again, this will be discussed fully in *Part II*.) Unless there is a compelling reason for doing so, you will not want to recommend anything that is over the client's stated budget — except, perhaps, as a "just in case" alternative. The best choice is a tour that is sufficiently *below* the client's stated price that he or she will feel that you are providing an especially good deal. If the client has suggested a range of prices, coming in at the middle to low end of that spectrum is a good idea.

    I am assuming, of course, that you will be able to meet the customer's expectations at the price you will quote. The client *must* understand the relationship between price and value. It may be important to make clear to the client what is possible given the budget. It may even be appropriate to suggest to a client that, for the price they want to pay, a stateside vacation might be more appropriate than the trip to the French Riviera that they envision. While it may be possible to send them there at their price by booking them into the Chateau Fleabag, you will not wind up with a happy customer.

That being said, the most important factors governing your choice of the products you will present to your client are as follows:

- **Preferred suppliers.** I am a firm believer in using your agency's preferred suppliers wherever possible — especially those with whom the agency has a direct relationship (as opposed to those with whom the agency gets a higher commission because they joined a consortium). This enhances your income, makes you more valuable to the agency, and provides you with a body of information and experience that makes you more efficient and therefore more valuable to your customers.

When you can't find a match between your client's needs and your agency's preferred suppliers, you can always use other suppliers. Or you can decide that you sell only the products of your preferred suppliers and direct your clients elsewhere.

- ■ *The 'personality' of the tour.* This applies primarily to fully escorted tours, where the personnel involved and the choices of sightseeing options can directly affect the quality of the experience. Three fully escorted tours, provided by three different operators, can cover the same ground yet provide radically different experiences — none of them necessarily bad. Knowing which tour operator's personality best matches your client can be tricky. As you gain more experience, debrief more and more returning clients, and go on fam trips yourself, you'll begin to get a sense of the styles of the various operators.

- ■ *Required form of payment.* As noted above, the form in which the tour operator requires payment may influence your ability to do business with them.

- ■ *The reliability of the tour operator.* Things go wrong when people travel. Flights get canceled. The reserved hotel room is unavailable when the traveler arrives. Tour operators strand people in far-off lands. In the first two examples, travelers are likely to blame the airline or the hotel. In the last example, they are likely to add you to the list of guilty parties. They might even sue you!

I go into this ghastly possibility a bit more in *Chapter 11*. For now, just remember that it is a good idea to guard against the possibility that the tour operator will go belly up or otherwise make your client's life miserable.

Sensible precautions

Since the viability and reliability of a tour operator are such important considerations, let's take some time to consider ways in which you can protect yourself (and your clients) from disaster. Just remember that none of the things suggested here offers an absolute guarantee that something won't go wrong. There is *always* that possibility. Still, some sensible precautions will increase your odds of being able to provide your customers with carefree vacations on a consistent basis.

- ■ *Preferred suppliers.* Your agency's preferred suppliers will tend to be the older, bigger, more stable companies — thus the ones least likely to leave your clients stranded. This is especially true of companies that are part of consortiums. It may be less true of suppliers with whom your agency has a direct relationship.

- **The trade press.** As mentioned earlier, it is a good idea to keep an eye on the trade press for distant early warnings that things may be amiss at certain tour operators. The letters to the editor columns in travel magazines and travel sections of newspapers may also contain horror stories about certain operators or destinations. Take heed and avoid them.
- **Your own clients.** In *Part II* we will discuss the importance of follow-up with your customers. One thing you want to find out is which suppliers your customers like and why. All things being equal, you're better off sending a client off with a supplier another client likes than trying out someone new.
- **Credit cards.** As I mentioned earlier, using a credit card can offer the client some protection if problems develop later.
- **Built-in tour insurance.** One of the reasons I've listed the membership of the United States Tour Operators Association (USTOA) in the *Resource Section* is that the Association has a program that indemnifies travelers against the failure of its members. The American Society of Travel Agents (ASTA) also has a program whereby tour operators insure the travelers' trip. Booking with these suppliers can provide an added level of reassurance.
- **Optional tour insurance.** If insurance isn't built in, encourage the client to take some out. If they choose not to, document that fact. (See *Chapter 11* for more on travel insurance.)

Making the sale

Three basics that we've discussed in the previous sections about "making the sale" apply to tours as well:

- Present the client with three choices — your recommendation and two fallbacks.
- Be prepared to discuss the trade-offs and differences among the choices.
- Lay out *all* the relevant facts about the booking.

Tours, however, differ from the products we've discussed so far (airlines, hotels, and rental cars) in a number of ways. Thus they require even more careful presentation to the client. You want to be absolutely sure that the client understands all the "rules of the game." Otherwise, you and the client may have some unpleasant surprises down the line.

Presenting the tour to the customer

"Presenting" is a very specific sales skill, which we will discuss in detail in *Part II* of this book. For now, it's important to remember that recommending a specific tour to a customer and asking that customer to make a decision to part with his or her hard-earned money to go on that tour is a serious business, which you should conduct in a thorough, orderly, and professional manner.

Our primary concern here is that the customer understand just what she will receive for her money. That means you have to make sure the customer understands, among other things, the following:

- ■ *What's included.* One reason to be thorough in this area is to present the product you are offering in all its glory; "A champagne cocktail reception on arrival" has a nice ring to it. On another level, it is plain common sense; you owe it to your customer to explain exactly what she is getting.

- ■ *What's NOT included.* Your list of what's included implies that everything else is not included. If the tour provides "some meals" that implies that most meals are on the client. If the tour includes "a half-day excursion to Tulum," that implies that it does not include "a half-day excursion to Chichen Itza." Still, it is often a good idea to spell out what the client can't expect, especially when there is the slightest possibility of a misunderstanding. Many people, to cite one small example, don't know what a "Modified American Plan" is. (It's breakfast and dinner but no lunch.) Similarly, if the brochure tells the customer he is going to "the Caribbean's biggest and best scuba diving resort," it might be a good idea to point out that the tour he is contemplating does not include any scuba diving, although it is available on-site for an additional charge. Telling customers what is not included can sometimes encourage them to add elements to the tour — which are commissionable, naturally!

- ■ *Payment terms.* This one is crucial. Make sure the customer knows when deposits are due (see "Get the check," below), when additional payments are due, and when the final payment is due. If there is enough lead time, you may be able to work out an installment payment plan.

- ■ *Restrictions and penalties.* You have to give the bad news along with the good. Make sure the customer knows what will happen if she backs out later. It is a good idea to point these items out in the fine print of the brochure, explain them to the customer, get her agreement that she understands, and then make a mark in the margin (a check mark or "OK") to indicate that the point has been covered.

"Get the check"

When I was preparing the manuscript of this book for publication, I ran it by some friends in the travel industry. One Certified Travel Counselor (CTC) kept writing in the margins of the previous chapters, "Ask for the check . . .Get the check! . . . Don't be shy. Ask for the check. . . Always get the check!"

I decided to save his sage advice for here. With airline tickets, most clients pay by credit card and are pretty certain they're actually going to make the trip before they get in touch with you. With hotels and car rentals, customers usually don't pay until they get there. Tours are another matter.

Because tours are relatively high-ticket items and because they are usually a discretionary purchase (no one has to go to the South Pacific!), there is always the risk of "buyer's remorse." This is common in all sorts of selling situations, and travel is no exception. Once the customer has made a buying decision, he immediately starts thinking, "Oh no, what have I done? I've parted with my hard-earned money. Maybe it wasn't the right decision. Maybe I could have gotten a better deal somewhere else. Maybe I can't really afford this. Maybe I better not go." If the client hasn't actually given someone a check, backing out becomes a very easy option. Moreover, because there are so many tour operators and travel agents out there seeking your clients' business, there is always the possibility that they may find a better deal — or at least a different deal that appeals to them more.

Those are just two good reasons to "get the check." Another is that the tour company demands it. Most tour operators want to get a deposit no later than seven days after the booking is made: No deposit, no booking. If the client decides to "firm it up" later, the price may have gone up — assuming, of course, there's still space left.

That is why it is always a good idea to conduct this phase of the booking process face-to-face with the client. That way, you can not only ask for the check, you can get it in your hot little hand. More on the nitty-gritty details and techniques of handling this kind of situation will be found in *Part II*.

Of course, the "check" may be a credit card. If that is the case, you will have to make arrangements to comply with your agency's policy on handling credit cards. You'll find this discussed in *Chapter 11*.

I am not suggesting that you "trap" or "hoodwink" or "pressure" your customers in any way. Even if they give you a check, they still have the option to cancel within the rules laid out by the tour operator. By asking for the check, you help your customer see the true nature of the decision you are asking him or her to make. Suppose you say to your customer:

"Would you like to take the Grand Tour of
Italy?"

A customer's "yes" answer to this question does not mean the trip will take place. The customer probably wants to do a lot of things, very few of which will actually get done. Suppose, on the other hand, you say:

"If you'd like to take the Grand Tour of Italy,
I'll need a deposit of $500 today to reserve
your space. Shall we go ahead and do that?"

If the customer responds affirmatively and writes a check, there is a much higher probability — not an absolute certainty, but a higher probability — that he or she will actually go.

Making the booking

You may have made a booking with the tour operator before getting the final go-ahead from the client. You would do this for the same reason you would book an airline seat before selling it — to hold the space. Many tour operators will give you a price quote which they will then guarantee for a certain period of time. Bookings can always be canceled — and frequently are.

There are so many tours, types of tours, and tour operators that it is almost inevitable that there are many different permutations, combinations, and subtleties in how individual companies operate. Fortunately, like the airlines, most of the larger tour operators have well-trained reservationists whose job it is to make it as easy as possible for you to book your clients on their tours.

Smaller companies, for their part, are often willing to walk you through the process of booking, even if it means calling in the owner to explain the procedures.

So, if you have any worries or uncertainties about making your first tour bookings, I would encourage you to remember the "magic words." If you can't remember what they are, here's a hint: They're in *Chapter 5: Getting Started.*

Above all, don't let your uncertainty or embarrassment keep you from asking what you might think are "dumb" questions. It's possible to make mistakes when booking tours, and you want to avoid that at all costs.

Information to give

Booking a tour is, in many respects, like booking an airline ticket. The reservationist will want to know:

- The name of the tour, as given in the brochure.
- The passenger(s) names(s).
- The departure date.
- The city of departure.

If your customer wants any add-on options (excursion to the ancient ruins, scuba diving package, tennis lessons, etc.), the reservationist will need to know about that, too. Some tour products will have an extensive list of options, so make sure you cover all the bases — with your customer and with the reservationist.

The reservationist will also want:

- Each passenger's address and phone number.
- The IATA or ARC number of your travel agency. (If you are dealing directly with the tour operator you may be using a "pseudo ARC or IATA number," which is just a number used internally by the tour operator to identify you and differentiate you from all the other agencies they deal with. More on this in *Chapter 11.*)
- Information about the passengers' citizenship and whether they have passports and any necessary visas.

Information to get

Among the things you will want from the reservationist are:

- ***Airline schedule.*** If the tour operator takes care of the air as well as the land portion of the trip, get a complete rundown of the customer's flight itinerary: airline, flight numbers, dates and times of departure and arrival. You may even be able to get seat assignments at this time.

- ***Confirmation number.*** As with other types of bookings, this specific tour booking will be identified by the tour operator with a unique confirmation number. You will need this for any future communication with the operator about the booking.

- ***IT number.*** The IT number is a number that identifies the tour product in the various computer reservations systems (CRSs). The same systems that carry all the data on airline schedules and fares can also be used to book many tour products, especially those of the major operators. If the tour you are booking is one of these, you may need the IT number to identify it to your agency and make it easier for them to claim and process the booking.

- ***Reconfirmation of payment schedule and amounts.*** Make sure you know when the deposit and the final payment are due. Usually, payment is a two-step process, but the routine may differ from operator to operator.

- ***When and how tour documents will be delivered.*** Documents are usually delivered after final payment and about two weeks before departure. It's best to have them delivered to you, if possible. Otherwise you'll have to make arrangements with your agency to pick them up there or have them forwarded to you in plenty of time to present to your client.

Relaying bookings & getting documents

Assuming that you are booking the tour in your capacity as an outside sales representative (as opposed to dealing directly with the tour operator under your own business name), you will have to relay the booking to your agency. Most agencies will give you a form they have developed specifically for this purpose. Your agency will need the information to process the booking properly (if that's necessary on their part) and to identify you as the appropriate person to pay when the commission comes in.

The term "tour documents" is used to refer to a grab bag of things sent to the passenger by the tour company. They include:

- Airline tickets.
- Coupons or vouchers for various elements of the tour such as meals, reception parties, excursions, vehicle rentals, etc.
- A printed itinerary and/or instructions for the tour. This information may be included in something with a fancy name like "Tour Membership Certificate."
- Guidebooks or pamphlets covering areas to be visited.

- Luggage tags and stickers with the tour company's name and logo.
- Shoulder bags, passport wallets, and such, also boldly emblazoned with the tour company's name.

If the trip is a fully escorted tour, items like luggage tags and stickers may be more than "little extras." They are often used by the people conducting the tour to identify luggage and people who belong to the tour. Consequently, using them isn't optional. Make sure your customers know the importance of displaying these tags and stickers — even if they are ugly and garish, which many of them tend to be.

When the tour documents arrive examine them carefully against your written records to make sure everything is in order — correct dates, flights, number of vouchers, etc. You may want to prepare your own additions to the package. Here are some suggestions:

- Your own list of things to see and do, restaurant recommendations, special instructions, and so forth.
- Brochures about the destination from the country's tourist office.
- A guidebook you feel will be especially helpful.
- A gift from you that will prove helpful on the trip.

Remember, you may be receiving several hundred dollars in commission on this trip. Spending a little time and a few extra dollars is an excellent investment in goodwill.

Getting paid

Tour commissions are typically paid to the travel agency about 30 days after the customer returns from the trip, and certainly not before departure. How soon the agency passes your share of the commission on to you depends on the agency's policies, efficiency, and goodwill.

Tour operators do not have the best of records when it comes to paying commissions. Delays, especially when credit card payments are involved, are widespread. Some agencies report waiting seven to eight weeks after the client's trip before receiving their commission. A move is afoot by ASTA to jawbone tour operators into improving their payment performance.

To protect yourself, make sure you know the tour operator's policy on paying commissions. Knowing when the agency *should* receive the commission lets you know when to start bugging them about getting your share. Here again, good record-keeping is essential. Tours are often booked many months before departure. If you don't keep on top of what's coming due when, you run the risk of missing out on what's owed you. Remember, no matter how nice the folks at your agency are, their primary duty is to run their business, not yours.

Chapter Ten: Booking Cruises

"The Lo-o-o-ve Boat!"

There can't be very many people who aren't familiar with *that* theme song. In fact, one cruise line bought the rights to it and uses the song in its commercials.

Cruises are a great travel product for the part-time travel agent to sell: They have broad "name recognition," as they say in the ad game. On top of that, they're a lot of fun. Cruise lines get phenomenal repeat business because the people who like them, really like them. The Cruise Lines International Association (CLIA) says that nine out of ten people who take a cruise report that their expectations were met or exceeded and two thirds of them rate cruising as superior to other types of vacations. Even those who have never cruised are thinking about it — six in ten, according to CLIA.

According to another source, 85% of those who take one cruise take another. Many people cruise twice a year, regular as clockwork. Moreover, cruise bookings have a wonderful way of being (or becoming) multiple bookings. One person in four cruises with friends, says CLIA.

Some other facts about cruising may surprise you. Half of all cruise passengers are under 40. First-timers are even younger, and fully one-third are single.

From the travel agent's standpoint, a cruise is like a tour, only more so. It's like a tour in that it combines a number of different elements in one package at one price. Most cruise fares combine air fare to the port of embarkation and back, a berth, all meals, and all entertainment. I say "only more so" because when you book a cruise you are, in effect, earning a commission on things (like meals and night club shows) you wouldn't share in otherwise.

While land-tours are very dependent on the destination, cruises are more about that elusive something called "the cruise experience." Just because someone loved the tour of Italy you sent them on last year, doesn't mean selling them a tour to China this year will be any easier. If someone loved their cruise of the Caribbean, however, selling them a Mexican Riviera cruise can be a snap. This aspect of cruises makes it easier to sell "cruising" as the product itself, without waiting for a customer to express an interest in going to a certain destination. You simply select a specific cruise that you think will appeal to your market and then go out and sell it through direct mail solicitations and "cruise nights" — gatherings to which you invite a sizable group of people interested in cruising and sell them on the benefits of this specific cruise, usually with the aid of videos and brochures from the cruise line.

In short, cruises are a great product — high-ticket (yet economical for the traveler), easy to explain and sell, and an excellent source of repeat business. Once your cruise business gets going, you should be able to look forward to a steady stream of cruise customers each year. Many will be repeaters who will require little selling.

By this time, you should have a pretty good idea of the process of gathering information and booking travel products. So in this chapter, I am going to concentrate more on the elements that make cruises different from other travel products. I will also discuss them more as an off-the-shelf product you can actively sell than as customized packages that you put together on an ad hoc basis to meet a particular customer's needs. Of course, if you specialize in a destination, you can sell tours in much the same way. (If you are skipping around in the book, you will find a lot of information in the previous chapters that will be useful when booking cruises.)

Gathering information

As with any travel product, it is important that you do a thorough and efficient job of debriefing your customers for the key information you need to match them with the perfect cruise. Assuming that someone comes to you expressing an interest in taking a cruise, you will want to know:

- ■ ***Who's going where, for how long, and why.*** This is not always as obvious as it might seem. Are they planning on taking the kids? (Cruising is a great family getaway!) Are they considering going with friends? (If so, you will want to make a strong case for handling the friends' bookings as well.) Cruises range in length from one day to several months, with four- and seven-day cruises being the average. The Caribbean is the stereotypical cruise destination for Americans, but Alaska, Hawaii, and the Mediterranean also offer wonderful experiences.

  Asking "why" the customer wants to cruise can give you valuable insights into what the customer is looking for in terms of budget and overall experience. If the customer is new to cruising, you will want to explore their preconceptions and misconceptions about cruises to help you sell them the right product.

- ■ ***Past experience and preferences.*** If they have cruised before, they may have a specific cruise line in mind. At the very least, their past cruising experience (what they liked and what they didn't) will tell you the *type* of cruise line and cruise experience that is most likely to appeal.

- ▪ ***Preferred and alternate sailing dates.*** Cruises tend to sell out. The availability of berths on any given cruise, however, is somewhat fluid until shortly before sail time. That's because reserved space gets canceled when no deposit is forthcoming. Thus, a cruise that's all booked up today may open up tomorrow. Still, it's best not to count on that when booking. Holding confirmed space is always preferable to being on a wait list.

- ▪ ***Budget.*** What the customer can pay is an important factor in determining the kind of experience you will be able to provide. With cruises, more so than with other travel products, you get what you pay for. So don't be afraid to "stretch" the budget a bit by presenting a cruise that's at the upper end of the customer's price range. While the cost may seem high at first glance to first-time cruisers, you'll be able to show them that cruises are actually very economical when you take into account their all-inclusive nature. Generally speaking, it's better to provide a great cruise at the upper range of the client's budget than to provide a disappointing experience at the bottom end of that range. If you know the kinds of cruises your customers have taken in the past, you will be able to ballpark their budget, even if they are reluctant to give specifics.

- ▪ ***Client preferences.*** Under this heading are things like inside or outside cabins (the inside are cheaper), a range of cabin categories they will accept (if they are experienced cruisers), the kinds of things they want to do (frequent port calls or more days at sea, for example), and preferred cabin layout. Along with budget, client preferences will tell you what cabin categories (see "Making the booking," below) you'll be looking at when selecting a specific cruise. For example, if your customers will not or cannot tolerate upper and lower berths, that will cut them out of the cheapest categories.

As I mentioned earlier, cruises can be marketed much more readily than many other travel products. Typically, a travel agent or agency will pick a sailing date for a specific ship and build a marketing campaign to sell berths on that cruise to as many people as possible. (We'll talk more about how that works a little later.) That means you can begin today to gather the information you will need to make decisions about which cruise lines and which cruises you might want to market to your customer base.

This is not as big a job as it might be with tours. Although the number of cruise options grows every year, the total number is still manageable, especially since you will probably narrow your search to a few key cruising areas —Alaska, the Caribbean, and the Mexican Riviera, for example. Here are some things you will want to consider as you look around for cruises to sell:

Booking Cruises

- ***Your own personal preferences.*** It's always easier to sell a product you know well and feel enthusiastic about. So if you are an old hand at cruising and you have a favorite cruise line, it makes a lot of sense to start your cruise business with that line. If you are new to cruising or don't have a strong preference, you will be well advised to follow your interests. If naturalist cruises to the Galapagos, Alaska, and Antarctica appeal, pushing the Caribbean may not be your best bet.
- ***What's popular.*** You can get a quick idea of what's selling in your market by looking at the ads in the travel section of the Sunday paper. The cruise destinations that show up again and again are "hot" in your market.
- ***Marketing help.*** Many cruise lines offer marketing assistance to help you sell their product. Knowing which lines provide the best backup may well affect your decisions. In fact, this consideration can be crucial when selecting a specific cruise to market.
- ***Preferred suppliers.*** Take a close look at the cruise lines with which your agency has a special relationship, either directly or through a consortium. If there's a match between what they offer and what you want to sell, then the added commission is an additional incentive.

Research

Long before the first customer asks you about cruises, you should be doing your research into this lucrative area. There are many good sources of information about cruising, cruise lines, and their individual ships. Among the sources are:

- ***The cruise lines themselves.*** I find that cruise line brochures make for wonderful reading. You can get booklets that cover all cruises in a specific area, brochures about a particular ship, and itineraries for individual sailings. Many cruise lines also provide videos that do a beautiful job of making the cruise experience come alive. Not only do they make superb marketing tools but the cost is so modest that they are worth buying just for your own research and viewing pleasure.
- ***CLIA.*** The Cruise Lines International Association can provide you with a wealth of information about cruises and how to sell them.
- ***Books and industry references.*** My favorite is the *Berlitz Complete Guide to Cruising and Cruise Ships,* but there are many others available. The *Resource Section* will point you in the right direction.
- ***Personal experience.*** Nothing substitutes for first-hand, on-the-spot experience. If you don't have it, you can get it by taking a low-cost cruise-seminar sponsored by an organization like OSSN. Get out on the high seas, let the salt air blow

through your hair, relax by the pool, take in the floor shows, graze at the midnight buffets — learn all you can about cruising. Like exploring destinations, it's a tough job. But someone has to do it, and it might as well be you.

These sources will help you decide which cruise lines might have a product line that is ideal to go out and sell to your customers and your marketplace. Once you have a live customer sitting in front of you asking specific questions about specific dates, specific cruising areas, and even specific cruise lines, however, you will have to narrow your research to the most appropriate sources. You'll find them by checking:

- *Your own "preferred suppliers."* If you have a number of cruise lines that you, personally, like to recommend, your first step would be to see if their offerings match the customer's needs and wants.
- *Books and industry references.* These are excellent sources of information when you need to respond to specific requests.
- *The trade press.* A good way to stay on top of what's currently available is through the trade press. *Travel Weekly*, for example, publishes a Cruise Guide supplement every few months, with a complete listing of sailing dates and itineraries. Some trade publications even specialize in cruises.

As soon as you spot likely cruises for your marketplace, go straight to the cruise lines themselves. The cruise lines' reservations departments will be able to tell you what's currently available and answer whatever questions you have. The reservationists I have dealt with have invariably been friendly, helpful, and patient. Don't be afraid to ask questions about anything that is unclear to you. And don't forget the "magic words." (See "Making the booking," below, for more information on the booking process.)

Here are some things to keep in mind when researching fares and availability.

- *Pricing.* Cruises are usually priced on a per-person, double-occupancy basis; that is, the fare quoted is for each person when individuals stay two to a cabin. A single person in one cabin pays a premium known as the "single supplement," usually considerably higher than the double occupancy rate but less than the cost for two people. Some, but not all cabins, can accommodate additional people. The third person in a cabin pays a lower fare and the fourth person a still lower rate. Many cruise lines have "guaranteed share" programs whereby a single passenger will be paired with a roommate of the same gender at the normal per-person, double-occupancy fare. If the ship can't make the match, the passenger travels solo at no extra charge.

  In addition to the fare, there are the inevitable "port charges," taxes levied on departing passengers and something over which the cruise lines have no control. Port charges are not commissionable. There may be additional, noncommissionable fees incurred at stops along the itinerary, which will also be passed on to the passenger. Usually, these will be lumped together with the fare so that the passenger has the convenience of paying for everything at once.

Finally, some cruises will have optional shore excursions, which are priced separately and usually are commissionable.

- **Cabin categories.** Just as airplanes have first-class, business-class, and coach, cruise ships have various cabin categories. A ship's cabins are typically divided into four to ten or more categories, usually indicated by letters of the alphabet. Typically, "A" will designate the best, most expensive category, with the following letters designating progressively cheaper accommodations with progressively fewer amenities. Usually, all the cabins in a given category will be either inside or outside cabins. This should be obvious if you have the ship's layout in front of you (it will be in the brochure). If for some reason you do not have this information available to you, make sure you know what the category designation means.

- **GG rates.** Most cruise lines have negotiated special rates, called "guaranteed group rates" or "GG rates," with certain travel agencies or consortiums. In simplified terms, the cruise line is saying to the agency, "We will give you the same, lower fare we offer to large groups for single bookings." One of the first things you will want to find out, then, when talking to the cruise lines is what is the best fare they will give you. That can mean identifying yourself (or, more accurately, your agency) as a consortium member or part of a larger chain of agencies that qualifies for a better fare.

- **Fending off the competition.** Cruises are a competitive field — competitive among travel agents, that is. Don't be surprised if your customer books with you and then shops around, finds another agency that offers the same cruise for a lower fare, books with it, and calls you back to cancel your booking. One way to prevent such cancellations is to ask the reservationist, "Will you protect my booking?" In other words, if you book Mr. and Mrs. Smith on this cruise today, will the cruise line guarantee to match, through you, any fare another agency quotes the Smiths? In effect, you are asking the cruise line to give you its lowest fare — but only if you'd lose the booking otherwise.

This won't always work but it's certainly worth asking at this stage of the game. Presumably, you are looking at a number of different alternatives for your client. Guaranteeing the booking will help the cruise line secure your business. If you do get a verbal guarantee, remember to ask for the reservationist's name so you can later say, "Carmen, guaranteed this booking on January 7th."

- **Option dates.** As with tours, cruises are typically paid for in two stages. First a deposit is due by a certain date — the "option date" — to guarantee the booking. Missing the option date doesn't always mean loosing the berth, but it usually means having to rebook. Make sure you are very clear on what is due when, and in what form, to avoid embarrassment later on.
- **Air fare alternatives.** Once you get to the point of researching fares, you may want to check the cruise-only pricing. This is a lower fare for passengers who will get to the port city on their own. Most cruise lines have a laundry list of air-inclusive fares that vary according to the passenger's departure point for the port city. In today's highly competitive airfare environment, you may be able to find an airfare that beats the air-inclusive fare quoted by the cruise line.
- **Always make a "just in case" booking.** Cruises have a way of selling out. There are only so many berths on a ship; when they're full, they're full. Always make a booking if you have gotten to the point of actually talking with a reservationist. You can cancel it if you don't sell it or the clients change their mind. In fact, you will probably find yourself canceling many more bookings than you confirm with a deposit. The cruise lines are used to this, so don't worry about it. Just make sure that you cancel the booking *immediately*, as soon as you know it's not going to happen, rather than waiting for the cruise line to "get the message" when the option date rolls around.

Picking the "perfect cruise"

There's no such thing as the perfect cruise. There are so many options available that one person's dream cruise will be another person's nightmare. Here are just a few of the variables that have to be weighed and sorted to determine which cruise will be right for which person:

- **The ship's "personality."** Every cruise line has a carefully designed and nurtured image, style, or personality that it hopes will appeal to a fairly specific slice of the marketplace. Some cruises go for up-scale "mature" folks, others for "swinging singles," still others for families with small children. In theory, then, different cruises should appeal to very different people. In practice, people of very different backgrounds, with very different tastes, can go on the same cruise and all have a wonderful time. They may even meet and discover they get along famously — even if they'd never *dream* of speaking to each other on shore. Still, the general rule is valid, and you should take care when matching cruise line with customer.
- **Cruising area.** Different cruise lines cruise in different parts of the world. Consequently, they appeal to different interests

and pocketbooks. Cruises to the Caribbean on the East Coast and the so-called "Mexican Riviera" on the West Coast are the most accessible to the greatest number of people and, therefore, appeal to the broadest range of tastes and budgets. But there are numerous other possibilities. There are cruises to Alaska and among the Hawaiian islands, and newer, so-called expeditionary cruises to places like the Galapagos and Antarctica. Tours of the real Riviera and the Greek islands have long been a romantic staple. Finally, riverboat cruising has recently come into its own in the U.S., thanks largely to relaxed state laws allowing casino gambling on board.

A rather specialized type of cruise is the "crossing," a cruise that goes across an ocean and is typically sold on a one-way basis with either the return or the outgoing leg on a plane. In this category are "repositioning cruises," which occur when a cruise line is moving a vessel from, say, the Mediterranean (at the end of the summer season) to the Caribbean (for winter cruising). Crossings and repositioning cruises are for those who relish long periods on the open seas.

- *Gambling, alcohol, and other "sins."* Cruises have always been seen as a way to let loose and have a little fun. Trouble is, people's ideas of a good time tend to differ. Gambling is now pretty nearly universal on the larger cruise lines, as is the sale of alcoholic beverages. There are people who shun cruises for precisely this reason.

  A growing number of cruises are being designed to cater to this "lost" customer base. You can even book your client's on cruises with support groups, seminars, and regular "AA" meetings.

  Other cruises cater specifically to single people in search of a mate — and another, and another. A growing number are being designed for gay and lesbian cruisers (no pun intended). If you, or your clients, are likely to be offended by booze, gambling, or alternative lifestyles, book with care.

- *Solo passengers.* We're not talking here about those in search of companionship necessarily but those who, by chance or choice, are traveling alone. Many solo travelers never consider cruises in the mistaken belief that cruises are designed specifically for couples. But, in addition to the "meet and mate" type of singles cruises, many cruise lines have programs that cater to the solo traveler — from guaranteed-share programs, to attractive single-supplement rates, to activities designed with the single person in mind.

- *Size.* The nature and quality of the cruise experience can differ rather remarkably depending on the size of the ship. Some people prefer the big ships; others like something a bit less hectic. There are two ways to gauge size: by total number of passengers and by the ratio of the number of passengers to the vessel's gross registered tonnage (GRT). Dividing the GRT by the ship's capacity results in a "space ratio," which can be used as an indicator of the "elbow room" available on a ship. The higher the space ratio, the roomier the ship. In an example given by CLIA, a ship with a GRT of 38,000 and a capacity of 1,116 passengers would have a space ratio of 34. A ship with a GRT of 21,000 and a capacity of 1,100, on the other hand, would have a space ratio of 19. The first ship then is much roomier, despite the fact it carries slightly more passengers. According to CLIA, a space ratio in the 20's or higher is an indicator of a spacious ship.

Making the booking

As I have mentioned before, which comes first — the booking or the sale — is not always clear. Sometimes you book a cruise (or a tour, or an airline ticket) just as if the customer were actually going and then "sell" it to the customer (that is, get their okay to spend the money). Sometimes, you will get the customer's firm go ahead and only then make the actual booking. Sometimes the two processes will go on in tandem — a little selling, a little conversation with the supplier, a little more selling, a little more talking with the supplier — until every thing is finalized.

In previous chapters I placed "Making the sale" before "Making the booking." I am reversing the order here because of the annoying tendency of cruises to sell out or become overbooked months in advance because other travel agents are holding space. So the rule of thumb in booking cruises is, "Book first, ask questions later."

While there are not as many differences among the policies and procedures of the various cruise lines as there are among tour companies, there are some. Eventually, you will find yourself dealing with the same handful of cruise lines again and again, and it will all become second nature to you. Until you become familiar with the way each works, however, throw yourself on the mercy of the reservationist; ask questions about anything that seems confusing to you.

Information to give

Booking a cruise is in many respects like booking an airline ticket, except that you get a cabin number instead of a seat assignment. Here's what the cruise line reservationist will want from you:

- **The name of the ship, the date of sailing, and category.** This is the first order of business. This information allows the reservationist to get the proper information in front of him to continue the booking process.

  Categories have a maddening way of being fully booked when you ask for them, so it's a good idea to have some flexibility when it comes to picking the category. This will only happen if you have thoroughly debriefed your customer. In some cases, however, you may have to do quite a bit of checking back and forth before the booking is finalized. The more you can do to avoid this, the better. Sometimes, the entire ship will be sold out (or the affordable cabins will all be booked, which amounts to the same thing). This is where alternate dates come in. Of course, you can wait list your passengers. But all things being equal, you are better off booking your people on a sailing you *know* they can take than risking their eventual disappointment.

- *The fare basis.* Will this be an air-inclusive booking or do you want the cruise-only price?

- *The names, ages, and nationalities of the passengers.* If there is a group of people involved, you might begin by telling the reservationist the total number of cabins you will need. Then you can go on to break down the list of names into standard double, or triple, or single cabins.

  If there is more than one cabin involved, you will have to know who goes in which cabin. Age becomes important with minors; many cruise lines will not let teenagers stay in a cabin without an adult. The nationality of passengers is important, too. Many cruise lines call at foreign ports, and the documentation required by the various governments involved varies widely. American citizens will not require passports for most cruises to Mexico or the Caribbean.

- *Who's paying.* In the case of a group of people, each cabin may be paid for by a different person. Or three cabins may be paid for by one family member and two additional cabins by another.

- *Odds and ends.* On larger ships, the reservationist will want to know which seating the passengers prefer at meals. (To accommodate the large number of passengers, cruise lines usually serve meals in "shifts." Typically, the first seating is at six and the second at eight.) Will they want an assigned table or general seating? There may be other items of information needed to complete the cruise line's records. If you don't have all this information, you will still be able to make the booking. However, you will have to get all the required information straight well before the sailing date.

- *Your agency information.* The reservationist will want to know who you are, who your agency is, and what its ARC, IATA, or CLIA number is, if appropriate.

Information to get

Among the things you will want to get from the reservationist are:

- *Booking details.* This would include such things as the precise cabin numbers (the customer will no doubt have the brochure and be able to find his or her cabin on the ship's layout), the *exact* pricing — after all the port charges and any add-ons have been figured in, and the payment schedule. Sometimes cabin assignments will be TBA (to be assigned).

- **Option date and payment procedures.** Even if you think you know, double-check when deposits and final payments must be received. If a credit card will be used, make sure you understand the procedure.
- **Confirmation numbers.** Most cruise lines book by the cabin and treat each cabin booking as a separate reservation with a separate confirmation number. Once issued, this number becomes the point of reference for all subsequent communication with the cruise line about the booking. In addition to the confirmation numbers, it is always a good idea to get the name of the reservationist who took the booking.
- **Airline schedule.** If this is an air-inclusive booking, you will want to know the precise air itinerary information so that you can pass it on to the customer. You will also want to know what arrangements will be made to get the passengers from the airport to the cruise ship. Usually, the cruise line takes care of that with air-inclusive bookings. Conversely, if this is a cruise-only booking, you will have to make a mental note to deal with the issue of getting the passengers to dockside.
- **When and how the travel documents will be delivered.** As with tours, documents are usually delivered to the travel agency after final payment and about two weeks before sailing. Again, you will have to make arrangements to get them from the agency and to the customer.

Making the sale

Everything that was said about making the sale in *Chapter 9: Booking Tours & Packages* applies to cruises. You will be well advised to reread that section. Here we will confine the discussion to some points that are peculiar to cruising or which bear repetition.

I am assuming that you have made at least some form of tentative booking with a cruise line before you get to the point of actually asking the customer to make a firm buying decision — by writing a check or making some other form of deposit. You may be able to confirm all of the details of the completed booking with the client in the process of making the sale. Or you may have to make additional arrangements or changes with the cruise line after making the sale. Or you may do a bit of checking back and forth before everything gets ironed out. Whatever the particular situation, it's always a good idea to recap the booking details with the customer after the booking is complete in the cruise line's records (in other words, after you have crossed all the "t's" and dotted all the "i's" with the reservationist).

A good way to present the cruise and ask for the sale is with a brochure of the cruise ship. On it, you can circle the customers' cabin and point out the various amenities they will be enjoying. You should also circle, underline, or highlight key portions of the "Terms and Conditions" of the cruise line to make sure the client knows what to expect. If you are selling to a couple, make sure you have a copy of the brochure for each person. This way you avoid "insulting" one or the other by making assumptions about who the real decision-maker is.

Among the things you will want to cover are:

- *Payment schedules.* Make sure the customer understands the payment process and all deadlines. Ideally you already have the deposit in hand. Make arrangements to get the rest of the money as well. You may even want to consider some sort of installment payment program (assuming the sailing is far enough off). If a credit card is to be used, get a signature guarantee (see *Chapter 11: Getting Serious*) and agree with the client on which day you will submit the credit card number for final payment.

- *Cancellation policies.* Review the fine print with the client. Make sure everything is understood. This can be a good time to pitch cancellation and other travel insurance, either the cruise line's or that of another provider (see "Travel Insurance" in the *Resource Section*).

- *Travel documents.* Since your customers may not be receiving any travel documents (airline tickets, etc.), be sure to review exactly what they can expect to receive and when. This will keep them from undue worry as the sailing date draws near.

Dealing with price resistance

One thing to be aware of when making a cruise sale is that the quoted cost of the typical cruise is noticeably higher than the quoted cost of a comparable land-tour of similar length. This is due to the all-inclusive nature of cruise pricing. Essentially, out-of-pocket expenses on a cruise are limited to alcoholic beverages, soft drinks, tips, casino losses, and any souvenirs you buy. The land-tour passenger — in addition to the above — may be paying for all or some of his meals, local transportation, admission to attractions, entertainment such as night clubs, and even a rental car. So while the total cost of the tour may be higher — even much higher — than the cost of the cruise, the cruise may appear more expensive when you quote the price.

Consequently, you should be prepared for some resistance. Make a point of underlining the many, many features of the cruise package when you present the cruise. That way, your customers are fully aware of just how much they will be getting for their vacation dollar. To emphasize that value, you may want to break down the total costs. For example:

*"The first two people in the cabin are $679
each. The fare for the third person is just
$449. That includes. . ."*

Additional tips for dealing with price resistance, whenever and for whatever reason it occurs, will be found in *Part II*.

Bear in mind, too, that the steps outlined in "Making the sale" and "Making the booking" may take place in a different order. In other words, you may make the booking (that is, the reservation with the cruise line) after you make the sale (present the cruise to the customer and get his or her acceptance). Conversely, you may have to go back and change or refine the booking after making the sale.

Finally, remember the wise advice given in the last chapter: "Get the check."

Relaying bookings & getting documents

While it is possible to develop a direct relationship with a cruise line, it is most likely that as a beginner you will have to route this booking through an agency to be able to collect a commission. This will be especially true if a credit card payment is involved, as it frequently is. If cruises become a major part of your business, however, you may want to consider joining CLIA and becoming a "cruise-only" agency — at least as far as the cruise lines are concerned. This would enable you to collect commissions directly from the cruise lines.

As with tours, most agencies will have a simple form that you can use to transmit your cruise bookings. Also as with tours, you can expect travel documents to arrive after the final payment has been received and about two weeks before the sailing date.

When the travel documents arrive, be sure to double-check them for accuracy. If this is an air-inclusive arrangement, instruct the customer to reconfirm the airplane reservations directly with the airline in case of any schedule changes.

In addition to airline tickets, cruise passengers receive a ticket for passage on the cruise itself. These tickets spell out the major details of the booking and usually have a sea of fine print on the back. Immigration forms, if required for ports of call, will also be provided and must be filled out by the passenger. Be sure to go over these points with the client to avoid misunderstandings later on.

Getting paid

Arrangements for cruise commissions vary widely. If the passenger is paying by check, you or your agency can sometimes take the commission out directly. It works like this: The passenger writes you (or your agency) a check for the deposit. You (or your agency) deposit it and immediately write another check for the same amount to the cruise line. When the passenger gives you a check for the final payment, you (or your agency) deposit that check and write a check for that amount *less your commission*.

Be aware that even if the whole transaction is handled by check, you cannot necessarily bypass your normal ticketing agency. In other words, the cruise line may be willing to accept a check from your agency, which has an ARC or IATAN number and with which, presumably, the line has been dealing for years. But it may not accept a check drawn on your personal account, or even your business account. One way around this is to ask the cruise line if they will accept a money order. Most will.

Sometimes, the cruise line will want to get the full amount and wait until the actual sailing date or later (just to make sure the person doesn't cancel) before paying your commission. In the case of a cancellation, even though the cruise line keeps part of the payment, the agent usually gets no commission. The exception is when there is some "commission protection" deal with the agency. Usually this will be in place if the agent has sold the passenger the cruise line's own trip cancellation insurance.

If payment is by credit card, you will have to ask the reservationist for the correct procedures and what sort of documentation the cruise line requires. They may require an MCO ("miscellaneous charge order"), which means that payment will be processed much as an airline ticket would be and run through ARC. Commissions on credit cards are invariably paid after the fact, typically 30 days after the passenger returns from the cruise.

Cruise lines have been getting better about paying commissions promptly, thanks to an aggressive lobbying campaign on the part of the travel agency community. According to ASTA, 60% of cruise lines pay the agency commission within two to three weeks after final payment is received. Of those that wait until the ship has sailed, many have taken to paying up within a week to ten days of sailing.

Chapter Eleven:
Getting Serious

There are many levels on which you can play the part-time travel agent game. That, as I've already pointed out, is one of its greatest attractions. You can book just your own travel and that of your immediate family, saving roughly five to seven percent on your annual travel bill. Or you can do it as an occasional thing, helping friends out when the opportunity presents itself, earning a little pin money in the process. Or perhaps you'll adopt my strategy and set yourself the goal of earning enough money — through commissions and/or the special deals available to you as a travel industry insider — to take a nice vacation or two each year. The material we've covered so far should enable you to do that quite nicely, if you put your mind to it.

Some of you, I am sure, will not be satisfied with such modest goals. You may be looking for a *real* second income — the kind you might be able to earn by finding some other, far less interesting job. You're wondering if you can earn that kind of income as a part-time travel agent. You may even be wondering if you could earn enough to support yourself by working as an outside rep full-time job. The answer to both questions (part-time and full-time) is "yes," assuming of course that you are willing to put in the time and effort. As I said in the introduction, this is not a get-rich-quick proposition.

Once you get past the phase of experimenting with this new lifestyle, however, the travel game is no longer a *game*, it is a *career*. Even if you pursue it only part-time, you should approach it with the same degree of seriousness and commitment that you would approach any other career. In this chapter, I will discuss some of the ways in which a part-time, "fun," avocation can grow into an important source of both income and personal and professional satisfaction. Along the way, I'll touch on some issues and pass along some tips that will be important to you regardless of how much or how little time you plan to put into this new lifestyle.

Being professional

I am fond of the corny old joke about the two country rubes talking about the local boy who's planning on going off to college to get one of those newfangled "eddycashuns." One of them has to explain the system to the other. "First, y'go off to some fancy pants college fer four years and they give you somethin' called a 'B.S.' An' y'know what that means, doncha?" he says. His friend allows as how he does, indeed, know the meaning of B.S. "But that's not enough," the first rube fumes. "Then they stay in school fer two, three years more and get an M.S. That stands fer More of the Same. Finally, they stay in school, studyin' they call it, fer four or six years more just to get somethin' called a P.H.D. — Piled Higher and Deeper!"

I think I like the joke because it speaks to my deep-seated prejudice that just because someone has a bunch of letters at the end of his name is no guarantee that he's either knowledgeable or competent. It's the same in all professions, travel included. Yes, there are travel schools and various certification courses that you can take. And they're all very good, I'm sure. But it has always seemed to me that the true hallmark of the professional is how he or she conducts his or her affairs. You can be a mere beginner and be professional. Or you can be an old hand and be an incompetent ninny — regardless of what your credentials say!

To me being a professional part-time travel agent means dealing with people ethically and honestly, never promising more than you know you can deliver, and making a sincere effort to educate yourself about the business and your role in it. All in all, that's not a difficult code to live up to.

The American Society of Travel Agents (ASTA) has promulgated a code for its member agencies to live by. You can't go too far wrong by adopting it as your own.

Preamble

We live in a world in which travel has become both increasingly important and complex in its variety of modes and choices. Travelers are faced with a myriad of alternatives as to transportation, accommodations, and other travel services. They must depend on travel agencies and others in the industry to guide them honestly and competently. Similarly, carriers, hotels, and other suppliers must provide to the traveler the product as it was advertised. All ASTA members pledge themselves to observe this spirit in all their activities and to conduct their business in accordance with the following Principles of Professional Conduct and Ethics.

Responsibilities of All Members

1. All ASTA members shall be factual and accurate when providing information about their services and the services of any firm they represent. They will not use misleading or deceptive practices which could be damaging to the consumer or the travel industry.

2. All ASTA members shall remit any undisputed funds under their control within the specified time limit. Reasons for any delay in providing funds will be communicated to the claimant in a timely manner.

3. All ASTA members will provide complete details about terms and conditions of any travel service, including, but not limited to, cancellation and service fee policies, prior to non-refundable payment being accepted for the booking.

4. All ASTA members will not make use of improperly obtained client lists or other confidential data obtained from agency personnel's former employers.

5. All ASTA members will cooperate with any inquiry conducted by ASTA to resolve any dispute involving consumers and/or another member.

6. All ASTA members will promptly respond to their clients' complaints. If the complaint cannot be resolved by the agency and/or client, it should be referred in writing to ASTA's Consumer Affairs Department.

7. All ASTA members shall consider every transaction for a client as a confidential matter and not disclose any information without permission of the client, unless such disclosure is required by law.

8. ASTA members operating tours shall provide all components as specified in their brochure or written confirmation, or provide alternate services of equal or greater value, or appropriate compensation.

9. ASTA members operating tours shall promptly advise the agent or client who reserved the space of any change in itinerary, services, features and/or price. If substantial changes are made that are within the control of the operator, the client shall be offered the opportunity to cancel without penalty.

10. ASTA members shall stand behind any program in which their names and/or logo are used with their permission for advertising or promoting travel.

11. ASTA members will not falsely represent a person's affiliation with their firm.

Conclusion

Adherence to these Principles of Professional Conduct and Ethics signifies competence, fair dealing and high integrity. Failure to adhere to these Principles may subject a member to disciplinary action, as set forth in ASTA's Bylaws.

The naysayers

I think it only fair to warn you that not everyone in the travel industry will welcome you with open arms. Some people, primarily those with strong ties to or ownership positions in what I call "traditional" agencies, will resent your presence. They will call you a "pseudo agent." They will accuse you of being unprofessional, ignorant, and incapable of providing competent service to your clients. They will question your motives in living this lifestyle, strongly suggesting that you're just trying to pass yourself off as a "real" travel agent in order to defraud travel suppliers out of discounted tickets and hotel rooms.

Some of this attitude can be attributed to well-intentioned concerns about the integrity of the profession and the best interests of the consumer. Most of it, I'm afraid, is born out of fear — fear of competition and fear of change.

My advice to you, when confronted by this nay saying, is to ignore it. Go about your business and do your job. Allowing yourself to get sucked in to someone else's negativity will only drag you down to their level. And one of the keys to success in this business (or any sales-oriented business for that matter) is to maintain a positive attitude.

Joining a professional organization

In *Chapter 4: Setting Up Your Travel Business*, I suggested joining OSSN or NACTA as a way of providing yourself with an instant support network and a place to turn for advice, answers, and continuing education. If you're truly serious about a career as an outside rep, part- or full-time, then joining a professional organization is a must.

So which one to join? That I'll leave up to you. I joined OSSN mainly because it was the first one I learned about, so I can't claim to have done a careful comparison. The most important thing about joining a professional organization, in my opinion, is the availability of regular, usually monthly, meetings. And since OSSN and NACTA are very specifically targeted to outside reps, they are the logical choices. Check them both out and ask about meetings in your area. You may even be able to attend a meeting as a guest before joining. If NACTA has an active chapter in your neck of the woods and OSSN doesn't, then NACTA is the better choice.

OSSN and NACTA are not your only choices. The Association of Retail Travel Agents (ARTA) says it welcomes outside agents. You could even join ASTA, if your parent agency is a member. I suspect, however, that their meetings are less oriented to the educational needs of beginning part-time travel agents than are those of OSSN and NACTA. There are also a number of local organizations formed by local travel agencies in their mutual interest. These may or may not provide a comfortable place for beginners; you'll have to check them out. You can find out if such an organization exists in your area by phoning local agencies and inquiring. The *Resource Section* lists a few of these organizations.

Getting the most out of meetings

The primary goal of OSSN and NACTA chapter meetings is "professional development." The OSSN meetings I have attended follow a predictable pattern. There will be refreshments (perhaps even a dinner), followed by a talk by a representative of one supplier or another, followed by a question-and-answer period. Usually there's a per-meeting fee to cover expenses. It is $10 or $20 well spent. These are working meetings not social events, although socializing is an important part of the experience. Often chapters will throw a special Christmas party where the emphasis is on fun and business is, for the moment, forgotten.

While these meetings are usually a great deal of fun, you should not lose sight of the very important role they play in educating you and helping you make more money. Plan to arrive early, come prepared, and pay attention. Here are some hints and tips that will make these meetings more productive for you:

- *Network, network, network.* Bring your business cards and exchange cards with as many people as possible. Some people find it helps to set a goal — "I will come home with the cards of ten other people." There may not be an immediate payback in this activity, but it will help you get a sense of the travel agent community in your area because most of the people there will be outside agents with local agencies. Collecting cards will help you remember who people are; over the course of several meetings you will develop relationships, even friendships, with your fellow agents. In my experience, the people you are likely to meet are friendly and helpful and more than willing to share their expertise and experience, even if it is limited. It can be very comforting to know that there's someone to call on when you have a question or problem. You also may be surprised at how quickly you become "the expert" and are able to provide sage counsel to others.

  Not all the attendees are agents. I have met representatives of locally based tour operators who attend these meetings as a way of increasing their visibility with local agents. You may also meet people who specialize in certain types of travel and who have contacts and special deals you can use for your own clients.

- *Record the talk.* A small, hand-held tape recorder is inexpensive and a great learning tool. You can record the presentations of industry representatives at these meetings and then play back the tapes at home or in your car as a sort of "refresher course." If you can't use a tape recorder, take good notes and file them somewhere you can find them when you need them. Also, collect any handouts the speaker brings. Sometimes they underestimate the demand and bring too few, which is another good reason for arriving early.

- **Ask questions.** Don't bite your tongue for fear of looking stupid. If you have a question in your mind, it's a good bet several others have do, too. Participating in the group also raises your profile with your fellow agents. It's hard to quantify the benefit of that, but it is real. If nothing else, it will help increase your level of self-confidence.

- **Get to know the speakers.** Make sure you get the speakers' business cards. Write them a thank you note after the meeting; you may be the only one who does. Find some reason to call them in the next week or so to clarify something mentioned in their talk or to request more information. Clarify their position within their company. Many of the people who speak at these meetings are sales reps themselves. Their job is to promote their products to the travel agent community and help travel agents sell more. If you need help with a large group, they are the ones to call. If you're having a problem with the company, they may be able to straighten it out. They may even be able to get you discounts or other perks. For all these reasons, they are good people to get to know.

  Be aware that if you are an outside agent for a distant agency, the sales reps you meet at these meetings may not be "your" sales reps. Reps usually cover a certain geographic territory. "Your" sales rep is the one who covers the territory in which your agency is located, even if that's across the country. That's another good reason for working with a local agency.

- **Volunteer.** Running these chapter meetings is a lot of work and a labor of love. The people who take on the responsibility *never* have enough hands. Getting involved and helping out in whatever way you can will earn you a lot of brownie points. Not only can getting involved be an enjoyable social experience, but you can also pick up useful leads, hot tips about special deals, and any number of other bits of inside information, all because you're in the right place at the right time.

Developing your product knowledge

Success in any selling endeavor depends on two things: product knowledge and selling skills. You have to know what you are selling and how to sell it. The category of selling skills can be further broken down into two additional categories: business skills and interpersonal skills. You have to know *how* your products are sold (business skills) and how to deal with the people who need those products and guide them to an appropriate buying decision (interpersonal skills).

In this section I will discuss ways in which to begin the on-going, never-ending process of expanding your product knowledge. Many of the things you will do to increase your product knowledge will also increase your business selling skills. In other words, as you read and carefully examine tour brochures and pore over the fine print, you will become clearer on the mechanics of dealing with tour operators. Some of the things you will do to expand your product knowledge will also help you develop your interpersonal selling skills. For example, a seminar on selling cruises may offer many useful tips on dealing with customers, presenting the cruise, overcoming misunderstandings, and so on.

Getting to know your preferred suppliers

Since you have to start somewhere, I strongly suggest you start with your agency's preferred suppliers. Make it a project: For the next month or so devote a certain amount of time each day to gathering material on these suppliers and familiarizing yourself with what they sell and how they operate. There are a number of reasons for this:

- *They're easily identified.* Your agency probably has already provided you with, at least, a list of who they are and how to contact them.

- *Detailed information may be close at hand.* If you're working with a local agency, they probably have a large library of brochures, videos, and other information on these suppliers. Load up and start reading and watching. Your diligence will be appreciated.

- *There are probably not too many preferred suppliers to handle,* although you may be surprised at how many there are. If your agency belongs to one consortium (see below), there will probably be about two dozen or so; if it belongs to more, the list will double or treble. In any event, if you research all of them thoroughly you will wind up with an awful lot of information (not to mention brochures to be filed).
  If the list of preferred suppliers available through your agency seems overwhelming, I would recommend researching the ones offering the highest commissions first.

- *They will cover all the major destinations and modes of travel.* Expect the list of suppliers to be heavy on companies that offer cruises, European escorted tours, and packages to warm places like Hawaii, the Caribbean, and Mexico. The reason for this is that these are the places most American tourists want to go. Once you've gotten a good handle on what your preferred suppliers do and where they go, you will have a ready response to most leisure-travel requests from your customers. You will also have a pretty good overview of leisure travel in general.

- **They offer you higher commissions.** As long as you're studying suppliers, why not study the ones with the highest payback potential?

Essentially a preferred supplier is any provider of travel products that offers special inducements to a travel agency (usually in the form of higher commissions or "overrides") in recognition of the volume of business the travel agency brings them. But not all preferred suppliers are created equal. It will help your understanding of the business — and your agency's (and your) place in it — if you draw distinctions among the various categories of preferred suppliers.

- **Consortiums.** There are a number of so-called travel consortiums that provide travel agencies with a ready-made list of preferred suppliers. By joining a consortium (for an annual fee), an agency gains access to better commissions from a list of suppliers the consortium has put together. The understanding is that, in return for the better commission deal (and other inducements such as co-op advertising funds), the agency will "push" the consortium's preferred suppliers.

- **Direct relationships.** Many travel agencies develop direct relationships with certain suppliers. That's because they send a lot of people to certain destinations and/or through a certain supplier. For example, a travel agency in Minnesota may find itself selling a lot of travel to Scandinavia and form close relationships with tour operators serving that market, or even with SAS, the Scandinavian airline. Remember the sales reps I mentioned when talking about organization meetings? Well, one of the reps' jobs is to get to know the travel agencies in their area that are doing high volumes of business with their companies. They reward these agencies by setting up a direct preferred-supplier relationship with them.
Another way a direct preferred-supplier relationship can come about is when an entrepreneurial travel agency hooks up with, say, a specialty tour operator in Germany or a hotel association on a Caribbean island. The two entities enter into a mutually satisfactory agreement. The agency agrees to promote the product or products in exchange for a preferred commission rate. The supplier for its part hopes the association with the travel agency will help it sell more of its product. In cases like this, the travel agency is being rewarded in hopes that it will produce more business.

- **An agency's own wholesale products.** An agency may take things a step further and become a wholesaler for certain travel products. It may even create its own tours and packages. It will then sell these not just to its retail customers but through other travel agents as well. Usually, although not always, it is products like this that offer you, the outside rep, the highest commissions of all.

Start educating yourself with brochures

If your agency can provide you with a supply of brochures and other information, so much the better. Otherwise, you will have to start calling the various preferred suppliers and gather your own collection of brochures. Tell them who you are — that is, a new outside sales rep with such-and-such an agency — and ask if they can send you a supply of brochures representing a good overview of their product line. Some companies will have truly enormous numbers of different tours and cruises, so restrict your initial requests to those you feel will be most helpful. Some companies will not send materials directly to your home. As I mentioned in earlier chapters, their policy is to send brochures only to agencies. In such cases, you will have to make arrangements with your agency to hold the brochures until you can pick them up or have them forwarded to you. Consider ordering more as soon as you get them; it can take quite a while for brochures to reach you.

- ■ *Read and analyze the materials.* Allow yourself some daydreaming about how wonderful it would be to visit the places depicted so artfully in the color pictures. But keep your travel agent's hat on as well. *Analyze this material.* Ask yourself questions. Would I take this trip? Why or why not? Who do I know who would *love* this place? Who would hate it? What is the intended market for this product — singles, young couples, families, seniors? To what special interests (art lovers, scuba divers) does it appeal?

- ■ *Think about the offer.* That is, what are they selling and how? Is there an all-inclusive price? What can visitors do there? What amenities are offered? What add-ons are available? What's the pricing like? Is the offer structured and presented in a way that makes it easy to present, explain, and sell?

- ■ *Pay particular attention to the fine print.* Here is where the learning curve begins. Do you understand everything? Are there any unfamiliar terms or buzzwords? If so, write them down and find out their meaning. You can always ask someone at your agency. Or you can turn to reference works like *The Intrepid Traveler's Complete Desk Reference*, which contains an extensive glossary of travel industry terms, abbreviations, and acronyms. If the brochure itself is unclear, don't hesitate to call the supplier to ask for clarification.

As I noted earlier, this little project will result in a largish collection of brochures. This is a good time to begin your filing system. Otherwise you will quickly be overwhelmed. The best way to file materials is by destination. Your headings can be as specific as "Acapulco, Mexico" or as broad as "Latin America." I use both. I file my brochures in a battered old file cabinet with drawers divided by continents. I keep general information about, say, "Europe" in the front, with more specific information filed first by country then by city or region. It is also a good idea to start a "Special Interests" section where you can file brochures and other materials that focus on themes like honeymoons, golf, tennis, skiing, and so forth. Your system doesn't need to be elaborate, just useful. For example, you'll want to be able to put your hands on outdated brochures quickly and replace them with up-to-date information. You'll never be able to find anything if you let your brochures become hopelessly mixed together in random piles.

Your continuing search for product knowledge

If you follow my advice and make a project out of getting to know your preferred suppliers, you'll probably find yourself, a month or so later, with a pretty solid grounding in what they offer in the way of travel products. But this is only the beginning. There is a great deal to learn, and expanding and refining your product knowledge will be an ongoing challenge and responsibility. Fortunately, there is also a lot of help out there if you'll just take advantage of it. Most of it is low-cost and a lot of it is free. Here are some suggestions:

- *The trade press.* In *Chapter 4*, I suggested that you subscribe to a few industry trade papers and magazines. Now that you've done that, read them! They are a treasure trove of helpful information. What's more, many of them present product information in such a way that it's easy to clip and save the material. Each issue of *Travel Weekly*, for example, has a section on travel products divided by destination. A page — or two or more — is devoted to each destination, and the top of each page is clearly flagged "Selling Las Vegas," or "Selling Hawaii," or whatever. Many trade publications regularly publish separate magazine-sized supplements covering specific destinations or types of travel.

  Don't overlook the advertising either. It's filled with helpful information about new products, as well as special commission deals and fun contests for you to enter.

- *Supplier seminars.* Among the things you'll find advertised in the trade press are traveling seminars sponsored by suppliers. These tour the major cities in the country and are designed to increase the knowledge of travel agents. They may be sponsored by a single supplier, such as a car rental company or a hotel chain, or they may focus on a destination and be sponsored by several tour operators, airlines, and cruise lines that serve that destination.

  These seminars are usually free (although some do charge a nominal fee). Typically they last a little longer than half a day and offer a free continental breakfast and lunch. The ones I have attended mix the learning with fun. There will be door prizes and contests in which the room is divided into teams, with prizes for the winners. I have left seminars loaded with upgrade coupons for myself and my clients.

  The suggestions I gave earlier for getting the most out of meetings of your local professional association also apply to these events. I would suggest going to as many as possible, early in your career, even if the subject matter doesn't seem immediately useful. For example, attend a seminar on Greece even though you have decided to specialize in the British Isles. Techniques used to sell Athens can be used to sell London as well. You also never know whom you will meet; you might make a valuable contact at an unpromising seminar. Later, when you have a better feel for the industry and the volume of business you are doing leaves you less free time, you can pick and choose the seminars that interest you most.

- ***OSSN cruise-seminars.*** The Outside Sales Support Network (OSSN) sponsors a regular series of cruise-seminars. They are held on prominent cruise lines, and the prices often represent a tremendous savings off the regular cost of such a cruise. While at sea, you attend seminars on subjects such as "How To Sell and Promote Cruises" and "Issues and Answers for the Independent Contractor." Occasionally a seminar will be held on land, but cruises seem to be OSSN's specialty. Seminars like this can be an excellent way to learn about a very profitable travel product (cruises), meet other outside reps from around the country, and have some fun. For a slightly higher fare you can even bring your spouse (who will, needless to say, be eternally grateful).

- ***Readings.*** There is a small but growing library of books about the travel business. There is a much larger library of guidebooks and books about far-off places and the adventure and excitement of travel. You will probably want to spend some time dipping into these books. The bibliography in the *Resource Section* will get you started.

- ***Video.*** Seeing is believing. Many suppliers will provide you with video cassettes about their products and destinations for a very moderate price. Some suppliers even offer sales training videos, designed to help you become a better salesperson for their products. For more information on using video to help you sell, see *Chapter 17: Presenting The Wonder Of Travel* in *Part II* of this book.

- ***Experience.*** Experience, some wise person said, is the best teacher. As your part-time travel agent career progresses you will learn quite a bit on your own. My advice would be to write a brief note to yourself every time you learn a new process or technique. For example, the first time I had to book a ticket for a client using a frequent flyer award for a companion ticket, the reservationist had to carefully walk me through the steps of the process. I didn't write it down. I regretted that a few months later when the same situation cropped up and I, of course, had forgotten the process.

- ***Travel schools.*** It is too early in your part-time career to decide whether or not a travel school is for you. It may never be. Or you may decide after you have learned a bit more about the business that the structured, detailed training they provide in highly technical areas such as booking on a CRS is just what you need. I have provided a list of ASTA-affiliated travel schools in the *Resource Section*.

Maximizing your income

One of the best ways to get serious about your part-time travel agent business is to cast a steely eye on the bottom line and get very clear about the things you can do to increase your income. One way of course is to sell more travel. But for now we will talk about squeezing more income out of the travel you sell.

In the simplest terms, this means paying less attention to low-commission products (5% commissions on car rentals, for example) and paying more attention to higher-commission products (city packages with a preferred supplier that carry a 12% commission *and* include a rental car). This is a matter of selling *smarter* rather than selling more.

The most obvious way to earn higher commissions is to book with your preferred suppliers whenever possible. More than that, book with the preferred suppliers that give you the best deal, since you may find that your agency's list of preferred suppliers contains a lot of different companies offering very similar products.

Be aware, too, that the commission structures offered by preferred suppliers can be confusing. It is not always easy to determine exactly what you will get out of the deal. The simplest possibility is that they will pay your agency a single (but enhanced) commission rate, say 11% or 12% on everything booked by that agency and its outside reps like you. So if you book a tour and your split with the agency is 50/50, you will receive half of 12% or 6%. The other possibility is that the preferred supplier operates on an override basis. This is where things get confusing. (In the examples cited below, we will assume your split with the agency is 50/50.)

An override is an additional payment, usually expressed in percentage points, that is added to a base commission. For example, the base commission may be 10% with a 2% override for your agency. That means the total commission is 12%. So far, so good. What gets confusing is how overrides are applied. Here are the possibilities:

- **The override is based on volume.** In other words, the supplier pays a flat 10% commission until the agency books a certain, usually annual, dollar volume with the supplier. Let's say, for the sake of discussion, that the volume level is $50,000. You book a tour, the fifth booked by your agency this year. The dollar volume is still below $50,000, so you get half of 10%. But suppose you book the 215th tour and the agency's dollar volume with the supplier is well over $50,000. You get half of 12%, right? Well, maybe not. Read on.
- **The override may be retroactive.** If it is retroactive, all bookings made prior to reaching the $50,000 level will be eli-

gible for an additional 2% commission once the $50,000 level is reached. If this is the case, how do you know whether you're in line for an extra 1% on your earlier booking? For that matter, how do you know that the 5% commission you receive on this booking really should have been 6% because the $50,000 mark was crossed months ago? The honest answer is that, like Blanche duBois in *A Streetcar Named Desire*, you are dependent on the kindness of strangers — in this case the person at your agency who figures this sort of thing out.

- ■ ***The override may not be retroactive.*** Once again you must trust your agency to do the right thing.
- ■ ***The override accrues only to the agency*** and not to individual agents. You may not receive the benefit in this case even if the agency's dollar volume is well above $50,000. Let's say the agency's volume goes over $50,000 and they receive a check for $1,000 (2% of the first $50,000). It's a lot easier to deposit that check in the agency bank account than to figure out how to divvy it up among the agents who booked with that supplier before the override kicked in.

This last situation can also arise when the override takes the form of a free trip or vouchers that can be exchanged for discounts. (Technically, these are not commission overrides, but they are similar in that they are based on volume.) Let's say that among them, six agents at your agency sell "x" number of cruise berths for a certain cruise line. The cruise line in a burst of gratitude writes the agency to say that a berth for two is theirs for the taking; the agency can sell it and pocket the entire sum or the owner and his wife (or someone else) can go for a cruise. Guess what happens?

Another word of warning: Remember that some agencies only share *base commissions* with their outside reps and keep all overrides for themselves regardless of the circumstances. This stipulation is usually buried in the fine print when you sign up, or is not mentioned at all. Get very clear on this point before you sign on with an agency — especially if they are asking you to part with a goodly chunk of change for the privilege of being one of their agents. If you discover this after the fact, you may want to consider switching to an agency that offers you a better deal.

If you find you are receiving 5% of the cost of a tour when you were expecting 6%, have a heart-to-heart talk with your agency about its override policies. To be fair to the agency, figuring out who's entitled to what can be hellishly difficult. I suspect that most agencies that wind up short-changing agents do so not so much because they are nasty and venal people but simply because sorting everything out in an effort to be "fair" is not cost-effective.

Booking with preferred suppliers

Hopefully, things will not become this complicated in most cases. You will simply make the booking; the supplier will pay your agency the higher

commission because of the preferred supplier relationship; and you will receive your fair share of that sum. However, for this to happen, the supplier must know that you represent one of their preferred agencies. So make sure the point sinks in. When you call to make a booking, say something like:

> *"Hi, this is Mary Jones, with The Very Big Agency. We're an Action 6 member, and I'd like to make a reservation."*

or

> *"This is Bill Smith with The Very Small Agency. I'd like to make a GEM booking, please."*

The idea is to let them know that your agency belongs to a consortium that earns it a higher commission rate. I like to double-check later in the conversation and make sure they've recorded the booking as an Action 6 booking or whatever. You can also say something like:

> *"I'm showing that we receive a 15% commission because you're a preferred supplier. Is that correct?"*

Sometimes the reservationist will have that information. Sometimes he or she will seem confused by the question. If so, ask to speak with a supervisor. You may feel a bit stupid doing this; but if you're operating on erroneous information, it's better to find out now rather than when you receive a too-small commission check. Be aware that both the relationships of suppliers with consortiums and the commission structures are constantly changing. If your agency handed you a list of consortiums, suppliers, and commission rates when you joined up, it may be out of date. The more time passes, the more incorrect information the list will contain. So checking with the supplier at the time of booking is always a good idea.

Bonuses, spiffs and special promotions

Like other vendors, suppliers of travel products sometimes run sales. Some of these sales cost you money — you get a commission on a reduced fare. Other sales are directed at you, the travel agent, and can actually put money in your pocket if you're in a position to take advantage of them.

These sales take the form of special promotions and bonuses (sometimes referred to as "spiffs"). They are inducements to the travel agent community to take notice of particular suppliers and book their products. They take a variety of forms such as:

- Sharply higher commission rates for a certain, limited period of time.
- A bonus payment of $10, $25, or more for every booking made within a certain period of time.

- Issuing vouchers or points for bookings. These can be redeemed later for free travel or cash payments.

From an agent's point of view, these promotions sometimes suffer from the same drawbacks as overrides: They accrue to the agency and not the individual agent. You may want to be a little pushy with your agency when that's the case. Let's say there was a promotion for a resort that offered a free vacation for two for every 50 bookings. Let's further suppose that you made 18 bookings during the promotion period. When the promotion was over, you could call the agency to see if the requisite 50 bookings were made and if your 18 bookings made you the most productive agent. If so, you might be able to make a case that you should go on the trip.

If the prize is not of any great value, you don't have to bother to justify yourself at all. Call up and ask, "Did the agency get any upgrade vouchers out of last month's Hertz promotion? Could I have some?"

Of course, like so much else in the part-time travel agent game, you have to keep on top of what's owed you. If vouchers (or whatever) are sent to the agency rather than directly to you, make sure you follow up and have them forwarded.

Here are some examples of promotions and bonuses taken from the trade press:

- Runaway Tours offered agents $10 vouchers for every booking to Mexico or Hawaii. The vouchers went to the agent, not the agency. Ten bookings earned the agent a round-trip ticket to either destination. The vouchers could also be exchanged for $10 checks. The promotion ran for nine months, giving agents plenty of time to qualify for the free trip.
- The Holiday Inn Downtown in New York City offered agents a 20% commission on all bookings during a one-month period. With room rates of up to $175 a night, this was a very attractive deal.

Contests and sweepstakes

Another way suppliers try to create a little excitement, grab some publicity, and (hopefully) sell more product is by running contests and sweepstakes aimed at travel agents. I cannot honestly justify contest participation as a sensible, business-like way of increasing your income. But contests are fun and, hey, the odds are better than in the state lottery.

Some contests and sweepstakes only require you to fill out an entry form and send it in. Often, this type of sweepstakes is to be found in the trade press and will require you to answer a few simple questions — the answers to which can be found in an ad or a brochure supplied along with the magazine. Other contests are open only to those who make bookings with the supplier sponsoring the game. Some actually require a fair amount of effort.

Here, to give you an idea of the kind of fun you can have, are some of the contests and sweepstakes that were offered recently:

- Agents booking more than $100 in Alamo car rentals during a one-month period were entered into a drawing for a $10,000 grand prize.
- The Marriott Castle Harbor Resort in Bermuda sponsored a contest inviting travel agents to submit brief stories, with photos, about their clients' honeymoon experiences at the resort. Winning entries garnered a free trip for both the agent (and companion) and the clients.
- Sheraton Hotels offered a five-day vacation in Paris as the prize in one of its sweepstakes for agents who booked clients into the chain's Sheraton Suites properties during a one-month period.

Getting paid

Of course, taking all these steps to maximize your commissions won't do you much good unless you actually receive them. In most cases, getting your money is a two-step process: The supplier pays your agency, which deducts its share and then passes the remainder on to you.

I will assume (as you should until you have reason to believe otherwise) that your agency is honest and aboveboard and wants to do the right thing by you. That being said, the agency will also, quite naturally, want to do what's best for it. That's why most commission sharing systems that I've seen are tilted in favor of the agency. First, they wait until they are sure the commission has been paid; don't expect your agency to advance you commission money on commissions they themselves haven't received. There are exceptions to this. My agency sends my commission check for airline tickets in the same envelope as the tickets. Technically, they don't have the commission yet, but they know they will receive it shortly. If any problem crops up, they can debit any subsequent payments to bring my account into balance.

Once the commissions have been paid and the checks have cleared, the next step is paying you and the other outside reps. Most agencies tend to hang onto commissions as long as possible before splitting them with you. This helps their cash flow; it also protects them against things like bounced checks from suppliers. Some agencies have found it is more efficient and cost-effective if they write checks once or twice a month instead of paying people as commissions arrive. So the first thing to get used to is that, even in the best-case scenario, your payoff is going to be down the road — usually after your customer's travel has taken place; sometimes well after your customer is back home. That increases the possibility that, through negligence or poor management, you will lose track of what you are owed. It's bad enough to lose a commission. Losing one you forgot you were owed is even worse.

Then there's the problem of late, lost, and unpaid commissions. It happens. Hotels used to be notorious for not paying commissions, although they're getting better. Tour operators on shaky financial grounds also are tempted to "forget" payments. If your agency will beat the bushes for missing commission checks, you're way ahead of the game. Most won't. Of course, if a commission well into three or even four figures is at issue, the agency may stir itself to go after it. If it's a $20 hotel commission or a 5% car rental commission, it's most likely your headache. That doesn't mean your agency won't help at all. At the very least, they should provide some guidance on whom to call and how to proceed. In most cases, after all, you will be hounding suppliers to cough up money that will go first to your agency. Some suppliers also help in this regard. Most of the big hotel chains and car rental companies have special numbers for tracking down disputed commissions.

Be systematic about tracking your commissions

All of this serves to make the point that it behooves you to have a reliable system in place for recording, tracking, and following up on your commissions. Every agency has its own system for tracking commissions and paying its outside agents; some systems are better than others. Some are faster. Some are easier to understand and monitor. I can't give you precise guidance on how to work with your agency's system, but I can offer some general guidance and suggestions on how to conduct this all-important aspect of your business, regardless of what the system is.

First of all, find out what your agency's system is and how it works. Familiarize yourself with its ins and outs, the rules and regulations. If there is anything you don't understand, ask about it. Ask to see the reporting forms you have to send to the agency (if any) and the reporting forms they send to you with your payments (if any). Make sure you understand your responsibilities and carry them out. For example, my agency asks its outside reps to provide information, on a regular basis, about the non-airline reservations they make — identifying the supplier, the dates of stay, the confirmation number, and any other information that will help the agency identify the payment when it eventually arrives. Also, find out what the procedures are for handling missing or disputed commission payments. If you can do all this before you select your agency, so much the better. If not, make the best of the system that is in place.

Second, learn about how other agencies deal with their outside reps. The best way to gather this intelligence is by talking with other independent contractors you meet through professional organizations. If you find an agency that has a better system or a better track record for timely and accurate payments, you may want to consider moving to that agency. Remember that you are an *independent* contractor. You have a right to deal with whichever agency you feel best serves your needs.

Regardless of what system your agency uses, you should have your own tracking system in place. This will serve to keep you up-to-date on what you are earning as a part-time travel agent. It will also serve as a check and balance on the agency's accounting; so design it with that use in mind. If your agency pays you once a month, your ideal system will be one that enables you to quickly compare their accounting with your own and identify which commissions have been paid and which remain outstanding.

Among the things your system should record are:

- Booking date.
- Key booking information: supplier, client, dates, etc.
- Confirmation numbers.
- Due date. The approximate date on which you should expect payment (for example, 30 days after the client's departure date from the hotel). This will alert you to start being on the lookout for payment.
- Payment date. The actual date you receive your check.
- Follow-up actions. If you are recording this information in table form (which is not a bad idea), you will want a column or two to record the calls you make to scare up overdue commissions.

As I said earlier, most agencies will not hound the supplier on your behalf when a commission is overdue. That's up to you. You should be able to reach customer service through the hotel's toll-free number. Needless to say, a hotel's record in paying you will affect your interest in recommending that chain to customers in the future. Many hotels, in response to persistent agent complaints, have instituted policies to respond promptly to queries about overdue commissions.

It is also possible that a hotel will be able to show you that they paid your agency; in that case, your beef is with the agency. Confronting them can be unpleasant but it must be done. Rather than assume the worst, assume that they simply overlooked or "lost" the payment (which may be perfectly true). Present the hotel's proof of payment and ask what went wrong.

Simply demonstrating to the agency that you will be persistent in tracking down payments due you will often be sufficient to encourage them to be scrupulous about paying you in the future. If, however, a pattern of late or missed payments develops over time, you have a real problem with your agency. Since it takes time and effort on your part to extract these payments (which, individually, may be for quite small dollar amounts), you should give serious thought to switching agencies.

Protecting yourself

Why do bad things happen to good people?

Wiser men than I have been wrestling with that one since time immemorial. I don't have the answer; but I've learned through bitter experience that bad things do, indeed, happen to good people. In fact, bad things have occasionally happened to one of the nicest people I know — *me*!

If you think bad things can't possibly happen to you in the part-time travel business, you're kidding yourself. Bad things probably will happen to you if you don't take sensible precautions. In fact, they can happen even if you take sensible precautions. But at least you'll have the slender consolation of knowing you did everything you could to avoid them.

Getting 'street legal'

For those of you who never customized a car in your misspent youth, the term "street legal" refers to the minimum things you have to do to your car so those spoilsports, the local police, can't ticket you for violating silly rules about things like brakes and taillights. Similar rules may apply to your part-time travel business. I say "may" because the rules vary from state to state. I touched on this topic briefly in *Chapter 4*. Let's revisit it here.

Several states, Florida and California prominent among them, have so-called "Travel Promoter Laws," which seek to protect citizens from various travel scams and rip-offs. Whether they will deter this type of crime is a subject of debate. What is less disputed is the fact that, for honest people in the business, they have the unfortunate result of adding another level of cost and complexity to what is already a low-margin business. Typically, these laws require registration, licensing, bonding, and what-not for "travel promoters" in the state. My very personal bias is that these laws are being pushed by the "organized, traditional" travel agent community to hamper competition by raising the cost of entry to the profession.

Are you affected by "travel promoter laws?" I don't know. Even the legislators who drafted these laws might have a hard time telling you how they affect you. As this book is being written, many of these statutes are new to the books and a great deal of uncertainty exists on how they will be implemented and enforced. Some people seem to think that, as an outside agent, you are covered by the registration of your agency. Others think that *everybody* must register, except perhaps outside reps for agencies headquartered out of state.

I strongly suggest that you contact a lawyer. You'll probably want one to look over your contract with your agency anyway. Find out, first, if your state has a travel promoter law and, second, what your rights and responsibilities are under the terms of that law. Along the way, your lawyer should also be able to fill you in about what you need to do to become and stay "street legal." Some of the topics that might come up include:

- **Segregation of funds.** Essentially this means maintaining a separate bank account, or "escrow" account, so that money being held in trust will be separated from your general operating funds. In other words, you are courting disaster if Jim gives you a check for $500 as a deposit on his honeymoon and you use it to pay the rent, with the thought that by the time the $500 is due at the tour operator's you will have received additional funds to cover that payment.
  Segregation of funds may be required by your state's laws. Even if it's not, keeping your client's money separate from your own is a good idea.
- **Licenses.** Some states and/or localities require licensing for any type of business you may want to run, even if you're running it out of a file box, at your home, for two hours a week. You overlook these "petty" regulations at your peril.
- **Independent contractor status.** If you follow my advice, you're going to be stuck with a legal bill anyway. So why not

make sure that you are doing everything you can to protect your status as an independent contractor? It can have important tax consequences, as we shall see.

I suspect that there are many outside reps who operate in cheerful oblivion when it comes to these and other state laws. Either they don't know about them or can't be bothered. I further suspect that most of these people are honest, well-meaning souls who operate in this fashion for years, providing good service, never getting into trouble with their clients or suppliers, and escaping the notice of the powers that be. Of course, one slip-up and their world can come crashing down around them.

If you want to operate in this fashion, that is your decision. Just don't go crying to Judge Wapner that I didn't warn you.

Credit cards

For most Americans, plastic is coin of the realm. If your customers are like mine, they'll all want to pay with credit cards. While credit cards offer the customer a great deal of convenience and protection, they can create problems for you and your agency. The following, made-up, story will explain why.

Bill asks you to get him two tickets to London, which you do. He gives you his credit card number, which you phone into your agency, which accepts it. (Actually, it is highly unlikely that your agency would do that, but this is just a story after all.) Two days before flight time, Bill's mother dies and he flies, not to London, but to California. He doesn't use his London tickets. When the credit card bill arrives, Bill decides to handle the situation by telling the credit card company that he never bought tickets to London and they should remove this charge from his account.

The credit card company, thinking Bill is the perfect gentleman and not the cad and bounder he actually is, does as it is told. It turns to your agency and asks them to cough up for the London tickets. This is what is known in the business as a "chargeback." Your agency protests. The credit card company says, "Prove it!" Your agency is stuck. They have no way to prove that Bill actually authorized the charge, other than your word, which the credit card company won't accept. Credit card companies will always believe the customer's version of events until it is disproved at excruciating length.

Because people like Bill exist, no travel agency in its right mind accepts credit card numbers over the phone in the fashion just described. Instead, they institute a policy, or series of policies, that will insulate them from chargebacks. One way they do that is to make you ultimately responsible for any and all bookings you make. For example, they may accept Bill's credit card number, but only if you "guarantee" it with your own credit card number. So if Bill stiffs them, they charge your card. They may even add teeth to this policy by asking you to give them written authorization to charge your card when the need arises. In fact, one instant agency, as part of its sign-up process, asks you to authorize them to charge not one but two of your credit cards for unspecified "fees and charges" — a scary thought indeed.

Or your agency may insist that you document all credit card transactions in some fashion, creating a "paper trail" that can be used to prove, should the need arise, that the customer actually did authorize the charge. Whenever you use your credit card in a store or restaurant, the merchant does this by running your card through a little countertop machine. It makes an imprint of your card on a charge form (the Universal Credit Card form or UCC), which you then sign. You, of course, don't have that little gizmo.

There are a number of ways of getting around that problem. All are rather cumbersome.

- **Photocopies.** Some agencies will ask for a photocopy of the customer's credit card and even his driver's license, accompanied by a signed statement that the customer authorizes the charge in question.

- **Signed statements.** Some agencies will accept the signed statement alone. It needn't be complex: "I authorize Joe's Travel to charge $400 to my Visa card, number 000000000, exp. 11/96, for airline tickets from Chicago to Memphis on Budget Airlines."

- **Power of attorney.** If you have clients with whom you regularly do business (and presumably you will), another possibility is to have them execute what is know as a "limited power of attorney" that authorizes your agency to make charges to their credit card for travel-related purchases on an as-needed basis. Once this document is accepted and on file at your agency, you won't have to bother your client for photocopies or a signed statement every time you book a trip.

Here is *one* example of a Limited Power of Attorney. It is provided for the purpose of illustration only. Your agency may have a format it prefers, or your lawyer may suggest a variation on the theme.

LIMITED POWER OF ATTORNEY

I am a client of [YOUR BUSINESS NAME] travel agency, which is affiliated with [THE AGENCY THROUGH WHICH YOU BOOK]. I hereby appoint the owner, manager, and all employees of [YOUR BUSINESS NAME] and [THE AGENCY THROUGH WHICH YOU BOOK], acting in their stead to be attorneys-in-fact for the purpose of signing all documents necessary to purchase and issue airline tickets and other travel documents as follows:

and to charge these purchases to my _____ credit card, account number _____, expiration date _____.

I agree I will pay for all such purchases and will not hold [YOUR BUSINESS NAME], or its affiliate [THE AGENCY THROUGH WHICH YOU BOOK], responsible for any of its actions pursuant to this power of attorney.

_____
Signature

_____
Printed name of client

_____
Date

The blank space in the middle of the form can be filled out in any number of different ways. You (or your client) might feel most comfortable having the wording here cover only a single trip. However, the form will be most useful when it gives you the power to issue airline tickets and such things as tour vouchers and cruise documents on an "as needed basis."

You could also have the power of attorney authorize you to charge travel documents to one of several credit cards, at your client's direction. You can type up a power of attorney form on your letterhead and fill it out as circumstances warrant.

There's no point in pretending that these measures won't seem odd and more than a little off-putting to your customers, because they will. In the wrong hands, a limited power of attorney, like the one above, is a license to steal. Carefully explaining to the customer why these measures are necessary will help.

I know that some outside reps finesse the credit card issue by guaranteeing their client's charges with their own credit cards. That way, the outside rep never has to raise the matter with the customer. That's all well and good until something goes wrong. The result can be a credit card bill for several thousands of dollars for which the rep will be liable.

The other alternative is to deal only by check or in cash. However, that's bound to cost you business.

Other sensible precautions

The other major way in which you can get in trouble is when something goes wrong on a client's trip and, rightly or wrongly, the client blames you. In the worst-case scenario, the client sues you for damages. The remainder of this section deals with this, admittedly ghastly, possibility.

Perhaps we should begin by saying that worst-case scenarios seldom come to pass. Moreover, the lawyers who bring these suits — and who make a handsome living doing so — are no dummies. Since (in my humble and uninformed opinion) they are after money, they will tend to ignore you. They will sue the tour operator, or cruise line, which presumably has the "deep pockets" — unless, of course, they think (or know) you are insured or they can't get the money from someone else.

The threat of legal action aside, it just makes good sense to take some simple and sensible precautions to lessen the odds of something going awry for you or your clients. Here are some rules of thumb. They are not applicable in all situations, and some travel agents break some of them with no ill effect. Still you might want to reflect on how you might apply them.

- **Do your job and do it well.** This is one rule that should never be broken. It means paying attention to details and making sure every aspect of a booking is A-OK. Less obviously, it also means keeping on top of things and being reasonably well-informed about what is going on in the travel industry (who's going bankrupt?) and the world (who went to war this week?).

- **Avoid suppliers in trouble.** Some travel agents will never, never, never book a client on an airline in bankruptcy. There's always the danger that the airline will fail in its attempts to salvage itself and go belly-up at the worst possible time, stranding clients in some far-off airport. Very, very few airlines that go into Chapter 11, as it is called, emerge whole again. The same is true of tour operators. Courts have held travel agents liable for damages because they "should have known" about an operator's precarious financial position, which had been widely reported in the trade press.

- **Stick with suppliers you know.** This is a variation on the previous rule. One reason some agents stick with their preferred suppliers is that, in addition to the higher commissions, they have a reasonable level of assurance — although not an absolute guarantee — that these firms are stable and in no immediate danger of going under.

- **Stick with suppliers who are insured.** Both the United States Tour Operators Association (USTOA) and the American Society of Travel Agents (ASTA) have programs that insure tour operators against default. We'll discuss insurance in more detail a bit later.

- **Avoid trouble spots.** It was no accident that American tourism to Europe and the Middle East dried up during the Gulf War of several years ago. It is also true that many travel agents booked some stunning bargains during this period. You will have to decide where your (and your clients') best interests lie. Many agents decide that, with so many fascinating places to see, it makes little sense to send clients to countries where fanatics are murdering tourists to make a point.

Disclaimers, disclosures and waivers

We live in strange times. Two juvenile delinquents, trying to break into their school in the middle of the night, fall through a skylight and sue the school for damages. (True story.) A woman goes on a cruise, slips on a wet rock during a shore excursion, and sues her travel agent. (True story.) It's no wonder that some travel agents are starting to get a little twitchy about protecting themselves from the litigation-prone and their ever-eager attorneys.

The legal justification (such as it is) for suits against travel agents seeking recompense for injuries suffered while traveling usually revolves around the assertion on the part of the client that the travel agent somehow "guaranteed" or "insured" their well-being by sending them on this trip. Or, clients may claim that the travel agent breached some putative professional duty by not fully informing them of the dangers involved ("He didn't tell me that wet, slimy rocks are slippery").

One way travel agencies seek to protect themselves from this sort of nonsense is by getting travelers to sign "disclaimers" or "waivers" saying that the travel agent is off the hook if something goes wrong. Tour companies, cruise lines, and airlines do something similar. If you read the fine print in their brochures or the tariffs filed with the government, you will see that these carriers say something to the effect that, by accepting a ticket, you (the passenger) acknowledge that you are traveling at your own risk and will hold them blameless if something awful happens.

One of the interesting things I've noticed about disclaimers is that they don't prevent lawsuits. All they really seem to do is give the sued party some basis on which to mount a defense — "I told 'em so." Often, the defense, whatever its logical justification, doesn't work. Judges and juries tend to be sympathetic to plaintiffs in full body casts.

So why bother? Good question. I don't have an answer other than, perhaps, to suggest that it is better to light a single candle than to curse the darkness. At the very least, a disclaimer creates a paper trail showing that you weren't misrepresenting your role in any way to the client. Here is one example of a disclaimer that I picked up at a professional meeting. It was printed on the agency's letterhead and is included with the tickets and other travel documents the agency gives its clients.

> "[NAME OF AGENCY] and its agents, in providing consultation, making reservations, and issuing airline tickets or any other documents relating to travel or transportation, is acting solely in its capacity as agent for the carrier(s). [NAME OF AGENCY] and its agents, neither guarantees nor insures the service to be provided by any carrier and shall assume no responsibility or liability for actions beyond its own control in connection with the service to be provided. [NAME OF AGENCY] and its agents, are not responsible or liable for any act, error, omission, injury, or any consequences resulting therefrom, which may be occasioned through the neglect, default, or any other action of the company, carrier, or person engaged in carrying out the purpose for which tickets have been issued. We highly recommend the purchase of trip cancellation insurance."

The above disclaimer doesn't ask the client to agree with the agency's position. Of course there's nothing to prevent you (or a lawyer acting in your behalf) from drafting a disclaimer that will ask the client to acknowledge with his or her signature that he or she understands and agrees with your position.

Another way of trying to avoid some of the same problems is with an insurance waiver. This is a document that says, "We offered the client insurance and she declined." The inference, of course, being that when she finds herself laid up after slipping on that rock, she has only herself to blame. Waivers, for some reason, seem to be less aggressive than flat-out disclaimer statements, perhaps because most people are used to signing them when they pick up a rental car. Here is an example of what such a waiver might look like:

[NAME OF AGENCY] INSURANCE WAIVER

Date of departure: _____ Date: _____

I have been offered the following travel insurance and I have declined the purchase of:

- ❏ Trip cancellation & emergency evacuation.
- ❏ Baggage.
- ❏ Travel accident/limited sickness.
- ❏ Flight insurance.
- ❏ All of the above.

I, the undersigned, will not hold this travel agency and/ or its agents responsible for any expenses incurred by me resulting from cancellation of my trip, accident, sickness, stolen or damaged baggage.

_____
Agent's signature

_____
Client's signature

Insurance for the client

One of the reasons that people sue travel agents (aside from the fact that a caring lawyer talked them into it) is that they find themselves in some sort of financial difficulty due to an injury or loss of baggage or whatever. On the theory that it's better to have someone else pay your bills than pay them yourself, they engage an attorney and sue.

That's one reason travel insurance makes a lot of sense for both travel agents and clients alike. From the traveler's perspective, if they are insured against whatever disaster has occurred, then presumably their financial worries are taken care of. For the travel agent, there are a number of nice things about travel insurance:

- ▪ Even if the client decides not to take any, the travel agent has at least gone on record as having advised the client of the possibility that something might go wrong. The travel agent may even be protected in some small measure from retribution.

- If the client takes out insurance and something goes wrong, the client will be looked after. And if the client is unhappy, his wrath will be directed at the insurance company, not the travel agent.
- Travel insurance is commissionable, often up to 35%! Selling travel insurance to your clients can be a highly profitable add-on to your travel business.

As the waiver form above suggests, there many different kinds of travel insurance. Among the things your clients can insure themselves for are:

- Trip cancellation/interruption.
- Travel delay.
- Medical emergencies.
- Baggage delay, loss, or damage.
- Emergency medical transportation.
- Legal help related to travel.
- Death, dismemberment, and similar misfortunes.

Many policies allow the insured to pick and choose among the things covered and the amounts of coverage. Others are sharply limited in both what they cover and for how much. Many tour operators and cruise operators offer optional insurance products, usually covering cancellation, trip interruption, and similar eventualities. Most of these policies are sharply limited in what they cover and under what circumstances. Insurance is also available from outside vendors specializing in travel insurance. (A list will be found in the *Resource Section*.) Their policies may provide somewhat more coverage for more eventualities (like medical evacuation) than those provided by the travel suppliers themselves.

Check with your agency to see with which travel insurer they have a relationship and what your share of the commission will be. Take the time to familiarize yourself thoroughly with the coverage offered. Read the fine print with a critical eye. Note the deductibles and the exclusions carefully. Travel insurance can seem expensive to the consumer, and it can be a tricky sell for the agent. But it makes a lot of sense. As I get older, I have become increasingly aware of the advisability of taking out insurance that will lay on an air ambulance should I come a cropper in some far corner of the globe.

The real trick with selling travel insurance is getting credit for having sold it. Most companies provide brochures containing sign-up forms that are coded in such a way that your agency can be identified when the form arrives at the insurance company. You can simply hand these forms to your customers and hope they will see the wisdom of signing up. Even if they do, however, that doesn't always mean that you, specifically, will get the credit. You may have to work that out with your agency. Another problem is that the brochures usually include an 800 number for the client's convenience. If they wait until the last minute to take out insurance — and many people do — they will call the toll-free number, use a credit card for payment, and there will be no record that you handed them the brochure — unless the company asks them for the code on their brochure, which in my experience they don't always do. If at all possible, sell the insurance face-to-face and get a check. You can also take the client's credit card number and forward it to the insurer. Position this as another service you provide the client, which in fact it is.

Another possibility is to create a direct relationship with a provider of travel insurance and collect the entire commission. This is relatively easy to do in some states, much harder in others. In some states you may expose yourself to various regulatory laws by the mere fact that you make travel insurance available to your clients. I'm sure you are an honest, well-meaning, and decent individual. Unfortunately, the regulatory agencies of your state may not be willing to grant you the same benefit of the doubt. Your agency may be able to tell you what the relevant laws and rules are; a representative of a travel insurance provider is another excellent source of guidance.

The various providers of travel insurance have sales representatives whose job it is to serve the travel agent community. They often speak at the meetings of organizations like OSSN. You might also call a provider, get the name of the sales rep covering your territory, and get some one-on-one advice. Whether you are certain you'd like to add travel insurance to your product line or are merely curious, I would urge you to attend a seminar on the subject when one is presented in your area.

Insurance for the travel agent

Travel insurance for the customer may solve some problems for the travel agent. But for the truly paranoid there is yet another alternative — errors and omissions (E&O) insurance. This is a type of professional coverage whereby the insurer accepts the fact that, as a human being, you are fallible and might neglect to do something you should have done (like tell a customer that Whoopee Tours was in Chapter 11 bankruptcy and might go under before their tour took place). What's more, they'll agree to cover your assets in the unlikely event that happens and the customer sues.

Insurance of this kind is very expensive unless you go in on it with a large number of others. You may be able to get E&O coverage through your agency. My agency, which has well over 1,000 outside reps, offers to put its agents on their policy for $200 a year. OSSN also has a program whereby its members can get coverage at a moderate cost.

Another form of business insurance, general liability insurance, covers you for such things as the client who comes to your home office and slips on your icy front stairs. It is available, usually at a modest cost, from any independent insurance agent. Check your household policy first, however. It may include general liability coverage.

Incorporation

Another strategy designed to protect the businessperson against unforeseen legal actions is incorporation. Instead of being Joe's Travel, you become Joe's Travel, Inc.

The idea behind incorporating as a means of protection from lawsuits is that the assets of a corporation are separate, legally speaking, from the personal assets of the person who owns or runs the corporation. Thus, the theory goes, if you were sued successfully, the plaintiffs could get the value of your corporation (a box of business cards and a bank account with $100 in it, presumably) but not your house and car. The problem is, more and more clever lawyers are figuring out ways to "pierce the corporate veil" and go after personal assets.

Incorporating your business can cost anywhere from several hundred dollars to several thousand. It adds considerably to your paperwork load and brings with it certain tax consequences. These don't make a lot of sense for many very small businesses. So-called "Chapter S" corporations, however, offer many of the benefits of incorporating, while retaining much of the tax simplicity of a sole-proprietorship. Consequently, they are attractive to many small businesspeople. Whether or not incorporation makes sense for you is a matter between you, your conscience, and (of course) your lawyer.

Precaution or paranoia?

Having gone on at some length about the awful things that can go wrong and the often uncertain ways you can seek to protect yourself, we must now ask whether we're talking about sensible business precautions or raving paranoia. As with most things in life, there are two schools of thought on the subject.

I happened to be privy to a conversation between two travel agents, a lady who was an outside sales representative and a gentleman who was a travel agency owner in addition to being a lawyer. The subject was whether or not she should spend $523 to take out errors and omissions insurance. She feared that the advice she rendered clients left her open to lawsuits. He countered that there was nothing she could possibly say that would leave her open to a valid suit. He did admit that the possibility of an invalid suit was always present. After much back and forth, the travel agent-lawyer said, "My advice, as an attorney, is to put the $523 in a bank and watch it grow. In ten years you'll have seven or eight thousand." She replied, "I like to sleep at night, and to me $523 is cheap for a good night's sleep."

That's where they left it, and so shall I.

The tax man cometh

You will be pleased to hear that there is actually good news to report on the tax front. But first, let's take care of some minor points that, while not exactly bad news, must be mentioned in the interest of completeness.

First, you have to pay taxes on any income you make as a part-time travel agent. That really shouldn't be news to you but I just thought I should remind you. Among other things, that means that you will have to keep complete and accurate records so that you can (a) report your income and expenses accurately and (b) defend yourself if and when you are audited.

Some agencies issue their outside agents 1099 Forms at the end of the year, assuming their income was high enough. These forms are a mechanism whereby the IRS seeks to track significant payments made by companies to people other than employees. Taxes are withheld from the wages of employees but not from payments made to consultants and other "independent contractors" such as yourself. If you receive a 1099 from your agency, the odds are close to 100% that the IRS received a copy of the same form. The IRS, naturally, will want to make sure that your tax return and the 1099 match up. To be more accurate, the IRS will want to see that you are reporting at least as much self-employment income as reflected on any 1099s you may have received.

Some agencies take the position that their outside agents are not independent contractors at all but "customers" and that the commissions the outside rep receives are, in fact, "overpayments" that the agency is simply refunding to the outside rep. These agencies do not issue 1099s. I'm not sure what the government's take on this distinction is. What I do know is that, just because you don't get a 1099 from your agency, you can't pretend that the income you received through that agency doesn't exist. If you *do* pretend that income doesn't exist, you are cruisin' for the proverbial bruisin' from Uncle Sam.

Finally, the slim possibility exists that you may receive a W-2 Form at the end of the year. If you do, take immediate action because something has gone very wrong. A W-2 Form is used to report the annual income of *employees*. If your agency sends you one of these, it is probably an error; they are using the wrong form to report your commission income. The problem is, the IRS will think you are an employee and treat you as an employee, which is a terrible thing, as we shall see.

The tax benefits (yes, benefits)

If you've never been in business for yourself, becoming a part-time travel agent will open up a whole new world of possibilities for you when it comes to settling accounts with the tax man. Congress, in its infinite wisdom, has decided that businesses should not have to pay taxes on money they spend to stay in operation. Consequently, small businesses, even teeny-tiny sole-proprietorships such as you, can deduct a whole laundry list of expenses from their gross income, paying taxes only on the net income that remains.

Here are just some of things you can deduct from your income as a bona fide part-time travel agent:

- *A home office.* If you have a room in your home that you *set aside* for conducting your travel agency business, especially if you meet clients there, then a portion of your total home expenses can be deducted. That includes a portion of your rent or mortgage and utilities. Note, however, that the rules require that the room be used *exclusively* for business purposes.
- *Family employees.* Transform your layabout teenager into a valuable asset. You can hire your kids to work for you (fil-

ing, cleaning the office, etc.), pay them a reasonable wage, and deduct the expense from your taxes.

- **Your car or van.** You can deduct the cost of using your family car in your business. Trips made for business purposes — picking up office supplies, going to your agency to get brochures or tickets, taking clients to the airport, driving to a nearby city to attend a seminar, etc. — are deductible. The simplest way to keep track is with a mileage log. At the end of the year, you can determine what *percentage* of miles driven were for business purposes and then deduct that percentage of insurance, repairs, maintenance, gas, and so forth.

- **Business-related educational expenses.** The government wants your business to be a success. Therefore, they let you deduct the cost of learning how to do a better job at your business from the income your business earns. That means that the cost of attending a fam/seminar given by OSSN aboard a luxury cruise line is a tax-deductible expense. So are the books you read to learn the business — including this one!

- **Business-related travel.** Not only can you deduct the cost of a seminar, you can deduct the cost of getting there and back. If you are on a fam trip as a travel agent, you can deduct any expenses you incur. If you have specialized in Hawaiian vacations, you can even make a case to the tax man that going there twice a year to check up on resorts is a legitimate business expense. There are limits to what you can deduct when traveling on business, but they are reasonable and relatively easy to track.

- **Entertainment.** If you treat a client to lunch while pitching that luxury cruise, or if you throw a "cruise night" party at your home, those expenses are at least partially deductible. Again, certain limits exist and your record keeping must be impeccable, but staying within the letter of the law is far from impossible.

- **Business loans.** If you'd like to invest in some equipment for your business but can't quite afford it, remember that you can deduct any interest you pay on a loan taken out for business purposes. If you borrow money from your kids' college account, you get a double benefit — deductibility for the interest that raises the principal in their account. (Check with a lawyer to make sure such loans are structured legally.)

- **A retirement fund.** As a self-employed individual you will have a new opportunity to set aside a portion of your income each year in a tax-deferred retirement account, where it will grow untaxed until you are ready to retire. With company pension plans dropping left and right, looking out for number one in this manner is an increasingly wise course of action.

- **And on and on and on.** Every aspect of running your business is tax-deductible — things like phone calls, business cards, postage, books, subscriptions, computer fees, and so forth. Just make sure you keep good records and retain all your receipts.

And speaking of retaining things, retain a good accountant, one who is knowledgeable about and sympathetic towards small businesses. He or she will be able to educate you further on this intriguing subject. If you can't afford an accountant, use the bibliography in the *Resource Section* in this book and begin to educate yourself about your rights and responsibilities as a tax-paying small businessperson.

Of course, you can't simply spend and spend and spend without any heed to the amount of money coming in. Only the government can do that. Once you start declaring a loss on your Schedule C (the IRS form used to report profit or loss from a business) you start raising eyebrows at the IRS. That doesn't mean you can't declare a loss. Businesses do it all the time. I am constantly amazed at the number of businesses, big businesses, that have been around for years and have *never* shown a profit. Still, the IRS tends to treat folks like you and me a little differently from major corporations.

Be prepared to prove to the IRS that you are serious about making a profit, even if you haven't managed to do so just yet. Otherwise, the IRS may rule that your business is merely a "hobby" and deny your deductions. Of course, showing a profit every now and again doesn't hurt — either your self-esteem or the government's view of your business.

Presumably, you will be showing a profit right from the start of your part-time travel agent business. I did. The important thing is to conduct yourself as a bona fide business and pay not a penny more in taxes than is your legal duty.

As your business evolves

Throughout this book, I try to operate on the assumption that your business will start simple and stay simple; that is, you will be dealing through one agency for all your ticketing needs and funneling all your business through it. One advantage of that, aside from the simplicity, is that it increases the likelihood of reaching an earnings' level that will qualify you for travel benefits (see *Chapter 12: Straight Talk On Travel Industry Benefits*).

However, as you already know, your part-time travel business doesn't have to be that simple, even at the beginning. And as you grow — in experience, in clients, in income, in ambition — it may become increasingly difficult or unwise to keep it simple.In this section, I will deal with some issues that might arise as your part-time travel agent business evolves.

Specializing

It may seem ironic that, in a section discussing ways in which your business might become less straightforward, I start off with the possibility of simplification through specialization. It's not as odd as you think. You can specialize and still have many of the permutations and combinations mentioned below.

Just be aware that, as your business expands and you gain more experience and knowledge in the travel industry, the advantages of specialization may become more apparent. Whether you wind up specializing and, if so, in what area, is up to you. I, for one, think specializing makes an awful lot of sense, especially from a sales and marketing standpoint. Does that mean I've done it? Of course not.

Whatever you do, don't make the mistake of thinking that just because you started out being a general-service agency you have to continue being one. It's true that you may lose some clients and some business by specializing. They might be clients and it might be business you don't mind losing anyway. Besides, you can always make exceptions to accommodate special customers. For more on specializing, review *Chapter 4.*

Dealing direct

You will always be dealing directly with suppliers as you make bookings for your clients. What I mean by "dealing direct" in this context, however, is establishing relationships in which the commission comes directly to you instead of going through an appointed travel agency, where it is divvied up.

Remember, the major reason for dealing through an intermediary (that is, the agency for which you are an outside rep) is because that is the only way to collect a commission. As an independent contractor you have the right to do business where, with whom, and how you please. That means you have the right to deal directly with suppliers when the circumstances and any relevant laws allow.

Let's look at some of the situations in which you might collect commissions directly from suppliers:

- *Hotels.* Larger hotel chains identify travel agencies by IATAN or ARC number and consolidate commission payments by computer. If you hope to get a commission from them, you'll have to get it through an appointed agency. Smaller hotels, b&b's, and many resorts, however, are individual properties or very small chains. They too pay commissions. (At least some of them do.) To them, your little operation, Mary Jane's Travel Boutique, looks pretty much the same as the Very Big Agency Network through which you do your airline ticketing. The odds of them paying don't change according to whose name's supposed to be on the check. This is a no-brainer. Deal direct.

- *Tour operators.* Smaller, newer, or more aggressive tour operators may offer an outside rep like you a full commission for any business you bring in. Of course, in doing so, they run the risk of alienating the agency through which you book. This has nothing to do with the legalities of your independent contractor relationship with the agency. It has everything to do with clout in the marketplace. The agency would maintain that it brings in a lot more business, as an agency, than does any of its individual reps. It would also maintain that it has made a much higher commitment to the supplier in terms of its visibility in the marketplace and, therefore, should get some consideration. It certainly doesn't expect the supplier to give away business the agency would otherwise get to low-overhead upstarts like yourself.

Most suppliers are in agreement with this line of thinking and are loath to offend larger agencies (like the one through which you book) by favoring smaller agencies (like you). So you have to ask yourself, "Why would this tour operator be willing to deal with me directly?" Often it's because they're hungry. They may figure your business (assuming they get some of it) is worth the rather small risk that your agency will get wind of it and complain. But, as I noted in *Chapter 3: Become A Travel Agent — Today!*, their willingness to deal direct may mean that they are on shaky financial footing. Exercise caution in a situation like this.

On the other hand, if you are bringing in a large group — especially if you are doing so on a regular basis — then you have a certain amount of bargaining power. In this kind of situation, even well-established operators will be interested in dealing with you direct on a discreet basis.

- *Cruises.* As with tours, the likelihood of a cruise line showing a willingness to deal with you directly will be a function of volume — and steady volume at that. If you are at the point where such a relationship makes sense, you are probably at a point where becoming a CLIA-member "cruise-only" agency makes sense. (See below.)

- *Airlines.* The most obvious example of dealing direct when it comes to airline tickets is getting a consolidator ticket for a client. You buy it, mark it up, and pass it along. However, it is possible for outside reps to form direct relationships with major airlines. When you get to that point, you and the airline will know it.

Be aware that many agencies will try to tell you that you and they have an "exclusive" relationship — that is, that you must book all your travel through them. This violates both the spirit and the letter of your independent contractor agreement, which you undoubtedly signed. The agency wants you to be an independent contractor so that they don't have to carry you on their rolls as an employee, withhold taxes on the money they send you, and be liable for unemployment insurance and a lot of other inconveniences. But when they insist they are your "exclusive" agency, they are attempting to control you as they would an employee. They are trying to have it both ways, and that's not fair. It's also probably not legal; but not being a lawyer, I won't try to call that one.

If your agency tries to claim "exclusivity," you have a number of options. You can refuse, perhaps even insist that the offending language in the agreement (if it is there) be changed. You can simply let them know that you disagree with their position and tell them that you reserve the right to make strategic alliances with whomever you choose — as befits your standing as a true independent contractor. Or you can say nothing, figuring (a) they'll never know of your other dealings anyway and (b), even if they do, there's nothing they can do about them.

Of course, you can *choose* to deal only with one agency, turning away offers from tour operators to deal direct or routing hotel reservations through your agency even when it's not absolutely necessary. You might do this just because it's easier or because you receive a great deal of support and training from the agency and you feel they deserve your unswerving loyalty. However, you should know that you are not bound to do so. The outside rep's relationship with the booking agency is arm's length in most cases. The agency has little contact with the rep unless and until a booking is made and little direct knowledge of the rep's activities.

Most outside reps I've talked to don't make much of issue of the matter of exclusivity. Rather they choose a line of least resistance. They go about their business, dealing as they wish, with whom they wish, figuring it's nobody's business but their own. I think they're right.

But let's say push comes to shove. Let's say your agency doesn't like the fact that you are maintaining direct relationships and makes an issue of it. I would recommend simply pointing out that, since you're an independent contractor, they cannot make such demands on you — unless they want to start paying your health benefits and withholding taxes like they do for their other employees. They are unlikely to want to do that, although who knows? If you have proved yourself a valuable asset, they may be willing to change the basis of the relationship. And you may be willing to entertain that possibility.

Of course, the agency can always decide not to do your ticketing if it is really annoyed with you. Most agreements give them the right to terminate the arrangement for whatever reason they choose. Even if you had a basis for legal action in a case like this (and you'd have to review the individual facts with a lawyer to find out), it probably would cost you more to mount a suit than it's worth. It's far easier to simply move to another agency for the ticketing you need.

Pseudo ARC (or IATA) numbers

By and large, getting to the point of dealing direct with a supplier presupposes that you are doing a fair amount of business with them on a regular basis — or at least that the supplier believes that you will be. In other words, we're talking about an on-going relationship rather than a series of one-shot deals.

If you are going to be treated by the supplier like a "real" travel agency, they will probably set you up with a "pseudo ARC number" or a "pseudo IATA number." The number they issue to your agency is used solely to identify your agency and distinguish it from all others in the supplier's computer system. It serves as a mechanism for identifying all bookings you make and assuring that you get your commissions in due course.

When a supplier assigns you a pseudo ARC or IATA number, it means that the supplier intends to treat you exactly like all the other travel agencies with which it has relationships. What it does not mean is that you now have an ARC or IATA number. Your pseudo ARC number is just that — pseudo, or pretend.

Cruise-only agencies

One way of going direct with cruise lines is to become a "cruise-only" agency. One way to do this is to decide that you are now a cruise-only agency and write a letter on your business letterhead to the various cruise lines announcing your new agency and asking them to set you up on their system. A far better way to do this is by joining CLIA, taking their training, and becoming an accredited cruise specialist. While this is not an absolute must, it will make it a lot easier to develop the confidence and credibility needed to book directly with the cruise lines. Making this move usually means you have committed to taking on more overhead. Going out and actively promoting cruises — which you will want to do as a cruise-only agency — can involve considerable marketing and promotional expenses.

Becoming a "cruise-only" agency does not mean you have to stop booking other types of travel. Many cruise-only agencies are outside reps for full-service agencies so that they can also book tour products and airline tickets.

Branch programs

Just as you can set up an agency that will let you deal directly with the cruise lines, you can become a full-fledged travel agency and deal directly with the airlines. But setting up an ARC- or IATA-appointed agency can be prohibitively expensive for many people. Fortunately, outfits like Leisure Resource are stepping into this niche by offering low-cost alternatives that allow you to have most of the benefits of an appointed agency (100% of the commissions, your own IATA number) without a lot of the headaches. They do that by setting you up as a "branch." For an annual fee of several thousand dollars, they handle all the nitty-gritty paperwork of the reporting required by ARC.

This is obviously not an option for everyone — you have to gross $167,000 a year just to break even in the deal with Leisure Resource. You also have to maintain a storefront and carry mandatory errors and omissions insurance. But for someone who has built up a viable business base, it can be an attractive alternative to buying a travel-agency franchise or setting up an independent agency.

Automation

Another issue that will arise as your business grows is whether or not you should automate. Elsewhere, I made known my opinion that beginners should steer clear of instant agencies that require them to automate from the outset. It's expensive and there's no guarantee you'll like the business — and no getting your money back if you don't.

If you already have a computer, great. Get a modem and hook up with an on-line service that will give you access to EaasySabre or TravelShopper. That's all you need for starters. If you don't have a computer, I would recommend that your first step toward automation be getting one and then following the course I just recommended.

Once you have a sense of what kind of travel you will be booking and how much, you can begin to make some informed decisions about becoming "automated" in the travel industry's sense of the word. This means buying the software (and maybe the hardware) of one of the industry's several proprietary computerized reservations systems (CRSs). The cost of the software can be modest ($275 or so) as can the cost of connecting to the system ($14 a month minimum for one system). Training, which you will almost certainly need, is another matter. It can cost anywhere from nothing to several thousand dollars. Which system you get depends on which agency you are booking through. Obviously you will need to be speaking the same electronic language, as it were. Some agencies use more than one system; others have made a choice and stuck to it.

While the most logical reason for having a dedicated CRS is to book airline tickets, proponents of automation are fond of pointing out that there is a lot of other information on these systems, and the amount and variety are growing daily. In addition to sending your Aunt Matilda to Dayton, you can tap into the latest industry news and check the availability of fam trips — an exciting wrinkle to the travel industry that we will discuss in the next chapter.

Switching or combining agencies

As I mentioned earlier, you may find it advisable to switch or combine agencies. There are any number of reasons why you might want to do this:

- *Getting a better deal.* You may decide the grass, or at least the commission, is greener elsewhere.
- *Convenience.* You may have joined an instant agency out of state as a way to get started quickly. Once you have some experience under your belt and a growing client list, you may want to market your services to a local agency.
- *Better service.* If your agency is slow in paying, or not paying at all, you may want to seek out one that is more fiscally responsible.
- *Getting the best of both worlds.* It's even possible to have relationships with more than one booking agency. For example, you may use the out of state instant agency with its better commission cut when the trip is a few weeks off, but book through a local agency with a less generous split when you need to pick up tickets today.

One thing I hope this book will give you is the confidence and know-how to be able to face the possibility of switching agencies with confidence. It can be done, and you owe it to yourself to give yourself the best deal possible.

Chapter Twelve: Straight Talk On Travel Industry Benefits

Many of the advertisements designed to attract part-time travel agent wannabes follow a predictable pattern: A picture of a lovely white sand beach, a beautiful young couple ("That could be me!") and lines like "As a Solid Gold Travel consultant, you'll receive all the benefits given to other travel professionals; you'll be eligible for free and reduced-fare trips." Wow! Where do I sign up?

As I was researching the opportunities for folks like you and me to get involved in selling travel on a part-time basis, I developed a handy rule of thumb: the more they stressed free and low-cost travel, the less seriously I should take the proposition. Not that these outfits can't set you up to be an outside agent — they can. It's just that with a pitch that's closer to Barnum than to Baedeker, they seem to be more interested in collecting your sign-up fee (which in some cases can be substantial) than in letting you make money, which is a necessary prerequisite to "free" travel.

Even responsible observers and organizations, like the Outside Sales Support Network (OSSN), tend to put on the rose-colored glasses when writing about the benefits that accrue to outside sales reps. My goal in this chapter is to give you the straight poop.

Let me begin by saying that there are, in fact, a lot of nifty benefits that come with getting involved in this exciting lifestyle. It is actually possible (although rare) to travel free. It is far more common to get discounts on your travel. What a lot of the people pitching the "be-a-travel-agent-and-travel-free" pipe dreams won't tell you is that all these benefits must be *earned* and many of them come with strings attached.

But before we get to the nitty-gritty, we'll have to review a little history.

Hurricane Connie

In 1993, the travel industry was turned on its collective ear by an "investigative" report on the CBS newsmagazine, *Eye To Eye With Connie Chung*. The upshot of the report was that, in the agent community's head-long rush to protect its honor and the airlines' desire to quash a public relations nightmare, the facts of the situation got lost in the shuffle. Here's what happened:

The report "revealed" that there was widespread abuse of travel agent benefits. People who weren't travel agents at all — in fact, people who had *purchased* phony travel agent ID — were presenting themselves at airline counters and flying for ridiculously low fares. The villains in the Chung report were — and this, I think, is the most interesting thing about the whole flap — well-heeled business executives who (the report strongly implied) paid big bucks to have an unscrupulous agency owner list them as agents on the agency's "ARC list," which I'll define a little later.

Travel agents ran around in circles, wringing their hands and insisting that a few rotten apples were besmirching the reputation of a noble profession. A few faint voices could be heard saying that the Chung report was sensationalized nonsense and that "abuse" was a tempest in a teapot. They were ignored.

Within a week, a few airlines announced, echoing Claude Raines' performance in *Casablanca*, that they were shocked — shocked! — that abuse of their discount policies was occurring. In the future, they said, only the IATAN card would be accepted as proof that an individual was, in fact, a travel agent. As the weeks passed, more and more airlines and hotel chains joined the bandwagon. The IATAN card or bust.

Now the travel agent community began wailing a different tune. Or to be more accurate, several different tunes. Instead of attacking the out-and-out phonies, like the ones fingered on *Eye To Eye*, the travel agent community went in for some internecine bloodletting. It was the "haves" against the "have-nots," with the haves being the larger ARC- and IATAN-appointed agencies and the have-nots being outside agents and cruise-only agencies. Although they never said as much, the haves were perfectly happy with the new developments. They saw the issue as one of "real" travel agents versus "phony" travel agents, the part-timers and independent contractors. Moving to the IATAN card as the open sesame to travel benefits could only discourage parvenus (like you and me) from getting into the business and thus hold down competition.

A growing chorus of have-nots was heard in the trade press. What about all the agencies that weren't members of IATAN but that were bona fide travel agencies nonetheless? What about cruise-only agencies? What about outside reps? Maybe there could be other cards accepted as well. Maybe there could be a new form of travel agent ID created. In short, everyone wanted the benefits but still wanted to protect the profession from this presumed onslaught by greedy con artists and the unscrupulous travel agents who aid and abet them.

That's pretty much where it stands now. The IATAN card is the "official" ID for "real" travel agents. IATAN, generous to a fault, agreed to sell its card to ARC-appointed agencies for a fee that — what a coincidence — makes it cheaper to join IATAN than to buy the cards if you have more than four agents. At last count, applications for the new Gold Card of the travel industry were coming in at the rate of 15,000 a month. One industry insider estimated that IATAN would make $10 million a year off its card's newfound prominence.

What really happened

Since time immemorial (which in the travel agency business means as long as anyone can remember), suppliers have been extending courtesies to travel agents. Something similar happens in just about every business where suppliers use retailers to get their products to the end-user.

In the case of the airlines, this professional courtesy takes the form of "AD75" or "quarter fares." That means that travel agents can fly at a 75% discount. Pretty impressive, right? Except that this is 75% off a fare few people ever pay — the full-coach (or "Y") fare. Most "super-saver" fares represent a 55% discount off full coach. So the discounts, while real, are not as huge as they might seem at first blush. Still, they're a pretty good deal — except for the blackout periods. The airlines aren't about to let agents travel cheap during peak travel periods — like Thanksgiving, Christmas, Spring Break, and most of the summer. Then there's the paperwork. Most airlines don't let an agent walk up and buy a ticket. A request has to be made, in writing, in advance, and approved.

For the airlines this is a good deal. First, they generate a certain amount of goodwill with travel agencies. They reward travel agents who have sent them business in the past and stroke agents who might send them more in the future. Second, they make money on the deal. That's because no travel agent ever sits in a seat that could be occupied by a customer who would pay a higher fare. While the airlines book these fares as "positive space," they reserve the right to bump the agent (without any "denied-boarding" compensation) if the flight is overbooked. "Positive space" simply means that the agent can book ahead and get a seat assignment, as opposed to being put on a standby list. So every time an agent (even a phony one) flew, the airline was getting a few hundred dollars it might not otherwise have gotten.

The *Eye To Eye* piece gave the impression that abuse of this system was a new phenomenon. Wrong. What was new was the more or less open marketing, by a few agencies, of "travel agent ID." People passing themselves off as travel agents was old hat — and relatively easy — long before. All that was required was an amenable travel agency owner.

For many years, the easiest way to "prove" to an airline that you were entitled to a travel agent discount was the "ARC list," named after a blank form included in the manual received by all travel agencies that were appointed by the Airlines Reporting Corporation (ARC). On this blank form, the agency owner could type the names of all agents employed by the agency. If the agency owner wanted to include the name of his Aunt Martha, he could, and frequently did. If the agency owner found himself short of cash, he could get a loan from a friend, who then became a "part owner" as far as the ARC list was concerned. Sure, ARC was supposed to police this sort of thing, and it probably made an effort to do so. But there are a great many travel agencies in the country and limited time and money to check up on them all. Also, the nature of the ARC list was such that a new one could be cooked up whenever the situation demanded it.

By the way, as a result of the Connie Chung controversy, ARC discontinued the ARC list form. So if someone tells you they can get you on the ARC list, they are . . . well, let's just say they're misinformed.

So if abuse of travel agent status was going on before *Eye To Eye* broke this hot story, did the airlines know and were they upset about it? Hard to say, but the answers are probably "yes" and "not very much." The airlines' rules said travel agents had to prove who they were. If proof of some sort was forthcoming, the letter of the rules was satisfied. The rules did not say the people who passed on these tickets had to be detectives.

In the aftermath of the *Eye To Eye* story, the airlines and other suppliers presented themselves as unwitting victims of a scam. The actuality was probably somewhat different. If a business is extending discretionary discounts, the primary responsibility for determining eligibility lies with that business. The airlines have plenty of mechanisms for monitoring the use and abuse of agent tickets. My guess is that this hadn't become an issue before because it wasn't an issue. There probably wasn't a great deal of abuse, and the abuse that was occurring was at least selling tickets.

In announcing that they were henceforth going to accept only the IATAN card as proof of agent status, the airlines were actually moving to prevent not travel agent abuse but a public relations embarrassment. They were worried that the viewers of Connie Chung's show, all upstanding, hard-working, honest Americans, would feel that the airlines were letting con men play them for suckers. Here they were paying (what they think of as) full fare while the airlines are letting crooks fly for (what they think is) next to nothing. In true tabloid style, *Eye To Eye* did everything it could to convey that very impression.

So, will moving to the IATAN card put an end to the abuse of agent privileges once and for all? Not on your life. The final arbiter of who is eligible for an IATAN card is still — guess who? — the agency owner, the same guy who was putting the dentist and the plumber on the ARC list. What probably will change is that the cost of becoming a pretend travel agent will go up a bit. But the "part owners" and the others will still have their IATAN cards. Many already do. IATAN says it plans to enforce the integrity of its cards and will no doubt make an effort to do so. But, as with the ARC list, time, money, and personnel are limited. And since IATAN makes money on every card it issues, there will be a built-in temptation to expand the number of card holders.

What will also undoubtedly continue to happen is that suppliers in the travel industry will extend courtesy discounts to members of the travel agent profession, on a discretionary basis, whether they have "proper" identification or not. If the supplier thinks it's okay to give you a discount, what IATAN has to say about you doesn't matter.

What's the fuss all about?

The Connie Chung flap echoes in the trade press to this day. There has been a great deal of huffing and handwringing, righteous indignation and second guessing. Most of it has to do with pride and ego ("I'm a travel agent and you're NOT!"), although the trade press seldom acknowledges that aspect of it. What I've found most intriguing, however, is how little is at stake besides wounded pride.

All that an ID card (whatever form it might take) entitles you to in the travel business is a discount. Percentages like 75% and 50% are mentioned frequently. But as I've already pointed out, these are discounts off artificially high fares or rates. Let's take a closer look:

- **Airlines.** Let's put aside the blackout dates and paperwork hassles of the AD75 fare and examine the dollar savings. Let's say the "unrestricted coach fare" for a given trip is $800 plus tax. That means the AD75 fare should be $200. A super-saver fare might be $360, with no blackout dates and no paperwork. Book that for yourself as an outside rep and shave off another $18 to $25 (your commission). So the person using the AD75 is saving about $140. Worth it? Obviously it is to some people. But considering the hassles, the restrictions, and the possibility of getting bumped, I don't think so — especially when the money I make booking travel for others can pay for my own.

- **Hotels.** Hotels will typically offer you 50% off the rack rate, which is the outrageous rate they charge when the big convention's in town and you don't have any other choice. In *Chapter 7: Booking Hotels*, I gave some guidelines on bargaining for the best rate at a hotel. When you ask for an "agent rate," the reservationist may simply pick a number out of the air — remember, they have considerable bargaining leeway. Often a little smart shopping or use of half-price hotel programs will get you as good a rate as your travel agent ID. One ploy would be to call ahead (which you should *always* do anyway as a simple matter of courtesy), identify yourself as an agent, and ask what the rack rate is, then ask what the agent rate is. If it's 50% or more of the rack rate, you've got a bargain. Occasionally, various hotels will offer special promotional rates for agents that really are bargains. They are announced in the trade press.

- **Car rentals.** Car rental firms vary widely in their use of agent discounts. Sometimes they will offer no more than 5% and sometimes you can get real bargains, like a flat rate of $10 a day with unlimited mileage. Again, since rates vary so widely from company to company, the agent rate at one may be more than a special promotion rate at another.

- **Tours and cruises.** While tour operators and cruise lines will sometimes extend straight discounts to travel agents, most reduced-rate travel for travel agents in these areas takes the form of "fam trips," which are discussed a little later.

"Real" travel agents (and you will be one by the time you've finished this book) get to know the ins and outs of the business. They learn how to smoke out the best deals, and they recognize a great rate when it walks up and bites them. I suspect that many people who buy into instant agent programs solely to save tons of money on their own travel, wind up disappointed. For a while, no doubt, they enjoy the thrill of thinking they're "getting away with something." They may even think they've got a great deal, paying $80 for that "$180" hotel room, little knowing that the fellow across the hall is paying a $79 promotional rate obtained by a travel agent. The agency through which they got their ID may even make them feel special by tossing a few cheapies their way — discounts the agency qualifies for based on its volume, which it then passes along to people who paid for their travel agent status. Eventually, I suspect, many of these people catch on that they've paid a lot for not a lot. They almost certainly won't be the least bit amused the first time they get bumped from an airline because travel agents must yield to paying customers.

Who's a travel agent?

There are any number of ways travel agents can "identify" themselves to suppliers and others in the industry.

- *Business cards.* Who doesn't have a business card? They can be plain and simple. Or they can be gold embossed with ASTA and ARTA logos. My guess is that many places that accept your travel agency business card in exchange for a discount are merely making a few extra bucks on a hotel room or a car that might not get used otherwise.

- *Agency ID cards.* Some agencies will issue you a spiffy laminated ID card that identifies you as one of their agents. It may even look just a little like the IATAN card. You'll almost certainly have to provide your own picture and pay a fee for it.

- *The IATAN card.* This, as I mentioned earlier is the "Gold Card" of travel agent ID. It looks a bit like a credit card, with raised lettering for your name, and it has your picture on it. To get the IATAN card, you must be an employee of, or outside agent with, an IATAN-appointed agency. You must also meet certain qualifications that will be discussed below. It, too, costs money — $25 per card at present, plus an additional fee paid by the agency.

- *Personal contacts.* If the person with whom you are dealing at the supplier's office knows you personally and knows you to be a travel agent — better yet, a travel agent who has produced business for the supplier — that is the best form of identification you can have.

Other things being equal, these forms of identification are important and useful in reverse order. In other words, personal contacts are best, followed by the IATAN card, followed by your agency's ID, followed by a business card, which anyone can have printed up.

Sooner or later you will probably have one or more of these forms of identification. All of them will open the door to discounts for you — in some situations, some of the time. My guess is that, after the dust settles from the current flap over the abuse of industry privileges, more forms of ID will be accepted by more suppliers in more circumstances.

Finally, if these discounts are important to you, and you feel you are entitled to them, then show your ID and ask for them. The worst they can say is "no." (If they do, ask why. You'll gather some valuable information for future reference.) The second worst thing they can say is "You can get the discount if you do such-and-such" — which may not be too hard to do. Sometimes, of course, you will get the discount with no problem at all.

Qualifying for travel benefits — really

In spite of all the brouhaha over "phony" IDs and "instant agents," there are lots of people out there who have a perfectly legitimate claim to industry discounts and other privileges. You can be one of them; it's not as difficult as you may be thinking. It does involve work selling travel; but that, after all, is what you want to do anyway.

There are two main ways part-timers and full-time outside agents can join the "pros" when it comes to travel benefits — get the IATAN card and establish direct relationships with suppliers.

Getting the IATAN card

First, let's talk about qualifying for the IATAN card. Assuming you are not going to con, cajole, or pay a travel agency owner to put you up for the card (none of which I recommend), you will have to earn your way to the card. You do that by selling travel to your friends and family, even to yourself.

To get in the running for an IATAN card you must first be affiliated with an IATAN-endorsed agency. For a while, IATAN will also let ARC-only agencies get the card. But in a move obviously designed to coerce these agencies to join IATAN, they will be closing that window of opportunity on December 31, 1994. This means, among other things, that if you have decided to sell just cruises and are working through a cruise-only agency — or have decided to start your own cruise-only agency — you can pretty much forget about the IATAN card. Also, if your agency hasn't joined IATAN and doesn't want to, you may be out of luck. That, of course, could change depending on how much heat is generated though agent organizations like ASTA and ARTA. Stay tuned.

The agency owner must also be willing to accommodate you as far as getting the card is concerned. This shouldn't be a problem, but you never know. It may be something you'll want to discuss when you are shopping around for an agency to hook up with. My experience has been that an agency will back up your application for the card as long as you meet the requirements. You should also expect the agency to pass through to you any costs associated with applying for the card.

IATAN's rules and regulations about who can qualify for the card went through some evolution in the months following the Connie Chung report. As this was being written, the rules looked like this:

Employees of a travel agency as well as independent contractors qualify for the card when they have annual incomes (salary and/or commissions) totaling the federal hourly minimum wage, times 20 hours, times

48 weeks a year. Currently, that comes out to $4,080 per year. (Should the federal minimum wage change, you'll be able to calculate the new earnings' threshold.) That means that if you are splitting your commission 50/50 with the agency you will have to sell approximately $81,600 worth of travel product during the course of a year (assuming a uniform 10% commission rate). If you get 60% of the commission, the figure would be $68,000. At 70%, it would be $58,285. All of which serves to underline the importance of shopping for and negotiating the best split possible.

Note that all of the income you earn through the agency should be included, not just your commissions on the air fares that IATAN is concerned about. Of course, if you receive some commission payments directly from the supplier, the agency will not have those payments on its records and, presumably, won't be willing to count that money towards your quest for the card.

Does this mean you have to wait a year to rack up the necessary earnings figures? Not necessarily. Some agencies will sponsor you based on your weekly performance. For example, one agency says, "We will list someone on the IATAN list when they are booking at the rate of at least $1,200 per week." This suggests that you could get your IATAN card based on several weeks or months of high volume. You may want to check with your agency to see what their policy is on this score. It could be that you could qualify for the card quickly if you have a burst of activity and an accommodating agency.

What happens when your earnings dip below the threshold *after* you get your card is one of those gray areas. Since IATAN expects to collect an annual $13.50 renewal fee for the card, you (or more likely, your agency) may be expected to "prove" your eligibility each year. Or this may prove to be a pro forma process, with existing cardholders being given the benefit of the doubt as to their continued eligibility. Only time will tell.

Finally, it should be noted that while IATAN and the IATAN card may be "king of the hill" for now when it comes to travel agent ID, that could change. There is some pressure growing in the industry to increase the number of ways in which bona fide travel agents can prove that they are just that. The day may come when, just as restaurants accept Visa, Mastercard or American Express, suppliers will accept a number of different IDs as proof that you are, indeed, a travel agent.

Direct relationships with suppliers

As I mentioned earlier, when someone in a position of authority with a travel industry supplier (airline, hotel chain, or cruise line) knows that you are a travel agent worthy of a discount or other special treatment, that is the best form of ID you can have. Many outside reps have just this kind of relationship with one or more suppliers.

I know of an outside rep in the Midwest who specializes in travel to Europe. She does most of her ticketing through an IATAN-endorsed agency but she tickets directly with one of Europe's major airlines. They have issued her a "pseudo ARC number" and send tickets directly to her just as if she were a "regular" travel agency. Why? It probably has to do with the fact that she sends over $350,000 worth of business their way every year. You can also best believe that when she needs to go to Europe, this airline will accommodate her, perhaps even let her fly for free.

This example serves to illustrate the central point of these relationships — it's very definitely a quid pro quo arrangement: You bring us the business, we'll reward you. It also depends on volume, although you don't always have to be up into six figures before you see a payback. Fairly typical is the story I heard from one fledgling outside rep who booked his first big group with a Caribbean tour operator. The tour operator called him up a short time later and offered him an all-expenses-paid fam trip to the destination — which he promptly took, of course.

Sometimes, you don't even have to demonstrate that you can produce sales for the supplier. Every agent who showed up at an educational seminar hosted by one car rental company left with an ID card that entitled him or her to agent rates at all the company's locations.

Most of these relationships develop naturally, almost by accident, but there's no reason you can't help the process along. If you are specializing in a destination — and most of these direct relationships develop out of agent specialties — get to know your sales rep. As mentioned earlier, most suppliers of any size have salespeople who service the travel agent community. Your agency may be able to tell you who they are, or you can simply call the supplier to find out. Bear in mind that the sales reps' territories are determined by where the agency is located, not where you are. So if you live in Illinois but book through an agency in Florida, your supplier sales reps will all be based down there. That doesn't mean you can't deal with them; it just means that it will be a long-distance relationship. When and if you develop a direct relationship, such as the one the Midwest agent has with the European airlines, you will deal with the supplier's local rep.

There are any number of ways to get to know your suppliers' sales reps:

- **Industry association meetings.** I have met many sales reps just by attending local chapter meetings of OSSN.
- **Sponsored seminars.** Many suppliers organize touring "dog and pony shows" to tout their wares and increase agent proficiency in selling them. When they come to your local area they are usually put on by local sales reps.
- **Trade shows.** Again, if the trade show is held near you, at least some of the people staffing the booths will be local sales reps.
- **Calling them up.** Like everyone else with a nine-to-five job, supplier sales reps have to justify their existence. If you call them up for general information or to help you solve a booking problem, that counts as a sales call for them. So don't hesitate to call. That's what they're there for.

Of course, most supplier sales reps are doing an awful lot more than just trying to look busy. They are genuinely committed to growing the sales of their employers' products, and you are a very good vehicle through which to do that. If you show any likelihood of bringing in more business, they will do whatever they can to help you out. In the process, they will get to know you; you will get to know them; and notice will be taken of your success. It also goes without saying that these folks are savvy enough to separate the productive agents from the rest of the herd. If you're just wasting their time, they'll catch on real quick.

Finally, and at the risk of seeming repetitious, the benefits of the kind of direct relationships we're talking about here are yet another good reason to specialize in your travel business.

Benefits for the beginner

There are a lot of you who won't get an IATAN card, or who won't develop the kind of direct relationship that comes with selling $350,000 worth of airline tickets. You probably don't want to devote that much time to your sideline. That doesn't mean you are out of the running for free travel or other nifty benefits of the part-time travel agent lifestyle. You just have to be realistic about what you can and cannot expect. It may help to redefine your terms a bit, as we shall see.

Here, then, is a summary of some things I've already mentioned and some new thoughts on how to maximize the benefits of your newfound, part-time career:

- *Tour conductor passes.* All in all, the fastest way to free travel for the beginner is the tour conductor pass, or teacher-counselor slot if you're doing educational tours. This was discussed in some depth in *Chapter 1: Becoming a Tour Organizer*.

- *Seminar benefits.* There are all sorts of nifty things you can pick up (besides knowledge and skills) by attending the many seminars that are sponsored by suppliers for agents. These can range from an agent ID card, qualifying you to special treatment by that supplier, to dollars-off or upgrade coupons, to free trips given as door prizes. Add that to the bedrock educational benefits, and there is no reason you shouldn't try to attend as many of these enlightening and entertaining events as possible.

- *"Fam/seminars."* Some seminars, such as those sponsored aboard cruise ships by the Outside Sales Support Network (OSSN), are, in effect, discounted travel packages. The discounts are not always spectacular, but they offer good value compared to "the going rate." Then, too, don't overlook the value of the seminars themselves.

- *Discounts for the asking.* Even with just a business card you may find some benefits available to you. It never hurts to ask.

- *Earn "free" travel with commissions.* One way to view the commissions you earn as a part-time travel agent is as earned credits towards a "free" vacation at the end of the year. I think this is a very healthy mindset for the beginning part-time travel agent. In other words, you may not earn the $4,080 that would qualify you for the IATAN card, but the $3,000 you do earn (money you wouldn't have had otherwise) will pay for a very nice holiday, especially if you can get a free airline ticket using the next suggestion.

- **Earn frequent flyer miles on other people's travel.** This is a very risky strategy. Every time I use it myself, I wonder if this is the time I'm going to get soaked. It works like this: When a customer books, say, an airline ticket, you accept payment from them by cash or check. You then put the cost of the ticket on your own credit card when you book with your agency. Of course, it has to be a credit card that gives you a mile of frequent flyer credit for every dollar you charge; mine is linked to American's AAdvantage program. The client's check covers the cost of the tickets you charged and everything's hunky-dory — unless, of course, the check bounces. That's why the strategy is risky and I can't say I wholeheartedly recommend it for everyone. I certainly don't use it with *every* client. Still, I figure I qualify for one free ticket each year that I might not otherwise have been eligible for without using this ploy.

  The clients, of course, still get their frequent flyer credits for the mileage they fly. So you're not taking anything away from them or doing anything underhanded. The risk is strictly to your pocketbook.

- **Tax-deductible travel.** In the last chapter, I mentioned any number of ways in which your part-time travel agenting will affect your tax situation. Much of the travel that used to be "just a vacation" will take on a whole new importance as an integral part of your new business. As such, you are entitled to tax deductions to the maximum extent allowed by law. Check with your accountant, or other competent professional, to make sure you are getting every deduction to which you are legally entitled.

Much of the relatively little that gets written about the quick and easy way of becoming a travel agent focuses on "free" travel and "fabulous" benefits. Far too much, in my opinion. In the final analysis, there's no such thing as a free lunch. All the benefits that accrue to folks in the travel industry are *earned*. And that goes for the full-time "old pros" just as much as it does for the part-time beginners. Keep that in mind and you will have a profitable and enjoyable experience as a part-time travel agent.

Fam trips

"Fam trip" is short for "familiarization trip." As the name implies, these are trips sponsored by suppliers to familiarize travel agents with the destinations they serve and the tour products they offer. Fam trips take a number of different forms. Most typical is the fam trip sponsored by a tour operator. A fam of this type will include air fare, transfers, hotels, a number of sightseeing excursions, and at least some meals. There are also "land-only" fams that require the travel agent to pay his or her own way to the destination. These are generally offered by tourist boards and "receptive tour operators," that is, tour operators and wholesalers who handle arrangements at the destination but don't get involved in getting the tourists there. Finally, there are special deals offered by individual hotels, resorts, attractions, or even carriers (air or rail). These are sometimes called fams but probably belong in a different category.

Very few fam trips are free. Your actual out-of-pocket costs will depend on which type of fam trip you take. While the industry itself does not tend to discriminate among types of fam trips, I group them into three general categories:

- *Run-of-the-mill fams.* Pricewise, these fam trips aren't big bargains. You could get approximately the same trip for yourself or a client for about the same amount and be free of fam obligations (see below). These fams are almost always announced in the trade press. They, too, require some proof of agent status, although I suspect that the standards of proof are not as high in this category as in others. Tour operators, after all, are under a certain obligation to prove to airlines, hotel owners, and motorcoach companies at their foreign destinations that they are actively promoting their wares. Sending a busload of travel agents through every once in a while is one way of doing that. You may even find yourself being solicited by tour operators when it starts to look like a fam trip won't attract enough warm bodies to make it economically viable.

- *Good-deal fams.* This is a term of my own devising which I use to distinguish fam trips that are offered at truly steep discounts. For example, I was once offered a seven-day fam trip to Chile that included air, transfers, hotels, visits to three cities, sightseeing, and almost all meals for $449. The airfare alone at the time was running about $1,000 round-trip. My rule of thumb is that, once the per-day cost for an air-inclusive fam drops below $100, the deal becomes attractive. Fam trips in this category may or may not be announced in the trade press. The best way to learn about them is to be in contact with tour operators and booking your clients with them (that's how I happened to be offered the Chile fam). Fams in this category are generally open to serious agents only. If you approach the tour operator, expect to be asked to justify your status as a bona fide travel agent.

- *By invitation only.* These are the cream of the crop and the most likely to be completely free. These fam trips are seldom, if ever, announced in the trade press. To get on one of them, the tour operator must ask you, not the other way around. Being asked is usually a function of the amount of business you have brought the supplier. It is possible, however, that a supplier might approach a largish agency with an offer of a fam trip in the hopes that the agency would begin sending business its way. But in that case, it would be unlikely that you, as an outside rep, would be given the slot.

Getting on a fam

As noted, the best way to get on a fam is to be asked. Failing that, you will have to approach the organizer of the fam and ask to be included. Most likely, you will learn about fams through the trade press. *Travel Weekly* and *Jax Fax* have regular features listing upcoming fams. There are also a number of specialized publications claiming to offer up-to-the-minute inside information on fams. They are listed in the *Resource Section*. Another possible source of information about fams is the agency through which you do your bookings. They may receive faxes or other notices from operators and suppliers about trips in the offing.

The best way to start the applications process is to phone the operator sponsoring the fam trip and ask for details to be faxed to you. I have yet to encounter one that couldn't or wouldn't fax complete information. In most cases, an application form will be included with the information they send.

Here is the information sent out by one tour operator offering a nine-day fam trip to Greece. It will give you a pretty fair idea of the shape most fam trips take. I have omitted the names of the companies involved but have left the spelling and syntax intact.

GREECE 'FAM' TRIP ITINERARY

Day 1: USA/Greece. Depart on [Airline]'s 747 non-stop flight to Athens, Greece.

Day 2: Athens/Greece. Upon your arrival in Athens, you will be met by [Tour Company] who will assist you through customs. You will then be transferred to your hotel in Athens. Rest of the day at leisure to explore this fascinating city on your own.

In the evening, you will have an orientation of the hotel and Greece. We will discuss the many optional tours that will be available to you.

Day 3: Athens. After breakfast, you will begin your sightseeing tour of Athens. You will see the House of Parliament, Theater of Dionysius, Philopappus Hill, The Acropolis, The Parthenon, The Erectheum, The Theseum, The Forum, Tomb of the Unknown Soldier and much more.

Cape Sounion. In the afternoon, you will begin your excursion to Cape Sounion. Drive along the beaches of Vouliagemni and Glyfada along the Saronic Gulf to some of the world's most breathtaking scenery you will ever see. Arrive at Cape Sounion and be greeted by the spectacular Temple of Poseidon. Cape Sounion is well noted for its magnificent sunsets.

Day 4: Ancient Delphi. After breakfast, you will begin your excursion to Delphi. Drive through Thebes, Levadia and Arachova on your way to Delphi. Arrive in Delphi, "Home of the Oracles." Visit the Sanctuary of Apollo, The Athenian Treasury and the Castalia Spring. This was where the future was fortold by the Oracles. See Ossios Lucas and of course the famed statue, "The Chareoteer," You will have lunch in Delphi and return to your hotel in the evening.

Day 5: One Day Three Island Tour. After breakfast, you will be transferred to Pallo Phallron to board your cruise ship. Set sail for HYDRA and visit the 300 year old Church of the Dormilion Virgin. Here you will have time for strolling, shopping and swimming. In the early afternoon, sail for POROS passing through the narrow straight separating the Peloponnesian Coast from the island of AEGINA. Poros, an island with its quaint houses and simple people. A typical island where life is enjoyed to its fullest. After Porus, we sail for the magical island of AEGINA, Upon arrival, you may swim or an optional tour to the Acropolis of ATHENA APHAIA. Return to Athens in the evening and transfer to your hotel.

Day 6: Day At Leisure. Day at leisure. After breakfast, you may take a cable car to the top of Mt. Lycabellus for a fascinating view of Athens and The Acropolis. Take a stroll thru The Flea Market in Plaka, the oldest section of Athens. Enjoy a swim along the Saronic Gulf or relax in the popular cafes in Constitution Square. You may also take an optional tour to Argolis (Corinth, Mycenae, & Epidaurius), visit Mt. Parnis, the Corinth Canal and much more.

Day 7: Athens. After breakfast, you will have the morning and afternoon free. You may also take an optional tour of "Athens By Night" which will be as follows: In the evening, you will be transferred to Plaka for your evening on the town. You will be driven through Athens on your way to Pnyx Hill, followed by a short drive to the open air Dora Stratou Theatre. You will then be driven to Plaka, where in Athens, the night life never stops. Here you will visit one of the many typical "Greek Tavernas" where you will encounter a variety of Greek Performers doing traditional Greek dances with its famous belly dancing show. You will enjoy a typical Greek Dinner with a bottle of Greek wine. The bus will be taking passengers back to the hotel at midnight. Passengers wishing to stay longer will return to the hotel on their own. Plaka and its many Greek night clubs are open till 5 am.

Day 8: Athens. After breakfast, you will have this final day to relax or to take another optional tour if you wish, such as Argolis (Corinth, Epidaurius and Olympia). Also time to catch up on last minute shopping or relaxing.

Day 9: Athens/Airport. After breakfast, you will be transferred to Athens airport for your return flight to the United States.

By the way, this fam was available for $595. And, speaking of costs, there are three cost categories that you will need to become familiar with:

- *Agent fare.* This is the price you pay.
- *Single supplement.* All fams are priced on a per person, double occupancy basis. That means that you will be paired with another agent with whom you will share a hotel room or cruise ship cabin. If you prefer to travel solo, you will have to pay the single supplement. This can range anywhere from a few hundred dollars ($250 on a base fare of $1,095 on one fam) to the complete agent price (in other words, a single room costs twice as much as sharing).

  Of course, there's always the possibility that you'll be the odd person out and get a single room at no extra charge. Also, tour operators will try to accommodate cases of obvious incompatibility (your roommate smokes cigars, for example).
- *Spouse/companion fare.* Tour operators try to make fam trips more attractive for agents by allowing them to bring along a spouse or "significant other." Their fare is typically a few hundred dollars more than the agent fare. For example, one 8-day fam trip to Bulgaria charged agents $690 and spouses just $130 more. A 12-day fam to China sported an agent fare of $1,390 and a companion fare of $1,590.

Once you have decided on a fam you want to take, the next step is to apply. Typically, the application form that accompanied the information you had faxed to you will ask you for two things: a down payment and proof of agent status. The down payment is usually in the $200 to $250 range. Payment in full is required anywhere from 15 to 45 days prior to departure. Most fams have cancellation policies similar to those of regular tours.

Travel Industry Benefits

As to proving your status as an agent, the operators will phrase it in a number of ways. "A copy of IATAN/ARC list," "a current IATAN list," and "business card and IATAN list" are all common phrases. In addition, some fam operators may require that the request come through your agency rather than directly from you. They may also specify payment via an "agency check" that corresponds to the agency whose IATAN number is being recorded as the agency of record.

In other words, you may (in fact, probably will) have your own separate business identity with a business checking account and checks with your business name on them. But if you seek to qualify for the fam trip as an outside agent for Acme Travel and give Acme's IATAN number, the fam operator may want the check to come from Acme rather than from you. Many fam operators, however, are quite familiar with the way outside agents operate; so this will not always be a problem.

In addition to satisfying the policies and procedures of the tour operator, there's your agency to consider. You will have to sound out your agency about their policy on fam trips. My agency, for example, doesn't want to hear anything about fam trips from outside reps who don't qualify for the IATAN list. Even if you meet the most stringent requirements, your agency may be less than overjoyed at the extra work involved.

My philosophy is that, if you honestly feel you are qualified to take a fam trip, you should apply anyway. Act as if your acceptance on the fam is a sure thing and see what happens. For one thing, what the fam operator says it wants on its application form and what it will actually accept may be two different things. You have no way of knowing just how strict or loose their policies are or how desperate they may be to fill slots for the dates you requested. Remember, too, that you are sending a check with your application. A bird in the hand being worth two in the bush, the operator may simply cash your check and not ask any further questions. If they do ask for more information, you can respond appropriately.

If you are not on the IATAN list, or haven't *quite* qualified for it, or are in the process of applying for it, and the operator questions your eligibility, simply explain your situation and send along what you do have. That might include your business card, a photocopy of any ID card issued by your agency or just a letter on your letterhead stating that you are an outside sales representative for such and such an agency, with IATAN number such and such. You might want to explain why you want to take the trip and why you think it would be mutually beneficial if you did. You could even provide additional information about how much business your agency does, but that's probably overkill.

The point is this: Ask and you may or may not receive. Don't ask and you definitely won't receive.

Fam trips are hard work

One thing that is important for *any* travel agent to understand is that fam trips are business trips. They are not vacations. The tour operator wants to sell its wares, and it fully expects you to sit up and take notice. Many fam trips shuttle agents about on exhaustive — and exhausting — visits to several resort and hotel properties in a single location. At every turn you may be expected to sit through yet another "orientation" session, in which all the wonderful features of the hotel, cruise ship, resort, tourist region, or whatever are extolled at great length and in great detail.

Far from being a penance, this is precisely what you have come on the fam trip for. At least this is what you *should* have come on the fam trip for. From your perspective, the fam trip offers you an unparalleled opportunity to gain the product knowledge and the first-hand experience to be able to go home and sell the dickens out of the location you just visited. (Indeed, some tour operators have deals whereby they will rebate a portion of the cost of the fam trip based on how much business you send their way during the next year.)

Go on the fam trip prepared to learn and to ask a lot of questions. Gather as much descriptive literature as possible. Gather in-depth information about the places you visit.

- How many rooms in the hotel? What configurations?
- How are rooms priced? Are suites worth the extra charge?
- Which amenities are provided? Which are extra?
- Is the hotel in a quiet part of town or is it noisy? Are interior rooms a better bet?
- How does it stack up against an American hotel? Some people find the "foreign-ness" of a hotel part of its charm. Others want a hotel room just like the ones at Holiday Inn back home.
- What are the hours of popular tourist attractions? How often do the guided city tours run?
- What restaurants can you wholeheartedly recommend to clients?

Remember that in addition to gathering all the basic information about the places you go on the fam trip, you are serving as the eyes and ears of your customers — both the ones you already have and ones you might have in the future. View every attraction, every hotel, every town and resort through the eyes of these customers.

- What's the clientele like? Young and hip or middle-aged and stuffy? Middle-aged and hip or young and stuffy?
- Are there lots of stairs to climb or is everything easily accessible?
- Is the water good for snorkeling? Or better for sailing?
- Does the hotel have a disco? Is that good or bad?
- How will your clients take to the guides and tour escorts?
- What about crime? What tips should you pass along?
- Is there golf nearby? Tennis? Opera? Theater?
- Is Paris *really* for lovers?

Personally, I find this kind of touring to be a lot of fun. I find I enjoy myself just as much being shown around a five-star French hotel by the owner as I do wandering through a chateau or museum. It also provides a unique opportunity to share ideas and experiences with other travel agents. If, on the other hand, you think that a fam trip offers a great opportunity to get away from the regular grind and relax for a week, you're in for a rude awakening. You'll also, not incidentally, make some life-long enemies along the way — not just the tour operators, but your fellow agents as well, most of whom take their profession very seriously indeed.

So if you prefer to investigate destinations in a less pressured, less hectic fashion, avoid fam trips. Do it on your own time and pay the going rate. With your newfound skills and knowledge, you should be able to find some good deals and negotiate some attractive rates — and you'll probably be able to write it off as well.

The Fine Art Of Selling Travel

Chapter Thirteen:
The Art & Science Of Selling

Monty Python, the British comedy group, once featured a skit about an enterprising encyclopedia salesman with a novel approach. He rang the doorbell of a suburban home and announced that he was a burglar. The suspicious housewife on the other side was unconvinced; she was certain he must be an encyclopedia salesman. No, he assured her, he was simply a burglar who wanted to come in, ransack her home, and steal a few things. Finally, convinced that he wasn't an encyclopedia salesman, she let him in — whereupon he launched into a high-pressure sales pitch for "a really fine set of encyclopedias."

The joke, of course, is that people would rather have their homes burglarized than talk to a salesperson. Like all humor, it has some basis in fact. There is an old-fashioned, down-the-street kind of selling that's not too far removed from the tactics employed by that encyclopedia salesman. Here are some of the distinguishing characteristics of what we might call the "traditional" approach:

- The product being sold is treated as a commodity — that is, it is seen as basically the same as other products in its category.
- The concerns of every customer are seen as being identical.
- Or worse — the concerns of the customer are *ignored*. Selling someone something they don't want or need is considered the height of success. (Have you ever heard the phrase, "He could sell iceboxes to Eskimos?")
- Every sales presentation involves a "pitch." The same words are used over and over, for every customer.
- Salespeople use flattery, glad-handing, and insincerity — and call it "building rapport."
- Salespeople like to describe themselves as "closers," who won't take "no" for an answer.
- The salesperson's goal is to intimidate the prospect and gain a position of superiority.
- The mastery of hard-sell techniques is considered a sign of an excellent salesperson.

High-pressure, in-your-face salespeople still exist. You may have some idea that if you ever get involved in selling you will have to become one of those people. Nothing could be further from the truth. Selling is actually a very normal human activity — something we all do at one time or another whether we know it or not.

Avoiding the "screaming me-me's"

I'm assuming you don't see yourself as a high-pressure salesperson. I'm also assuming you have no desire to transform yourself into one. My guess is that you are simply someone who loves to travel and sees an opportunity to benefit both yourself and others by sharing your enthusiasm for seeing more of the world. But even if you have the best intentions in the world, it's easy to fall into a trap I call the screaming me-me's.

Many people who start a new business venture — like becoming a part-time travel agent — are so excited about what they are doing that they can talk of little else.

> *"**I'm** a travel agent! **I** can get you airline tickets anytime you want them! **I** can book you on a cruise! **I** know all about these great tours! **I've** found a great island resort!"*

Or they get so excited about the prospect of making a sale (and getting that commission) that they focus only on the end result.

> *"Let **me** book it for you. You're going to go to a travel agent anyway, why not let **me** do it. Come on, what's the difference, give **me** your business. You'll love this cruise! Take it! Do it for **me!**"*

They make the mistake of thinking only of themselves and forget that it is their customer who makes all things possible. Now there's nothing wrong with getting excited about what you can do and how you can benefit in this new lifestyle. But when you're in front of a potential customer, you will do well to remember: They don't care what's in it for me!

The only thing your customers care about — think about it — is what's in it for them. That doesn't mean that people are selfish beasts. Far from it. It's just human nature that when your customers are considering a decision that may eventually involve parting with some of their hard-earned cash, their charitable feelings toward you are not foremost in their minds.

As long as the question foremost in your mind is "What's in it for me?" you will never reach your full potential as a provider of travel services.

Take a "you" turn

I have had the opportunity to study dozens of high-performing salespeople in a range of industries. If there is one characteristic that links them together it is their single-minded focus on the customer — on what the customer's situation is, on what the customer needs, on what the customer thinks, on what the customer will feel comfortable with.

These are people who have stopped thinking "me, me, me" and started living "you, you, you." By committing themselves completely to servicing the best interests of their customers they have, at the same time, reached truly amazing sales goals. You can do the same.

So, if you are single-mindedly pursuing your own selfish interests, slow down and take a "you" turn. The next time you are with a potential customer — and in this business that means virtually anyone you happen to meet — get to know him or her.

> *"Tell me about yourself. What do **you** like to do when **you're** on vacation? Where do **you** like to go? What are **your** favorite sports?"*

Getting to know your customers means not just asking questions but really *listening* to the answers — and then remembering them. Take the time to truly get to know your customers before you even begin to think about "selling" them something. You may decide that you have nothing to offer them!

As a general rule, the more questions you can ask and the longer you can go without pulling out a brochure or suggesting that they book a flight with you, the more successful you will be. That may seem odd now, but it will make more and more sense as you read the chapters that follow. For the moment, remember that the secret to success in sales is to concentrate as fully as possible on your customer. If you do, your needs will have a wonderful way of taking care of themselves.

The importance of goals

Selling is a goal-directed activity. Even though much is made of the importance of "motivation" in sales, you must have a clear idea of where you are going and what you want to accomplish to be a success at selling. All the motivation in the world will do you no good unless it is directed toward a goal. Goals on the other hand, can get you going even in the absence of obvious motivation. Goals, in fact, are great motivators.

To be effective in producing sales results your goals must be:

- **Challenging.** Set yourself a goal that will give you a feeling of genuine pride when it is achieved. Something you can do with one hand tied behind your back is an excuse, not a goal.
- **Realistic.** On the other hand, don't set yourself up for crushing disappointment. Be wary of any tendency you may have to set your goals too high as a subconscious way of proving to yourself that something is impossible.

- *Measurable.* If you can't put a precise number to your goal, how will you be able to tell you've reached it?
- *Time-limited.* Good goals come with a deadline. A real deadline. A *drop dead*line. If you give yourself forever to accomplish your goals, that's exactly how long you'll take.

Start now to set yourself some challenging, realistic, measurable, time-limited goals. Set them for the near term (what you'll accomplish tomorrow), short term (what you'll accomplish this week or month), and long term (what you'll accomplish this year). Keep them simple and remember that they can always be adjusted, up or down. Indeed, that's the whole point. Goals should constantly be adjusted so that you are always doing just a little bit more than you did last time.

Start with activity-based goals such as:

- Contacting ten suppliers this week.
- Introducing yourself as a travel agent to 50 friends and acquaintances this month.
- Subscribing to two trade papers before Wednesday.
- Going to the library to research the industry reference books listed in the *Resource Section*.

Then, move on to results-oriented, or sales-based goals such as:

- Making three bookings this week.
- Making 20 bookings this month.
- Earning $500 in commissions in one week within the next two months.

At first, setting your goals will take a bit of guesswork. As you gain experience, you should become quite adept at setting reachable goals that will keep you energized and excited about your new lifestyle.

What Part II is all about

In *Part II*, I will attempt to provide you with a comprehensive look at the specific selling skills, tools, and techniques that can help make your part-time travel agent business a success. I'll begin at the beginning ("Where do I find my first customer?"). Then I'll proceed through the selling process in more or less logical steps, from your first contact with a customer, through making the sale, to following-up. These steps are discussed in the following chapters:

- *Chapter 14: Prospecting.* Before you can sell anything, you have to find someone to sell it to. In this chapter, I'll tell you how to find your best prospects.

- *Chapter 15: Spreading The News About Your Travel Business.* To be successful, you need an on-going program for identifying and approaching people who are likely to become your customers. In this chapter, I'll provide you with a rich menu of possibilities for reaching your customers.

- **Chapter 16: Qualifying.** Once you have a prospect in front of you, you have to learn enough about that person to know what he or she is likely to buy and for how much. In this chapter, I'll show you how to get to know your customers and create a treasure trove of information that will pay you dividends for years to come.

- **Chapter 17: Presenting The Wonder Of Travel.** Travel products don't often sell themselves. They depend on you to present them in such a way that your customers are eager to buy. In this chapter, I'll show you how to present your wares professionally and persuasively, whether it's to one person across the table or to dozens of people at a time.

- **Chapter 18: Handling Your Customers' Concerns.** People are naturally hesitant about making a buying decision. They have questions and need reassurance. In this chapter, I'll show you how to turn all sorts of objections, stalls, and excuses into closed sales.

- **Chapter 19: Closing The Sale & Follow-Up.** Selling travel is a repeat business. In this chapter, I'll show you how to turn customers into customers-for-life.

Some general considerations

Some of you may want to keep your part-time travel agent business quite small, while others may be looking for a regular part-time business that occupies 20 or more hours a week. Still others will want to go whole hog and make this new lifestyle their sole source of income. In order to make this part of the book useful to the greatest number of people, I have had to make some decisions about how best to present the material. I have chosen to make the discussion in *Part II* more, rather than less, inclusive — that is, I am operating on the assumption that you will want to maximize your opportunities in this lifestyle.

Therefore, although the basic principles will apply to everyone, some of the specific strategies and tactics I'll discuss will be inappropriate for some of you. It shouldn't be too difficult to pick and choose the suggestions that are best for you or to modify strategies to better suit your needs. Here are some things to bear in mind:

- **The scope of your business.** Your business need only be as big as you want it to be. Don't feel you have to try *everything* I suggest. Do just as much as you feel comfortable doing.

- **Computers.** I have already suggested the wisdom of acquiring a computer if you don't already have one. In *Part*

II, I make the assumption that you have a computer. If you don't, there are pencil and paper alternatives to everything I suggest.

- **Cost.** Even simple expenditures can add up. For example, if you have a customer base of a thousand people and you send each of them a postcard four times a year, you will spend $760 on postage alone, at 1994 rates. You can — and should — promote your business only to the extent you feel it will pay off in additional business. Don't be afraid to start off small and then add elements as your confidence increases and your income grows.

Chapter Fourteen: Prospecting

If you are new to sales, the word "prospecting" probably conjures up images of a grizzled old desert rat and his heavily laden pack burro heading into the Sangre de Christo Mountains in search of the mother lode. Salespeople, of course, know that prospecting refers to the constant and never-ending process of finding new people who might become customers. When you start your part-time travel agent business, prospecting will be your top priority. "Nothing happens 'til somebody sells something," the old saying goes, and to sell something you have to have someone to sell it to.

Where do these prospects come from? The beauty of the travel business is that virtually everybody travels at least every once in a while. That means that your potential supply of prospects is limited only by your get-up-and-go and, to a certain extent, by geography. But as you will quickly discover, just because everyone travels doesn't mean that all of them will become your customers. All prospects are not created equal. That is one reason why many sales professionals like to distinguish between "suspects" and "prospects."

Using this approach, you would look at your "territory" (the geographical area in which you want to practice your travel agent trade) and first eliminate all those who don't travel for one reason or other. Everyone else is a suspect.

Start with your friends

If you're new to the travel business and new to selling, the best place to begin looking for customers is among your friends and family. In fact, even if you aren't new to travel or selling, it's still a pretty good place to look! Why? For a lot of reasons. You know who your friends are. You know where they are and how to get in touch with them. You already know something about them, their likes and dislikes. You have a built in reason to contact them and start a conversation. They like you and are probably going to be willing to give you the benefit of the doubt. Some of your friends actually love you and will be willing to put up with your bumbling first efforts and give you their business anyway. And, finally, there are probably enough of them to keep you busy for a while and give you the practice you need to hone your selling skills.

The first thing you will want to do as an organized salesperson is to make a list of prospects. You need to start keeping track of people in a somewhat more organized, professional manner than you may be used to. Start with your address book. Transfer every name in it to your prospect list. Rather than use a piece of scrap paper or a yellow pad, put your prospects on 3x5-inch index cards or in a computer database. This way you will be able to sort them into categories and move them around later.

For now, keep it simple. Name, address and phone number will do. Your task is simply to get some idea of how many people *might* become your customers. Later I'll show you how to build up a veritable gold mine of information about your prospects and customers.

Once you've transcribed your address book, you have identified your hard-core prospects — family, friends, and associates. These are people important enough, for one reason or other, for you to record their phone numbers. If you're thinking, "Gee, I don't have that many friends," wait. You're not finished.

Now go through the list again. For each person, ask yourself, "Whom do I know through this person?" For example, when you look at Aunt Matilda's card you may realize that you also know her three grown children, your cousins. Add them to the list. Or when you look at the Smiths' card, you may remember the Joneses whom you meet every time the Smiths have a barbecue. Add them to the list. Your doctor and dentist have receptionists and nurses. Add them to the list.

You know more people than you think

By now you should have assured yourself that you do have a lot of friends. It's just that not all of them made it into your address book. The fact is that we all know many more people than we think we do.

Let's take this prospect-finding game a step further. Consider for a moment your acquaintances and associates. These are people you either come into contact with on a regular basis or with whom you have some point of connection. A good way to identify these people is to mentally walk through your daily activities. Where do you shop? You probably have a nodding acquaintance with many store owners and their employees. Whom do you meet at church or synagogue? Whom do you see everyday when you drop your kids at the day-care center? Who works in your office with you? Who are you in contact with in other parts of your company? Keep asking yourself questions like this until you think you've identified everyone you could possibly know. Then ask some more. If you and your spouse are thinking of working together in this lifestyle, make it a game; see which one can come up with the longest list of prospects.

You've probably got a pretty long list by now. And everyone on it is someone who, if they don't know your name, at least recognizes you on sight. In other words, these are all people who are not going to put up automatic defenses when you speak with them. But don't stop now. There are a lot of other people whom you may not know by name, and who may not recognize your face but whom you can contact easily and talk to openly after just a short introduction. These people might include:

- High school or college classmates.
- Fellow club members.
- Fellow parishioners or congregants.
- Neighbors — folks on your block or in your apartment building.
- Parents of your children's classmates.
- PTA members.

These are people to whom you can say, for example, "Hi, we're in the same congregation," and expect a friendly smile in return. The goal, at the beginning, is to make life as easy as possible by concentrating on people you will have no trouble approaching and talking with about your services as a travel consultant.

Other sources of prospects

To begin with, I would recommend sticking to folks you know and can approach easily — especially if you are new to the selling game. It's just easier that way. Eventually, however, you will probably have to or want to widen your search for prospects to include people you've never met before and who will not be immediately predisposed to chat with you about your travel business. Here are some ideas about how to find these people. Along the way, you may get some ideas you'll want to put to use sooner rather than later.

- *Everyone you meet.* From now on, every one you meet for the first time is a potential customer!
- *Advertising.* Not the glossy, four-color, full-page ads you see in magazines but the simple ways of getting your name out there — by circulating your business card, for example.
- *Engagement announcements in the local newspaper* are a great source of prime prospects for you. These are people who will be taking honeymoons, remember. That means cruises, resorts, foreign destinations — big commissions!
- *Small town papers* sometimes feature chit-chat about who's doing what, including where folks have been on vacation. These columns not only give you the names of potential prospects but valuable information about the kind of travel that appeals to them.
- *Lists of associations, clubs, organizations.* These are excellent prospects for group travel opportunities.
- *Referrals.* Everyone who becomes a customer knows people they think might benefit from your services. But there's a catch: They won't tell you who they are unless you ask them!

How many prospects do I need?

Good question. The answer is, "It depends. . ." Among other things, it depends on how many customers you want, which travel products you choose to sell, how much money you want to make, how much time you want to spend making it, and how good you are at converting prospects into customers. Assuming you're just getting started, you won't have the answers to all those questions; in fact, you won't have them for quite some time. But now is the perfect time to lay the groundwork for answering them.

Begin by asking a question you probably can answer now: "How much money do I want to make?" The answer might be $5,000 a year, $15,000 a year, $50,000 a year or a free trip with an educational tour. Don't be afraid to dream a bit here. No one's going to hold you to it later.

The next step is to figure out what each sale is worth to you. In the case of the educational tour operator who gives you a free trip for every person you sign up, the answer is simple — each sale is worth one-sixth of a free trip. In other situations, it's more complicated, especially if you sell a variety of travel products. For example, today you may book your friend Susie on a flight to Kansas City and back and earn a commission of $15. Tomorrow you may book a retired doctor and his wife on a luxury cruise and earn a commission of $1,000. Over the course of time — three months, six months, a year — you can add up all your commissions, divide the sum by the number of bookings you made, and arrive at an average. This is what each sale is worth to you. Obviously, the number will fluctuate. Some months are better for sales than others. But after your first year in this lifestyle, you should have a pretty useful figure to work with. You should expect to make at least this much per sale in your second year, hopefully more because your skills will be improving.

Starting today, I strongly urge you to keep meticulous records of your sales activities — how many people you talk to each day, what you talk about, and the results. If you do that, it's a relatively simple matter to work backwards from each sale and determine what you had to do to make it. To keep things simple, let's assume that you have decided to specialize in selling cruises. Over time, you may learn that to make one booking you have to give a formal presentation to three couples. To find those three couples you have to invite 16 people to a "Let's Take A Cruise" party at your house. To get those 16, you may have to invite 32 people you have determined are good prospects. And to locate those 32 prospects you might have to chat with 100 different contacts. In other words, you'll need 100 prospects to make one sale!

If you want to make $30,000 a year and each cruise booking brings you $500, then you have the answer to the question "How many prospects do I need?" — 6,000!

If that scares you, good! In my experience, more salespeople fail because of poor prospecting habits than from any other reason. We can see why by looking at the two major metaphors that salespeople use to illustrate the importance of constant prospecting — the "funnel" and the "pipeline."

You can look at the sales process as a funnel, but a funnel with holes in it. You put in lots of prospects at the top but only some come out the bottom as customers. The others slip through the holes: They decide not to take a vacation this year; they get a better price somewhere else; whatever. This image brings home the importance of having many more prospects than you need customers.

The pipeline metaphor illustrates the importance of planning. If you put oil in one end of a pipeline, you'll get oil out the other end. But it takes time to get from one end to the other. To the salesperson, this means that if you want sales next month, you have to start filling the pipeline *this* month. If you are happy to rely just on "walk-in" business, fine. But if you want a steady income, and you know that selling a tour or a cruise takes two months from first contact to the actual booking, then you have to get busy in April to guarantee you'll have bookings in June.

There is another lesson to be learned from the made-up example we just used. If you don't like your numbers you can change them! For example . . .

- If you can't imagine digging up 6,000 prospects in the course of a year, maybe you've set your earnings goal too high. Adjust it downwards until things look a bit more doable.
- If, on the other hand, you *must* have that $30,000, you now have a pretty good idea of what kind of activity level you will have to maintain to reach that goal. That knowledge in itself can be a powerful motivator.
- In the example given, you had to present to three couples to make one sale. What if you could increase your presentations skills so you'd be making two sales for every three couples? Or what if you could throw better parties and wind up presenting to four of five couples instead of three? The more you improve your basic selling skills the fewer prospects you will need to make each sale.
- You can also examine your sales strategy and see if making changes might improve things. It might be that "Let's Take A Cruise" parties are not the best way for you to sell in your market.
- Finally, you might want to change your "product mix" and sell travel products other than cruises, or sell different types of cruises that might provide a higher commission or have greater appeal to your clientele.

What's a customer worth?

Before you start thinking that the cards are stacked against you, consider the value of repeat business. Yes, it may be difficult to get the 60 couples you need to make $30,000 selling cruises. But the good news is that people who take cruises love the experience and do it again. According to one source, 85% of people who take one cruise take another. That means that of the 60 couples you book this year, some will cruise again

next year. Another percentage will cruise the following year, and still another group will cruise in year four.

Only experience will tell you exactly how many. But let's say 20% of them will cruise again in year two. That's 12 couples or $6,000 in commissions. You're already well on your way to your $30,000 a year goal before the year has even started! That means that to earn the same amount of money, you will need to add fewer prospects to your pipeline.

The travel business is a repeat business and, dollar for dollar, it repeats more frequently than most. There are people who will buy a $15,000 car once every five years who will spend $4,000 a year on leisure travel. Many people take a cruise twice a year. Some couples seek out a different foreign destination each year. Others prefer all-inclusive resort vacations in the States. Many business people make at least one business trip each month, requiring a plane ticket, a hotel, and a rental car.

The patterns will differ with each individual, but once someone becomes a customer you will have a fairly good idea of how much business to expect from them each year. As time progresses, you will start to get an idea of how long the average person remains a customer. (Remember, people die, relocate, stop traveling for one reason or another, or shift their allegiance to another provider.) Now you know the lifetime value of a customer.

The cyclical nature of prospecting

Prospecting does not just mean identifying potential customers, it means contacting them. Moreover, you need to contact them again and again, until calling on you for all their travel needs becomes a reflex. Marketing guru, Dr. Jeffrey Lant, preaches what he calls the Rule of Seven. By that he means that a prospect must be contacted seven separate times before they make a buying decision.

While you may not have to contact everyone on your prospect list seven times before making a sale, you will be well advised to be persistent. Otherwise, you'll lose easy bookings that might otherwise have been yours.

Here's a typical example: You run into your old acquaintances Bill and Marilyn in June. You tell them all about your new lifestyle as a travel agent. They're impressed. Naturally, you tell them that whenever they need to make any travel plans they should call you. They assure you they will. The next time you hear from Bill and Marilyn is when you get their Christmas card. "We're off on a cruise to the Bahamas in early January!" they announce.

Cruise? What cruise? Why didn't you hear about it? What happened? Well, it's probably a safe bet that the reason Bill and Marilyn failed to call you wasn't because they don't like you. If that were the case, they wouldn't send you a Christmas card would they? There is a very slight possibility that they didn't book through you because they think you're an incompetent ninny who would have just screwed up their booking. It's more probable that they didn't book with you because they already have a travel agent with whom they are perfectly satisfied and to whom they are very loyal. But my guess is that the *real* reason they didn't book with you is that they forgot you were now a travel agent! Had you contacted them in the early Fall, reminding them that the cruise season was fast approaching, you might have snagged the booking you lost.

One of the challenges of your new lifestyle as a part-time travel agent, then, is going to be finding ways to keep reminding folks that you exist and that you are ready, willing, and able to assist them with their travel needs. This is true not just of people who have never booked with you but with people who have as well. In fact, your present customers are your best source of new business.

Managing your prospecting activity

A professional prospecting program, because of its cyclical nature, requires careful management. You'll need to set up a prospect-management system to ensure that you make calls, mail out letters, and follow up every lead in a timely manner. The best way to do that is with your computer.

There is a growing supply of so-called "contact management" programs, a subset of database programs, which are specifically designed to help salespeople keep in touch with their prospects and customers. Essentially, these database programs are Rolodexes on steroids. In addition to basic information about your clients and prospects, these programs allow you to record key demographic information, follow-up dates, client history, and other data.

Once you've entered basic data about a client, you can go back into the program and pull up the information in a variety of useful ways. Most programs will automatically alert you when a follow-up call is due. Or you can search the database for things like people who are interested in cruising or people who have wedding anniversaries coming up.

In *Chapter 16: Qualifying* I will introduce you to a *Client Profile Form* that you can use to record a wide variety of information about your customers. It, too, can be computerized, although you will probably have to put it into a separate database program: Contact management programs usually aren't designed to hold as much information as you will want to have on each of your customers.

If you are not computerized, you can create a simple prospecting system using index cards and a box with 12 dividers, one for each month of the year. Most well-stocked business stationery stores will carry index file-boxes and dividers with the months printed on them. The cards carry the names, addresses, and phone numbers of your prospects. As you contact them, you record the date and results on the card and then place it two, three, or four months back in the pack, where it will serve as a reminder that the time has come to contact this person again. In a computer program, this task is automated.

Getting started

At this stage of the game, you shouldn't worry too much about how many prospects you'll need. This is no time to get caught in the "paralysis of analysis." The important thing is to get out there and start.

If you followed the suggestions earlier in this chapter, you probably have a list of 50 people, maybe 100 or more. You certainly don't need more than that to get started spreading the word about your new venture. For some ideas on how to do that, turn to the next chapter, *Spreading The News About Your Travel Business.*

Chapter Fifteen:
Spreading The News About Your Travel Business

Once you have allied yourself with an agency as an outside sales representative, the time has come to begin letting the world know that your new venture exists and that it is there to make their travel dreams come true. You have entered the world of advertising and marketing.

Advertising and marketing have a variety of definitions, depending on who's using the terms and in what context, so the definitions I give here may vary from the ones you have in your college marketing textbook. Don't worry about it. They will serve for our purposes in this chapter.

Advertising is the process of announcing the availability of a product or service to the greatest possible number of people. By definition, it is virtually impossible to predict who will see or respond to your advertising. Advertising your travel business may provide you with great customers, but it may just as easily provide you with poor customers (buyers of cheap travel, for example) or time wasting tire-kickers.

Marketing is the process of defining very precisely to whom you will sell and then devising strategies to reach that well-defined market. Marketing weeds out the unwanted customers and the tire-kickers. Unlike advertising, it never reaches out to them in the first place.

My recommendation is that you do very little advertising and a great deal of marketing. The two most obvious forms of advertising for a small retail business are the Yellow Pages and space ads taken out in local publications. Both of them are poor bets for the part-time travel agent. A business phone (a prerequisite for a listing in the Yellow Pages) is a useless expense for the beginner. Space ads are an equally frivolous expenditure. Advertising gains power only through repetition, and that's neither cost-effective nor, for most people, feasible at the outset of an outside travel-agent career.

Another form of advertising with which most of us are familiar is the flyer, one-page ads, cheaply printed on colored paper and posted on bulletin boards, slipped under windshield wipers, slid under doors, handed out on street corners, and so forth. While advertising of this sort might seem to make sense if, for example, you are trying to sell a large block of cabins on a cruise, it can better be used in the context of a direct marketing campaign, which I will describe a little later.

Your business card

The one form of advertising which I wholeheartedly recommend is the broad distribution of your business card. As I mentioned in *Part I*, the best place to splurge when setting up your travel business is in the design and printing of your business card. A well-designed card should sell you, sell your business, and sell the excitement of travel.

Make it one of your goals to get your business card in the hands of as many people as possible. From now on everyone you meet should receive one. In fact, give them several with the suggestion that they pass the extras along to friends, family, and business associates. Many people put a business card in every piece of mail they send out, including their monthly bills. Don't be stingy with your card. If you meet someone four times in a month, they should get your card each time.

Giving business cards is also a great way of gathering information because it puts you in a position to ask for one in return.

Observation: Many stores, especially office supply stores, have bulletin boards on which folks can post their business cards. While it can't hurt, my experience is that these boards produce next to no response, and the people who do respond are going to be more likely to want to sell you something than to travel.

Defining your market

We spoke a bit about defining your travel business in *Chapter 4: Setting Up Your Travel Business*. Much of that discussion was about making marketing decisions; you might find it helpful to review that section from time to time. As you gain more experience in the travel game, you will bring new insights to the discussion.

There are two major ways to define your market:

- *Geographically.* While it's possible to have clients scattered across the country, you will probably want to restrict yourself to a manageable geographic territory, centered on where you work or live. The key idea is accessibility to your clients. That might mean concentrating on the five-mile radius around your home and the five-block radius around your current place of employment.
- *Demographically.* Within your geographic market are any number of demographic markets, although several will probably predominate. Demographics is the science of grouping people by factors such as age, income, interests, ethnicity, and so forth. If your community is composed primarily of older people, your travel business will (or should) take on a different emphasis than if your community is primarily young marrieds. One of the most important de-

mographic indicators for the purposes of your travel business is income. The bigger the paycheck, the greater the disposable income. Professionals with incomes of $50,000 or more do a lot more cruising than laborers with incomes of $18,000.

The geography and demographics of your area are givens; there's nothing you can do to change them. In a very real sense, they determine what is possible and not possible in your area. You can examine the demographics of your geographic market and make shrewd decisions as to which travel products will sell best and how best to market them. Or you can decide to run your travel business according to what appeals to you and pretty much ignore the message of the market. There's nothing wrong with that. But be aware that, unless there just happens to be a match between the market in your area and what you want to do, your business will be less prosperous than if you had consciously tailored it to the needs and wants of your neighbors.

The other major way to define your market and guide your marketing efforts is through segmentation. By this I mean that you will subdivide (or "segment") your larger geographic and demographic markets by concentrating on selling such things as cruises, a specific destination or destinations, or travel built around a special interest such as golf, scuba diving, hiking, archeology, art, music — the list is virtually endless.

If you go this route, your own personal likes and dislikes will undoubtedly take precedence over the numbers (that is, what the demographics tell you). Again, there's nothing wrong with that. Just be aware that if you want to sell cruises in an area that doesn't generate much cruise business, you'll have to dig a lot harder.

Learning about your market

Very few people who get involved in the travel business rationally analyze their market. So don't feel too bad if you don't either. However, if you'd like to learn a bit more about your market — who lives there, how old they are, how much money they make, and what they like to do — help is at hand. There are two great sources, both eager to help you.

- **The library.** The reference librarian at the main branch of your public library is the best person to contact first. Tell the librarian you'd like to study the demographics of the area; get to know more about the income and spending habits of the various neighborhoods; and so forth. Don't be shy about explaining why you want this information. The librarian may just know where to find a market study on the travel habits of your neighbors. He or she will certainly be more than happy to point you in the right direction. (And don't forget: The librarian is a prospect!) If you live near a business school, the library there might also have good, targeted information about the local area.

■ ***The Chamber of Commerce.*** This alliance of local businesses is dedicated to growing the local economy. They will be happy to share information with you.

Doing this kind of research will not necessarily make you rich. But it can be fun in itself and it might offer some valuable insights that you can put to work for yourself.

Your first sales calls

As I mentioned earlier, from now on, everyone you meet is a prospect and should receive your business card. That means that every meeting you have with your friends and family in the coming weeks is going to be (or should be) a sales call. That doesn't mean it has to be anything less than informal, friendly, and fun. Indeed, the best sales calls are always just that. All it means is that these meetings will have a purpose.

Generally speaking, these initial meetings or encounters are not about selling travel. Of course, you never know a person's situation until you ask, so you may walk away from some of these meetings with a booking. However, that is not your main purpose. The primary purpose of these first attempts is to sell the idea of establishing a client/consultant relationship with you.

You want to let this person know . . .
■ You are a travel agent.
■ Using your services makes sense.
■ You are serious about making the person to whom you are talking a customer.

Like any good sales call, these first meetings with your prospective customer should have a structure and an agenda. Here's a time-tested strategy I urge you to use:

Step One: Introduce yourself and your company

If you're approaching a friend or family member (as I strongly suggest you do at first), they will obviously know who you are. What they will not know is that you have a new identity as a travel agent. Don't be shy. Share the good news.

> *"I just wanted you to know that I've become
> a travel agent with the Very Big Travel
> Agency. I'm going to be specializing in tours
> and cruises, but I'll be able to book any kind
> of travel you might need.
> Here's my card."*

That tells people what you are doing and with whom. It also gives them a rough idea of the scope of your business. Or you might say:

"Hey, I've just started a new job as a travel agent. I'll be working as an outside rep, which means I can come to you, or you can call me anytime you need some travel advice. Here's my card."

Step Two: Generate interest with a benefit statement

It's possible that your friend will reply, "Say, that's great! Susie and I want to take a cruise in November. Can you handle that for us?" There's a greater chance he won't. So, your next challenge is to create some interest in speaking with you a bit more about what you can do for them.

You do that with something known in the sales business as a "benefit statement," any interest-generating statement that offers a potential pay-off (or benefit) to the listener. There are two kinds of benefits, general and specific:

- **General benefits.** A general benefit is one that would be of interest to most people who travel.

  "Very Big is part of the Mega Chain of agencies; so we can offer you terrific savings on most tours and cruises."

  "To celebrate my new venture, I'm offering free rides to the airport to everyone who books with me this month."

  "Since I'm an outside rep, I'll be hand delivering all tickets and travel documents directly to my customers."

- **Specific benefits.** If you know something about your prospect, you can often tailor your benefit statement to their specific needs, desires, or interests.

  "Very Big has super rates on all Circus Line Cruises. That's your favorite cruise line, right?"

  "So the next time you want to visit your daughter, you can call me and I'll bring the tickets right to you."

Step Three: Deal with skepticism, if necessary

I would be less than honest with you if I didn't point out that not everyone will fall all over themselves to turn over their travel business to you. Some people will be skeptical. Some people will reflexively put you off because they sense this is a sales call. These are what are known as stalls by professional salespeople. They do not necessarily mean that the person speaking will never do business with you (although that may eventually prove to be the case). Most often they are simply subconscious requests for more information.

Be prepared to respond when you hear a stall. Here are some examples of stalls and responses:

*"**Come on. You? A travel agent?**"*
"That's right. I've been accepted as an outside rep by a $20-million a year agency. I'm in training now."

*"**Don't you need a license or something to do that?**"*
"Absolutely. And my agency is fully accredited and a member of ASTA, the travel agency association."

*"**You don't know anything about being a travel agent.**"*
"Actually, I've learned quite a bit. And I have someone in the travel business [that's yours truly!] showing me the ropes."

*"**I already have a travel agent.**"*

This last statement may be a stall, but it is an important one. I will deal with the best way to respond a little later, in *Chapter 18: Handling Your Customers' Concerns.*

Step Four: Ask for a commitment

No sales call is worthy of the name unless the salesperson "asks for the business." That doesn't always mean asking for a booking or getting the prospect to hand over his or her hard-earned cash. But is does mean asking the prospect to make some decision or commitment that will carry the selling relationship forward.

To do that, you have to ask a question that will be answered "yes" or "no." What you ask for will depend on the situation, how well you know the person, and so forth. However, here are some things you might ask. In fact, you might ask several of them.

"Do you have any immediate travel plans? Can I handle those for you?"

"Will you be willing to book all your travel through me?"

"Would you be willing to fill out this travel survey so I can learn a little more about your travel preferences?"

"I'd like to start a Client Profile Form on you so when you make your first booking, I'll have all the information I need at hand. It'll take just a few minutes. What do you say?"

All of these are what are known as "closes" by professional salespeople. Any question you ask of a prospect that requires a "yes" or "no" answer is a close. To distinguish them from the final close, which asks for the check, these earlier questions are sometimes referred to as "trial closes." You are simply asking the prospect if they are ready and willing to move to the next phase of the selling relationship.

The trial close you use here must be a genuine request for a genuine decision. Offhand remarks like . . .

*"So if you ever need anything, you know
where to find me, right?"*

or

*"So, I'd be happy if you'd think of me next
time you need something, okay?"*

. . . are just that — offhand remarks. People can say "Sure" or "Will do" without feeling they have made any commitment, because they haven't.

If you didn't hear a stall before, you might hear one when you make this trial close. In fact you may hear a bona fide concern or objection. Those will be discussed in *Chapter 18*. For now, let's assume that you will get a positive response. If you do, you will have a very tentative commitment or a very firm commitment, or something in between. Unless the prospect has immediate travel needs, you will need to contact them again on a regular basis until the commitment you got today evolves into an actual booking.

You don't have to rush through the four steps I've just outlined. In fact, going through them one after the other is not a good idea at all. Instead, they should occur naturally, in the course of conversation. For example, you might spend some time chatting about why you decided to get involved in selling travel between steps one and two or between steps two and three. Don't rush it. Let it happen naturally.

After each of these initial contacts, run a little review. Ask yourself:

- Did I use all four steps?
- What stalls did I hear? How well did I answer them? Could I have responded better?
- What benefit statements seem to work best for me?
- What should I do differently the next time?

The point is not to beat yourself up about your failures. Instead, you want to identify what went right so you can do it again, and what went wrong so you can change it next time.

You also may have noticed that many of the trial close questions above solicited more information from the prospect, either about their future travel plans or about their travel interests in general. This is the beginning of a process known as "qualifying." We will talk about that, along with travel surveys and the *Client Profile Form*, in the next chapter.

Direct mail marketing

Direct marketing is marketing aimed directly to the specific person you wish to address. You can market directly by mail, by phone or fax, or through a computer network. When direct marketing is done through the mail it is called — surprise, surprise — direct mail.

Direct mail can be an excellent and efficient way of letting the people on your prospect list know that you are in business. It is not a substitute for face-to-face selling. Instead, the two complement and reinforce one another. When you send out a mailing to a large number of people, you should plan on following within a reasonable period of time with a sales call, either in person (preferable) or on the phone (okay, but not great).

Contacting friends

A direct mail piece (to use the jargon of the direct mail industry) to your friends and family should be informal and chatty, just like a personal note — which it is. You can type it on the letterhead of your new business (if you've become an outside rep for a distant agency), or use the letterhead of the local agency you've hooked up with (if that's okay with them), or just use your personal note paper. In any event keep it simple.

"Dear Jim,

Hi! Just wanted to share the great news. I'm now affiliated with the Very Big Travel Agency as an outside sales representative. Very Big covers the entire world, but offers some extra special good rates on Caribbean resorts and cruises.

I'm enclosing several of my new business cards. I hope you will pass them along.

I'm also enclosing a brochure for the January 18th sailing of the *Fantasia II*. Thought you and Sharon would love the chance to get away.

But whatever your travel needs, feel free to call me,
day or night. Providing personal service is what my
new business is all about.

All the best,"

This is just a sample. Feel free to use it or adapt it. The Outside Sales Support Network (OSSN) provides its members with sample direct mail letters you might want to consider. Or just use your imagination to create a letter that sounds like you.

Including a brochure with your initial letter is not necessary. But it does provide a built-in reason for contacting the prospect to follow up: "What did you think of that cruise? Not interested? Well, what are your vacation plans this year?"

Here are some other thoughts on contacting your friends:

- You can automate the process on your computer. If you do, be sure to craft a letter that will apply to everyone on your list. Or be clever and design it so you can use the computer's "mail merge" functions to personalize each letter.
- Form letters and computer-generated stick-on labels are efficient and time-savers but they lack that personal touch. In fact, if you send friends a letter on your new stationery using a stick-on label on the envelope, they may just toss it in the trash, without ever knowing it came from you.
- By handwriting or typing each letter and hand-addressing the envelope, you increase the odds the letter will be opened, read, and well-received. This, of course, is more time-consuming; but that may actually be a benefit. . .
- If you stagger your letter-writing (as opposed to sending out hundreds of letters at once) you make the job of follow-up easier. For example, send out 20 letters this week and make 20 follow-up calls in two weeks. That way, you get into a routine: 20 letters and 20 follow-up calls each week.

Contacting people you don't know

One advantage of direct mail is that it is an excellent way of getting in touch with people you don't know, but who should know you. For example, the doctors, dentists, lawyers, and other professionals who have offices near you are excellent prospects. What's more they are easily located just by picking up the Yellow Pages or walking around the neighborhood.

A letter to them should be a little more formal than one to your friends.

"Dear Dr. Harris,

I am writing to announce a new and innovative
travel service that can save you time and money.

As a Travel Consultant with the Very Big Travel Agency, I specialize in bringing the services of a full-time travel agency to you. Now you can make all your travel arrangements in the comfort of your own home or office and have tickets and travel documents hand delivered to you.

I am enclosing several business cards for you to keep and share with your friends and colleagues. I am also including a brochure for a Winter sailing of the M/S Colossal, for which I can provide very attractive rates.

Whether you are traveling to a professional conference or looking for that very special getaway, please call me for all your travel needs at [phone number].

Sincerely,

P.T. Agent
Travel Consultant

P.S. I am adding your name to my list of preferred clients. This will assure that you are alerted to special travel opportunities and always receive the best fares on all your travel."

A letter like this will benefit immensely from a nicely printed letterhead, either your own travel-business letterhead or that of the agency with which you are affiliated. If you are using the agency's letterhead, be sure to include your own business address and phone number and let recipients know that they should contact you directly. If a prospect contacts the agency, there will probably be no way of knowing that your letter was the cause; so the client will become the agency's and not yours.

As with the letters to your friends, a letter like this requires follow-up. If you are mailing only to professionals in your immediate area, a personal visit will not only be advisable but easy to handle. The sooner your prospects can put a face to your business the better.

When making this type of call on a doctor or dentist (it's called a "cold call" in the selling business), try to drop in at off hours — before the office opens or just as it's closing. The doctor is more likely to have time to chat with you then. Your time together is likely to be short, however, so plan on using the four initial-call steps outlined above —and plan on using them quickly.

Take care with your appearance during these calls. A good rule of thumb is to dress as your prospects do. In this case, that would mean dressing like a highly paid professional person, in business attire. A good-looking briefcase to carry brochures and other materials is also a nice touch.

It is appropriate to ask a series of closing and qualifying questions during this follow-up call. Some of the things you might want to know include:

- When is the doctor planning her next vacation?
- How does she book travel now? Would it be more convenient to have someone come to her office?
- Is she planning on attending a conference in the near future? Where? When? Can you do the booking?
- Would her patients enjoy some travel brochures left in the waiting area (with your business card attached, of course)?

Don't worry about seeming pushy. Doctors and other professionals receive regular visits from salespeople selling them things. If anything, a call from a travel agent will seem a novelty and perhaps a welcome change of pace, especially if you bring along brochures or even travel videos that you can lend. Remember, too, that you will likely encounter other potential prospects during these calls — the doctor's staff and patients. Be prepared to give something to them as well. In return, attempt to get their names and addresses for your mailing list. At a minimum, you should record the names of the doctor's secretary and assistants. You can always reach these staff people at the office.

Summary

You have begun what will (or should) become a regular practice — contacting people in your customer base to let them know you are a professional travel consultant and to ask for their business. In this way, you turn your liability as an outside agent into an advantage. Here's what I mean:

The traditional agency, with its storefront offices and windows filled with alluring travel posters, may seem to have the advantage over you. But it is hampered by its lack of mobility. Like the venus fly trap, it depends on people wandering close enough to be attracted by its displays and coming through the door. Very few traditional agencies do the kind of active selling I just discussed. For many of them, meeting the high costs of their overhead and their investment in newspaper advertising leaves precious little money for any kind of direct marketing campaign.

You, on the other hand, are free to roam your territory — meeting people, getting to know them, inquiring about their travel plans and interests, and offering your services on a regular basis. The simple act of "keeping in touch" will be a major ingredient in your success.

But keeping in touch is only part of it. Ultimate success demands that you:

- Ask for the business, and

- Ask for the business, and
- Ask for the business, and
- Ask for the business, and
- Ask for the business, and
- Ask for the business, and
- ASK FOR THE BUSINESS!!

Chapter Sixteen: Qualifying

When you believe in the products and services you provide, you want to see to it that the greatest possible number of people become aware of and experience the many benefits they offer. You may even begin to think that *everyone* should do business with you.

Enthusiasm is a tremendous asset, but not when it blinds us to certain bedrock business realities. The truth is that no travel agent can possibly do business with every person in his or her potential market. Instead, every travel agent in a given geographic market will do business with a certain percentage of the potential market. That's what's called *market share*, and it's a natural (and healthy) byproduct of competition.

It follows that of all the people who *could* become your clients, only a certain percentage will. Some won't become your clients because you will choose not to work with them. They might include:

- People who shop you to death, calling back several times a day to ask for a lower fare or have you research yet another itinerary.
- People's whose needs outstrip your capabilities, such as business clients who need the services of someone extremely well-versed in the area of corporate meetings.
- People who need short-haul airline tickets, when you have decided to specialize in cruises, tours, or a specific foreign destination.

In some cases you will simply discourage business from certain people (politely, I would hope). In other cases, you will refer people to a more appropriate source, sometimes, perhaps, for a commission (as when you refer a corporate account).

Then there are those people who will choose not to work with you. They will make that decision for any number of reasons:

- They may have an ongoing relationship with a travel agent they like and see no need to switch.

- They may not trust you, as an outside rep, to provide the same level of service they have come to expect from "traditional" travel agencies.
- Some people don't like mixing business with friendship, on the theory that if something were to go amiss with their travel arrangements, the friendship would be jeopardized.
- They book all their own travel. Always have, always will.

Those of you with sales experience may look on this list as a list of objections and not as a list of reasons not to do business with you. True enough. But for now let's acknowledge that not all objections can be overcome. There will be some people who won't become clients.

Between these two extremes there are a great many people who will become your customers. Some will become better, more frequent customers than others. Your challenge, as a salesperson, is to separate the wheat from the chaff — to eliminate the people who won't or shouldn't be your customers, concentrate on those who will or should, and identify the real winners in that group. This is the process that's known as qualifying. It is something that begins when you start compiling the list of prospects we discussed in *Chapter 14: Prospecting* and continues throughout your business life.

What is qualifying?

Qualifying is the logical, structured process of getting to know more and more about your potential customers and your current clients. It is not something you do once; you are constantly qualifying — or should be. The major stages of qualifying are:

- ***Pre-qualifying.*** Sometimes you can pre-qualify suspects before you make contact with them. Presumably, you did that as you drew up your list of prospects by eliminating people you felt were very poor candidates and making sure to include those who travel frequently.
- ***Qualifying.*** When sales professionals speak of "qualifying," they are most often referring to this phase of the process. In this stage of qualification you make contact with the prospect to determine whether or not the person should remain on your client list. You can determine that by asking a handful of questions. Just how much specific information you will need to know will vary from situation to situation and from client to client. Note that qualifying is not entirely selfish on your part. You will be saving the prospect's time as well as your own by eliminating those who aren't real prospects from your list of potential customers.
- ***Qualifying the situation.*** Just because it proves worth your while to talk to a prospect does not mean that you will succeed in making a sale every time you approach them about a particular travel opportunity — or even every time they ap-

proach you, expressing a desire to take a trip. That is why, for each individual sale, you must take your qualifying a step further. You must know the prospect's specific needs to provide appropriate travel solutions.

Exploring and analyzing needs is sometimes called "qualifying the situation." This process is what I was referring to under the heading "Gathering information" in the chapters on booking various types of travel products. (*Chapters 6 through 10* in *Part I*.)

- **Long-range qualifying.** Qualifying is an on-going process and is crucial to the success of your long-term relationship with customers. In a very real sense, you can never know too much about your clients. That is what the *Client Profile Form*, at the end of this chapter, is all about. This type of long-range qualifying will enable you to compete effectively against larger, traditional agencies. Too many people in the travel business make the mistake of taking current accounts for granted. Always be on the lookout for changes in your clients' situations that might create new travel needs for them and opportunities for you. It never hurts to review your basic information about your current customers every six months. If you have established a good working relationship, you should have no problem in getting your clients' help in expanding and updating your records.

Why qualify?

The simple answer is: To save time — your own and your customers'. In the early stages of your part-time travel agent career, you will want to know who, out of the several hundred people who may be on your prospect list, are most likely to deal with you, so that you can concentrate your efforts on them. When you are dealing one-on-one with potential customers, you will want to know enough about their needs and wants to select the right products for them. That way, to use a small example, you will not research and present a resort property without tennis courts to a tennis player. Later on, when your client list has grown large, the qualifying you have done and recorded on your *Client Profile Forms* will let you quickly select those people who are the most likely to be interested in a special cruise or in staying at that all-inclusive resort that is running a special promotion for travel agents.

Remember that travel is a repeat business. Once the people on your "prospect" list become "customers," they are still "prospects" — prospects for a cruise next year, prospects for a European tour and a trip to their kid's college town the year after, and so on, and so on. Never stop qualifying.

Who's qualified?

You will no doubt take on all comers in the early days of your new lifestyle as a part-time travel agent. As you gain experience and learn the ropes of selling and booking, however, I would encourage you to look on your business as an exclusive club to which only those meeting certain qualifications can belong.

Qualifying is sort of like a scoring system. Those with higher scores go to the head of the class, as it were, and become your best prospects, your best customers. Many professional salespeople like to rank their prospects using an A-B-C method. "A" prospects (or customers) get the most attention, "B" prospects a little less, and so on. In adapting that system to selling travel, we must distinguish between those people you might sell travel to in the future and those people to whom you are speaking at this very moment. Once a customer is in front of you asking you for help on a trip to visit relatives, attend a conference, or whatever, they become your primary concern. On the other hand, when you look at the ever-growing list of people who have booked through you before or who have yet to book through you, you can begin sorting them into categories.

Early in your travel career, you will probably want to score people against some or all of the following qualifying criteria:

- ■ *An immediate travel need.* Someone who has an immediate need for travel advice and bookings is a far better prospect than someone who may take a trip sometime next year.
- ■ *A willingness to work with you.* Don't kid yourself. You will meet with some skepticism at first. That is why it is important to find those people who are willing to give you the benefit of the doubt and start booking through you. As you gain experience with these people, you will gain credibility with others.
- ■ *Straightforward travel needs.* In other words, don't try to land a corporate account, or send a group of 127 on a ten-country independent tour of Europe, your first week out. Armed with the information in *Chapters 5* through *10,* you should be able to handle most normal requests.

As your travel business grows, you will start to notice differences among your customers and prospects. You will start qualifying and categorizing them according to certain demographic and lifestyle criteria. For example:

- ■ *Frequency of travel.* Those who travel three times a year are better prospects than those who travel once a year.
- ■ *Budget.* This could mean the average amount of money spent per trip. If your records show that the Bakers spend an average of $5,000 each year to take a vacation, while the Coopers spend $2,000, it doesn't take much figuring to know which family is the better prospect for that $6,000 cruise.
  It could also mean annual income. Those who earn over $50,000 a year are better leisure travel prospects than those who earn less. Those making over $100,000 are better prospects still.

- *Price sensitivity.* People who will trust you to get them a good deal on a trip are better customers to have than those who nickel and dime you to death.
- *Life situation.* Many retired people are active travelers, while young families may be limited in their discretionary income. A small business owner may make travel decisions for several members of his or her staff in addition to her own leisure travel, while an executive at another company may be so snowed under that he never has time to get away.

These are only some of the ways in which you can qualify and rank your customers and prospects. You no doubt will develop your own criteria that apply to your market, the type of business you run, and the types of travel products you sell.

The importance of qualifying the situation

So far we have been discussing qualifying primarily as it relates to money — whether prospects will part with money, how frequently they will part with it, and how much they'll part with. That is only part of the qualifying picture. Once your prospects are sitting in front of you to make a buying decision about a trip, you must qualify the situation — gather the information you need to match this specific prospect with the right travel product or combination of products.

At this stage of the game, the actual sale may not be in doubt. Of course, the customer might decide that what you ultimately present is not suitable and take their business elsewhere. This is especially true with leisure travel, when the customer may be speaking to several different travel agencies and suppliers. (In fact, one of the most important things to qualify is whether the customer is talking to other travel agents or if they have made a decision to book through you.)

Let's assume, for the sake of discussion, that the sale is not in jeopardy, that the customer has made a firm decision to book their business trip or vacation through you. While qualifying the situation will not affect whether or not you make the sale, it is still vitally important to the future health of your travel business. Travel is a repeat business: Every sale you make has a direct impact on your ability to make more sales in the future.

Provide people with a wonderful travel experience and they will come back. Book them into an overpriced fleabag hotel on a filthy beach and they'll go elsewhere to book next year. That's why all the qualifying information you gather at this stage (aisle or window, smoking or non smoking, ocean view or garden view, tennis or golf, and on and on) is crucial to matching this prospect with the ideal travel product.

Not only will this produce a happy client who will bring you a continuing stream of business, but it will create a walking advertisement for your business. People have a way of talking about their good experiences (especially if you encourage them to do so). Also, the information you gather during this process can be recorded on the *Client Profile Form* for easy reference the next time you work with this customer. Your efficiency and in-depth knowledge of the person's preferences will be noticed. It will further establish your reputation as a professional and reliable travel agent with whom it is a pleasure to do business.

Asking qualifying questions

In certain situations — such as when you are trying to determine just which tour product is right for a particular customer — qualifying can involve gathering a great deal of information. That is why it is helpful to approach the task in an orderly and professional manner. These four steps should suffice in most situations:

1. ***Explain the need for qualifying.*** Avoid any possible misunderstanding by letting the customer know what you are doing and pointing out that there's something in it for them.

   *"What I'd like to do is get a general idea of
   the sort of things you like to do on vacation.
   That way, we'll be sure to pick just the right
   tour for you. Okay?"*

2. ***Keep the questions friendly and conversational.*** When you are gathering a lot of information, there's a danger that customers will feel like they are being interrogated. This is especially true if you are working with a form — the *Client Profile Form* included. There is a tendency to just go down the list, firing questions at the customer. A far better strategy is to start a wide-ranging, general conversation, noting down specific facts as they emerge naturally. You can always go back later and fill in the blanks. See the discussion of types of qualifying questions, below, for more tips.

3. ***Handle stalls as necessary.*** There is a slight possibility that the customer may be hesitant about providing certain information or may not understand the purpose of some questions. If so, you will have to reassure the customer and proceed. (See "Handling stalls," below.)

4. ***Thank the customer.*** Always acknowledge the customer's role in what is, in fact, a joint effort of investigation and information gathering.

   *"Thanks a lot. You've certainly made my job
   a lot easier. And I think I'll be able to come
   up with just the sort of vacation you're
   looking for."*

As a general strategy, you should begin with the big picture and then progressively narrow the focus until, finally, you are dealing with the small details. There are three basic types of questions you can ask to facilitate this process. Ask them in order, as you move from the very general to the very specific.

- **Open questions.** Although, technically, an open question is any question that cannot be answered "yes" or "no," some open questions are more productive than others. Try to begin with broad, open questions to get the customer talking freely about their situation and their needs. The broader and more general the better.

> *"Why don't you tell me a bit about what you have in mind."*

> *"If you could design the perfect vacation, what would it look like?"*

- **Reflective questions.** Reflective questions bounce off what the customer has already said. They are designed to encourage him or her to share more information. They can be very simple questions like "Uh-huh?" "And . . . ?" "What else?" or "Could you expand on that a bit?" Sometimes, you may want to be more specific.

> *"You said you like to 'learn a little about the culture' on a trip. How have you done that on previous vacations?"*

- **Closed questions.** These are the ones that can be answered "yes" or "no" or with a simple one- or two-word answer. For example:

> *"Do you prefer the window or the aisle?"*

> *"Smoking or non?"*

> *"Do you have any dietary restrictions?"*

> *"Would you like me to look into theater tickets in London?"*

Don't ask these kinds of nitty-gritty, closed questions until you have to. The answers to a lot of the questions on your list (or in the *Client Profile Form*) will emerge naturally in the course of the conversation. Be alert for them and record the information as the client provides it.

Handling stalls

Prospects or customers will sometimes show some resistance to answering qualifying questions. Usually this is a reflex reaction and not a serious objection. Sometimes it may signal that the conversation has gone on too long. Most of the time, you will not have a problem if you have remembered to give a reason for asking a series of qualifying questions. But if you hear a stall or a put-off, follow this simple process:

- **Respect the prospect's position.** Don't try to brush aside or belittle the resistance. Instead, say something like,

  "I can understand how you feel."

  "I certainly don't want to waste your time."

- **Give a good reason.** If you are a professional, you will have a number of excellent reasons why asking these questions is a benefit *to the prospect*. But first, ask a clarifying question.

  "Is there a problem?"

  "What's your concern?"

  The answer will allow you to select the *precise* reason, or to reassure the prospect.

- **Ask again.** As soon as you have provided a good reason for asking your qualifying questions or soothed a concern, *immediately* ask another question that will move the process forward.

If the customer still shows resistance, don't push it. You may be able to get the information at a later time. Remember that this prospect will become your customer for many years. You will be able to pick up more and more information over time.

Surveys and questionnaires

Asking questions in the course of a conversation is not the only way to gather qualifying information about your prospects and customers. Many travel agents use surveys and questionnaires of one form or another to speed up the qualifying process.

Surveys and questionnaires have the advantage of saving time for the agent and allowing a large number of prospects to be qualified at once. On the downside, they run the risk of alienating or offending some people. Handle them with care and carefully consider what information to request, how much information to request, and under what circumstances to request it.

Conducting a travel survey

One way to introduce yourself to your market and gather some valuable pre-qualifying information at the same time is with a Travel Survey. This is nothing more than a short form requesting a modest amount of information, which the prospect can fill out and return to you. One of the most effective forms a travel survey form can take is a self-addressed postcard (addressed to you, that is) that the prospect can simply fill out and drop in the mail.

You can include a Travel Survey card in every introductory letter you send out. Invite your prospects to fill it out and send it back, but don't be surprised if very few do. A return of 1% is considered excellent in the direct mail business. Since your initial list will be heavily front-loaded with the names of friends and family, you may get a higher return.

The very fact that someone has taken the time to fill out a survey form and return it is, itself, an important qualifier. The fact that this person has taken some action to further the selling relationship with you indicates that they are more likely to book with you than others who received the card and didn't return it.

In addition, the travel survey can be used to gather simple information that will start to tell you who your best prospects are. What information you solicit is up to you. There are no hard and fast rules. Gary Fee, Chairman of the Outside Sales Support Network (OSSN), in his *Official Outside Sales Travel Agent Manual*, which is included with membership in the organization, suggests asking the following questions:

- Are you planning a vacation this year?
- Does anyone in your family travel on business?
- Have you ever taken a cruise vacation?
- If so, where and on what ship?
- What was your favorite vacation spot?
- If you could choose to travel anywhere in the world, where would that be?
- Where did you go on your last vacation?
- Where did you stay?

These are all good questions. There are not too many of them and they are not threatening in any way (unlike a question such as "How much money do you spend each year on travel?"). They solicit information about upcoming needs ("Are you planning a vacation this year?"), possible regular bookings ("Does anyone in your family travel on business?"), and a lot of information about likes and dislikes. To an experienced agent, the answers to these questions will speak volumes. For example, a person who has never taken a cruise vacation is less likely to take one than someone who has. If the person cites a particular ship, the agent will have a good idea of their budget range and tastes. The same applies to questions about past vacations and hotels in which they've stayed.

To encourage prospects to reply, be sure to put a stamp on the reply card. Once your business grows large enough, you may want to consider applying at the Post Office for Business Reply Mail privileges. These are the preprinted post cards and envelopes you receive all the time from companies soliciting your business; In the place where the stamp usually goes, they say "No Postage Necessary If Mailed In The United States."

Using questionnaires

Another way to gather qualifying information is with a questionnaire. Handing a prospect a questionnaire usually implies that he or she has already committed to entering into a business discussion — that is, the customer is actively looking for your assistance in making a booking. A questionnaire allows you to gather accurate information quickly and the customer may actually prefer that to being asked a series of questions.

Your questionnaire might include some of the kinds of questions listed earlier, but it also might solicit other, drier information that will prove helpful now that the prospect has become a customer. That might include such intelligence as frequent flyer programs to which the prospect belongs; airline seating preferences; preferred hotels, rental car companies, and airlines; etc. In short, it would ask for the kinds of information you will want to record on your *Client Profile Form*.

I do not recommend that you simply hand a *Client Profile Form* to every prospect. There may be a few people (your best friend, your mother) who will sit still and fill one out just to oblige you. Most people will have better uses for their time. Besides, there is some information on the *Client Profile Form* that, while having no sinister purpose, might raise questions in your prospects' minds. Instead, you should create a separate questionnaire that excerpts key information from the Form. You may even want to create several questionnaires for different occasions (for example, one for tour booking, one for cruises). Of course, there's nothing to prevent you from creating a long questionnaire from the *Client Profile Form* and using it with people you think will have the patience to fill it out completely.

You can use a questionnaire the first time you sit down with a prospect to discuss a booking. You can use it as a sort of "assumptive close." In other words, you are acting on the assumption that the prospect fully intends to become a long-term client and won't hesitate to provide you with information about his likes, dislikes, and frequent flyer numbers. If he cooperates, terrific; you have just further qualified this prospect. If he hesitates, no problem. You simply explain that the questionnaire is optional and move along to other matters. Another occasion on which you might use a questionnaire is when you have developed an on-going client-consultant relationship. You could send a questionnaire in the mail along with a short letter or note, and a stamped, self-addressed return envelope.

"Dear Bill,

First of all, let me thank you for letting me handle your travel needs this past year. Serving you has been a privilege — and a great deal of fun as well.

I am sending you a short questionnaire that will help me serve you even better in the future. I hope you will be able to take a few minutes to fill it out and return it in the enclosed stamped, self-addressed envelope.

As a small way of saying "Thanks" I am also enclosing an upgrade coupon from Acme Rent-A-Car, which is valid until March 31st.

Best wishes,

PT Agent
Travel Consultant"

Whether you use questionnaires and, if so, in what circumstances, is entirely up to you.

The Client Profile Form

On the following pages you will find the *Client Profile Form*. It is intended to serve as the definitive repository of all the information you will collect about your customers over the years. The information it contains will help you sell to them more effectively and satisfy their needs more fully. It contains a great deal of information. Obviously, you will not gather it all at one time. Even if you could, doing so would probably not be advisable; you'd end up sounding like the Grand Inquisitor

You should feel free to use the Form just as it is. Or you can adapt it in any way you see fit, dropping or adding sections to better reflect the way you do business with your clients.

I also suggest that you either computerize the entire Form or the key portions of it. By entering this data in a database program you will be able to do some revealing analyses of your customers and their travel habits. You also will be able to identify the ideal prospects for special deals that come your way. A database program will allow you, for example, to produce a list of all those customers who play golf and have expressed an interest in visiting Hawaii. Many database programs can be designed to print out the information in any variety of ways, including a complete form that will look very much like a filled-in version of the one on the following pages.

Notes on the Client Profile Form

Most of the information on the Form is self-explanatory. However, some elements may require further explanation.

Will refer? Make a note of whether this client is willing to serve as a "proof source" for you. In other words, will they be willing to talk to other people about the benefits of a cruise or a tour or a resort they booked through you.

Birth Date. Get the precise day and year of birth. You can use this information, for example, to chat with a wife about taking her husband somewhere special for his 50th birthday.

Marriage Date. Again, get the day and year in which they were married. Recording this information (as opposed to just the anniversary date) lets you market a splurge trip for those very special 10th, 20th, and 25th anniversaries.

Honeymooned in. Most people are sentimental about the place they honeymooned. It can be an ideal destination for an anniversary trip.

Children. Don't overlook the possibility of "Sweet Sixteen" trips or other gift vacations that can be tied to a child's birthday.

Income. You'll probably be guessing here but the data can prove useful when marketing high-ticket cruises or tours.

Memberships. Tracking this kind of information will prove helpful when you start going after group business.

Personal Interests. Keeping track of this information will help you look good when describing potential destinations. It will also help you avoid miscalculations like recommending a resort with no golf course.

Travel History. Keeping this section up to date can be troublesome, but an in-depth knowledge of a client's past travel history is an excellent tool for predicting future travel destinations.

Business Travel. Note that some people must book their business travel through a company-approved agency.

Leisure Travel. Knowing your clients' leisure travel patterns will help you market to and service them better.

Airlines, etc. Keeping track of frequent flyer, frequent lodger, and other affinity programs will save you and the client time in subsequent bookings and aid you in selecting travel vendors.

Booking History. Taking the time to make a brief note here each time you book a client will tell you, in due course, who your best customers are. It will also give you a very accurate guage of their budgets for various types of travel.

Client Profile Form

Personal Data

Name: _____ Will refer? _____

Address (home): _____

(office): _____

Telephones: _____
            (home)   (office)   (fax)

Birth date:_____ Marriage Date:_____ Honeymooned in: _____

Spouse (age & DOB): _____

Children (ages & DOB): _____

_____

Profession: _____

Income: ❑ <$25K   ❑ $25-$35K ❑ $35-$50K ❑ $50-$100K ❑ >$100K

Memberships in professional organizations and clubs: _____

_____

_____

_____

Health considerations when traveling: _____

_____

Personal Interests

	Self	Spouse		Self	Spouse
Music/Dance	❑	❑	Hiking	❑	❑
Art	❑	❑	Golf	❑	❑
Antiques	❑	❑	Tennis	❑	❑
Theater	❑	❑	Skiing	❑	❑
Opera	❑	❑	Swimming	❑	❑
Museums	❑	❑	Snorkeling	❑	❑
History	❑	❑	Scuba diving	❑	❑
Archaeology	❑	❑	Surfing	❑	❑
Genealogy	❑	❑	Windsurfing	❑	❑
Religion	❑	❑	Rafting	❑	❑
Gourmet food	❑	❑	Sailing	❑	❑
Cooking	❑	❑	Cycling	❑	❑
Wine	❑	❑	Spelunking	❑	❑
Sightseeing	❑	❑	Ecotourism	❑	❑
Gambling	❑	❑	Soft-adventure	❑	❑

Travel History

	Has visited	More than once	Would return	Will never visit	Would like to visit
Northeast	❑	❑	❑	❑	❑
Cities: _____					
Florida/South	❑	❑	❑	❑	❑
Cities:_____					
Midwest	❑	❑	❑	❑	❑
Cities: _____					

	Has visited	More than once	Would return	Will never visit	Would like to visit
Mountain States	❑	❑	❑	❑	❑
Cities: _____					
West Coast	❑	❑	❑	❑	❑
Cities: _____					
Alaska	❑	❑	❑	❑	❑
Cities: _____					
Hawaii	❑	❑	❑	❑	❑
Islands: _____					
Canada	❑	❑	❑	❑	❑
Cities: _____					
Caribbean	❑	❑	❑	❑	❑
Islands: _____					
Mexico	❑	❑	❑	❑	❑
Cities: _____					
West Europe	❑	❑	❑	❑	❑
Countries/cities: _____					
East Europe	❑	❑	❑	❑	❑
Countries/cities: _____					
Middle East	❑	❑	❑	❑	❑
Countries/cities: _____					
Africa	❑	❑	❑	❑	❑
Countries/cities: _____					
Asia	❑	❑	❑	❑	❑
Countries/cities: _____					
Central America	❑	❑	❑	❑	❑
Countries/cities: _____					
South America	❑	❑	❑	❑	❑
Countries/cities: _____					

Other: _____

Future Travel Plans

"Dream" Destination(s): _____

_____

Is there anywhere you NEVER want to go? _____

_____

Business Travel

How Many Trips/Year: _____ Average Length: _____

Destinations: _____

_____

❑ Pre-paid by company   ❑ Paid by client & reimbursed   ❑ Company-approved agency

Comments:

Leisure Travel

Time of Vacation: ❏ Winter ❏ Summer ❏ Spring ❏ Fall ❏ Varies
Length of Vacation: ❏ 1 week ❏ 2 weeks ❏ 3 weeks ❏ 1 month ❏ Longer ❏ Varies
Preferred Destinations: _____
Type of Leisure Travel:

	Always	Sometimes	Never
Independent	❏	❏	❏
Fly/drive	❏	❏	❏
Escorted tours	❏	❏	❏
All-inclusive resorts	❏	❏	❏
Cruises	❏	❏	❏

Travels on Vacation with: ❏ Solo ❏ Spouse ❏ Girl/boyfriend ❏ Children ❏ Friends ❏ Varies
Type of Vacation: ❏ US ❏ Foreign ❏ Warm in winter ❏ Cool in summer ❏ Beach
❏ Mountains ❏ All-inclusives ❏ Sightseeing ❏ Active Sports ❏ Skiing ❏ Tennis ❏ Diving
❏ Sailing ❏ History ❏ Archaeology

Airlines

Preferred Airline(s): _____

_____

Frequent Flyer Information (airline, number):

_____
_____
_____
_____
_____

Seating: ❏ First ❏ Business ❏ Coach ❏ Aisle ❏ Center ❏ Window ❏ Smoking ❏ Non
Special Requests: _____

_____

Car Rentals

Preferred Companies: _____

_____

Frequent Renter Programs (company, number):

_____
_____
_____

Type of Car: _____

_____

Comments: _____

Hotels

Preferred Hotel(s): _____

_____

Frequent Lodger Programs (hotel, number):

_____
_____
_____

Preferences for general and business travel:

	Required	Preferred	Optional
All-suite	❏	❏	❏
Non-smoking room	❏	❏	❏
"Green" room	❏	❏	❏
King	❏	❏	❏
Double	❏	❏	❏
Two beds	❏	❏	❏
Suite	❏	❏	❏
Junior suite	❏	❏	❏
Wheelchair accessible	❏	❏	❏
High floor	❏	❏	❏
Low floor	❏	❏	❏

Preferences for leisure travel:

	Required	Preferred	Optional
Deluxe	❏	❏	❏
Moderate	❏	❏	❏
Budget	❏	❏	❏
"Old world charm"	❏	❏	❏
Modern facilities	❏	❏	❏
Resorts	❏	❏	❏
Villas, castles, etc.	❏	❏	❏
Inns, b&bs	❏	❏	❏
All-suites	❏	❏	❏
Ranches, farms	❏	❏	❏

Comments: _____
_____

Cruises

Preferred Cruise Line(s): _____
_____

Preferred Cruise Area(s): _____
_____

Ship Type: ❏ Large ❏ Medium ❏ Small ❏ Windjammer
_____

Cabin Location: ❏ Forward ❏ Midships ❏ Aft ❏ Upper deck ❏ Mid deck
❏ Lower deck ❏ Suite ❏ Outside ❏ Inside
_____

Comments: _____
_____

Booking History

Date	Booking Details	Total Cost

Chapter Seventeen:
Presenting The Wonder Of Travel

Some travel selling situations are pretty straightforward. A customer calls you up and says, "I'm going to Fort Lauderdale for a medical conference. I have to leave the third of March and return the sixth. I want to stay at the Marriott Harbor Inn Resort, and I'll need a rental car." You pull the client's *Profile Form*, make the bookings, and that's that.

In other situations, you'll have to do some selling. When a client has asked your help in selecting a tour or a cruise, or when you have decided to go out into the marketplace and actively promote a specific tour or cruise, you will be faced with the challenge of presenting your wares in such a persuasive and professional manner that the prospect will be convinced that this is the right buying decision.

While this chapter covers the skills and techniques of making professional — and successful — sales presentations to a single person or a couple, the techniques discussed can be applied when you are presenting to a small group in your living room or to dozens of people at a formal sales meeting.

Gathering information, developing needs

In *Part I*, we discussed the process for booking airlines, hotel, rental cars, tours, and cruises. Each of the chapters devoted to these products discussed the importance of gathering information from the client so that you would know which specific product to book. By now, you should also realize that, by gathering this information, you are qualifying the prospect. You are learning about her likes and dislikes in general and you are also "qualifying the situation," learning what specific elements must be in place for this *specific* journey. In addition, you are finding out what the prospect *needs*.

In the strictest sense, no one buys anything they don't need. I know you can immediately think of exceptions to this supposed rule — how about that candy bar you picked up yesterday? Or the fourth drink you had at the bar last night? You didn't need those. True, perhaps. But something inside you, the "inner shopper," convinced you that you *did* need those little luxuries. So you bought them.

When selling travel, everything that the prospect tells you he or she wants — an aisle seat, a subcompact car, and so forth — is a need. Successful sales are concluded when the seller (you) matches the customer's needs with the right products. The customer needs an aisle seat and a subcompact car. You provide it. Sale made. Everybody's happy.

Determining needs and satisfying them is not always that simple. With complex travel itineraries or higher-ticket discretionary purchases (like tours and cruises), more complex needs come into play. It's no more a matter of just aisle seats or a compact car. The traveler, for example, might have a need to be reassured that connections will go smoothly and that all aspects of the itinerary have been taken care of. A would-be cruiser may have a need to achieve total relaxation and freedom from care.

Those are a higher-order of needs than the basic elements of the booking. If it's true that meeting needs earns sales, then it is also true that the more needs you meet and the more important those needs are, the greater the likelihood of making the sale.

Most travel agents do a pretty good job of meeting the basic needs (the right seat on the right airline, for example). What distinguishes the great travel agents from the rest of the herd is their ability to identify and sell to their customers' higher-order needs.

What are those higher-order needs and how do you find out about them? Higher-order needs tend to be very personal, emotional, and specific to the individual. Some of them may apply in most or all travel situations. For example, some people have a need to feel they are always getting the best deal available. Others may want to use travel as a sort of "fashion statement," spending a little (or a lot) extra to get the very best. Still others have a need to be made to feel special, a need that you might meet by hand delivering tickets, providing them with extensive notes on what to do in Singapore, driving them to the airport, and so forth.

Other needs are specific to a particular journey and are best discovered by asking, "Why are you taking this trip?" The answers you receive will provide you with your most valuable information on how to sell this trip to *this* customer. For example, if a customer is taking a business trip to try to close a major deal, you may have uncovered a need for a first-class hotel and a full-size rental car to impress the people he's meeting. If you learn that someone is inquiring about a trip to the Caribbean to celebrate a twentieth wedding anniversary, you have probably uncovered a need for a very special, romantic experience. Of course, you will have to ask the right questions to uncover and pin down specific needs. But once you have this powerful information in hand, you will be able to tailor a highly persuasive presentation for this client, as we shall see.

Features, functions and benefits

One of the keys to successful selling is understanding the difference among features, functions, and benefits and how they relate to needs. Let's start off with some working definitions.

- **Needs.** A need is something for which a prospect or customer *has expressed a desire.* Strictly speaking, if a prospect hasn't told you that he needs a beachfront room, he has no need for a beachfront room.

- **Features.** A feature is any aspect, element, or part of a product. It is also the name given to that element. In the case of a travel product that means things like an "oceanfront room," a "tour guide" on the motorcoach, an "optional excursion to the archaeological ruins," "First Class" on the airline, and so forth.
- **Functions.** A function is what the feature does. The function of "transfers" (a feature of a tour) is to provide transportation from the airport to the hotel and back.
- **Benefits.** A benefit is the positive outcome the prospect will enjoy from the feature. *Every feature offers a benefit!* Many features offer more than one benefit. It is the benefit that fulfills the prospect's need and convinces the prospect that this is the right product.

That last point bears repeating, so let's repeat it. *It is the benefit that fulfills the prospect's need and convinces the prospect that this is the right product.*

Qualifying the situation, as I just mentioned, is a process of developing needs. Of course, there are such things as unexpressed needs. The problem is, from your point of view, it is very difficult to sell to an unexpressed need. If the client wants to play tennis on vacation and hasn't told you, then you may present a tennis-less resort, lose a sale, and never know why. Now you might say, "If she wanted to play tennis, why didn't she tell me?" The answer is, "Because you didn't ask." *It is the travel agent's responsibility to elicit complete information about the client's needs.* That is what you get paid for.

The features of any travel product are the suppliers' answers to the needs of the traveling public. The Modified American Plan, to cite just a single example, is a feature of a resort hotel. Its function is to provide vacationers with breakfast and dinner every day for a set price. The benefit is that vacationers don't have to worry about where they will eat breakfast and dinner or what it may cost them, leaving their days completely free for sightseeing and shopping at their leisure.

The selling power of benefits

Unless you're flat out lying to your customers, a feature is always a feature and a function is always a function. Yes, this hotel does have five pools. Yes, the Modified American Plan at the hotel does provide breakfast and dinner every day. That's the plain truth and nothing can change it.

But is a benefit always a benefit? The answer is, "No."

Unlike features and functions, which are defined by the product, a benefit is defined by the customer and the customer alone. Consequently, what is a benefit for one customer may actually be a drawback for an-

other. For example, an ocean-front room may seem like a dandy idea. It has the benefit of giving immediate access to the beach. But if the room faces East, the sun will come pouring in at dawn. To a late-riser that could be a drawback.

That is why only benefits make sales. Not features. Not functions. Benefits!

Still, many travel agents make the mistake of overloading their prospects with features. One reason for this is that features are easy to find. The brochure lists them for you. It requires no particular skill or imagination to simply rattle them off. Professional salespeople have a term for this tendency to fling features at a customer — "feature vomit." Avoid it like the plague. Just remember that:

- Features alone provoke little interest.
- Features and functions spur moderate interest.
- Features and functions linked with specific benefits create high interest and lead to successful sales.

Choose specific benefits

Any given travel product may have literally dozens or scores of features. Each of those features may have several benefits, depending on the customer. You simply don't have time to present all the benefits of a given cruise or tour. Even if you did, it would be a terribly inefficient way to sell to your customers.

So what benefits should you present? How many should you present?

You should present only those benefits that fulfill specific needs expressed by the customer. You should present them in the order of their importance to the customer. And you should present only enough of these benefits to make the sale.

Caution: You will remember from the chapters on booking travel products that there is important information you must relay to the customer. Much of this information concerns the features and functions of the travel product. I am not suggesting that you stop providing information once the sale is made. What I *am* suggesting is that when you sense the client is ready to make a buying decision (write a check, for example) you should stop presenting and conclude the sale. Then you can continue to provide information about the product the customer has just purchased. Only now, you can do so in a somewhat abbreviated fashion because the sale is no longer in doubt.

How will you know which specific benefits to present? You will know because you have taken the time to qualify the situation.

Distinguishing features, functions, benefits

I am convinced that selling benefits is the key to all successful selling, whether it's travel products or anything else. Unfortunately, not everyone can distinguish a feature from a function, or a function from a benefit. I have seen example after example of cruise and tour sales materials that claim to list "benefits" and actually list "features." Take it from me, "great service, spacious cabins, elegant decor, and an early booking discount" are features and not benefits!

I have also learned from training hundreds of salespeople, many of them accomplished professionals, that distinguishing among features, functions, and benefits is not always easy. One way to do so is to use the "So what?" test. If you state what you consider a benefit and the prospect can plausibly reply, "So what?" you haven't gotten to the real benefit yet.

Many travel agents continue to offer their customers features. Some offer functions, in the mistaken belief that they are benefits. Some offer generic benefits when they could very easily tailor the benefits to the specific, expressed needs of their clients. Truly creative travel agents — and I hope you will become one of them — offer their customers powerful benefits that match and meet very specifically the customers' expressed needs and desires.

Because I feel so strongly about the importance of selling benefits, as opposed to features or functions, and because I want you to succeed, I am going to take a moment to further illustrate the point with the following table of features, functions, and benefits. I have chosen the features more or less at random. The functions, hopefully, are self-explanatory. In the final column, I have listed *possible* specific benefits. In other words, much of this is made up. Some benefits listed may be benefits for one person but not another. You can probably think up additional benefits for most of these features (in fact, I encourage you to do so). Just remember, you can never know if a benefit is appropriate for a particular customer until you have thoroughly qualified the situation and developed their needs through artful questioning. The number of possible specific benefits is limited only by your customers' needs.

Feature	Function(s)	Possible Specific Benefits
First Class (airline)	Provides more comfortable, spacious seating, free cocktails, better food, higher level of service.	• Pamper yourself. • Reward yourself for a successful business year. • Surprise your new bride on your honeymoon. • Arrived relaxed and "psyched" to do business. • Be more productive because you'll be able to work in flight.
Escorted tour	Provides a guide throughout the trip. Handles check-in, check-out, and all details of the trip. Explains sights and attractions.	• Learn more about the culture than you could on your own. • Make sure you see all the highlights of the museums and castles you visit.

Feature	Function(s)	Possible Specific Benefits
Escorted tour (continued)		• No worries about speaking the language. • No dragging your bags around, so you can concentrate on having a good time.
"Cashless" cruises	All on-board expenditures are signed for. You get one bill at the end of the cruise.	• You can forget about money for a week. • You can wear nothing but a swimsuit if you wish because you don't need pockets. • You'll know exactly what you spent and for what (final bill).
"All-inclusive" pricing	Lodging, meals, and activities included in a single price. Very few extra expenditures.	• You can forget about money for a week. • You can wear nothing but a swimsuit if you wish because you don't need pockets. • You know what the trips costs *before* you go, not after you get back and count up the bills. • Easy to budget, pay for.
"Day at leisure"	On a tour, provides a day when no activities are scheduled. You are on your own.	• Let's you get the benefit of an independent tour at a package tour price. • Not tied down to someone else's schedule. • Private time for you and your spouse. • Perfect opportunity to splurge on a 4-star restaurant or go shopping. • You can visit attractions, museums, theater, or sporting events not on the regular tour. • Let's you take a break and sleep late.

This is just a start. There are literally thousands of features associated with the travel products you will be selling. However, I hope this table serves to illustrate the differences among features, functions, and benefits. I would encourage you to practice making these distinctions. Take a hotel or tour brochure at random and make your own table. For each feature, describe its function. Then ask yourself, "So what?" Use your imagination and come up with as many possible answers as you can. Envision different types of travelers and imagine what would be a benefit *to them*.

The more skill you develop in translating features into powerful, *specific* benefits for your customers, the more successful you will be as a travel agent, especially when it comes to booking those high-ticket, high-commission tours, honeymoon packages, and cruises.

A presentation model

As with so much of what we discuss in this book, presenting the wonderful benefits of the travel products you sell will be a lot easier if you approach the task in a professional and orderly fashion. Over the years, sales professionals have developed a highly effective way of providing information to their clients in such a way that the client sees — even experiences — the wisdom of making an immediate buying decision. This method is built around a simple, four-step process:

Probe — Present — Prove — Close

This method works best if you fully qualify the situation first, research available travel products, and then present your solutions to the client. It works in both informal settings and formal group presentations. Let's take a look at each step in turn.

- *Probe.* Ask a question — preferably one to which you know the answer — that addresses an expressed, known, or strongly suspected need of the customer. Obviously, expressed needs will be the strongest motivators. But you may know about your customers' needs based on past experience with them. Also, some needs can be inferred; for example, it is reasonable to assume that a need to escape the chill of winter to a Caribbean island is shared by an audience in upstate New York that is attending a Cruise Night you sponsored.
  When the customer answers the question, he will be reinforcing the need in his own mind, conjuring up a mental picture of whatever it is in his life that is lacking.
- *Present.* Your question sets the stage for you to present a specific benefit or group of benefits of the travel product you are offering.
- *Prove.* While not always necessary, your presentation of benefits will be stronger if you have some way of backing up what you say with proof. That proof can take the form of your own

personal experience with a cruise line, that of other satisfied customers, the pictures in a brochure, or slides or a video you can show the customer.

- ■ *Close.* Once you have presented the benefit and proved its worth, you should make a trial close to test that the customer has accepted the benefit as valid.

Let's take a look at how this process might be played out in a typical selling situation.

Travel Agent:	Now, you said that peace and quiet was important to you, right? *(Probe)* [The agent, we can assume, has elicited the customer's feelings about peace and quiet while qualifying the situation.]
Customer:	Is it ever! Work's been a madhouse lately. I just want to get away from everything and chill out for two weeks.
Travel Agent:	*(Present)* Then I think there are some things about the Ends of the Earth Resort that you'll find particularly appealing. It's located on 478 acres of private land, with the nearest town over 25 miles away *(Feature)*. Unless you leave the resort itself there are absolutely no signs of civilization *(Function)*. You're completely removed from the cares of the world *(Benefit)*. The individual cabanas are spread around the grounds, separated from one another by lush tropical vegetation *(Feature),* so it's impossible to see or hear anything from your neighbors *(Function)*. You'll have absolute quiet *(Benefit)*. Best of all, the rooms have no telephones *(Feature)*. So if there's an emergency at the office, that'll be just too bad. No one will be able to reach you *(Benefit)*.
Customer:	Wow!
Travel Agent:	Here's a map of the resort. See how the cabanas are spaced? And there's the beach. It's possible to go for hours without seeing another soul. *(Prove)*
Customer:	That's great.
Travel Agent:	Is that the sort of peace and quiet you had in mind? *(Close)*

As you can see, in this example the travel agent bases the presentation of the resort's quiet, out-of-the-way atmosphere as a benefit that addresses a specific need — the customer's expressed desire to get some real peace and quiet.

In theory, you could carry on a dialog like the one above for every element of the booking. ("Now, you said you wanted an aisle seat, right?")

In practice, you will want to go into this depth and detail only for those aspects of the product that address the customer's major needs. That could mean the higher-order needs uncovered when you asked "Why are you taking this trip?" Or it could mean those benefits that, through the process of qualifying, you have determined are the most crucial to making this sale.

The example above suggests a benefit by benefit approach, and there's nothing wrong with that. You can continue to probe, present, prove, and close, covering one benefit after another, until you have made your most persuasive case. This, however, is not your only alternative. For example, you might begin a presentation to a couple looking for a winter vacation this way:

> *"As you asked me, I've been researching some vacation possibilities in the Caribbean. And I think I've come up with three choices that fit the bill. Today, we can choose the one that's best for you and put down a deposit to secure your booking. Now you told me there were three major considerations for this trip: You wanted something sophisticated, without a lot of honky-tonk or loud, raucous people. You were also looking for something that would give you the widest choice of activities and allow you to try out some new sports activities. You also said that some of your previous trips wound up costing a lot more than you'd anticipated so you wanted to budget very carefully on this one. Does that about sum it up?"*
> [They agree that it does.]
> *"Is there anything else you'd like to add to this list?"*
> [They say there isn't.]
> *"Fine. Then let me start by presenting what I feel is the preferred choice for you. But, remember, the decision is yours. You pick the one you like best."*

This approach isolates the three major benefits that will make the sale — sophistication, a wide choice of activities, and good pricing. Presumably, if the travel agent can make a persuasive case that these criteria have been met, then the customers have no real reason not to put down a deposit. (By the way, notice how the agent made it very clear that the purpose of this discussion was to make a *buying* decision, not just to chat. I like that.) That doesn't mean the agent will ignore the other benefits of the packages he recommends. But the prime thrust of the presentation will be aimed at fulfilling those three major needs.

Presenting The Wonder Of Travel

The cost/value ratio

One of the major considerations for just about anyone considering a major leisure travel expense such as a tour or a cruise is the cost/value ratio. In other words, is this product worth what they are going to charge me for it? This consideration is separate from, but related to, budget. A customer may have the budget for (be able to afford) a specific tour but not be convinced that the trip is worth the price (the cost/value ratio doesn't make sense). On the other hand, many people will be willing to pay a little more than they had anticipated if they are convinced that the extra money will provide an enhanced travel experience. I am convinced that more travel sales fall through because the cost/value ratio isn't there than for any other reason.

The problem is, the cost/value ratio is a slippery concept. It can't be found in any reference book. It exists only in the minds of your customers. It changes from person to person and it can change from day to day or minute to minute for any individual. One of your goals in presenting travel products, then, is to create the most favorable cost/value ratio possible in the customer's mind. You want the prospect to feel, after your presentation, that the several thousand dollars he is being asked to part with to finance this cruise is the bargain of the decade.

Think of the cost/value ratio as an old-fashioned balance scale with two trays. On one side is the cost, tipping the scale down. On the other side is a tray for all the benefits you will provide. Each one evens the scale just a little more. At some point, the cost on one side and the benefits on the other will become even. Keep adding benefits, or add "heavier" ones, and the value becomes much greater than the cost. That's your goal.

Obviously, this can be taken to absurd extremes:

> *"And on the flight down you will receive the
> soft drink of your choice, served by an atten-
> tive and highly trained flight attendant.
> Each soft drink will be accompanied by a
> beautiful foil-wrapped portion of the finest
> dry-roasted peanuts — all at no additional
> cost to you!"*

Still, the point is valid. The more value you can build into your presentations with specific benefits, the less the cost will seem.

Visual aids and how to use them

One nice thing about selling travel is that the suppliers do such a good job of helping you out with eye-popping brochures, videos, slides, and posters. Depending on the kind of travel business you eventually evolve, you may even create your own visual aids — for example, slide shows of tours you have led in the past.

While there is no doubt that visual aids can be of immense help to the travel agent, they do not relieve you of the responsibility to be in charge of the presentation. In this section, I will discuss the most common forms of visual aids and give some pointers on how to use them to best advantage.

Whatever visual aids you use, you must use them *interactively*. That is, they are not a substitute for talking with your customers but a spur to further discussion. So get the prospect involved with the visuals you use. Ask questions about the pictures or slides you show. Have prospects choose among alternatives ("Which of these hotels looks the nicest to you?"). Have them point to the pictures that most appeal. Encourage them to *imagine* themselves in the photos or in the video.

Studies have shown that people remember 25% of what they hear and 50% of what they see. But they remember fully 85% of what they see, hear, and interact with.

Brochures

When you are using a brochure to make a presentation to a client, there are two salespeople involved — you and the brochure. You (presumably) are constantly working to improve yourself, but the brochure, once printed, will never get any better. In fact, it will get worse with age as it becomes dog-eared from use, or as the information it contains becomes outdated, or as the hairdos on the models in the photographs grow out of style. Unfortunately, the brochure is one aspect of the presentation over which you have no control. Well, almost no control. You can control which brochures you choose to present to your clients.

To help you make good choices, here are some insights gleaned by the Martin Agency of Richmond, VA, in focus groups with travelers. Use them to evaluate the brochures that come across your desk.

- The photographs are the most important single aspect of a travel brochure. The more beautiful and evocative the pictures, the more interest your customers will have. But no matter how beautiful they are, the pictures must also look recent. If they appear to be years or decades old, the customer will become suspicious that the property can't stand up to current scrutiny.
- The quality of the travel experience is also conveyed to the customer through such seemingly minor details as the quality of the paper on which the brochure is printed.
- A simple, open layout, with large, easy to read type will convey the idea that going there will also be a relaxed and pleasurable experience.
- Brochures with lots of information are appreciated because many people take the brochures with them on their trips and use them as guides.

You can factor in your evaluation of the brochure when you make your decisions about which resorts, hotels, and destinations you will be recommending to your clients. Jamaica (to cite a random example) is chock-full of resorts. Why not sell only those which make the best impression on would-be guests with sleek, professionally designed and produced marketing materials? Of course, we all know that photos can lie and your clients won't be comforted by the knowledge that the brochure looked lovely when the actual trip is a horror show. You'll have to assure yourself that the brochure adequately reflects the reality — that's what fam trips are all about. But all else being equal, a fine resort with a fine brochure will be an easier sell than a fine resort with a mediocre brochure. It's a small point perhaps, but one worth bearing in mind as you choose properties to recommend to your customers.

Using brochures as part of a sales presentation requires a modicum of care and attention to details. Here are some tips:

- Don't simply hand your customers copies of the brochures at the beginning of your presentation. They will read the brochures while trying to listen to you. As a result, neither you nor the brochure will communicate effectively.

- Use the brochure as a sort of slide show, to illustrate points you are making, as you make them. When talking about the beach, have open the page with the beach picture. When talking about the amenities of the hotel room, point to the photo of the typical suite or a map of the resort's layout.

- If presenting to a couple — a fairly typical situation — sit between them, with the brochure on the table in front of you. That way, you can all see what you're pointing out. You can present the brochure across the table, with the brochure facing the clients and you behind it, but it requires some practice.

- Highlight, underline, circle, or otherwise mark key elements in the brochure as you cover them in your presentation. This is especially important when discussing such matters as cancellation policies (the "fine print"). It serves as reminder to both you and the client (see below) that these matters were explained. Keep this copy for yourself.

- At the end of the presentation, hand out fresh copies to the client, containing appropriate highlightings and marginal notations that you've made in advance. For example, next to the cancellation policy you might write, "Very Important!" If you are presenting to a couple, give each of them a copy; that way you avoid insulting the "decision-maker" by giving the brochure to the wrong spouse.

- Practice your presentations so that you become comfortable using the brochure. Enlist a spouse or friend or use the always accommodating mirror.

Videos and slide shows

Many tour and cruise suppliers will provide you with video cassettes at very modest cost. Videos may also be available from foreign tourist bureaus, commercial suppliers, or your local public library.

Video cassettes can be given to a prospect to be viewed at home, shown in your own living room to a group of friends, or used as the centerpiece of a presentation to a larger group. Here are a few simple things to bear in mind when using videos with a group.

- *Always pre-screen the video.* This may seem obvious, but some agents forget to do it. You want to make sure you can answer any questions that the video might generate from your audience. You also want to make sure that you can deliver on everything that the video promises, or seems to promise. If there are parts of the video that don't apply or that may be misleading you may want to stop the video in midstream rather than risk confusing your audience.

- *Make sure the screen is visible to everyone.* In a living room, this might mean moving the set so that it is at shoulder height. When arranging seating, it is better to place people a little farther back than too far to the side.

- *Dim, but do not completely turn out the lights,* when showing videos. Try to position yourself in such a way that you can observe reactions during the screening.

- *Adjust the volume.* Set it slightly higher than you would if you were watching for your own enjoyment. The somewhat louder soundtrack will help focus attention squarely on the video (much as it does in a movie theater). Of course, the sound should never be so loud as to be uncomfortable.

- *Introduce the video.* Tell people what they are going to be seeing. You might, for example, give a brief summary of the video's highlights. Or suggest that, as they watch, viewers pick out which of the locales shown is their favorite. Or pose a question, the answer to which will be found in the video. Strategies such as these will encourage audience attention to and involvement in the video.

- *Schedule a short break before playing it* if the video is longish (say, over 20 minutes). That way people can help themselves to refreshments or make that important visit to the rest room

Much of the advice that applies to videos applies to slide shows as well. However, there are few items that are peculiar to slide presentations:

- *Position yourself correctly.* If you are going to be speaking as you present the slides, stand in front of the audience to the left of the screen (from the audience's point of view). Since people read left to right, positioning yourself to the left puts you in a stronger position. Use a remote control device to advance the slides, or have an assistant do it. Standing at the back of the room and advancing the slides yourself is not a good idea; you and the slide show become two separate elements in the minds of the audience.

- **Check your materials.** Always check your slides, their order, and orientation just before each presentation. I don't why it is but practical jokers seem to have a special affinity for slide trays.
- **Know your equipment.** The best slide machine is the one you know intimately and bring yourself. If you are using rented or borrowed equipment, get there early, test it out, do a couple of dry runs, and have a back-up plan in case of emergency.
- **"Clear the visual."** If your slide show includes slides that contain nothing but text, be sure to "clear the visual" immediately whenever such a slide appears. In other words, read the text aloud before proceeding, because your audience will do so whether or not you allow time for it. Typically, a text slide will have a major subject heading and three or so bullet points. Once you have read through the material on the slide, you can return to the beginning and expand on each point separately, knowing that your audience is with you.

Selling through visual imagery

Don't think that just because you have all these wonderful visual aids at your disposal, you have all the pictures you need. Some of the best pictures that travel agents use are the ones they create in their prospects' heads through the use of visual imagery and powerful, evocative words. Here are some of the ways you can paint those pictures:

- **Modifiers.** Adjectives, adverbs, and short phrases are all modifiers; that is, they define or describe other words. Select modifiers that are particularly evocative yet still describe your products and services accurately. Can you offer savings or tremendous discounts off the regular fare? Do you provide fast delivery of tickets or personal delivery to your customers' homes? Do you book cruises or glamorous cruises of the sunny Caribbean?

  The optimum adjectives and descriptive phrases for you will, of course, depend on your area of specialty and the mix of travel products and services you are offering. They will also depend on what you feel comfortable with. Make an effort to search them out. Once you have found them, use them!

  Using vivid adjectives and descriptive phrases will add power to any sales presentation. One caution: Avoid adjective pollution. You can overdo it if you're not careful. Don't use three adjectives when one will do nicely. Check yourself periodically to make sure that the words you are using accurately convey your meaning. For example, which is bigger — "huge" or "colossal?"
- **Romance words.** Certain words are especially romantic. In fact, the word "romantic" is one of them. People who sell travel

often use the term "romance words" to refer to those adjectives that do a special job of capturing the allure of the products and experiences they are selling. You can find plenty of romance words in the brochures and videos put out by the various suppliers. Which of them will work for you is a matter of taste; what sounds great on the page may sound corny or trite coming out of your mouth. Nonetheless, you should start searching for romance words that will work for you. Find words and phrases that you can use convincingly and unselfconsciously to describe and promote your travel products.

- **Setting the scene.** If people buy benefits (which reflect their selfish interests), it follows that helping them envision those benefits working for *them*, on *their* trip or vacation, providing the specific benefits *they* are seeking, will make it easier for them to make the right buying decision.

  So, when presenting the wonder of travel, set the scene: "Remember, that tour of Italy you told me about when . . . ." Now the prospect is seeing that pleasant episode in his mind's eye. When you present your tour of Ireland, he will automatically "see" it as providing a similar, even superior, experience.

- **The telling detail.** Another way to bring your presentation to life in the prospect's mind is to use crucial information that you gathered while qualifying the situation. Suppose your client had told you that she was looking for a vacation where she could "sit on a beach, sip a margarita, and watch the perfect sunset." During your presentation of a resort brochure, you could linger over a photo of a picture-perfect beach and say, "Wouldn't this be the perfect spot to relax, sip a margarita, and watch that perfect sunset?" Whether the prospect remembers her earlier remark or not, she will be subconsciously reminded of her desire for the perfect getaway and move one step closer to firming up her booking.

- **The sizzle, not the steak.** There's a line from the world of advertising that you may have heard: "Sell the sizzle, not the steak." The idea is that people are looking not so much for the product itself but the *feelings* that are associated with it — the benefits, if you will. The word pictures you create, then, should evoke the emotions and feelings rather than the nuts and bolts. "Like an elegantly furnished country cottage" is more evocative than "a one thousand-square-foot junior suite" although both may describe the same thing.

The power of words

While we're on the subject of words, let's take a moment to consider how they affect another important aspect of your success as a travel agent. Some 80 years ago, Benjamin Whorf, a language scholar from Yale, discovered that the way people talk actually affects the way they think and act. He was studying the language of the Hopi Indians, but his insights have implications for present-day travel agents and other salespeople.

Your choice of words affects not only your prospects' view of you but, even more important, your view of yourself. Listen to two travel agents:

Agent #1:   Gee, I'm really not too sure. Would this be okay? I'll try to find out; and if I can get the information, I'll try and get back to you.

Agent #2:   I don't have that information, but I'll be happy to get it for you. I'll call you back tomorrow morning at eleven, or would two in the afternoon be more convenient for you?

Not only will Agent #1 *seem* tentative, uncertain, and indecisive, the odds are overwhelming that he or she will *behave* in precisely the same way. Agent #2, on the other hand, not only comes across as decisive and proactive but he or she is committed to a plan of action.

So, speak positively! If you do, you'll act positively!

Chapter Eighteen:
Handling Your Customers' Concerns

Nothing puts fear into the heart of a novice salesperson like the sound of a customer saying, "Yeah, but . . . ." To many beginners, this signals the arrival of an "objection," an "obstacle" to the sale that must be "overcome." They are on the defensive. Their products or, even worse their honesty and integrity, are being called into question. The customer is fighting them.

Nothing could be farther from the truth. If anything, these so-called "objections" signal the prospect's high level of involvement in the selling process. After all, if a prospect is truly uninterested, why would she bother asking questions about the tour or cruise you are presenting?

By and large, travel agents don't have to face the heavy resistance that some other salespeople must contend with. There are a number of reason for this:

- *People come to you.* In many cases, the only reason you are talking to someone is because they have decided to take a trip. The sale is never in doubt. All that remains to be done is iron out the details.

- *The product range is vast.* Most salespeople are limited to a greater or lesser degree by their product lines. Not so the travel agent. If your customer *hates* escorted tours, you can arrange a fly/drive package, an all-inclusive resort package, or a cruise.

- *Qualifying avoids objections.* Another bonus you receive from your huge product line is that you can eliminate most objections through the qualifying process. In other words, you avoid an objection to escorted tours by learning the customer's likes and dislikes and recommending something else.

- *Your customers are in a buying mood.* Most of the people you deal with are actively looking for reasons to take the trip, not searching for excuses to avoid going.

In spite of everything you have going for you, I would be doing you a disservice if I were to suggest that all will go smoothly from first contact to

final sale. The selling process runs into a variety of hitches, bumps, and glitches along the way. Very few of them are full-fledged, sale-busting objections, in the sense that most salespeople use the term. Therefore, I prefer to call them concerns. But whatever we call them, and no matter when or why they come up or how serious they may be, there is a way to handle them — as we shall see in this chapter.

One note of caution to those of you who have decided to specialize in any way or have made a conscious decision to restrict your product offerings for any reason: Because you cannot easily shift to a product you don't usually offer, you may have to be a bit more aggressive in selling the products you do offer. Here's an example:

Vacation getaways to the Caribbean are a huge market. Some part-time travel agents may decide that rather than sell the hundreds (even thousands) of resorts in the Caribbean, they will specialize in a dozen or so properties that offer a good selection, covering most tastes and budgets. When a client requests a Caribbean holiday, they select the one or two most appropriate destinations and present those. For these agents, having the customer pass on both choices presents something of a problem. Of course, the agents can always research another, more suitable property for the client, but that defeats the purpose of specializing. Therefore, these agents have a built-in incentive to push just a little harder to sell the properties of their choice.

The same goes for the person who decides to specialize in Scandinavia. While she *could* sell a tour to Spain, she'd rather not. Her goal is to convince people that Scandinavia offers the kind of vacation experience they're looking for. A travel agent in this kind of situation may want to handle customer concerns a bit more aggressively.

The truth about customer concerns

Because a certain amount of . . . well, *concern* . . . exists about concerns, let me make a few of points up front:

- Concerns don't mean you've failed. Just the opposite. The expression of a concern by the customer usually means that they are seeking more information, in the hope that the answer will provide them with the reason to make a positive decision.
- Concerns don't slow down the selling process, they accelerate it. Once you have successfully handled a customer concern, you are closer to the sale than you would be had the concern not been expressed.
- Concerns signal involvement. Whatever else, an expression of concern by the customer at least means they are listening and engaged. They are not dismissing you out of hand.
- Concerns often tell you the final decision is close at hand. Always be ready to close for the booking after handling a concern.
- Concerns expressed early in the sales cycle are not really concerns at all. They are reflex reactions, and you shouldn't try

to close on them. Once interest is aroused, these stalls and excuses tend to melt away.

- Handling concerns can be fun. It's really all about solving problems and helping people. What can be bad about that?

Handling customer concerns

Concerns cannot be ignored, brushed aside, or minimized. To the customer, *every* concern is a serious matter and should be treated as such. Nor can you hope to make much headway by meeting your customers' expressed concerns with a burst of cheery enthusiasm. That will just raise their hackles and reconfirm all their prejudices against pushy salespeople.

Here is a simple, four-step method that you can use to answer just about any customer concern, whenever and for whatever reason it comes up.

- *Clarify the concern.* Make sure you *really* know what the customer's concern is. Even if you're sure, it's a good idea to encourage the customer to expand on their thinking.
- *Empathize with the concern.* Show that you respect the customer's point of view, even if you don't necessarily agree with it.
  Note: Sometimes these first two steps can be reversed. It depends on the situation and your personal style.
- *Answer the concern.* Solve the customer's problem. If necessary, provide appropriate proof that what you are telling the customer is actually true.
- *Check for agreement.* If the customer doesn't agree that the concern has been satisfied, then it hasn't.

Step One: Clarify the concern

Many travel agents make the mistake of responding to concerns they do not fully understand. Avoid this trap. Never assume you know what the customer means. Even if you are "right" you will lose a valuable opportunity to build rapport and trust with your customer.

Ask questions that probe beneath the surface. There are a number of reasons to do so:

- You want to understand the customer's feelings as well as the facts of the situation.
- You want to know if this is a mild concern or a serious problem.
- You want to know if it is something that arises from a misunderstanding or incomplete information, or if it involves a real drawback that you can't easily solve.
- Questions give the prospect a chance to talk through his or her own thinking. Many times, the customer will handle the concern for you!
- You gain valuable time to choose your best strategy and formulate an effective response.

For example, you can ask questions like:

> *"Could you explain that a little more?"*
> *"Why do you see that as a problem?"*
> *"What do you think would be the result?"*
> *"How would that make you feel?"*
> *"I'm not sure I understand exactly what
> you're concerned about."*

Step Two: Empathize with the concern

Once you know the nature of the concern and see how easily you can explain it away, there is a great temptation to jump ahead and explain it with a smile and a flourish. This is a mistake. Instead, take a moment to show that you understand and accept the customer's feelings.

This does not have to involve an elaborate show of concern on your part. Indeed, you should avoid anything that would strike customers as inappropriate to the situation. You can express empathy in a number of simple but effective ways. Just paying attention — nodding your head and saying, in a sympathetic tone, "Uh-huh." — will tell customers you are on their side.

The important thing here is to signal to the customer that you are not going to fight them on this point. If they were raising their defenses, they will lower them now. They will become receptive to your point of view and give your response a fair hearing. Here are some things you might say to convey empathy for the customer's point of view:

> *"That's a good point you've brought up."*
> *"Well, I can certainly understand why you'd
> feel that way."*
> *"We certainly wouldn't want that to happen."*
> *"I see what you mean."*
> *"That's only fair."*
> *"A lot of people feel just as you do."*

Anything you say that tells the customer you are listening, you are open, you are fair-minded, sends a powerful message that encourages trust and rapport.

Just remember that empathizing with a concern does not mean agreeing with it. You wouldn't want to say something like. . .

> *"You're absolutely right. The fares are outra-
> geous. But, hey, what can you do? That's
> what cruising is all about — spending a lot
> of money."*

Remember, too, that you can sometimes empathize before clarifying the concern.

[Empathize]*"No one wants to pay more than*
a tour is worth.
[Clarify]*What is it, specifically, that makes*
you feel the tour is over-priced?"

Step Three: Answer the concern

By empathizing with and clarifying the customer's concern, you have not only made the customer receptive to your point of view, you have gathered the information you need to effectively answer the concern.

You may also have to *prove* to the customer that your solution to their problem is in fact a solution and not just a glib response meant to put them off. There are any number of ways to offer proof.

- Your own word should suffice in most instances. Assuming the customer trusts you (and they should), they will be willing to accept your reassurance on minor concerns. More serious concerns will require — indeed, demand — proof.
- Citing an authority can serve as a proof source, even if you don't have actual documentation. For example, the customer should accept your statement that a particular cruise ship received a sanitation score of 99 from the U.S. Public Health Service even if you cannot produce the actual report.
- Materials from the supplier can be used to clear up concerns where a misunderstanding or lack of information is the cause.
- Your own experience and that of other customers can also reassure clients that their concerns are unfounded. If you can suggest that the customer call Joe Smith to ask how his vacation went, it can be a very powerful proof source.
- Some concerns respond well to paper and pencil. For example, jotting down pricing comparisons between travel alternatives is a good way to reassure customers that they are, in fact, getting the better deal with the product you are promoting.
- Finally, some serious concerns may require a bit of research on your part to produce proof that will be acceptable to the customer.

We will deal with some specific ways of answering concerns a little later.

Step Four: Check for agreement

Finally, make sure that the customer is satisfied — that the concern has been handled to their satisfaction. Ask questions like:

"Does that answer your question?"
"That doesn't seem to be a problem, then,
does it?"
"Are you more comfortable now?"
"Are you reassured on that point?"

If the customer doesn't respond positively, all is not lost. She is simply telling you that the concern has not yet been handled to her satisfaction. Use the same process to find out what you missed and deal with the situation accordingly.

Some additional points

Before we continue, let's make a few additional observations about concerns and how to handle them:

- The process outlined above can be abbreviated. Many low-level concerns or misunderstandings can be cleared up without using the complete four-step process. This is a judgment call. However, should you discover that you've miscalculated and the customer *does* have a serious concern, switch to the four-step method immediately.
- Don't try to pound square pegs into round holes. Some concerns are valid objections that mean the particular travel product you are trying to sell is not appropriate for this prospect. Don't fight the inevitable. It is far easier to go back to the qualifying phase and find the right product for this person than to try to talk them into something they don't want or need.
- Handling concerns is about helping people not hoodwinking them. If you find yourself in a struggle with a customer over a booking, your problem does not really lie with the customer. It lies with your qualifying skills. Figure out where you went wrong in the qualifying phase and apply the lessons learned. If you do, you will sharply decrease the odds of a similar situation arising in the future.

Types of concerns

One of the keys to knowing how to answer a customer's concern is knowing what type of concern it is. Sometimes you know this immediately. Other times you will have to clarify the concern to get a better handle on it. Here are the major types of concerns:

- *Stalls.* A stall, putoff, or excuse, as I have noted elsewhere, is usually a reflex reaction rather than a valid concern. Stalls are an expression of that quirk of human nature that doesn't enjoy change. If the customer is not in a sales discussion he would rather not start one (even if he knows there might be something in it for him). If a customer has not yet made a deposit, she will tend postpone doing so (even if she really wants to go).
- *Misunderstandings.* Most concerns you will deal with will arise because the customer is working with incomplete or faulty information or has misunderstood the information you have provided. These are the easiest concerns to deal with.

- ***Drawbacks.*** Some concerns revolve around drawbacks in your offering. The customer wants something you can't provide. Or an otherwise acceptable offering contains an element the customer doesn't like. Drawbacks may be minor and easily resolved, or they may be major and hold the potential of killing a booking. Concerns in this category require creative solutions.
- ***Cost concerns.*** Concerns about cost may be the result of misunderstandings or they may be real drawbacks. Because they tend to come up late in the sales process and can be troublesome to customer and agent alike, we will discuss them separately at the end of this chapter.

Answering customer concerns

There is an "answer" to every objection.

Sometimes the answer is that the prospect is quite right, the cruise or tour you are offering is not for them. In that case, your best strategy is to recommend an alternative that does meet the prospect's needs and make that booking. You haven't lost a sale, you have gained a friend. You can rest assured that the next time they need the services of a travel agent, you will be likely to get the call.

Sometimes the "answer" is a snow job. By cleverly twisting words, telling half truths, or outright lying, the agent tricks prospects into believing their concerns have been dealt with. Travel agents who use such tactics tend to have a high turnover of customers.

Most of the time, however, the prospect has been well qualified by you. You know the prospect has a need for the tour or package you are presenting. In these cases, your challenge is to guide the prospect to a favorable decision — favorable for them; favorable for you.

The successful travel agent has at his or her disposal a number of techniques to answer customer concerns. Here are some of them:

Explain it away

Many objections are the result of simple misunderstandings. You haven't explained something well. The prospect hasn't heard what you said. The prospect has heard something from another source that is not true. Some important piece of information is missing. By following the four-step method outlined above, you will be able to spot these misunderstandings. In that case, it is a simple matter to explain the objection away.

> *"Mr. Jones, you'll be happy to know that all the hotels on this tour have fully functioning modern toilet facilities and not just a 'hole in the ground out back.'"*

Here are some other examples:

Prospect:	I dunno. All that shuffleboard and bingo. I'm not sure a cruise is for me.
Travel agent:	I know what you mean. I don't much care for bingo myself. You know, they have bingo right here in the city.
Prospect:	Yeah. But I never go.
Travel agent:	Well, that's pretty much how it is on a cruise ship. Just like a city. There's an awful lot going on, and you pick those things you like to do. What are some things you think you might like to do on a cruise?

* * * * *

Prospect:	I'm a diabetic. I couldn't handle all those big, rich meals.
Travel agent:	You're right to be concerned, and I certainly wouldn't want you to put your health in danger. That's why you'll be happy to learn that the M/S Big Ship's kitchens can cater to all dietary requirements. I'll just make a note of your special needs and you'll get the same superb cuisine, except tailored to your diet. How does that sound?

Outweigh it

Sometimes your prospect will point out a real drawback in your offering. It may not seem like a drawback to you, but that's hardly the point. It is the customer who must be satisfied. In this situation, you must attempt to outweigh the negative of the tour's (or cruise's, or package's) shortcomings with the many positives of its strengths.

> *"Well, Mr. Jones, it's true that none of these hotels have microwave ovens in the rooms. However, wouldn't you agree that doing without microwave popcorn is a small price to pay for seeing the wonders of the Himalayas from the back of an elephant?"*

Here are some other examples:

Husband:	Looks like there's a lot of museum-going on this tour.
Travel agent:	Is that a problem?
Wife:	Oh Harry, don't be such a slob! Pay no attention to him. I *love* art. That's one of the main reasons we're going to Paris.

Husband:	Look, I'm just as cultured as the next guy, but a little art goes a long way with me.
Travel agent:	Well, I can see both your points. Perhaps there's a way to keep everybody happy. What would you like to do, Harry?
Husband:	I'm more of a people watcher. I could have a good time just sitting at a sidewalk cafe, sipping a glass of wine, and watching the gir . . . watching the world go by.
Wife:	We are going to the museum!
Travel agent:	Well, you know, one stop is the Pompidou Center, which not only has a great collection of modern art . . .
Husband:	I *hate* that crap.
Wife:	Harry!
Travel agent:	. . . but it also has a great street scene outside. There are singers, and mimes, and jugglers. It's like a free circus. Now I'm sure you'll want to give Martha the benefit of the doubt and check out the museum, Harry. But if you decide you don't like it, you can wait outside and have a terrific time.
Husband:	Hmm.
Wife:	Well . . .
Travel agent:	And another thing you'll be happy to know: The Louvre has a *terrific* cafe. Great wines, very reasonable prices, and some of the most interesting people in Paris. So it would seem that you can stick together and both be happy, wouldn't you say?

* * * * *

Prospect:	I dunno. It's a little more than I'd hoped to spend.
Travel agent:	Really? About how much over is it?
Prospect:	About 500 bucks.
Travel agent:	Well, that's certainly a consideration, especially when you were expecting to pay less. On the other hand, let's look at what we're getting for our money.
	[The travel agent would then list all the *agreed-on features and benefits* that had been elicited during the qualifying process. At each step, she would check for agreement. The client did want a golf course so he could play every day, didn't he? He had specified a junior suite so he wouldn't feel cramped, correct? And so on.]
	And on top of all the amenities, wouldn't you agree that the El Luxo Magnifico qualifies as the sort of special anniversary trip you were looking for?

| Prospect: | Well, it certainly is fancy. |
| Travel agent: | And when you think about it, the extra money comes to less than $50 a day. Doesn't it seem worth it to pay a little bit extra to assure you get the vacation you want? |

Feel-Felt-Found

Sometimes prospects' objections are the result of doubt, uncertainty, or fear. They've never experienced the benefits of a cruise, for example, and just aren't sure it will be as much fun as everyone says it will. You can help reassure them by pointing out that others have been in the very same position, taken the plunge, and are now very happy.

*"Mr. Jones, I understand exactly how you **feel**. That's exactly the way I **felt** before I took my first cruise. And I **found** that there was so much to do that I was hardly in my cabin at all, except to change clothes and sleep."*

This "feel-felt-found" technique is not only one of the simplest ways to handle your customers' concerns, it's also one of the most effective. The technique works well because you express empathy and understanding for the client's point of view. You make it all right for the client to feel the way he does. By sharing with the client that you felt the same way once, you become equals in discussing the matter. Now you have an attentive audience for your presentation of the benefits of cruising.

You don't always have to use the exact words feel-felt-found to use the technique. For example, you might say,

"I can understand why you say that. I hear that a lot from first-time cruisers. But when they get back they can't stop talking about all the things they found to do on the cruise. They were hardly in their cabins at all!"

You can add some extra punch to this technique if you can refer the client to a third party. For example:

*"I know just how you **feel**. One of my best cruise customers is Joe Smith and he **felt** the same way you do before he took his first cruise. He **found** it wasn't a problem at all, and now he's one of the biggest cruising fans in the city. Why don't I give you his number? I'm sure he'd be happy to talk to you about it."*

Talking to Joe Smith may give the client an extra level of assurance. After all, Joe has no financial interest in the sale. Of course, you should make sure that Joe is willing to chat with reluctant cruisers before you give out his number to people.

And if you don't already have a list of satisfied customers willing to answer questions for other would-be travelers, start compiling one now!

"I already have a travel agent."

Early in your career as an independent travel consultant, you may hear those words a lot. One way to deal with them may be to say, "Okay. But if you're ever interested in changing agents let me know." I don't particularly recommend that you take that stance, but if you do, I won't hold it against you. You may feel that it's easier to find people who will be eager to deal with you rather than try to change somebody's mind about a travel agent with whom they have an on-going and presumably satisfactory relationship. It may be that you will find plenty of people who don't already have a travel agent and that they will bring you all the business you want to handle.

You should be aware, however, that just because someone already has a travel agent docsn't mean you can't become their new travel agent. The statement "I already have a travel agent" is, technically speaking, an objection. As such it can be dealt with using the four-step method outlined above. Here's how:

Prospect: I already have a travel agent.

Travel Agent: Great. Having a regular travel agent is important. [Empathize] Which agency do you use? [Clarify]

Prospect: The Traditional Travel Agency down on Main Street.

Travel Agent: I've heard good things about them. [Empathize] How do you like them? [Clarify]

Prospect: They're okay.

Travel Agent: Who do you deal with down there?

Prospect: No one in particular. Just whoever happens to be free.

Travel Agent: Uh-huh. What is it you like about them?

Prospect: Well, they seem to know what they're doing, and I've been pretty happy with the fares I get.

Travel Agent: I see. So a knowledgeable travel agent and good prices are important to you then? [Clarify]

Prospect: Yeah. Of course.

Travel Agent: Are they easy to work with? I mean, how do you usually book through them? [Clarify?]

Prospect: I call up and tell them what I need and if I need to look at brochures or something I go down and check 'em out. Then they tell me when the tick-

	ets are ready and I go pick 'em up, or they mail them to me.
Travel Agent:	Well, let me ask you this: Say the Traditional Agency assigned you your own personal travel agent, so you'd be dealing with someone who really got to know you and how you like to travel. And say they came to you with the brochures, instead of your going all the way down to Main Street. And say they hand-delivered the tickets to you. Would you be likely to continue doing business with them? [Clarify]
Prospect:	Well sure.
Travel Agent:	I'm glad to hear that because that's just the level of service I want to provide for the neighborhood. My agency has access to all the same suppliers and brochures as Traditional, so with the help of my agency I can answer any travel question you have. Plus, I make a personal commitment to gain an in-depth knowledge of all my clients' travel preferences. And I can come to your house when it's most convenient for you and Martha to look at brochures and discuss your plans, and I'll hand-deliver your tickets. [Answer the concern] Isn't that the kind of service you'd like to get from your travel agent? [Check for agreement]
Prospect:	Well, when you put it like that . . .
Travel Agent:	Will you let me handle your next booking? [Check for agreement]

Let's analyze what happened here. First, the agent — let's call her Sue — empathized with the objection by noting that it's a good idea to have a regular travel agent (which it is). Then she began a process of learning more about the prospect's situation and how strongly attached he is to his current agent.

Asking the name of the agent can provide Sue with some valuable information. She may know quite a bit about the Traditional Agency, how big it is, what its specialties are, and so forth. She may even have looked into becoming an outside rep there. Also, by asking questions like this, she will start to get an idea of who her main competition is. At the very least, she will get an idea of how far the prospect has to go to get travel assistance; convenience, after all, is one of the biggest things the part-time neighborhood-based travel agent has to offer.

In further clarifying the objection, she learns that the prospect's loyalty to his agency is not particularly strong. "They're okay," he says. And the fact that he doesn't have a personal, on-going relationship with a specific person there also speaks volumes about the strength of his commitment. If it turned out that the prospect had a much stronger relationship with the agency, Sue might well decide not to push so hard for his business.

In the process of clarifying the objection, Sue tries to find out what is important to this prospect when it comes to dealing with a travel agent. She also finds out the basic nature of the prospect's dealings with Traditional. Reading between the lines here, we can determine (as can Sue) that this prospect deals with Traditional not so much because of their great level of service but because he hasn't found anything better. Many people continue dealing with the same travel agency year after year out of simple inertia. If you examine your own buying habits, you may find you do much the same thing. All of this leads me to the conclusion that, most of the time, when you hear the words, "I already have a travel agent," you are not hearing a super-serious objection.

Sue next asks a question to which there is only one answer: "Say the Traditional Agency assigned you your own personal travel agent, so you'd be dealing with someone who really got to know you and how you like to travel. And say they came to you with the brochures, instead of your going all the way down to Main Street. And say they hand-delivered the tickets to you. Would you be likely to continue doing business with them? "

What's he going to say? "No?"

Of course, the prospect may see exactly what Sue is doing here, and that's just fine. After all, she is merely feeding back, in slightly different form, what the prospect has told her. She is restating Traditional's negatives as positives. That puts her in a position to state her case for her own travel consultancy. She is offering the prospect features his current travel agency doesn't offer. These are all perfectly good reasons for switching agencies, at least on a trial basis.

Not only does Sue check for agreement ("Isn't that the kind of service you'd like to get from your travel agent?"), she does it twice. The second check is a strong closing question — "Will you let me handle your next booking?"

Overcoming initial skepticism

Ideally, the prospect will say, "Sure, Sue, I'll let you handle my next booking. In fact, Martha and I are thinking about a Caribbean cruise this winter. Why don't we talk about that?"

On the other hand, the conversation could continue along these lines:

Travel Agent:	Will you let me handle your next booking?
Prospect:	We-l-l-l. I dunno, Sue.
Travel Agent:	Is there a problem?
Prospect:	I dunno. You're kinda new at this, right?
Travel Agent:	About a month now. Are you concerned that I might not have the knowledge and experience to handle your bookings?
Prospect:	Well, I'd hate to put it like that.
Travel Agent:	Phil, don't worry. It's a perfectly valid concern and I understand completely. Believe me, the last thing I want is for you to be left in the lurch because of a mistake on my part.

Prospect:	I'm sure you're very good. It's just that . . .
Travel Agent:	Well, I certainly haven't gone into this half-cocked. I did a lot of research and training before I started asking for business, and I continue to go to seminars and association meetings to build my knowledge. And the agency I book with double-checks all my bookings for accuracy, so there's very little chance of things getting fouled up. Does that help reassure you?
Prospect:	A little.
Travel Agent:	I can see why you'd be hesitant. Let me ask you this: How did you find out the Traditional Travel Agency was right for you?
Prospect:	I just tried 'em out a few times and they seemed pretty good.
Travel Agent:	Sounds sensible. Why don't you do the same with me? Try me out a couple of times and see how you like the service. How about letting me book your next vacation?

Once again, we can see how Sue applies the same four-step process — clarify, empathize, answer, check for agreement — and then asks a strong closing question to move the sales relationship forward.

There are some other lessons about how to handle your customers' concerns to be learned from this little exchange between our travel agent, Sue, and her prospect, Phil.

- **Respect the prospect's position.** Sue always showed that she respected Phil's point of view: "Having a regular travel agent is important." "It's a perfectly valid concern." These reassurances will make Phil comfortable, so he'll be receptive to Sue's ideas. Notice, too, that when she found that Traditional was lacking in certain areas, she didn't try to make Phil feel bad about it by saying something like, "Come on! You call that service? They probably don't even know your name!"

- **Don't knock the competition.** If Sue had said something like, "Traditional!? That fly-by-night outfit? How can you deal with them?" she would have, in effect, been calling her prospect a jerk. Sometimes you may have to point out why you feel a particular travel product is inappropriate for a customer. When that's the case, do so objectively — with facts and figures and proof — rather than with a sweeping condemnation.

- **Don't be afraid of concerns and objections.** Phil was reluctant to come right out with his concern, but Sue wasn't afraid to bring it into the open. The only objection that can hurt your sales is the objection that remains hidden and is never identified or discussed.

- **Be persistent.** Many people might have walked away from this discussion as soon as Phil said, "I already have a travel agent." But Sue persisted past several expressed concerns on Phil's part. She was successful because she kept her cool, focused on Phil's point of view and his needs, and remained polite. Polite persistence will invariably be respected. But let the discussion degenerate into an argument ("Traditional is a lousy agency and I can prove it.") or a shouting match ("I'm better than they are any day!") and you have lost.
- **Don't beg.** Sue kept the discussion on a professional level, giving solid, businesslike reasons for doing business with her. Don't succumb to the temptation to say things like, "Come on, Phil. I'm your *friend*. How do you expect me to get any business if my own friends won't work with me? Ple-e-e-ase!"

Concerns about cost

Concerns about the cost of travel products are troublesome. They tend to crop up late in the selling process, after you have invested a fair amount of time and energy. Worse, they have the potential to sink the sale and, for that reason, can be stressful. Here are some thoughts on dealing with your customers' concerns about the cost of travel.

The best way to handle cost concerns — avoid them

If you have done a good job of qualifying the situation, cost concerns should not be a problem — in theory. In practice, people get cold feet at the last minute and use cost as an excuse. Still, the theory is valid. Once you know the prospect's budget range, you can present only products that fall within that range. Elsewhere, I recommended that you try to propose something in the middle to lower end of the customer's range, holding in reserve a higher-priced alternative. That remains good advice.

The problem, then, is how do you determine the prospect's price range? By asking the right questions, of course. "How much do you want to spend?" is a good place to start, but it will not always get you the best answer. Here are some other things you can say. Try them out and see how they work for you.

"What did you pay for your last cruise? Would you like to spend about the same this year, or upgrade a bit?"

"As a rule of thumb, I figure that a trip like this costs $1,000 per week per person. Is that about what you had in mind?"

"I can serve you best if I have a clear picture of what you want to spend. That way, I can

make sure you're not in for any unpleasant surprises."

"Tours of this type tend to range from $2,000 to $5,000. Where would you like to be on that scale?"

"Are you looking for a splurge, or would you like to keep the costs down?"

"Without doing a lot of research, my guess would be that this will come in at about $3,500. Would you like me to look for something a little fancier or shall we keep it at the $3,500 level?"

"Is there a price level above which you definitely don't want me to make any recommendations?"

Through careful, polite, and persistent questioning, you can usually arrive at a pretty clear idea of what the prospect is willing to spend. Armed with that information you can select the right product, a product that might even be seen as a bargain.

In presenting that product, you will want to follow the suggestions in *Chapter 17: Presenting The Wonder of Travel* to create the most favorable cost/value ratio in the prospect's mind. In this way, you can nip cost concerns in the bud.

Compared to what?

If a customer thinks the price you've quoted is too high, the first thing you will want to know is, "Compared to what?" Clarify the concern to make sure the customer is comparing apples to apples instead of apples to oranges, which is more often the case.

- *What's included?* Sometimes the concern occurs because the customer has not taken into account all the things that are included in the price. This is especially true of cruise vacations and all-inclusive resorts. Take the time to list all the things that might cost extra on a "regular" vacation but are included in this product's quoted price.
- *What level of quality?* This is the apples to oranges problem. If the customer tells you they've seen "the same" tour advertised at a lower price, clarify the source. Usually, they are referring to a discount tour operator's product. There may be some differences in the itinerary ("What's included?"), but this is more often a matter of quality. Some tour operators specialize in lower-priced tours. They do this by using smaller,

less luxurious hotels, skimping on meals, using older buses, and hiring cheaper tour guides who may be less qualified. It's not necessarily that the lower-priced tour is *bad*. It's just been designed for a different market, much as Motel 6 attracts a different traveler than the Hyatt Regency chain.

- ▪ ***Adding it up.*** Sometimes you'll have to prove the value of what you're offering by doing a side-by-side, pencil and paper comparison. You might, for example, compare the cost of air, hotel, and car booked separately to the cost of a package. Or you might ask a couple to estimate what they actually spent on last year's independent trip through Europe ("About how much did you spend each day on restaurants? How about gas for the car?") to illustrate that the cruise they are now considering may actually cost less, even though it seems more expensive at first blush.

Cushioning the blow

Not all major travel expenses have to be paid all at once. Typically, customers pay a deposit for tours, cruises, and many packages followed by a final payment-in-full some time later. Stating the total cost as two separate payments due at different times can sometimes lessen the potential for "sticker shock." Here are some other ways of either making the cost seem less oppressive or spreading out the burden.

- ▪ ***Point out the self-financing opportunities.*** If the customer is paying by credit card, they don't have to pay the entire amount at once. Sometimes, you can arrange that two (or more) payments appear on the customer's credit card bill in different months. Some resorts let guests charge the final payment to their credit card at check-out, postponing the day of reckoning until well after the trip has taken place.

- ▪ ***Put it in perspective.*** Point out that a $2,000 trip costs just $200 a day, or a mere $100 a day for each person, or even less if a child is sharing a room for free. If this is an annual vacation, point out that it's like setting aside just $40 a week ($2,000 divided by 50). If it's a *paid* vacation, point out that their boss is, in effect, offsetting some of the expense of their holiday. Compare the price to the event — it's your honeymoon; it's your anniversary; it's the only time in your life you'll visit China.

- ▪ ***Spread out payments.*** Depending on the timing, you might want to consider getting the full payment in installments, a few hundred dollars each month. Usually, this will mean the client is paying by check. Make sure the client understands that if the full payment is not made for any reason, the deposit may well be forfeited.

- ▪ ***Get financing for the customer.*** It is also possible to arrange financing for your customers. Approach a local finance

company and explain that you would like to offer your clients financing on their vacations. If the finance company is willing to work with you, they will provide you with applications you can give your clients. If their credit is approved, the finance company will pay for the trip and the client will then be responsible for monthly payments to the finance company. It is also possible to set up arrangements like this with the savings department of a bank (a "Cruise Club"), although finance companies seem to be more receptive to dealing with folks like you and me. Of course, you can always suggest that the customer set up his own savings program to pay for a vacation or cruise. Setting up a savings program requires forethought, however. It is seldom a good solution to a last-minute cost concern.

Chapter Nineteen:
Closing The Sale & Follow-Up

For those of you who are new to sales, the word "closing" and terms like "trial closes" and "close the sale" may be unfamiliar. So let's start this chapter with some definitions.

Closing is any question you ask or action you take that requires the prospect to make a decision. At the end of the sales process that decision will be whether or not to give you a deposit or a credit card number and authorize you to make a booking. Earlier in the sales process, you will be asking the prospect for any number of decisions — whether they prefer an aisle or a window seat, whether an all-inclusive resort sounds like a good idea for their vacation, and so on. Closing, then, is the simple process of reaching an agreement with another person and confirming that agreement.

Building agreement with trial closes

Many travel agents truly believe that they don't close until they actually ask for the deposit. That is because for most of the sales process they gather information, answer questions, show the customer a selection of brochures, or arrange to send the customer more information. Yet, whether they know it or not, they are constantly closing throughout every conversation they have.

If you think you only "close" at the end of the sales process, consider this. . .

- When you say, "May I ask you a few questions for my records?" you are closing.
- When you say, "Do you want me to check availability?" you are closing.
- When the prospect says, "Do they have triple rooms?" and you respond, "Do you want a triple room?" you are closing.
- When you finish reviewing a brochure by saying, "Is that the kind of resort you're looking for?" you are closing.

Any question you ask or action you take that requires the prospect to agree or commit to continuing the conversation is closing. These preliminary closes are called "trial closes" because they tell you how close you are to the "real" close: asking for the order. Don't underestimate the importance of trial closes. They are the glue that cements your relationship with your customers.

Creating a sense of urgency

In many industries, salespeople qualify their prospects by the *urgency* of their need. In other words, someone who needs a new widget immediately because theirs just broke is a better prospect than someone whose widget is six months old and still working well (even though it will eventually need replacement).

The same principle holds true in the travel industry. But the nature of the travel business works in your favor because a sense of urgency is built into virtually every product you sell. When the cruise is full, it's full. When the airline sells all its seats, there aren't any more. Most air fares aren't guaranteed at all. The price quoted today could go up 20% tomorrow. Other fares expire 30, 14, or seven days before flight time. With other products (like widgets), the factory can simply add another shift and crank out some more to meet increased demand.

One of your responsibilities as a travel agent is to remind your customers of these built-in deadlines. Don't think of this as a high-pressure sales tactic. You are doing your customer a favor by pointing out that you can nail down this air fare or this stateroom *now*, but might not be able to get it at all tomorrow. You can often use the sense of urgency to secure at least a tentative booking by making a reservation (which you might have to cancel tomorrow). This is a trial close, and signals that the customer is more likely to go through with the booking than would be the case had he decided against making the reservation at all.

The greater the sense of urgency you create, the more likely the customer will make a buying decision. There is an art to this, however. Reminding the customer of deadlines is one thing, hounding the customer is something else again. If you cross the line and harp on it too much, then it really does become a high-pressure tactic. The customer will get annoyed and simply start dealing with another travel agent who doesn't put him under so much stress.

Asking for the check

Asking for a deposit or the customer's credit card doesn't have to be a difficult or stressful event. It is, in fact, the natural conclusion to your sales conversations. Closing the sale should be easy for a number of reasons, some of which have been mentioned before:

- **People come to you.** Why would they be here if they didn't want to give you money? At the very least, they are open to the *possibility* of giving you money.

- **Qualifying avoids the odds of hearing "no."** By qualifying budget and selecting appropriate travel products, you should be able to make the sale a "sure thing."
- **Your customers are in a buying mood.** Most of the people you deal with are actively looking for reasons to take the trip, not searching for excuses to avoid going.
- **People expect you to ask.** No one is going to be surprised or feel "waylaid" when you ask for a deposit.

Still, no matter how easy it might be for travel agents (as opposed to other types of salespeople) to ask for the order, the fact remains that you have to ask. You can't finish a presentation and then hope that the customer will just naturally reach for her checkbook.

I am a big advocate of setting up the eventual close by making it clear to the client (and yourself!) at the very beginning of the meeting that the meeting's purpose is to reach a definite buying decision.

> *"As you asked me, I've been researching some
> vacation possibilities in the Caribbean. And
> I think I've come up with three choices that
> fit the bill. Today, we can choose the one
> that's best for you and put down a deposit to
> secure your booking."*

If that opening seems familiar, it's because you read it in *Chapter 17: Presenting The Wonder Of Travel*. While a statement such as this puts the prospect on notice, I think the psychological effect on the travel agent is just as important.

Starting the call is one thing. Ending it with a clear, unmistakable request for the check is another. Let's turn our attention to how to ask for the order.

The alternate-choice close

Elsewhere, I have recommended presenting the customer with two or three choices. This is actually a form of alternate-choice close. The question is not whether the customer is going to take a tour. The only thing to be resolved is which tour she will take. But presenting three tours is only part of the process. You still have to ask:

> *"Which of these tours shall we book?"*

> *"You seemed most interested in the Trafalgar
> Tour. Shall I book that, or would you prefer
> the Tauck Tour?"*

> *"Which of these hotels shall I book?"*

*"Will you be putting that on a credit card, or
would you prefer to write a check?"*

The direct close

Sometimes the best way to ask for the check is . . . to ask for the check.

"I'll need a check for $150 to hold the cabin."

*"Which credit card number do you want to
use?"*

The assumptive close

In this close, you *assume* that the answer is "yes" and proceed accordingly.

*"I'll book these flights and put it on your
Amex card."*

*"I'll go ahead and firm things up with Mega
Tours. I'll need the full $200 deposit by
Monday."*

You can also use the assumptive close for add-on business. For example, if a customer has booked a flight to Cleveland, you might say:

*"Which hotel would you like? What size
rental car will you be needing?"*

The booking-form close

This is a type of assumptive close. You can use paperwork provided by the supplier or your own form. Here's how it works.

Travel agent:	So you prefer the May 16th sailing?
Prospect:	Yeah, that looks like the better deal.
Travel agent:	Okay. Let me just get my booking form. Ah, here it is. Now which name will you want on the booking, yours or your husband's?
Prospect:	Use Bill's name.
Travel agent:	And I have the address. And the phone. Okay. That was an outside cabin in Category C, right?
Prospect:	Right.

Simply go down the form, whatever it is, and fill in the blanks, asking for input from the prospect as needed. You are operating on the assumption that the sale is closed. The more information the prospect lets you fill in, the surer the sale.

Eventually, of course, you will have to deal with the deposit. Perhaps an alternate-choice close would work nicely.

"Now the minimum deposit is $200. Or shall I put down $300, so your final payment will be smaller?"

Follow-up

Perhaps this chapter should have been called "Follow-Up & Closing The Sale & Follow-Up." Follow-up is a constant activity for travel agents both because success in selling travel depends a great deal on repeat business and because travel agenting is above all a service business. You have to follow up before the sale and after the sale, with prospects and with customers.

Follow-up involves activities that can be classified as sales, marketing, and customer service — and some that are a blend of all three. In this section, we will discuss some of the many ways you can use follow-up to power your successful travel business.

Follow-up before the sale

Not all sales happen with one phone call or meeting. Some sales take weeks, even months to conclude. And there are some sales you might begin plotting years in advance — a twentieth anniversary "second honeymoon" or landing the group business of a local fraternal organization or church group. Making sales happen requires persistent, creative, but always polite and professional follow-up on your part. Here are some of the things you will find yourself doing, along with some tips on how to do them.

- **Nailing down dates.** Before you can book anything, you need firm dates of departure and return. Some prospects can be maddeningly vague about just when they are going to take that vacation they need so desperately. Call periodically with tantalizing references to great packages you have been finding. When they ask for specifics, say that you really need to know when they want to book before you can proceed.
- **Following up on brochures.** Sometimes you will send clients a selection of brochures. Follow up to find out which ones appealed. Close for a meeting to discuss their favorite choices and finalize the booking. An alternate-choice close works well here.

"I'm glad you narrowed it down! We should pick one and book it before it's too late. I can

*stop over tonight at eight or would tomorrow
night be better for you and Phil?"*

- **Mailings.** Periodic mailings to your client base are an excellent way to generate a steady flow of bookings. Each card or letter they receive reminds your clients of your travel business (people do forget, believe it or not) and can get them to pick up the phone if they have an immediate or short-range need. Your mailing can also be used quite effectively to promote specific tours and cruises that offer a high payback to you.

- **Following up on mailings.** Most mailings deserve a follow-up call —either in person or over the phone (unless of course your client list has grown so large that this is impossible). In *Chapter 15: Spreading The News About Your Travel Business*, we talked about sending out a mailing announcing your new travel consultancy. That mailing definitely requires follow-up. And within a reasonable time, too. Calling three months later to say, "Remember that letter I sent you?" won't suffice. Follow-up calls like this are sales calls. They should end with a closing question.

- **Keeping your promises.** If you tell your customer that you will research available Hawaii packages and get back to him in three days, do it! If a client has a question you can't answer immediately, get the information as quickly as possible and get back to the customer. Developing a reputation for quickly fulfilling requests and meeting promised deadlines will go a long way to building a loyal repeat following.

- **Servicing your customers.** You can take care of your clients even when you are not selling them travel. Alert them to articles about their favorite destinations. Pass along upgrade coupons that might come your way. Send a free informative brochure (the government and trade associations print this kind of thing all the time). The ways of keeping in touch are limited only by your imagination and determination to follow up.

- **Never stop prospecting.** One thing that requires constant follow-up is your prospecting program. Review *Chapter 14: Prospecting* and recommit to making those calls, turning out those letters of introduction, making new contacts, getting referrals (which we will discuss in more detail shortly), and keeping your pipeline full of prospects who will turn into bookings next month, the month after, and every month of the year.

Follow-up after the sale

Once you have made a successful booking, it is not time to relax. There is still a lot of work to do. What you do after the sale can be your most effective marketing tool. It can certainly differentiate you from run-of-the-mill travel agents who make the booking and promptly forget the customer exists. Here are some of the things you will (or could) do *after* the sale is made.

- **Deliver tickets.** If at all possible, hand deliver the tickets and other travel documents. It's a level of service most people are not accustomed to. It also gives you an opportunity to review the details of the booking with the customer in person.

- **Review the details of the booking.** Now is not the time to make false assumptions. Make sure the customer understands everything about the booking. This is especially true of tours and cruises and doubly true when it's the first such experience for the traveler. Go over what will happen, step-by-step. Make sure the client is comfortable with the procedures and feels secure that everything has been taken care of.

- **Provide pre-trip assistance.** Your client may need assistance and guidance with things like passports or visas, even immunizations or other health concerns. In some cases, you may even want to volunteer to go shopping with the client for that special dress she'll wear on the cruise.

- **Customize the trip.** You may be able to add value to the tour or package you have booked by providing personal advice, based on your actual experience or research — a list of romantic restaurants in Paris; tips on using public transportation in Rome; your own guide to the sights of Vienna, complete with your personal observations and insider's secrets. Even if you can't write your own mini-guidebook, you may be able to recommend guidebooks, historical accounts, even novels that will add to the client's travel experience.

- **Market to their interests.** Once a client shows a predilection for a certain type of travel, he or she should be on the "A" list to receive notices for any future opportunities that might come up. A prime example would be the retired couple who go cruising once a year. Once you have their business, you should make it a priority to keep it by attentive and creative follow-up.

- **Monitor the booking.** Things change. It's the agent's responsibility to make sure the client is kept posted about changing schedules and the like.

- **Give them a going-away present.** A bouquet in their stateroom, a bottle of champagne in their hotel room — gestures like these are appropriate when you've secured a major booking. They will also be appreciated and remembered.

- **Be a chauffeur.** Some agents build fantastic customer loyalty by driving their clients to the airport and picking them up on their return.

- **Keep the home fires burning.** Why not volunteer to keep an eye on the clients' home while they're away? Pick up the mail, change the position of curtains to deter intruders, feed their pets.

■ *Debrief them after the trip.* Once your clients have returned from a trip or cruise, give them a call to ask how things went. Not only is this a welcome way for you to keep in touch, it will give you valuable intelligence for your own use and that of future travelers. Get their opinions about hotels, restaurants, sights, the trip in general. What did they like and what could they have done without? Far from feeling put upon, most clients will welcome the opportunity to provide you with a complete and detailed report on their trip.

Asking for referrals

Referrals are the hallmark and the lifeblood of any first-class sales organization — and a travel agency is no exception. There are several times during your sales relationship with a client when you can ask for a referral:

1. When you've failed to make a sale.
2. When you've made a sale.
3. When the client returns from the trip.

You will find that the quality of referrals you solicit will get better as you move from 1 to 3.

Of course, you can always ask for referrals by saying, "Know of anyone else who might be interested?" But the odds are that this approach will produce very few names. You will do better if you repeat the benefits of the product. For example. . .

*"I can understand how this cruise might not
be right for you. But perhaps you know
someone else who is just itching to spend
thirteen peaceful days away from everything
on a cruise to Lisbon."*

This approach still has the problem of asking the client to draw a name or two out of a very big group of people — everyone he knows or might be acquainted with. Many salespeople find that both the quantity and quality of their referrals increase when they narrow the field. You might say, for example,

*"I bet there are some folks you know down at
the legion hall who'd be interested in a tour
of Normandy. Can you think of anyone?"*

If the client shows a willingness to search his or her mental database for you, you can keep probing.

"How about down at the office?"

This way, your clients can focus in on a small group of people and begin to visualize faces and personalities. When that happens, there's a better chance they will see a match between someone they know and the travel product you're offering.

The best time to get high-quality referrals is immediately after a client has returned from a positive vacation experience. This is also the appropriate time to ask if they'd be willing to share their enthusiasm with other people who might be considering taking the same type of vacation or visiting the same destination. If they're willing, be sure to ask how many calls from would-be travelers they'd like to answer. Don't push it. Better to have 12 people who'll talk to reluctant cruisers once a month than one person who'll have to answer 144 calls a year!

Folks like this are called "champions." They have a genuine love for the experience and relish the chance to share it with others. Ideally, you should have a number of champions for each travel product in which you specialize — champions for Alpine ski trips, champions for cruises, champions for escorted cultural tours, and so forth.

Once you've located a champion, take care of him or her. If you refer another client to them for a chat, follow up to see how it went. If they show any signs of wearying of the task, back off. Show your appreciation for their assistance by giving them first crack at special fares and discounts. If someone has produced a lot of business for you through their enthusiastic recommendations, you should consider rewarding them with a tour conductor slot if you can.

Following up on what you've learned

We are ending this discussion of the art and science of selling pretty much where we began — prospecting for new business, this time through referrals. The cycle has come full circle. The process begins anew.

And although the *Resource Section* lies ahead, you have come to the end of the learning portion of this book. But, like selling travel, learning about the travel business is not something you do once. It is something you do over and over again for as long as you live this fascinating, romantic, and rewarding lifestyle.

So now that you have come this far, I urge you to follow up. Follow up on what you have read here. Follow up on the ideas that leapt into your mind as you read. Follow up on the excitement that thinking about your new lifestyle has generated. Follow up by reading more. Follow up by joining a professional association. Follow up by subscribing to the trade publications. Follow up by attending the many informational seminars offered by suppliers.

The *Resource Section* will help you do just that kind of follow-up. But the main text of this book is also a resource section for your future development. I urge you to use it as a ready reference. Return periodically to the text and reread it. If you are new to the travel industry, to sales, to self-employment or to all three, things that you breezed over on the first reading will take on new meaning once you have some experience under

your belt. A colleague and I have also put together *The Intrepid Traveler's Complete Desk Reference* so that you can have a one-stop source for the inside information — supplier contacts, airport and airline codes, industry jargon, and so on — you will need to book travel and work smoothly with the suppliers' reservation departments.

However, the real job is yours. I can tell you about the wonderful opportunities that exist in this lifestyle. Only you can make them happen.

Remember, a dream is just a dream.

A dream you act upon is a reality.

III

Resource Section

Chapter Twenty: "Instant" Agencies

In describing the Leisure Resource system in *Chapter 3: Become A Travel Agent — Today!*, I discussed how *one* agency works with outside sales reps. Of course, Leisure Group is not the only agency offering people like you and me the chance to become an outside rep regardless of geographical location or previous travel industry experience. In fact, there seems to be a growing number of companies extending this opportunity to the general public.

I am calling these "instant agencies" because, although the term is used derisively by many traditional travel agents, it is descriptive. For the most part, the agencies listed here will take you on no questions asked, no matter where you live — as long as you pay whatever fees they charge, in full and on time. Some of the listed agencies screen applicants, although I suspect that some are more serious about doing so than others.

Before we get to the meat of the matter, here are a few personal observations and caveats about evaluating any instant agent opportunity:

- *Are they a travel agency?* This may seem obvious, but the whole point of becoming an outside rep is that only bona fide travel agencies (i.e., those "appointed" by ARC or IATA) can collect certain types of commissions and share them with you. If an outfit offering you the chance to become a travel agent is not a travel agency, then you are being taken for a ride. Ask them the name of the appointed agency through which you will be dealing. Ask them for the ARC or IATA number of that agency and then check with ARC or IATA. If they are reluctant to give this information, ask if they belong to ASTA. If so, you can check them out with ASTA. If you have any doubts that they are a bona fide appointed agency, run, do not walk, in the opposite direction.

- *"Free" travel come-ons.* Yes, it is possible to travel free once you become a travel agent. Yes, it is possible to travel at greatly reduced rates as a travel agent. I tell you all about it in *Chapter 12: Straight Talk on Travel Industry Benefits*. But these

perks must be *earned*. A growing number of "instant agent" operations hold out the lure of instantaneous free travel benefits. The outright claim or subtle implication is that, once you sign up, you get an "official" travel agent ID that will immediately open the doors to super savings and free trips. It just ain't so. In my humble opinion, the more they go on about the free travel benefits, the less seriously they should be taken. (See *Chapter 12* for a fuller discussion of the use and abuse of travel agent perks.)

- **How much automation do you need?** Many instant agencies require you to be fully automated from the start. By "fully automated," I mean that they want you to use the same proprietary CRS system (Sabre, Apollo, etc.) that their agency uses. Not only is this expensive (many of them overcharge in my opinion) but you have no way of knowing if you'll be generating enough volume to justify the on-going cost of these systems. You also may find that you *hate* these systems with their Byzantine procedures and cryptic codes. A lot of people do. The fact of the matter is, it is possible to be very productive as a travel agent without being automated. In fact, in some very profitable areas of the travel business (cruises are the premiere example) automation is almost never necessary. In *Chapter 6: Booking Airlines* I show you how to do quite nicely, thank you very much, without a dedicated CRS (although a home computer and access to an on-line service certainly helps!). In evaluating many of these instant agent opportunities, you'll have to decide if automation is for you.

- **What about training?** The biggest justification I can see for paying a hefty fee to become an instant agent is the training you'll receive. The question then becomes, what kind of training is it? If it is simply training in how to operate the CRS, then it may not be nearly enough. Obviously, if you'll be using a CRS, then it will help to know how to use it. But if you don't know how to sell travel and negotiate with suppliers then a CRS is of limited utility. It's rather like learning how to use a typewriter before learning how to spell or mastering the rules of grammar. Then, too, there are all those areas of the travel business that don't require a CRS. Take a long hard look at the training being offered. Ask hard questions about what is and is not included.

- **What kind of support can you expect?** Another good justification for an up-front fee and monthly or annual charges is caring, on-going support. If you can call someone whenever you have a question and get a good answer, that's a definite plus. If you can call on a toll-free number, that's even better. Many of these operations, however, want to have as few "problems" with you as possible. That means little support. Some adjust the commission split according to how much "help" they provide you.

- **_Cost._** This is a business proposition, after all, so it makes perfect sense to keep your eye firmly fixed on the bottom line — your bottom line. Ask yourself, "How much travel will I have to book to recoup my initial investment and any ongoing charges?" Then take a long hard look at what you can *realistically* expect to book your first year out. This can be a tough call. For some people, knowing they have to book $30,000 in travel just to break even on their investment can be a powerful incentive. Others will get started, find out it's harder than they thought, become discouraged, and give up. It is my strong suspicion that some instant agent operations don't really care if you ever book a single trip; they do quite well on the sign-up fees alone.

- **_What's the split?_** As I mentioned in *Chapter 3*, it's important to get *very* clear on how the commission will be split. Be aware that some agencies figure the split on *base commission only*, and keep any overrides for themselves. Make sure you know, in detail, what the deal is in this all-important area.

- **_Can the terms change?_** Some agencies that start out offering a very generous split or a low, low sign-up fee find it's hard to make ends meet on such low margins and change the terms of the deal. Of course, once you've paid your fee, it's paid. If your commission split shrinks or an annual fee is raised or instated, however, you feel the consequences immediately. It is worth asking to what extent, if any, the agency will guarantee the terms it is offering. When Leisure Resource changed its split with outside agents, the existing agents were "grandfathered." That is, their split remained the same. The new, less generous split applied to new reps only. Of course, when an agency changes the terms on you, you always have the option to switch to another agency offering a better deal.

I mention all this not to discourage you or dissuade you but simply to give some context to your investigations. There are probably other considerations of importance to you — location, chemistry, etc. — that you will want to bear in mind as you weigh your choices.

Finally, some notes about the listings themselves:

- Obviously every agency will have its own unique policies and procedures. You should not assume that any of the operations listed below will operate in the same way as Leisure Resource. It will be up to you to contact them and learn more about their policies and procedures.

- The agencies listed here run the gamut from small operations that exist largely (or exclusively) to create a network of outside sales reps to major chains that use outside reps selectively as part of their selling mix. Some will take you on no

questions asked, others are looking for experienced travel professionals only. Some charge no sign-up fee, others charge several thousand dollars. All will send you information on request.

- A more complete discussion of the agencies listed here (as well as some others) will be found in the Special Report, *A Shopper's Guide To Outside Travel Agent Opportunities*. This report, which will be updated on a regular basis, provides an unbiased analysis of the policies and procedures of the growing number of companies offering outside agent opportunities. It is available for $19.95, plus $3.00 postage and handling, from The Intrepid Traveler, P.O. Box 438, New York, NY 10034-0438.

- To the best of my knowledge, all the companies listed here are bona fide ARC- or IATA-appointed agencies and are engaged in nothing illegal — although one, World View International, has come under sharp attack from the travel industry for what some see as its questionable marketing tactics. A complete account of the on-going controversy over World View will be found in *A Shopper's Guide To Outside Travel Agent Opportunities*.

- This list is not exhaustive. There are other companies offering similar opportunities. New ones pop up all the time. You can find them through classified advertisements in travel industry publications like *Travel Weekly*, in the business or Sunday travel section of your local newspaper, or in magazines that appeal to either frequent travelers or entrepreneurs. In addition, the Sunday *New York Times* and *The Wall Street Journal* occasionally carry ads for this type of opportunity and are available at most well-stocked libraries. If you know of other instant agent opportunities, I would appreciate hearing about them. You can drop me a note care of The Intrepid Traveler, P.O. Box 438, New York, NY 10034-0438.

- Please don't assume that this listing means that I think you *should* become an outside rep with one of these companies. As I said elsewhere in this book, I personally feel that your best option is to form an outside relationship with a local agency that will provide you with support and guidance. However, for some people, seeking out an "instant agent" opportunity may be their best (or only) option for getting started in this exciting lifestyle. If you do decide to go this route, I suggest that you start your investigations with agencies near you and work your way out (in terms of distance) until you find one that suits your needs.

- A listing here in no way implies a recommendation or warranty on my part. Exercise caution and seek expert advice before forming any business relationship.

Directory of "instant" agenices

Alamaden Travel Managers
Go Travel Managers
Sandra Molloy
6477 Alamaden Expressway
San Jose, CA 95120
(408) 997-1100
(408) 997-0329
(408) 977-9731 fax

Destinations Unlimited
Joe Banasiak
5208A Sunshine State Parkway
Ft. Pierce, FL 34951
(407) 465-9001

Eagle Travel Services, Inc.
Frank W. Burks
P.O. Box 1046
Crossville, TN 38557
(800) 777-5867
(615) 484-0180
(615) 484-9602 fax

Groups Only
Traveling Taj, Inc.
Al Noor
964 Third Avenue
New York, NY 10022
(212) 223-3333

HMI Travel
(Holiday Marketing Inc.)
Stan Phillips
1175 Herndon Parkway, Suite 100
Herndon, VA 22070
(703) 318-8183

Home Travel Associates, Inc.
TravelLine 24
Gene Schaedel
519 North Howard Avenue
Tampa, FL 33606
(800) 940-3699
(813) 254-3699
(813) 254-9218 fax

Incentive Connection Travel, Inc.
Robert Siamon
12601 North Cave Creek Road
Suite 110
Phoenix, AZ 85022
(602) 867-9606
(602) 867-9216 fax

Independent Travel Makers
Malcolm MacDonald
3107 Fillmore Street
Suite 304
San Francisco, CA 94123
(415) 398-3822
(415) 398-6184 fax

Leisure Resource
344 West Main Street
Milford, CT 06460
(800) 729-9051
(203) 874-4965

Leisuretyme Travel
Keith C. Monen
1467 East H Street
Chula Vista, CA 91910
(800) 322-8963
(619) 482-7878
(619) 482-8025 fax

Omega Travel Affiliates
Goran Gligorovic
Omega World Travel
3102 Omega Office Park
Fairfax, VA 22031
(800) 756-6342
(703) 359-0200
(703) 359-8889 fax

Premier Travel, Inc.
John Dimmock
P.O. Box 5008
Hopkins, MN 55343
(800) 228-0244

(612) 938-7527
(612) 938-7942 fax

Prestige Travel Services
Anita LaScala
4100 West Kennedy Boulevard
Suite 100
Tampa, FL 33609
(813) 289-7772
(813) 289-5663

Select International
525 Boulevard
Kenilworth, NJ 07033
(800) 842-4842
(908) 276-2000
(908) 276-1896 fax

Solid Gold Travel
648 North New Street
Bethlehem, PA 18018
(800) 435-4642
(215) 691-6443

Solo Incorporated
Murdock Travel Management
Dean L. Hill
36 South State, Suite 900A
Salt Lake City, UT 84111
(800) 678-8614
(801) 328-5465
(801) 266-6668 fax

TN Travel Link
Bill Prusso
675 Ygnacio Valley Road
B202
Walnut Creek, CA 94596
(510) 947-0222
(510) 947-4903 fax

TPI Travel Services
Bernhard Benet
3030 North Rocky Point Road W
Suite 100
Tampa, FL 33607
(813) 281-5670
(813) 281-2304 fax

Travel Business Opportunities
Civic Center Travel
Ronald Harris
142 West Grand Avenue
Escondido, CA 92025
(800) 626-4485
(619) 741-3833
(619) 480-1433

**Travel Entrepreneur Network
(T.E.N.)**
Scott Winsten
184 Fifth Avenue
New York, NY 10010
(800) 825-8728
(212) 242-2277

Travel Executives
Charles J. Givens Organization
921 Douglas Avenue
Altamonte Springs, FL 32714
(800) 333-4168

Travel Network
Michael Brent
560 Sylvan Avenue
Englewood Cliffs, NJ 07632
(201) 567-8500
(201) 567-4405 fax

Travel Professionals International
Gary Bays
15080 South West Bangy Road
Lake Oswego, OR 97035
(503) 624-9406

World View International
Tim Donlon
4225 Executive Square
La Jolla, CA 92037
(800) 234-1217
(619) 558-3100

... *And one you might want to avoid*

Of all the opportunities I looked into, only one raised serious red flags in my mind:

Independent Travel Agencies of America Association, Inc.
(ITAA)
1945 East Ridge Road
Suite 23
Rochester, NY 14622
(800) 947-4822

ITAA has been in trouble with the Attorney General of New York for false advertising and not refunding the membership fees of disillusioned members. Not too surprising.

To begin with ITAA is not a travel agency. For a hefty fee of $2,870 (plus $40 annual "dues") ITAA claims they will "certify" you to deal directly with suppliers. Unfortunately, almost no suppliers recognize ITAA's "certification." Also, the fee seems to vary widely according to when you contact ITAA, they contact you, or whom you talk to. One confusing brochure cited a $3,870 "standard" price for full membership, marked down 50% to $1,935. The same brochure mentioned an "ITAA Insider Membership" on sale for $179!

I was able to talk with one (former) member of ITAA. Here is what he told me:

"For your $2800, here's what you get:

1. A home study course to become a "certified" travel agent, consisting of nine volumes of course study. Covers how to book hotels, airlines, car rentals, and cruises. Mainly basic stuff but enough to get you started. Reference material with names, addresses, and phone numbers of suppliers airlines, hotels, tour operators etc. After completion of the course you take a open book test and if you pass (hard not to) you are sent a certificate stating you are recognized as an industry certified travel agency.

2. A listing of "preferred" suppliers willing to take your bookings and pay commissions directly to you (usually 10%).

3. One-year subscriptions to *Travel Age* and *Travel Trade* magazines.

4. A help line to call with any problems you might have with bookings.

5. A monthly in house mag with tips, ads, and fam trips. (I received one copy and it stopped.)

6. A one-year guarantee to refund your $2800 if not totally satisfied.

7. One-week free use of a condo (picked from a list from all over the world)

8. A promise to book any booking for you if you have any trouble with suppliers and pay you the full commission."

So far so good, except maybe for the high fee. But, wait! There's more, My informant went on:

"Here's what I got out of the deal with ITAA (some good, lots bad):

1. The industry "certificate" is a lark. ITAA is the only one that will honor the "certificate." In fact a lot of suppliers won't even send you brochures unless you have a ARC or IATA number.

2. I tried to do business with some of the "preferred" suppliers on the list sent with my course, and some claimed not to even know ITAA, however to be fair I was able to book with a few of them and others did send me their brochures.

3. The help line was available for assistance and the people manning it were friendly and helpful. You call in and give your name and type of problem and they call you back usually the same day

4. The trade mags did come and are useful.

5. I made one cruise booking through ITAA before I got my CLIA certification. The booking went through OK but I only received 10% of the commission NOT the whole 10% commission. I called (several times) and got nothing but the run around, every time I call they are "checking on it"

6. The condo deal is a scam. You call and they ask for 30-day notice which is understandable, but nothing is ever available. I tried to get a condo in August and asked for anything in the state of California or Baja Mexico. They said nothing was available for August in either area. I tried again for September and again nothing available.

7. I tried to get my money back after reading in the trade mags that ITAA was in trouble with the State Attorney General of New York for false advertising. To make a long story short, to date I still have not received my money."

That was enough to scare me off! It also serves to underline an important point about researching and getting involved in these instant agency relationships — *Caveat emptor!* That's Latin for "Let the buyer beware!" (which shows that scam artists have been around at least since the Roman Empire).

Chapter Twenty-One:
Guide To Travel Suppliers

One of the great things about the part-time travel agent business is that the suppliers of travel products are eager to help you succeed. One way they do that is by providing you with a quick, cost-free way of getting in touch with them. At the other end of the toll-free numbers listed here you will find well trained, professional reservationists ready to help you make money by booking their products.

The contact numbers listed here will help you get started. I have tried to list the most important suppliers, especially those connected with the various consortiums. A more complete listing of toll-free supplier numbers will be found in *The Intrepid Traveler's Complete Desk Reference*, available from the Intrepid Traveler for $14.95, plus $3.00 shipping and handling, P.O. Box 438, New York, NY 10034-0438.

Airlines

Here is a listing of major domestic and foreign carriers. The fares and schedules of most (if not all) of these airlines are available on EaasySabre and TravelShopper. However, if you want to start from scratch, the reservationists at these numbers will be more than happy to guide you in constructing an itinerary. All of the numbers listed here are (800) numbers.

Aer Lingus	223-6537	Air Portugal TAP	221-7370
Aero Costa Rica	237-6274	Alaska Airlines	426-0333
Aero Mexico	237-6639	Alitalia	223-5730
Aeroflot	995-5555	All Nippon	235-9262
Air New Zealand	262-1234	Aloha Airlines	367-5250
Air Aruba	882-7822	America West	292-9378
Air Canada	776-3000	American Airlines	543-0460
Air France	237-2747	Austrian Airlines	448-9400
Air India	223-9850	Avensa	428-3672
Air Jamaica	523-5585	Avianca	284-2622

British Airways	247-9297	Mexicana	531-7921
British Midland	788-0555	Midwest Express	452-2022
BWIA	327-7401	Morris Air	444-5660
Canadian Air	426-7000	Northwest Airlines	225-2525
Carnival Airlines	824-7386	Olympic Airlines	223-1226
Cathay Pacific	233-2742	Philippine Airline	435-9725
Cayman Airways	422-9626	Private Jet	949-9400
China Air	227-5118	Qantas	227-4500
Continental Int'l	231-0856	Reno Air	736-6247
Continental Dom.	525-0280	Sabena	955-2000
Delta Internat'l	241-4141	SAS Scandanavian	221-2350
Delta Airlines	221-1212	Singapore Air	742-3333
Finnair	950-5000	Southwest Airlines	435-9792
Hawaiian Air	367-5320	Swiss Air	221-4750
Iberia	772-4642	Thai Airlines	426-5204
Icelandic	223-5500	Tower Air	221-2500
JAL Japan Airlines	525-3663	TWA	221-2000
Kiwi	538-5494	United Airlines	521-0810
KLM	374-7747	USAir	428-4322
Korean Air	421-8200	Varig	468-2744
Lufthansa	645-3880	Virgin Atlantic	862-8621
Mark Air	544-0181		

Tour Operators

This is a listing of some of the larger tour operators in the various markets discussed in this book. The idea is to give you a place to start where the odds will be in your favor. In other words, these outfits have been around for a while and seem to be reputable organizations. Therefore, there is less chance that you will wind up dealing with a financially shaky operation that could go belly up and leave your clients stranded in some distant land. Of course, I cannot *guarantee* the trustworthiness of any of the operators listed here. Seemingly stable businesses fail all the time. As always, exercise caution and protect yourself in whatever ways you can.

Educational Tours

These tour operators specialize in putting together tours aimed (primarily) at the high school market. They are more than happy, however, to have college students or even senior citizens on their tours. As explained in *Chapter 1: Becoming A Tour Organizer*, educational tours offer the quickest route to free travel. Often it is possible to travel free just for signing up five paying customers.

ACIS
American Council for International
Studies
19 Bay State Road
Boston, MA 02215
(617) 236-4703
(800) 888-2247
One free chaperone for every six
students.

CHA
Cultural Heritage Alliance
Falcon Building
107-115 South 2nd Street
Philadelphia, PA 19106
(215) 923-7060
(215) 923-5583, fax
One free chaperone for every six
students.

EF Educational Tours
One Memorial Drive
Cambridge, MA 02142
(800) 637-8222
One free chaperone for five students
the first time and for six after that.

ET Educational Tours, Inc.
104 Wilmot Road
Deerfield, IL 60015
(800) 962-0060

(708) 374-0088
(708) 374-9515, fax
One free chaperone for every 15
students.

Great Escape Tours
8 Olive Street
Waterford, CT 06385
(800) 365-1833
(203) 443-1889
(800) 727-9843, fax
One free chaperone for every 10
students.

Passports
389 Main Street
Spencer, MA 01562-1908
(508) 885-4600
(800) 332-7277
(508) 885-0329, fax
One free chaperone for every 6
students on most trips.

U.S. Educational Tours
4450 Hugh Howell Road, Suite 4
Atlanta, GA 30084
(800) 772-6661
(404) 938-1722
(404) 934-6699, fax
One free chaperone for every 10 students, plus a stipend on some trips.

College Tours

These operators specialize in low-cost tours aimed at college students.
They all work through campus organizers as described in *Chapter 1*. They
will also deal with travel agents.

AESU Travel
2 Hamill Road, Suite 248
Baltimore, MD 21210-1807
(800) 638-7640
(410) 323-4416
(410) 323-4498, fax
Tours to Europe for 18- to 35-year
olds. On prepackaged tours, gives
one free trip for every 15 paid, or one
half-price for every 7 paid.

Student Holidays
650 Village Trace Parkway
Building #17 Paper Mill Village
Marietta, GA 30067
(800) 360-8747
(404) 952-2353
(404) 952-0949, fax
Offers warm-weather destinations
during Spring Break. Gives one free
trip for every 25 paid.

Student Travel Services
120 N. Aurora Street
Ithaca, NY 14850
(800) 648-4849
(607) 272-6963
Offers charter service to the warm-weather destinations Jamaica and Cancun during Spring Break. Departure cities are in the East and Midwest. Gives one free trip for every 19 paid.

United States Tour Operators Association (USTOA)

USTOA is made up, primarily, of the heavyweights in the tour business. Its 33 active members, however, represent only a tiny fraction of the total number of tour operators. Chances are you'll be able to find a USTOA member who can get your clients to where they want to go, although some less "discovered" areas are underrepresented. You may have to turn to a non-USTOA operator to satisfy some client needs.

Why USTOA? Mostly because they have an insurance program to protect your clients against default by member organizations — a nice, extra layer of assurance. If you want to check to see if a tour operator you're looking at might have joined the organization recently, or to check on the current status of their insurance program, call USTOA at (212) 750-7371.

Here is a current list of active members, as provided by USTOA:

AAT King's Australian Tours
(800) 353-4525
(818) 843-7161
(818) 843-7361, fax

Abercrombie & Kent
(800) 323-7308
(708) 954-2944
(708) 954-3324, fax

ACV Tours
(800) 634-5555
(305) 357-4664
(305) 357-4611, fax

African Travel, Inc.
(800) 507-7893
(818) 507-7893
(818) 507-5802, fax

ATS Tours
(800) 423-2880
(310) 643-0044
(310) 643-0032, fax

Australian Pacific Tours
(800) 290-8687
(818) 840-9122
(818) 840-8039, fax

Brendan Tours
(800) 421-8446
(818) 785-9696
(818) 902-9876, fax

Central Holidays
(800) 935-5000
(201) 798-5777
(201) 963-0966, fax

Certified Vacations
(800) 233-7260
(305) 522-1440
(305) 357-4672, fax

Collette Travel Service, Inc.
(800) 832-4656
(401) 728-3805
(401) 728-1380, fax

Contiki Holidays
(800) CONTIKI
(714) 740-0808
(714) 740-0818, fax

DER Tours
(800) 782-2424
(310) 479-4140
(310) 479-2239, fax

Donna Franca Tours
(800) 225-6290
(617) 227-3111
(617) 266-1062, fax

Funway Holidays Funjet
(800) 558-3050
(414) 351-3553
(414) 351-1453, fax

Gate 1 Ltd.
(800) 682-3333
(215) 572-7676
(215) 886-2228, fax

Globus & Cosmos Tourama
(800) 221-0090
(303) 797-2800
(800) 239-4646, fax

Haddon Holidays
(800) 257-7488
(609) 273-8997
(609) 273-8997, fax

Holland America Line-Westours, Inc.
(800) 426-0327

(206) 281-3535
(206) 281-7110, fax

Insight First Class Vacations
(800) 582-8380
(617) 426-6666
(617) 482-2884, fax

Islands in the Sun
(800) 828-6877
(310) 536-0051
(310) 536-6266, fax

Isram World
(800) 223-7460
(212) 661-1193
(212) 370-1477, fax

Japan & Orient Tours
(800) 877-8111
(619) 282-3131
(619) 283-3131, fax

Jet Vacations
(800) 538-0999
(212) 474-8740
(212) 586-2069, fax

JetSet Tours, Inc.
(800) NET-FARE
(213) 290-5800
(213) 294-0432, fax

Mayflower Tours
(800) 323-7604
(708) 960-3430
(708) 960-3575, fax

MTI Vacations, Inc.
(800) 635-1333 (Hawaii)
(800) 323-7285 (Florida, Las Vegas)
(708) 990-8028
(708) 990-3353, fax

Pacific Bestour, Inc.
(800) 688-3288
(201) 664-8778
(201) 664-1497, fax

Pacific Delight Tours, Inc.
(800) 221-7179
(212) 684-7707
(212) 532-3406, fax

Pleasant Holidays
(800) 242-9244 (Hawaii)
(800) 448-3333 (Mexico)
(818) 991-3390
(805) 495-4972, fax

Runaway Tours
(800) 622-0723
(415) 788-0224
(415) 391-6643, fax

Special Expeditions, Inc.
(800) 762-0003
(212) 765-7740
(212) 265-3770, fax

Tauck Tours, Inc.
(800) 468-2825
(203) 226-6911
(203) 221-6828, fax

TBI Tours
(800) 223-0266
(212) 489-1919
(212) 307-0612, fax

Trafalgar Tours, Inc.
(800) 854-0103
(212) 689-8977
(212) 725-7776, fax

Visitours, Inc.
(800) 3-ORIENT
(212) 243-9500
(212) 243-1902, fax

Cruise lines

The cruise industry is small — at least, compared to airlines and tour operators. Here is a listing of all the major cruise lines in the United States, as well as a few from other countries. Remember to dial 1-800 before each of the listed numbers.

American Family Cruises	232-0567	Majesty Cruise Lines	532-7788
American Hawaii Cruises	765-5555	NCL Norwegian Cruise Line	327-7030
Carnival Cruise Line	327-9501	Oceanic Cruises	545-5778
Celebrity Cruises	437-3111	Orient Lines	333-7300
Chandris Cruise Lines	423-2100	Pearl Cruises	556-8850
Commodore Cruise Lines	277-5361	Premier Cruise Lines	327-7113
Costa Cruise Lines	462-6782	Princess Cruises	421-0522
Crown Cruise Lines	822-5220	Regency Cruises	388-5500
Crystal Cruises	446-6645	Royal Caribbean Cruise Lines	327-6700
Cunard Crown	528-6273	Royal Cruise Line	792-2992
Delta Queen	543-1949	Royal Viking Line	422-8000
Diamond Cruise	333-3333	Seabourn Cruise Line	929-9595
Dolphin Cruise Lines	222-1003	Seawind Cruise Line	258-8006
Epirotiki Cruises	221-2470	Seven Seas Cruise Line	285-1835
Fantasy Cruises	423-2100	Silversea Cruises	722-6655
Holland America/ Westours	426-0327	Sun Line Cruises	872-6400
		Windstar Cruises	258-7245
		World Explorer Cruises	854-3835

Hotels

Hotels are becoming friendly toward travel agents. In other words, they're paying their commissions with more regularity than was the case in the past. It would be virtually impossible to list every hotel, so I'll just list the major U.S. chains with their (800) numbers. For a more complete listing, including resorts, spas, and hotel booking agents, invest in a heavy-duty reference like the *Hotel & Travel Index*, listed in *Chapter 25: Further Reading*.

Best Western	334-7234	Marriott	228-9290
Budgetel	4-BUDGET	Courtyard	228-9290
Quality Inns	228-5151	Residence Inns	228-9290
Comfort Inns	228-5150	Omni Hotels	THE OMNI
Sleep Inns	221-2222	Penta International	225-3456
Clarion Hotels	CLARION	Radisson Hotels	333-3333
CIGA Hotels	221-2340	Ramada	441-1255
Concorde Hotels	888-4747	Red Lion Hotels	547-8010
Embassy Suites	362-2779	Regent International	545-4000
Fairmont Hotels	527-4727	Rockresorts	223-7637
Guest Quarters	424-2900	Rodeway Inns	228-2000
Hampton Inns	HAMPTON	Sonesta Hotels	SONESTA
Hilton	445-8667	Sheraton	325-3535
Holiday Inn	HOLIDAY	Stouffer Hotels	HOTELS-1
Hyatt	228-9000	Super 8 Motels	800-8000
Knights Inn	843-5644	Travelodge	255-3050
La Quinta Inns	231-9860	Westin Hotels	228-3000
LHW	223-6800	Wyndham Hotels	822-4200

Rental cars

Like the cruise industry, the rental car business is small in comparison to some other areas of the travel industry. That makes it easy to keep on top of who's who and what's being offered. Here are the major U.S. chains and a few companies that specialize in overseas rentals. Again, all numbers listed are (800) numbers.

Advantage	777-5500	General	327-7607
Alamo	327-9633	Hertz	654-3131
Auto Europe	223-5555	Kemwel	678-0678
Avis	331-1212	Kenning	227-8990
Budget	527-0700	National	328-4567
Dollar	800-4000	Payless	PAYLESS
Enterprise	325-8007	Thrifty	FORCARS

Travel Insurance

The savvy traveler recognizes the importance of travel insurance. Moreover, selling travel insurance to your clients can be highly lucrative. Commissions go as high as 35%! Here is a list of providers of travel insurance. All of them work through travel agencies. Be sure to check with your agency to see if they have a preferred travel insurance provider and to see if they meet state requirements to sell travel insurance. Note, too, that not all insurance products are available in all states. For more information about selling travel insurance, see *Chapter 11: Getting Serious.*

Access America
Subsidiary of Blue Cross-Blue Shield
6600 West Broad Street
Richmond, VA 23230
(800) 284-8300

Carefree Travel Insurance
Berkely Group
100 Garden City Plaza
Garden City, NY 11530-3366
(800) 537-3386

Group HealthCare Abroad
Wallach & Co. Inc.
107 West Federal Street
Suite 13
P.O. Box 480
Middleburg, VA 22117-0480
(800) 237-6615
(703) 255-9800

Tele-Trip Co., Inc.
Subsidiary of Mutual of Omaha
Mutual of Omaha Plaza
Omaha, NE 68175
(800) 228-9792

Travel Assistance International
1133 15th Street NW
Suite 400
Washington, DC 20005
(800) 821-2828

Travel Guard International
1145 Clark Street
Stevens Point, WI 54481
(800) 826-1300
(715) 345-0505
(715) 345-0525, fax

Travel Insurance Services
2930 Camino Diablo
Suite 200
Box 299
Walnut Creek, CA 94596
(800) 937-1387
(510) 932-1387
(510) 932-0442, fax

Travel Insured International
P.O. Box 280568
East Hartford, CT 06128-0568
(800) 243-3174
(203) 528-7663

Tripguard Plus
M. H. Ross/Doud
16933 Parthenia Street
Sepulveda, CA 91343-4552
(800) 423-3632
(213) 872-3693
(818) 891-7811
(818) 892-6576, fax

Chapter Twenty-Two:
On-Line Services

On-line information services offer you low-cost access to computerized reservations systems (CRS) for airlines, car rentals, and hotels. They also afford an opportunity to network with like-minded individuals about the ins and outs of the travel business or just about travel in general.

Listed below are the four major on-line services. All of them offer access to at least one CRS system, usually EaasySabre. Which one you choose will depend on your preferences. Weigh cost against features and features against your needs and interests. For example, if all you want an on-line service for is to access a CRS, then it makes no sense to pay a higher monthly fee to a service that has a lot of forums or bulletin boards you'll never use. Recently, with all the media talk of the "information superhighway," the on-line services business has become fiercely competitive. So look for special low-cost sign-up deals.

America On-Line
8619 Westwood Center Drive
Vienna, VA 22182
(800) 827-6364

GEnie
P.O. Box 6403
Rockville, MD 20902
(800) 638-9636

CompuServe (CIS)
5000 Arlington Centre Boulevard
P.O. Box 20212
Columbus, OH 43220
(800) 848-8199

Prodigy
The Prodigy Information Services
445 Hamilton Avenue
White Plains, NY 10601
(800) PRODIGY (776-3449)

In addition, American Airlines lists the following on-line services through which you can gain access to their EaasySabre CRS. Note that not all of these services are compatible with all brands of computers:

ALEX	(416) 350-ALEX	(Canada)
AT&T EasyLink	(800) 227-6364	
BASELINE	(800) CHAPLIN	(212-254-8235 in New York)

BellSouth	(404) 847-2900	
DELPHI	(800) 695-4005	
Dialcom, Inc.	(800) 628-3497	
DTC DUAT	(800) 243-3828	
GTE Main Street	(617) 449-7676	
IBM Info Network	(800) 727-2222	
iNET 2000	(416) 581-4900	(Canada)
Minitel Services	(212) 399-0080	
National Videotex Network	(800) 336-9096	
Omnet/SCIENCEnet	(617) 244-4333	
PC-Link	(800) 827-8532	
Q-Link	(800) 827-8444	
SNET	(800) 272-SNET	(Connecticut only)
StarText	(817) 390-7905	
Travel by Modem	(800) 876-5551	
U.S. West Community Link Service	(800) 645-4654	

Chapter Twenty-Three:
Travel Industry Organizations & Associations

There are many, many organizations that involve themselves with the travel industry in one way or another, as this list proves. Some represent travel agents, some represent suppliers, others represent business travelers who deal with travel agents and suppliers, some represent people who work in the travel industry, some are government agencies.

There will probably be a number of associations and organizations listed here that you will want to contact for one reason or another — part of any trade organization's mission, after all, is to dispense information about its area of expertise to the general public. There may well be some organizations listed here that you will want to join.

I have tried to restrict this listing to those associations and organizations that will be most interesting and helpful to the part-time travel agent. A much more comprehensive listing of travel-related organizations and associations will be found in *The Intrepid Traveler's Complete Desk Reference*, available from The Intrepid Traveler for $14.95 (plus $3.00 shipping and handling), P.O. Box 438, New York, NY 10034-0438.

Academy of Travel and Tourism
235 Park Avenue South, 7th floor
New York, NY 10003
(212) 420-8400
A non-profit organization that develops travel career prep programs for high school students.

Air Transport Association of America (ATA)
1301 Pennsylvania Avenue NW
Suite 1100
Washington, DC 20004-1707
(202) 626-4000
(202) 626-4181, fax
A lobbying and trade organization which represents the interests of the airline industry.

Airline Reporting Corporation (ARC)

1530 Wilson Boulevard

Suite 800

Arlington, VA 22209

(703) 816-8000

A separate corporation created by the Air Transport Association (ATA) to manage the complex business of monitoring the sale of airline tickets. ARC "appoints" agencies so that they can gain access to ARC's bank-like system of collecting payments for airline tickets and disbursing commissions to agents. For more on ARC and how it operates, see *Chapter 2: The Outside Sales Rep*.

Alliance of Canadian Travel Associations (ACTA)

1729 Bank Street

Suite 201

Ottawa, Ont., K1V 7Z5

CANADA

(613) 521-0474

Alliance of Westchester Travel Agents

284 South Main Street

New City, NY 10956

(914) 638-4422

(914) 638-6183, fax

A professional association of local retail travel agencies.

American Automobile Association (AAA)

1000 AAA Drive

Heathrow, FL 32746-5063

(407) 444-7967

Promotes the interests of America's car owners. Publishes an excellent series of regional guide books.

American Hotel and Motel Association (AHMA)

1201 New York Avenue NW

Washington, DC 20005-3917

(202) 289-3100

A federation of associations in the hotel and motel industry. Represents the industry's interests to Congress and the public. Publishes a directory of every hotel, motel, and resort chain with more than three units.

American Society of Travel Agents (ASTA)

1101 King Street

Alexandria, VA 22314

(703) 739-2782

The largest travel trade organization for the travel agent community, with 22,000 members, seeks "to enhance the professionalism and profitability of member agents through effective representation ... education and train-

ing, and by identifying and meeting the needs of the traveling public."
They publish a magazine and wide variety of helpful travel-related information for the general public. ASTA now accepts outside reps of member agencies as associate members.

Association of British Travel Agents (ABTA)
55-57 Newman Street
London, ENGLAND WlP 4AH
071-637-2444

Association of Retail Travel Agents (ARTA)
1745 Jefferson Davis Highway
Suite 300
Arlington, VA 22202-3402
(703) 413-2222
(703) 413-2225, fax
A feisty trade and lobbying organization representing travel agents. "The Association that fights for the rights and dignity of travel." ARTA welcomes independent contractors as members.

Association of Travel Marketing Executives (ATME)
P.O. Box 43563
Washington, DC 20010
(202) 232-7107

Caribbean Hotel Association (CHA)
18 Marseilles Street
Suite 1-A
Santurce, PR 00907
(809) 725-9139
This association promotes Caribbean tourism in general and the interests of its members in particular.

Caribbean Tourism Organization (CTA)
20 East 46th Street
New York, NY 10017
(212) 682-0435
(212) 697-4258, fax
A regional tourism bureau which promotes the joys of the Caribbean in the United States.

Central Ohio Travel Professionals
c/o McMurray Travel Service
787 South State Street
Westerville, OH 43081
(614) 899-1979
A professional educational, networking, and support group for travel professionals in the central Ohio region, including outside sales reps.

Commercial Travelers Association (CTA)
P.O. Box 76400
Atlanta, GA 30358
(800) 392-2856
(404) 993-1155
Representing the "average business traveler," CTA describes itself as "a non-profit contract negotiation and advocacy group." It is seeking, among other things, to end the airlines' requirement of a Saturday stay-over to qualify for the lowest fares. Dues are $15 a year.

Condominium Travel Associates, Inc.
2001 West Main Street
Suite 140
Stamford, CT 06902
(203) 975-7714
(203) 964-0073, fax
A membership travel agency consortium offering a comprehensive product and marketing program that helps position travel agents to become "the condo vacation specialist in their market areas."

Cruise Lines International Association (CLIA)
500 Fifth Avenue
Suite 1407
New York, NY 10110
(212) 921-0066
A marketing organization created by the cruise industry to promote cruise vacations in general and provide training and educational support to the travel agent community.

Department of Transportation (DOT)
400 7th Street SW
Washington, DC 20590
(202) 366-4000
This government agency oversees transportation (including tourism) and fields complaints from the public.

Elderhostel
75 Federal Street
Boston, MA 02110
(617) 426-7788
This organization promotes educational and cultural enrichment travel for senior citizens. Most trips feature visits to and lodging at institutions of higher learning.

European Travel Commission (ETC)
c/o Donald N. Martin Company
630 Fifth Avenue
Suite 565

New York, NY 10111
(212) 307-1200
This company promotes travel to Europe on behalf of its European counterpart. The New York office serves as a clearinghouse and can point you toward the resources you need.

Institute of Certified Travel Agents (ICTA)
148 Linden Street
P.O. Box 812059
Wellesley, MA 02181-0012
(617) 237-0280
(617) 237-3860, fax
A professional organization dedicated to excellence in the travel agent profession. Administers the rigorous Certified Travel Counselor (CTC) certification program, as well as other programs for the professional development of travel agents at all career stages.

International Air Transport Association (IATA)
International Airlines Travel Agents Network (IATAN)
2000 Peel Street
Montreal, Quebec
CANADA H3A 2R4
(514) 844-6311
(514) 844-5286, fax
IATA administers the system of airline and airport coding. IATAN appoints travel agencies and issues an increasingly important form of travel agent identification card. For more on these interrelated associations see *Chapters 2* and *12*.

International Association for Medical Assistance to Travellers (IAMAT)
417 Center Street
Lewiston, NY 14092
(716) 754-4883
With sufficient notice, travelers can contact IAMAT and receive a wide variety of health-related information. Their information is especially helpful on the health hazards of foreign countries to which your clients might be traveling.

International Association of Convention and Visitor Bureaus (IACVB)
P.O. Box 6690
Champaign, IL 61826-6690
(217) 359-8881
(217) 359-0965, fax
Promotes "an awareness of the convention and visitor industry's contribution to communities around the world." Works to improve professionalism within the industry.

International Federation of Women's Travel Organizations (IFWTO)
13901 North 73rd Street
Suite 210B
Scottsdale, AZ 85260
(602) 596-6640
(602) 596-6638, fax

International Forum of Travel and Tourism Advocates (IFTAA)
693 Sutter Street, 6th Floor
San Francisco, CA 94102
(415) 673-3333
(415) 673-3548, fax
This group of attorneys has allied itself with others in the travel industry to promote their mutual interests.

Long Island Travel Agents
c/o Travel With Joy
2961 Merrick Road
Bellmore, NY 11710
(516) 783-6441
(516) 783-6785, fax
A regional association of approximately 125 owners of local retail travel agencies.

Midwest Agents Selling Travel (MAST)
15 Spinning Wheel Road
Suite 336
Hinsdale, IL 60521
(708) 323-0770
(708) 323-2662, fax
A large, regional association of retail travel agencies.

Mobility International
P. O. Box 10767
Eugene, OR 97440
(503) 343-1284
(503) 343-6812, fax
A not-for-profit organization promoting international educational exchange and travel for persons of all disabilities and all ages.

National Air Carrier Association (NACA)
1730 "M" Street NW
Suite 806
Washington, DC 20036
(202) 833-8200
A trade organization representing smaller, low-cost and charter carriers.

National Air Transportation Association (NATA)
4226 King Street
Alexandria, VA 22302
(703) 845-9000

National Association of Business Travel Agents (NABTA)
3255 Wilshire Boulevard, Suite 1514
Los Angeles, CA 90010-1418
(213) 382-3335

National Association of Commissioned Travel Agents (NACTA)
P.O. Box 670963
Dallas, TX 75367-0963
(214) 739-2868
Formed in 1990 to "furnish a voice in the industry for the outside sales agent." Publishes a quarterly newsletter, offers fam trips and other benefits for its membership. Dues are $25 a year.

National Association of Cruise Only Agents (NACOA)
3191 Coral Way
Suite 630
Miami, FL 33145
(305) 446-7732
This organization provides professional support and development to cruise-only agencies.

National Business Travel Association (NBTA)
1650 King Street, Suite 301
Alexandria, VA 22314
(703) 684-0836
(703) 684-0263, fax
A lobbying and educational organization servicing corporate business travel managers.

National Tour Association (NTA)
546 East Main Street
Lexington, KY 40508
(800) 755-8687
(606) 226-4444
Trade organization of operators of escorted bus tours in the United States and Canada. Publishes a consumer's guide and offers a Consumer Protection Plan which protects travelers in case of default of a member.

National Travel and Tourism Awareness Council
1133 21st Street NW
Suite 800
Washington, DC 20036
(202) 293-1433

Organizations
& Associations

An industry coalition which promotes and publicizes the economic contribution of travel and tourism.

Outside Sales Support Network (OSSN)
1061 East Indiantown Road, Suite 410
Jupiter, FL 33477
(407) 575-7327
(407) 575-4371, fax
"The national association for independent contractors and outside sales travel agents." Provides cruise fam/seminars to educate outside reps. Local chapters hold monthly meetings featuring industry speakers.

Pacific Asia Travel Association (PATA)
Telesis Tower, Suite 1750
1 Montgomery Street
San Francisco, CA 94104
(415) 986-4646
(415) 986-3458, fax
A trade organization which promotes travel and tourism to the nations of the Pacific Rim.

Professionals In Travel, Inc. (PITI)
79768 Arnold Palmer Drive
La Quinta, CA
(800) 433-3060
An association of individuals in the travel agency business, focusing on the needs of people in travel rather than companies. Offers members a range of professional services, insurance, consumer goods at discount, and a newsletter.

Society for the Advancement of Travel for the Handicapped (SATH)
347 Fifth Avenue
Suite 610
New York, NY 10016
(212) 447-7284
(212) 725-8253, fax
Promoting the needs and interests of disabled travelers. Provides information on facilities available to the disabled in foreign countries.

Society of Travel Agents in Government (STAG)
6935 Wisconsin Avenue NW
Suite 200
Washington, DC 20815
(301) 654-8595
An association of in-house travel agents at various governmental agencies.

Tourism Industry Association of Canada (TIAC)
1016-130 Albert Street
Ottawa, Ontario, K1P 5G4
CANADA
(613) 238-3883
Promotes the interests of the tourism industry in Canada.

Travel Agents of the Carolinas
8224 Creedmoor Road
Suite 101
Raleigh, NC 27613
(919) 676-0400
(919) 676-8211, fax
A professional association of local retail travel agents.

Travel and Tourism Government Affairs Council (TTGAC)
1133 21st Street NW
Washington, DC 20036
(202) 293-5407

Travel and Tourism Research Association (TTRA)
10200 West 44th Avenue
Suite 304
Wheat Ridge, CO 80033
(303) 940-6557
(303) 422-8894, fax
An association dedicated to educating those within and outside the travel industry about tourism. Membership comprises representatives from all aspects of the travel industry, from travel agents to convention and visitors bureaus.

Travel Industry Association
2 Lafayette Center
1133 21st Street NW
Suite 800
Washington, DC 20036
(202) 293-1433
Promotes travel to and within the United States. Membership consists of hotels, attractions, state travel councils, and other members of the travel industry. Publishes a useful series of special reports and directories.

Travel Data Center
2 Lafayette Center
1133 21st Street NW
Washington, DC 20036
(202) 293-1040
This government agency conducts research in the travel industry and disseminates the results to the public.

Travel Information Service (TIS)
c/o Moss Rehabilitation Hospital
1200 West Tabor Road
Philadelphia, PA 19141-3099
(215) 456-9600
Provides information by phone for disabled travelers.

United States Tour Operators Association (USTOA)
211 East 51st Street
Suite 12B
New York, NY 10022
(212) 750-7371
(212) 421-1285, fax
A trade association of mostly large tour operators. Represents the interests of the industry and insures travelers against member default.

United States Travel and Tourism Administration (USTTA)
15th Street & Constitution Avenue NW
Room 1862
Washington, DC 20230
(202) 482-4904
Promotes tourism to the United States by foreign visitors.

Western Association of Travel Agents
21060 Homestead Road
Suite 108
Cupertino, CA 95014
(408) 720-8686
(408) 736-8912, fax
A regional association of retail travel agencies.

Chapter Twenty-Four:
Travel Schools

Learning the travel business—really learning the travel business—is not something that can be done overnight or with one hand tied behind your back. By now you probably have some appreciation for the complexity of the industry. Certainly just learning to navigate through the codes and rigamarole of one of the competing CRS systems is a daunting task by itself.

You don't need a college degree to be a successful part-time agent but you can't be completely ignorant either. This book gives you the basic information you need to get started. There is a lot more to learn, especially if you want to get automated and start churning out airline tickets in large numbers. There are several ways to learn the many ropes of the up-to-date, automated agency. One way is by hooking up with a going agency as an outside rep and getting them to teach you. Often, the agency will be more than happy to have an extra set of hands, even if it is a slow set, at the keyboard punching out tickets.

For some people, however, a formal school is the way to go. There's the companionship of your fellow students, the structure and discipline of regular classes, and the steady progress of a set curriculum. There are also the teachers who, in theory at least, are paid to be patient with you and answer your many questions.

There are hundreds, perhaps thousands, of schools teaching travel. Some are obviously better than others. What follows is a state-by-state list of travel schools that are members of the American Society of Travel Agents (ASTA). While this may be taken as an indicator of the schools' seriousness, it is not an absolute guarantee of quality. As with any substantial purchase, you should carefully investigate any travel school before plunking down your hard-earned cash.

ALASKA
SST Travel Schools of Alaska
4609 Business Park Boulevard
Anchorage, AK 99503-7121
(907) 563-8585

ARIZONA
American Express Travel School
120 North 144th Street
Suite 200
Phoenix, AZ 85034-1822
(602) 244-2660

International Society of Meeting
  Planners
8383 East Evans Road
Scottsdale, AZ 85260
(602) 483-7400

CALIFORNIA
Los Medanos Community College
353 California Drive
Burlingame, CA 94010
(415) 439-2181

Condie Junior College
1 West Campbell Avenue
Campbell, CA 95008
(408) 866-6666

Travel West Academy
2505-B Zanella Way
Chico, CA 95928
(916) 893-1388

Coastline Community College
Travel & Tourism Department
2990 Mesa Verde Drive East
Costa Mesa, CA 92626
(714) 751-9747

Travel & Tourism Institute
5252 Sunrise Boulevard
Suite 5
Fair Oaks, CA 95626-3505
(916) 967-7007

Academy Pacific
1777 North Vine Street
Hollywood, CA 90028-5218
(213) 462-3211

American College of Travel
501 Pine Avenue
Long Beach, CA 90802
(310) 491-0811

Long Beach Community College
4901 East Carson
Long Beach, CA 90808
(310) 420-4325

Trans World Travel Academy
1543 Shatto Street
Los Angeles, CA 90017

American Travel Institute
28201 Marguerite Parkway
Mission Viejo, CA 92692
(714) 364-2264

Desert Institute of Travel
41-995 Boardwalk
Suite A3
Palm Desert, CA 92260-2758
(619) 346-7755

Canada College
4200 Farm Hill Boulevard
Redwood City, CA 94061-1099
(415) 364-1212

Echols International Travel Training Course
1390 Market Street
Suite 218
San Francisco, CA 94102-5404
(415) 861-1922

International Tour Management
  Institute (dba ITME, Inc.)
625 Market Street
San Francisco, CA 94105
(415) 957-9489

San Francisco School of Travel
414 Mason Street
Suite 602
San Francisco, CA 94102
(415) 956-5622

San Francisco State University
1600 Holloway Avenue
San Francisco, CA 94132-1722
(415) 338-1205

Pacific Travel School
2515 North Main Street
Santa Ana, CA 92701-1330
(714) 543-9495

Empire Business College
3033 Cleveland Avenue
Suite 102
Santa Rosa, CA 95403
(707) 546-4058

Watterson College
5121 Van Nuys Boulevard
Sherman Oaks, CA 91403-1718
(818) 990-4070

Westem College of Travel Careers
1700 North Broadway
Suite 206
Walnut Creek, CA 94596-4138
(415) 945-0790

COLORADO
Mountain States Travel Training
   Institute
3131 South Vaughn Way, #124
Aurora, CO 80014
(303) 695-1947

The Travel School of Boulder
1745 15th Street
Boulder, CO 80302-6323

Blair Junior College
828 Wooten Road
Colorado Springs, CO 80915
(719) 574-7082

Metropolitan State College
HMTA Department
Box 60
1006 11th Street
Denver, CO 80204
(303) 556-3152

Parks Junior College
9065 Grant Street
Denver, CO 80229-4339
(303) 430-8511

The Travel Trade School, Inc.
7921 Southpark Plaza Street, #105
Littleton, CO 80120
(303) 493-8287

CONNECTICUT
Stone Academy
1315 Dixwell Avenue
Hamden, CT 06514-4136
(203) 288-7474

Briarwood College, Inc.
2279 Mt. Vernon Road
Southington, CT 06489
(203) 628-4751

School of Hotel, Restaurant &
   Tourism Administration
300 Orange Avenue
University of New Haven
West Haven, CT 06516
(203) 932-7357

DELAWARE
Brandywine College of Widener
   University
Box 7139 Concord Pike
Wilmington, DE 19803-0139
(302) 477-2046

DISTRICT OF COLUMBIA
McGraw-Hill Continuing Education Center
4401 Connecticut Avenue NW
Washington, DC 20008
(202) 244-1600

Travel Schools

FLORIDA

Webber College
Babson Park, FL
(813) 638-1431

Florida Atlantic University
MT-l, Division of Continuing
    Education
Boca Raton, FL 33431-0991
(407) 367-3179

Art Institute of Fort Lauderdale
1799 SE 17th Street
Fort Lauderdale, FL 33316-3000
(305) 463-3000

Sheridan Vo-Tech Center
5400 Sheridan Street
Hollywood, FL 33021
(305) 985-3220

Lorraine Travel School, Inc.
1001 NW Le Jeune Road
Miami, FL 33126
(305) 649-8129

Florida International University
    School of Hospitality
    Management
NE 151st Street & Biscayne
    Boulevard
North Miami, FL 33181
(305) 948-4500

Associated Schools, Inc.
1110 NE 163rd Street
North Miami Beach, FL 33162
(305) 944-4236
(800) 343-7309

Career Training Institute
2120 West Colonial Drive
Orlando, FL 32804
(407) 843-3984

Sarasota Travel School
307 South Orange Avenue
Sarasota, FL 34236-6803
(813) 957-4880

New Horizons School of Travel
6019 SE Federal Highway
Stuart, FL 34997
(407) 283-7117

National Career Institute
3918 US Highway 301N, #200
Tampa, FL 33619
(813) 620-1446

HAWAII

Traveler's Choice School of Travel
838 South Beretania Street, #206
Honolulu, HI 96813
(808) 523-5811

World Travel Academy
3626 Lower Honoapiilani Highway
P.O. Box 5399
Lahaina, HI 96761-5399

ILLINOIS

Parks College of St. Louis
    University
500 Falling Springs Road
Cahokia, IL 62206-1998
(618) 337-7500

Chicago City-Wide College
226 West Jackson Boulevard
Chicago, IL 60606-6997
(312) 855-8235

Echols International Travel and
    Hotels School, Inc.
676 North St. Clair, #1950
Chicago, IL 60611-2922
(312) 943-5500

Robert Morris College
180 North LaSalle
Chicago, IL 60601
(312) 836-6442

Trans World Travel Academy
225 North Michigan Avenue
Chicago, IL 60601

Careers In Travel, Inc.
3008 North Water Street
Decatur, IL 62526-2465
(217) 875-5640

Elgin Community College
1700 Spartan Drive
Elgin, IL 60123
(708) 888-6901

College of Dupage
Lambert & 22nd Street
Building A, Room 1031
Glen Ellyn, IL 60137-6599
(708) 858-2800

United American College of
   Travel & Tourism Careers
550 East Devon, # 170
Itasca, IL 60143
(708) 250-8866

Lincoln College School of Travel
715 West Raab Road
Normal, IL 61761
(809) 452-0500

Regal School of Travel
6420 West 127th Street, #213
Palos Heights, IL 60463-2265
(708) 389-6900

Moraine Valley Community
   College
10900 South 88th Avenue
Palos Hills, IL 60465
(708) 974-5708

INDIANA
National Business Academy
5881 East 82nd Street
Indianapolis, IN 46250
(317) 571-0047

IOWA
Hamilton Business College
1924 D Street SW
Cedar Rapids, IA 52404
(319) 363-0481

AIC Junior College
1801 East Kimberly
Davenport, IA 52807
(319) 355-3500

Midwest Travel Institute
1301 West Lombard Street
Davenport, IA 52804-2101
(319) 322-1690

American Institute of Business
2500 Fleur Drive
Des Moines, IA 50321
(515) 244-4221

Iowa Lakes Community College
3200 College Drive
Emmetsburg, IA 50536
(712) 852-3554

KANSAS
Cloud County Community College
1514 Country Club Drive
Concordia, KS 66901
(913) 243-1435

National College
630 Minnesota Avenue
Kansas City, KS 66101
(913) 371-0420

The Travel Academy
11902 Santa Fe Trail Drive
Lenexa, KS 66205
(913) 541-1700

KENTUCKY
Shawnee High School
Travel/Tourism Department
4018 West Market Street
Louisville, KY 40212
(502) 473-8356

Sullivan Junior College of Business
PO Box 33-308 3101
Bardstown Road
Louisville, KY 40205
(502) 456-6504

LOUISIANA
Ayers Institute, Inc.
PO Box 3941
Shreveport, LA 71105-3941
(318) 868-3000
(800) 284-6085

MAINE
Casco Bay College
477 Congress Street
Portland, ME 04101
(207) 772-0197

MASSACHUSETTS
Travel School of America
1047 Commonwealth Avenue
Boston, MA 02215-1001
(617) 787-1214

Salem State College
Salem, MA
(508) 741-6224

Marian Court Junior College
35 Little's Point Road
Swampscott, MA 01907-2840
(617) 595-6768

Quinsigamond Community College
670 West Boylston Street
Worcester, MA 01606-2031
(508) 853-2300

MICHIGAN
Conlin-Hallissey Travel School,
   Inc.
3270 Washtenaw Avenue
Ann Arbor, MI 48104-4250
(313) 769-2318

Suomi College
Quincy Avenue
Hancock, MI 49930-1882
(906) 482-5300

Lansing Community College
45 Hospitality Systems
PO Box 40010
Lansing, MI 48901-7210
(517) 483-1532

Aviation Career Center
38705 7 Mile Road, #270
Livonia, MI 48152-1056
(313) 953-0094

Dorsey Business Schools
30821 Barrington Avenue
Madison Heights, MI 48071
(313) 585-9200

American Institute For Travel and
   Tourism
17515 West Nine Mile Road, #225
Honeywell Center
Southfield, MI 48075
(313) 559-8040

MINNESOTA
Albert Lea Technical College
2200 Tech Drive
Albert Lea, MN 56007-3499
(507) 373-0656

Brainerd Staples Technical College
300 Quince Street
Brainerd, MN 56401-4096
(218) 828-5344

The McConnell School, Inc.
831 Second Avenue South
Minneapolis, MN 55402-2861
(612) 332-4238

Rasmussen College System
12450 Wayzata Boulevard
Minnetonka, MN 55343-5631

Dakota County Technical College
Travel Planner Program
1300 East 145th Street
Rosemount, MN 55068-2932
(612) 423-8430

MISSOURI
Columbia College
10th & Rogers Streets
Columbia, MO 65216-0001
(314) 875-7580

Maple Woods Community College
2601 NE Barry Road
Kansas City, MO 64156
(816) 436-6500

Trans World Travel Academy
11500 Ambassador Drive
Kansas City, MO 64195

Trans World Travel Academy
502 Earth City Plaza, #204
St. Louis, MO 63045
(314) 291-6321

NEBRASKA
Spencer School of Business
410 West 2nd
Grand Island, NE 68801
(308) 382-8044

Calvin T. Ryan Library
Kearney State College
Kearney, NE 68849
(308) 234-8545

Lincoln School of Commerce
1821 K Street
Lincoln, NE 68508
(402) 474-5315

Travel Careers Institute
9777 "M" Street
Omaha, NE 68127-2008
(402) 339-1200

Universal Technical Institute
4001 South 24th Street
Omaha, NE 68107
(402) 345-2422

NEW HAMPSHIRE
Hesser College
3 Sundial Avenue
Manchester, NH 03103
(603) 668-6660

NEW JERSEY
Bergen Community College
400 Paramus Road
Paramus, NJ 07652-1595
(201) 447-0525

Montclair State College
Commercial Recreation & Tourism
    Program
Upper Montclair, NJ 07043-1624
(201) 893-5254

NEW MEXICO
National College
1202 Pennsylvania NE
Albuquerque, NM 87110
(505) 265-7517

NEW YORK
Genessee Community College
College Road
Batavia, NY 14020-9704
(716) 343-0055

State University of New York
    College of Technology
MacDonald Hall, #124
Delhi, NY 13753
(607) 746-4189

Tompkins Cortland Community
    College
PO Box 139
Dryden, NY 13053-0139
(607) 844-8211

Travel Schools

Herkimer County Community
College
Herkimer, NY
(315) 866-0300

Sullivan County Community
College
P.O. Box 269
Department of Travel & Tourism
Loch Sheldrake, NY 12759
(914) 434-5750

LaGuardia Community College
31-10 Thomson Avenue
Long Island City, NY 11101-3083
(718) 482-5619

Brugger, Inc.
dba Travel Institute
15 Park Row
Suite 617
New York, NY 10038
(212) 349-3331

National Academy Foundation
660 Madison Avenue
Suite 1804
New York, NY 10022
(212) 754-0044

New York University
Management Institute
School of Continuing
Education
48 Cooper Square
New York, NY 10003
(212) 998-7215

Trans World Travel Academy
2 Penn Plaza
New York, NY 10121

Travel Careers International, Ltd.
184 Fifth Avenue
New York, NY 10010
(212) 242-2277

Institute of Travel, Hotel, & Restaurant Administration
Niagara University
Niagara Falls, NY 14109-9999
(716) 285-1212

Paul Smith's College
Routes 30 & 86
Paul Smiths, NY 12970
(518) 327-6218

Monroe Community College
1000 East Henrietta Boulevard
Rochester, NY 14623-5789
(716) 292-7900

Rockland Community College
145 College Road
Suffern, NY 10901-3699
(914) 356-4650

NORTH CAROLINA
Lucas Travel School
2201 Coronation Boulevard
Charlotte, NC 28227
(704) 847-6005

Lucas Travel School
7817 National Service Road, #508
Greensboro, NC 27409
(919) 665-0210

Lucas Travel School
5540 Centerview Drive
Raleigh, NC 27606-3363
(919) 851-2900

OHIO
Bowling Green State University
102 North Main Street
Bowling Green, OH 43402
(419) 372-8181

Rets Tech Center, Inc.
116 Westpark Road
PO Box 130
Centerville, OH 45459
(513) 433-3410

Tri State Travel School
4600 Montgomery Road
Suite 210
Cincinnati, OH 45212
(513) 841-5588

Columbus State Community
    College
Hospitality Management
    Department
550 East Spring Street
Columbus, OH 43215
(614) 227-2579

Sinclair Community College
444 West Third Street
Room 5141-A
Dayton, OH 45402
(513) 226-2964

Travel Agents Training School
5356 Pearl Road, Side Entry
Parma, OH 44129
(216) 845-0304

Toledo Travel School
2034 South Byrne Road
Toledo, OH 43614-5198
(419) 385-3161

OKLAHOMA
Demarge College
3608 NW 58th
Oklahoma City, OK 73112
(405) 947-1425

OREGON
Trend Colleges - Eugene
1050 Green Acres
Eugene, OR 97401
(503) 342-5377

Emmett Travel School
10250 SW Greenburg Road
Portland, OR 97223-5494
(503) 293-2323

Northwestern College of Business
1950 SW Sixth Avenue
Portland, OR 97201-5226
(503) 224-6410

PENNSYLVANIA
Northampton Community College
3835 Green Pond Road
Bethlehem, PA 18017-7568
(215) 691-8489

Harcum Junior College
Program Director, Hospitality -
    Tourism
Bryn Mawr, PA 19010
(215) 526-6073

Keystone Junior College
PO Box 50
LaPlume, PA 18440-0200
(717) 945-5141

Luzerne County Community
    College
Prospect & Middle Road
Nanticoke, PA 18634-3814
(717) 821-1514

Martin School of Business
2417 Welsh Road
Philadelphia, PA 19114-2206
(215) 677-6110

The Boyd School
One Chatham Center
Pittsburgh, PA 15219
(412) 456-1800

ICM School of Business
10 Wood Street
Pittsburgh, PA 15222-1977
(412) 261-2647

Trans World Travel Academy
2250 Butler Pike
Suite 130
Plymouth Meeting, PA 19462

Reading Area Community College
PO Box 1706
Reading, PA 19603
(215) 372-4721

Central Pennsylvania Business
   School
College Hill Road
Summerdale, PA 17093-9999
(717) 732-0702

York Technical Institute
3351 Whiteford Road
York, PA 17402-9017
(717) 757-1100

RHODE ISLAND
Johnson & Wales University
Abbott Park Place
Providence, RI 02903
(401) 456-1475

SOUTH DAKOTA
National College
321 Kansas City Street
Rapid City, SD 57701
(605) 394-4943

Black Hills State University
1200 University
USB 9082
Spearfish, SD 57799-9082
(605) 642-6734

TENNESSEE
Edmondson Junior College
3635 Brainerd Road
Chattanooga, TN 37411-3693
(615) 698-3885

Southeast College of Technology,
   Inc.
2731 Nanconnah Boulevard
Memphis, TN 38132
(901) 345-1000

TEXAS
International Aviation & Travel
   Academy
300 West Arbrook
Arlington, TX 76014-3105
(817) 784-7000

Capitol City Careers
4630 Westgate Boulevard
Austin, TX 78745
(512) 892-4270

Pace Travel School
1106 Clayton Lane, #130E
Austin, TX 78723-1033
(512) 459-1241

American Airlines Travel Academy
PO Box 155391
Fort Worth, TX 76155-5391
(817) 963-3480

North Harris County College
20000 Kingwood Drive
Kingwood, TX 77339
(713) 359-1646

SST Travel Schools of Texas
4502 Centerview, #602
San Antonio, TX 78228
(512) 736-4299

UTAH
Bryman School
1144 West 3300 South
Salt Lake City, UT 84119
(801) 975-7000

June Morris School of Travel
240 East 2430 South
Salt Lake City, UT 84115
(801) 483-6417

Murdock Travel School
36 South State, 9th floor
Salt Lake City, UT 84111-1452
(801) 521-7850

VERMONT

Champlain College - Travel &
  Tourism
163 South Willard
Burlington, VT 05401-3950
(802) 658-0800

VIRGINIA

Commonwealth College, Hampton
  Campus
1120 West Mercury Boulevard
Hampton, VA 23666
(804) 838-2122

National Business College
Travel and Airline Careers
PO Box 6400
Roanoke, VA 24017-0400
(703) 986-1800

Commonwealth College
4160 Virginia Beach Boulevard
Virginia Beach, VA 23452-1744
(804) 340-0633

Lucas Travel School, Inc.
184 Business Park Drive
Virginia Beach, VA 23462-6533
(804) 499-7522

WASHINGTON

Academy of Travel Careers
10900 NE 8th Street
Suite 900
Bellevue, WA 98004
(206) 462-5703

SST Travel Schools of Western
  Washington
1474 - 112 Avenue NE
Suite 200
Bellevue, WA 98004
(206) 451-3990

SST Travel Schools
3400 - 188th Street SW
Suite 125
Lynwood, WA 98037
(206) 771-3245

Art Institute of Seattle
Management in Travel & Tourism
2323 Elliott Avenue
Seattle, WA 98121
(206) 448-0900

The Fox Travel Institute
520 Pike Street
Suite 2800
Seattle, WA 98101-4000
(206) 224-7800

SST Travel Schools of the Pacific
  Northwest, Inc.
18000 Pacific Highway South
Tower 1, Suite 411
Seattle, WA 98188
(206) 244-9200

Bates Technical College
1101 South Yakima
Tacoma, WA 98405
(206) 596-1689

Clover Park Vocation
  Technical Institute
4500 Steilacoom Boulevard SW
Tacoma, WA 98499-4098
(206) 756-5649

International Air Academy
2901 East Mill Plain Boulevard
Vancouver, WA 98661
(206) 695-2500

WISCONSIN

Academy of Travel, Ltd.
12700 West Bluemound Road
Elm Grove, WI 53122-2637
(414) 782-9191

The Milwaukee College of Business
161 West Wisconsin Avenue
Milwaukee, WI 53203
(414) 272-4736

Stratton College
1300 North Jackson Street
Milwaukee, WI 53202-2602
(414) 276-5200

Chapter Twenty-Five:
Further Reading

In this section, I have listed magazines and books that you might find helpful as you embark on your new lifestyle as a part-time travel agent. Learning the travel business is a lifetime commitment. The range of topics to master is so wide that I cannot pretend that this list is anywhere near all-inclusive. For example, I have not even attempted to cover the thousands upon thousands of books that cover the many world-wide destinations to which you will be sending your clients.

So rather than attempt to be exhaustive, I have tried to point you to a number of resources in a number of directions you may wish to explore. The magazines, both trade and consumer, will provide an on-going resource and up-to-the-minute information. The books listed will provide a beginning. As your own studies progress, you will, I am sure, uncover additional resources that will prove helpful.

Trade publications

These publications are intended for those within the travel industry, primarily retail travel agents. Obviously, you won't want to get them all — you wouldn't have time to read them — but subscribing to a few will give you a feel for the travel agency business and make you feel like a pro. Don't expect these publications to teach you the business, however. That is best accomplished through seminars, professional organizations such as OSSN, and actual experience. What they *will* do is keep you up-to-date on trends and issues in the industry and alert you to new tour and cruise packages that you might want to sell.

I have annotated some of the listings. However, don't assume that because a publication isn't annotated, it is not worth a look. You can always call or write the publication and request a sample issue and then make up your own mind. Information in quotation marks has been supplied by the publication itself.

Some of these publications are free to qualified professionals. Once you have established an outside sales relationship with an agency, you may want to see if you can get a complimentary subscription. On the subscription form, give your agency's IATA number; ask your contact at the agency how to answer the questions on the form about agency volume and so forth. Be honest and bill yourself as an outside sales rep and ask to receive the subscription at your home. There's no guarantee, but it's worth a try.

ASTA Agency Management
Pace Communications, Inc.
1301 Carolina Street
Greensboro, NC 27401
(919) 378-6065
(800) 828-2712
Monthly; $36/year (for non-members).
This is the magazine for members of the American Society of Travel Agents who receive it as part of their membership dues. Covers travel industry trends (the ecological impact of increased tourism, what's new in automation, etc.) and agency issues (why agents are cutting back on fam trips). Also features how-they-did-it success stories that might fire your imagination. If you're an outside rep for an ASTA agency, you might want to ask to be put on the distribution list for their copy.

Better Business Traveling
25115 West Avenue Stanford
Valencia, CA 91355
(805) 295-0175

Business Travel Management
Coastal Communications
488 Madison Avenue
New York, NY 10022
(212) 888-1500

Business Travel News
CMP Publications,
600 Community Drive
Manhasset, NY 11030
(516) 365-4600
Semi-monthly; "free to qualified corporate travel arrangers," $95/year otherwise.
As the name implies, the focus here is on the business traveler, with an emphasis on in-house travel agencies of large corporations, meeting planners, and relationships between suppliers and major business customers.

Canadian Travel Press Weekly
310 Dupont Street
Toronto, Ontario M5R 1V9
CANADA
(416) 968-7252

Corporate Travel
1515 Broadway
New York, NY 10036
(212) 869-1300
Monthly, $36/year.

Cruise Travel
990 Grove Street
Evanston, IL 60201
(708) 491-6440

Cruise and Vacation Views
60 East 42nd Street, Suite 905
New York, NY 10165
(212) 867-7470
A controlled circulation magazine which is free for qualified travel agents.
It covers the leisure market.

GTC Fam Facts
1454 East Hinchman Road
Berrien Springs, MI 49103
(800) 695-2156
Monthly; $60/year, $89.95/two years.
A newsletter listing familiarization trips, agent incentives, contests, complimentary hotel rooms, and such. The price of the subscription includes
"three annual directories listing over 400 pages of agent reduced rates" on
a variety of domestic and international travel products and services. Information on fams is generally available elsewhere in the trade press or
through your agency. There's a 60-day money-back guarantee.

Jax Fax Travel Marketing Magazine
Jet Airtransport Exchange, Inc.
397 Post Road, P.O. Box 4013
Darien, CT 06820-1413
(203) 655-8746
(203) 655-6257, fax
Monthly; $12/year, $20/two years, $25/three years.
A thick, information-packed monthly that focuses on what's available from
various travel suppliers. A goldmine of information on deep-discount consolidator fares. Just look up the destination you (or your client) wants and
find out who's offering the best deal. Also features information on the latest in cruises, tours, and fam trips.

Les Romantiques
E&M Associates
211 East 43rd Street, #104
New York, NY 10017
(800) 223-9832

(212) 599-8280
Published three times a year, this newsletter highlights "the best romantic hotels" around the world. Aimed at travel agents (it's free to agents with IATA number), the publication features only properties paying at least 8% commission and reachable through an 800 number.

Tours and Resorts
990 Grove Street
Evanston, IL 60201
(708) 491-6440

Tour and Travel News
CMP Publications, Inc.
600 Community Drive
Manhasset, NY 11030
(516) 562-5000
Weekly; free to qualified travel agents, $95/year otherwise.
This "newspaper for the retail travel industry" offers a mix of articles on what's going on in the travel biz, from fare wars to agency bankruptcies, coupled with destination stories highlighting new tours.

Travel Age (East, West, Midwest editions)
888 Seventh Avenue
New York, NY 10019
(212) 237-3000
Weekly; free to qualified agents, $10/year otherwise.
Published in regional editions, this magazine-sized weekly features general travel industry news, with a regional focus. One nice feature is the Discount Corner, listing discounts available to travel agents. There is also a separate listing of fam trips and seminars being offered around the country.

Travel Agent
801 Second Avenue
New York, NY 10017
(212) 370-5050
Weekly; $79/year.
Slick, weekly newsmagazine in the mold of *Time* or *Business Week*. Bills itself as "The National Newsweekly of the Travel Industry." Provides a good overview of the industry and its trends with an emphasis on reporting (as opposed to reprinting press releases). Profiles of agencies sometimes provide good how-to tips.

Travel Counselor
CMP Publications
6000 Community Drive
Manhasset, NY 11030
(516) 562-5000
Quarterly, "a supplement of *Tour & Travel News*."

This magazine is "directed solely to the graduates of ICTA," Certified Travel Counselors (CTC), and Destination Specialists (DS). It describes itself as dedicated to "the continuing education of Travel Counselors, covering marketing communications, career growth, legal issues, research, and travel counseling opportunities."

Travel Expense Management Newsletter
American Business Publishing
3100 Highway 138
Wall Township, NJ 07719-1442
(908) 681-1133
Twice monthly; $397/year.
Aimed at corporate travel managers, this eight- to ten-page newsletter covers a range of issues of importance to people overseeing the corporate travel function. It is of little use to agencies, unless they are into the corporate travel scene in a major way, and the high ticket price will discourage browsers. An allied publication, the *Travel Expense Management Guide*, is published periodically for approximately $85, and is available to non-subscribers.

Travel Industry Indicators
P.O. Box 6627
Miami, FL 33154
(305) 868-3818
Monthly; $95/year.
Tracks and analyzes statistical trends in the travel industry with easy-to-read graphs in a no-nonsense newsletter format.

Travel Life
Whittle Communications
505 Market Street
Knoxville, TN 37902
(615) 595-5000

Travel Management Daily
Reed Travel Group
500 Plaza Drive
Secaucus, NJ 07094
(201) 902-2000
Daily (with special convention issues); $735/year, $420 for six months.
Covers essentially the same ground as *Travel Weekly* (it's owned by the same company), but provides its information on a more timely basis.

Travel Trade
15 West 44th Street
New York, NY 10036
(212) 730-6600
Weekly; $10/year.

Further Reading

A no-nonsense business-oriented weekly tabloid — it likes to call itself "the business paper of the travel industry." Among its better features are a lively "Letters to the Editor" column and the "Business Features Showcase," which offers tips and suggestions from industry pros, some of which can be put to use by part-time and outside reps.

Travel Weekly
500 Plaza Drive
Secaucus, NJ 07094.
(201) 902-1500
Twice weekly; $19/year.
A lively, glossy, tabloid style publication that combines travel industry news (who's doing what) with regular features on specific destinations (which can alert you to tours and cruises you might want to sell). There are regular supplements that give extended attention to various destinations (Hawaii and Europe are the most frequent, but less familiar areas like the Maya region of Central America are covered, too). Occasionally carries classified ads from agencies looking for outside reps. A good, cheap way to get a feel for the business.

Travel World News
One Morgan Avenue
Norwalk, CT 06851-5017
(203) 853-4955
Monthly; free to qualified subscribers, otherwise $25/year.
Similar to *Jax Fax* in look, feel, and layout. Covers the usual mix of industry news, new tours by region of the world, consolidator fares, cruises, fams, and so forth.

U.S. Rail Update
U.S. Rail Corp.
c/o D.P. Wilkinson
86-25 Van Wyck Expressway
Briarwood, NY 11435
(718) 526-9067
(718) 526-0609, phone/fax
Monthly; $19.50/year, $35/two years.
This newsletter covers developments on the domestic rail scene and provides advice on issuing rail tickets.

Consumer publications

These magazines and newsletters are targeted primarily to consumers (your clients!). That doesn't mean that the part-time travel agent won't find a lot of interest here, especially if a publication zeros in on an area that you are interested in. Many times, a consumer publication can not only help you identify a great vacation for a client, but it can help you sell it as well.

Andrew Harper's Hideaway Report
P.O. Box 50
Sun Valley, ID 83353
Monthly; $100/year.
The granddaddy of luxury travel newsletters. Harper (not his real name) tours super-luxury resorts, hotels and spas and writes unbiased and highly opinionated critiques. The circulation is held to 15,000 to heighten the exclusivity of the letter and there is sometimes a waiting list for new subscribers. The articles can serve as useful sales aids when dealing with well-heeled clients.

Anthony Osborne's Discoveries
1761 Heritage Lane
Sacramento, CA 95815
(800) 727-7727
(916) 923-0585
(916) 923-0663, fax
Monthly; $49/year.
A clone of the *Hideaway Report*, covering similar properties and aimed at a similar readership. It offered an 18-month, charter "membership" to the travel trade for $39.

Business Traveler International
41 East 42nd Street
New York, NY 10017
(212) 697-1700
Monthly.

Caribbean Travel and Life Magazine
8403 Colesville Road, Suite 830
Silver Spring, MD 20910
(301) 588-2300

Conde Nast Traveler
P.O. Box 57018
Boulder, CO 80322-7018
(800) 777-0700
Monthly; $12/year.
A glossy monthly with an emphasis on the upscale travel experience. Appeals to the well-to-do traveler and the not-so-well-to-do dreamer.

Consumer Reports Travel Letter
P.O. Box 53629
Boulder CO 80322-3629
Monthly; $37/year.
Geared to the upscale penny-pincher, this no-nonsense newsletter gives the low-down on the best deals in travel, covering things like consolidators, travel clubs, round-the-world fares, frequent flyer programs, and so

Further Reading

forth. Destination coverage is confined to one- or two-page articles on major world cities, featuring capsule information on what to see, where to stay, and what to eat.

The Discerning Traveler
504 West Mermaid Lane
Philadelphia, PA 19118-4206
(215) 247-5578
Bi-monthly; $50/year.
This newsletter is a labor of love by a husband-wife team. Each issue focuses in-depth on one vacation area on the East Coast. Back issues (which come with updated information, when available) may be ordered separately.

Freighter Travel News
3524 Harts Lake Road
Roy, WA 98580
Monthly; $18/year.
Readers of this newsletter provide first-hand accounts of trips aboard passenger-carrying freighters. Offers an interesting look at an off-beat corner of the travel world but of limited use to the travel agent.

International Travel News
520 Calvados Street
Sacramento, CA 95815
(916) 457-3643
Monthly; $16/year.
On a pennies-per-word basis, *ITN* has to be the best buy in travel magazines. Printed on cheap newsprint-like paper, this 100-pager appeals primarily to the more adventurous budget traveler. Its pages are filled with tips from readers on the best flophouses in Malaysia and articles on how to bargain on Beijing's "O.K." Street. While it may be a little too "hippie-dippie" for some tastes, it makes for fun reading and could be a good source of information if your travel business leans to the adventure or eco-tourist market.

Islands
Island Publishing Company
3886 State Street
Santa Barbara, CA 93105
(805) 682-7177

The Mature Traveler Newsletter
P. O. Box 50820
Reno, NV 89513-0820
Monthly; $24.50/year.
Tips and discounts for the 49+ crowd. Subscription includes four "special reports" on topics like lodging and airline deals.

National Geographic Traveler
P.O. Box 2895,
Washington, DC 20077-9960
(202) 857-7000
Monthly; $17.95/year.
Covers the world, much in the style of *Conde Nast Traveler* or *Travel & Leisure*, although with perhaps more of an outdoorsy sensibility.

Travel and Leisure
1120 Avenue of the Americas
New York, NY 10036
(800) 888-8728
(212) 362-5600
Monthly; $32/year.
A slick, thick luxurious look at the world of (generally) luxury travel, with an accent on good writing and honest appraisals.

Travel Confidential
88 Bleecker Street
New York, NY 10012
(212) 254-1069
Monthly; $95/year.
This newsletter made a mark for itself by publishing the special "event codes" airlines use to designate discount fares to conventions, association meetings, seminars, and the like. If you have the code, you can get a client a last-minute fare to an event city at 45% off. American Airlines has sued the newsletter for revealing the codes, even though it says it is discontinuing event fares. *Travel Confidential* also publishes the "lowest available" consolidator fares for destinations around the world.

Travel Holiday
28 West 23rd Street
New York, NY 10010
(212) 633-4660
10 times a year; $12.97/year.
A somewhat less glamorous version of *Conde Nast Traveler* and *Travel & Leisure*, with an accent on how-to information and tips.

Travel Smart
40 Beechdale Road
Dobbs Ferry, NY 10522
(914) 693-8300
Monthly; $44/year.
Newsletter offering short bits of information on travel tips, low fares, hotel discounts, last-minute deals, and the like. Also runs what to do-see-eat features on destinations, with an emphasis on the U.S. Although the masthead promises "No Advertising," each 12-page issue has three pages of ads!

Further Reading

Books about travel & the travel business

Anolik, Alexander, *The Law and the Travel Industry*. San Francisco: Anolik, 1990.

Boe, Beverly, and Phil Philcox, *How You Can Travel Free as a Group Tour Organizer*. Babylon, NY: Pilot Books, 1987.

Boniface, Brian G. and Christopher P. Cooper, *The Geography of Travel and Tourism*. New York: Fairchild, n.d.

Boyd, Wilma, *Travel Agent*. Englewood Cliffs: Prentice-Hall, 1989.

Bryant, Carl L., et. al., *Travel Selling Skills*. Cincinnati: South-Western Publishing Co., 1991.

Cassidy, Maggie B., *Taking Students Abroad: A Complete Guide for Teachers*, rev. ed. Brattleboro, VT: Pro Lingua Associates, Inc., 1988.

Cournoyer and Marshall, *Hotel, Restaurant, and Travel Law*, 3rd ed. Albany: Delmar Publishers, 1988.

Davidoff, Doris, and Philip Davidoff, *Air Fares and Ticketing*, 2nd ed. Englewood Cliffs, NJ: Prentice-Hall, 1991.

Davidoff, Doris, and Philip Davidoff, *Financial Management for Travel Agencies*. Albany: Delmar Publishers, 1986.

Davidoff, Doris, and Philip Davidoff, *Sales and Marketing for Travel and Tourism*, 2nd ed. Englewood Cliffs, NJ: Prentice-Hall, 1994.

Davidoff, Doris, and Philip Davidoff, *Worldwide Tours: A Travel Agent's Guide to Selling Tours*. Englewood Cliffs, NJ: Prentice-Hall, 1990.

Davidoff, Philip G., *Tourism Geography*. Englewood Cliffs, NJ: Prentice-Hall, 1988.

Davidoff, Philip G., *Tourism Geography Workbook*. Englewood Cliffs, NJ: Prentice-Hall, 1992.

De Souto, Martha Sarbey, *Group Travel Operations Manual*, 2nd ed. Albany: Delmar Publishers, 1993.

Dervaes, Claudine, *Travel Agency Computerization*. Tampa: Solitaire, 1992.

Dervaes, Claudine, *Travel Agency Computerization Software*. Tampa: Solitaire, 1990.

Dervaes, Claudine, *Travel Training Workbook, The*, 6 vol., 5th ed. Tampa: Solitaire, 1994.

Enggass, Peter M., *Tourism and the Travel Industry: An Information Sourcebook*. Phoenix: Oryx Press, 1988.

Fee, Gary, and Alexander Anolik, *Official Outside Sales Travel Agent Manual, The*. St. Louis: Travel Support Systems, 1992.

Fink, Martha Norman, *Successful Travel Marketing*. Daly City, CA: Blue Ribbon Productions, 1993.

Ford-Woodcock, Jean, *Advanced Domestic Ticketing and Tours*. Glen Ellyn, IL: Bridgewater Publishing, 1987.

Ford-Woodcock, Jean, *Introduction to Airline and Travel Agency Operations*. Glen Ellyn, IL: Bridgewater Publishing, 1986.

Ford-Woodcock, Jean, *Introduction to Domestic Airline Ticketing*. Glen Ellyn, IL: Bridgewater Publishing, 1986.

Ford-Woodcock, Jean, *Introduction to International Airline Ticketing*. Glen Ellyn, IL: Bridgewater Publishing, 1987.

Foster, Dennis L., *Business of Travel, The: Agency Operations and Administration*. New York: Macmillan, 1990.

Foster, Dennis L., *First Class: An Introduction to Travel and Tourism,* 2nd ed. Westerville, OH: Glencoe, 1993.

Foster, Dennis L., *Sales and Marketing for the Travel Professional*. New York: Macmillan, 1990.

Fremont, Pamela, *How To Open and Run A Money-Making Travel Agency*. New York: John Wiley & Sons, 1983.

Friedheim, Eric. *Travel Agents: From Caravans and Clippers to the Concorde*. New York: Universal Media, 1992.

Godwin, Nadine, *Complete Guide To Travel Agency Automation,* 2nd ed. Albany: Delmar Publishers, 1987.

Gold, Hal, *The Cruise Book: From Brochure To Bon Voyage*. Albany: Delmar Publishers, 1990.

Goldsmith, Carol, and Ann Waigand, *Building Profits With Group Travel*. San Francisco: Dendrobium, 1990.

Gregory, Aryear, *The Travel Agent: Dealer in Dreams,* 2nd ed. Englewood Cliffs, NJ: Prentice-Hall, 1985.

Hayes, Greg, and Joan Wright, *Going Places: The Guide to Travel Guides*. Harvard Common Press, 1988.

Heckler, Helen. *Directory of Travel Agencies for the Disabled*. Vancouver, WA: Twin Peaks Press, 1993.

Hoosen, Chris, and Francis Dix, *Travel Agent Training Series*. Clinton Turnpike, MI: Travel Text Associates, 1989.

Howell, David W., *Passport: An Introduction to Travel and Tourism Industry*. Cincinnati: South-Western Publishing Co., 1988.

Jansz, Natania, *Real Guide for Women Travelling*. Englewood Cliffs, NJ: Prentice-Hall, 1990.

Jung, Gerald, *A Practical Guide to Selling Travel*. New York: Prentice-Hall Travel, 1992.

Krygel, Barbara, *Basic Ticketing,* 3 vol., 2nd ed. Turnpike, MI: Travel Text Associates, 1983.

Makower, Joel, ed., *The Map Catalog*. New York: Random House, 1986.

Maxtone-Graham, John, *Crossing & Cruising: From the Golden Era of Ocean Liners to the Luxury Cruise Ships of Today*. New York: Scribner's, 1993.

Middleton, Victor T. C., *Marketing in Travel and Tourism*. New York: Fairchild, n.d.

Mitchell, Gerald E., *How to Design and Package Tours*. Englewood, FL: G.E. Mitchell & Associates, 1992.

Monaghan, Kelly, *Consolidators: Air Travel's Bargain Basement*. New York: The Intrepid Traveler, 1993.

Monaghan, Kelly, *Insiders Guide To Air Courier Bargains, The,* 3rd ed. New York: The Intrepid Traveler, 1994.

Monaghan, Kelly, *Shopper's Guide To Outside Agent Opportunities, A*. New York: The Intrepid Traveler, 1994.

Morrison, Alastair M., *Hospitality and Travel Marketing*. Albany: Delmar Publishers, 1989.

Nwanna, Gladson I., *Americans Traveling Abroad: What You Should Know Before You Go.* Baltimore, MD: The World Travel Institute Press, 1993.

Ogg, Thomas, *How To Buy Or Sell a Travel Agency.* Valley Center, CA: Travel Business Investments, 1988.

Poynter, James, *Corporate Travel Management.* Englewood Cliffs: Prentice-Hall, 1990.

Poynter, James, *Foreign Independent Tours.* Albany: Delmar Publishers, 1989.

Poynter, James, *Travel Agency Accounting Procedures.* Albany: Delmar Publishers, 1991.

Reilly, Robert T., *Effective Communication in the Travel Industry.* Albany: Delmar Publishers, 1990.

Reilly, Robert T., *Handbook of Professional Tour Management*, 2nd ed. Albany: Delmar Publishers, 1991.

Reilly, Robert T., *Travel and Tourism Marketing Techniques*, 2nd ed. Albany: Delmar Publishers, 1988.

Rice, Susan, *Welcome to Worldspan: Pars Edition.* Indianapolis: Travel Careers, n.d.

Roberts, Graeme, compiler, *Computerised Reservations System Words and Phrases.* Holmes Beach, FL: Wm. W. Gaunt & Sons, 1991.

Semer-Purzicki, Jeanne, *A Practical Guide to Fares and Ticketing.* Albany: Delmar Publishers, 1990.

Semer-Purzycki, Jeanne, *A Practical Guide to SABRE Reservations and Ticketing.* Albany: Delmar Publishers, 1992.

Simoney, Maggie, ed., *The Traveler's Reading Guide.* New York: Facts on File Books, 1987.

Stevens, Laurence, *Guide to Starting and Operating a Successful Travel Agency*, 3rd ed. Albany: Delmar Publishers, 1990.

Stevens, Laurence, *Guide to Travel Agency Security.* Albany: Delmar Publishers, 1982.

Stevens, Laurence, *Travel Manager's Personnel Manual, The,* 2nd ed. Albany: Delmar Publishers, 1990.

Stevens, Laurence, *Your Career in Travel, Tourism, and Hospitality*, 6th ed. Albany: Delmar Publishers, 1988.

Tepper, Bruce, *Incentive Travel, The Complete Guide.* San Francisco: Dendrobium, 1992.

Thompson, Douglas, *How To Open Your Own Travel Agency,* 3rd ed. San Francisco: Dendrobium, 1992.

Thompson, Douglas, *Profitable Direct Mail for Travel Agencies.* San Francisco: Dendrobium, 1992.

Thompson, Douglas, and Alexander Anolik, *Personnel and Operations Manual for Travel Agencies, A.* San Francisco: Dendrobium, 1993.

Thompson-Smith, Jeanie M., *Travel Agency Guide to Business Travel.* Albany: Delmar Publishers, 1988.

Todd, Ginger, *Selling Travel 1-2-3.* Indianapolis: Travel Careers, 1990.

Todd, Ginger, and Susan Rice, *Travel Perspectives: A Guide to Becoming a Travel Agent.* Albany: Delmar Publishers, 1992.

Travel Industry Association of America, *Discover America Package Tour Handbook*. Washington, DC: TIAA, 1993.

Ward, Douglas, *Berlitz Complete Guide to Cruising and Cruise Ships: Where to Cruise and How to Choose*. New York: Berlitz, 1993.

Webster, Susan, and Ralph Phillips, *Group Travel Operating Procedures*. New York: Van Nostrand Reinhold, 1983.

WHO staff, *International Travel and Health: Vaccination Requirements and Health Advice*. World Health Organization, c/o Chicago: ASCP Press, 1993.

Woodring, Carol, and Gail S. Huck, *Reservations and Ticketing: Apollo*. Albany: Delmar Publishers, 1991.

Zvoncheck, Juls, *Cruises: Selecting, Selling & Booking*. New York: Prentice-Hall, 1988.

Travel industry reference books

The books listed here are published periodically and provide highly targeted, up-to-date information for the professional or part-time travel agent. As a result, most of them are fairly expensive. Sometimes, you can get a good price on the more expensive tomes when they are offered to the membership of organizations like OSSN.

Business Travel Planner. Official Airlines Guides, 2000 Clearwater Drive, Oak Brook, IL 60521-9953. Quarterly; $136/year.

Hotel & Motel Redbook, European Edition. Official Airlines Guides, 2000 Clearwater Drive, Oak Brook, IL 60521-9953. Quarterly; $136/year.

Hotel & Motel Redbook, Pacific Asia Edition. Official Airlines Guides, 2000 Clearwater Drive, Oak Brook, IL 60521-9953. Quarterly; $136/year.

Hotel & Travel Index. Reed Travel Group, 500 Plaza Drive, Secaucus, NJ 07096. Quarterly; $125/yr.

Intrepid Traveler's Complete Desk Reference, The. New York: The Intrepid Traveler, P.O. Box 438, New York, NY 10034-0438, 1994; $14.95.

OAG Cruise and Shipline Guide. Official Airlines Guides, 2000 Clearwater Drive, Oak Brook, IL 60521-9953, bi-monthly; $106/year.

OAG Desktop Flight Guide (North American Edition). Official Airlines Guides, 2000 Clearwater Drive, Oak Brook, IL 60521-9953. Monthly and bi-weekly; $238 - $415/year.

OAG Desktop Flight Guide (Worldwide Edition). Official Airlines Guides, 2000 Clearwater Drive, Oak Brook, IL 60521-9953. Monthly; $270/year.

OAG Pocket Flight Guide. Four separate editions: North American; Europe/Africa/Middle East; Pacific/Asia; and Latin American/Caribbean. Official Airlines Guides, 2000 Clearwater Drive, Oak Brook, IL 60521-9953. Monthly; $82/year.

Official Hotel Guide. 44 Cook Street, Denver, CO 80206.

Official Tour Directory. Thomas Publishing, One Penn Plaza, New York, NY 10119. (212) 290-7355. Bi-annual; $28.

OHG Cruise Directory. 44 Cook Street, Denver, CO 80206.

Travel Industry Personnel Directory. Fairchild Books, 7 West 34th Street.

New York, NY 10001. 1993; $30.

Worldwide Brochures. 1227 Kenneth Street, Detroit Lakes, MN 56501. Annual, $39. (800) 852-6752.

Mail order sources for travel books

Travel books, especially guides to out of the way places, are sometimes hard to come by locally. Here are some travel-oriented catalogs that might prove useful if you are not located near a large metropolitan area. They will be most helpful in locating guidebooks and general travel books. By and large, they do not carry specialized books about the travel business or travel industry directories and reference works.

Bon Voyage!
2069 West Bullard Avenue
Fresno, CA 93711-1200
(800) 995-9716

Book Passage
51 Tamal Vista Boulevard
Corte Madera, CA 94925
(800) 321-9785
(415) 927-0960
(415) 924-3838 Fax

The Complete Traveller Bookstore By Mail
199 Madison Avenue
New York, NY 10016
(212) 685-9007

Travellers' Bookstore
75 Rockefeller Plaza
(22 West 52nd Street)
New York, NY 10019
(212) 664-0995

Books for the home-based business

Arden, Lynie, *The Work-at-Home Sourcebook.* Boulder, CO: Live Oak Publications, 1987.

Boone, Louis E., and David L. Kurtz, *Contemporary Marketing*, 6th ed. Tacoma Park, MD: Dryden Press, 1988.

Brabec, Barbara, *Help for Your Growing Home-Based Business.* Naperville, IL: Brabec Productions, n.d.

Brenner, Gary, *Complete Handbook for the Entrepreneur.* Englewood Cliffs, NJ: Prentice-Hall, 1989.

Contrucci, Peg, *The Home Office: How To Set It Up, Operate It, and Make It Pay Off!* Englewood Cliffs, NJ: Prentice Hall, 1988.

Cornish, Clive G., *Basic Accounting for the Small Business*. Seattle: Self-Counsel, 1984.

Davidson, Jeffrey P., *Breathing Space: Living and Working at a Comfortable Pace in a Sped-Up Society*. New York: Master Media, 1991.

Davidson, Jeffrey P., *Marketing for the Home-Based Business*. Holbrook, MA: Bob Adams, Inc., 1990.

Davidson, Jeffrey P., *Marketing on a Shoestring*. New York: John Wiley & Sons, 1988.

Debelak, Don, *Total Marketing: Capturing Customers with Marketing Plans that Work*. Homewood, IL: BusinessOne Irwin, 1989.

Dudley, George W., and Shannon L., *The Psychology of Call Reluctance: How To Overcome the Fear of Self-Promotion*. Dallas: Behavioral Science Research Press, 1986.

Edwards, Paul, and Sarah Edwards, *Best Home Businesses For The 90s*. New York: Tarcher/Perigee, 1991.

Edwards, Paul, and Sarah Edwards, *Getting Business To Come To You*. New York: Tarcher/Perigee, 1991.

Edwards, Paul, and Sarah Edwards, *Making It On Your Own*. New York: Tarcher/Perigee, 1991.

Edwards, Paul, and Sarah Edwards, *Making Money With Your Computer At Home*. New York: Tarcher/Perigee, 1993.

Edwards, Paul, and Sarah Edwards, *Working From Home*. New York: Tarcher/Perigee, 1994.

Fleming, Lis, *Electronic Cottage No. 1: Running a Home Business with Your Computer*, rev. ed. Davis, CA: Fleming, Ltd., 1988.

Fleming, Lis, *The Electronic Cottage Handbook II: Making Money With Your Home Computer*, rev. ed. Davis, CA: Fleming, Ltd., 1989.

Fletcher, Jan, and Charlie Fletcher, eds., *Growing a Business — Raising a Family: Ideas and Inspiration for the Work-at-Home Parent*. Seattle: Next Step Publications, 1988.

Frohbieter-Mueller, Jo, *Your Home Business Can Make Dollars and Sense*. Radnor, PA: Chilton, 1990.

Gerber, Michael E., *The E Myth: Why Most Small Businesses Don't Work and What To Do About It*. New York: Harper, 1986.

Gillis, Phyllis, *Entrepreneurial Mothers*. New York: Rawson Associates, 1984.

Goldstein, Arnold S., *Starting on a Shoestring*. New York: John Wiley & Sons, 1988.

Golomb, Stan, *How To Find, Capture, and Keep Customers*. Atlantic City, NJ: Raphel Publishing, 1993.

Gray, Douglas A., *The Entrepreneur's Complete Self-Assessment Guide*. Seattle: Self Counsel, 1986.

Holmes F. Crouch, *Being Self-Employed*. Saratoga, CA: All Year Tax Guides, 1993.

Holtz, Herman, *The Complete Work-At-Home Companion*, 2nd ed. Rocklin, CA: 1994.

Hopkins, Tom, *How to Master the Art of Selling*. New York: Warner, 1988.

Hopkins, Tom, *Tom Hopkin's Guide To Greatness in Sales*. New York: Warner, 1993.

Kamoroff, Bernard, *Small Time Operator: How To Start Your Own Small Business, Keep Your Books, Pay Your Taxes & Stay Out Of Trouble!* 12th rev. ed. Laytonville, CA: BellSprings Publishing, 1992.

Kanarek, Lisa, *Organizing Your Home Office For Success*. New York: Penguin, 1993.

Kern, Caralee Smith, and Tammara Hoffman Wolfgram, *How To Run Your Own Home Business*. Lincolnwood, IL: VGM Career Horizons, 1992.

Lant, Jeffrey, *Cash Copy: How to Offer Your Products and Services So Your Prospects Buy Them ... Now!* Cambridge, MA: JLA Publications, 1989.

Lant, Jeffrey, *The Unabashed Self-Promoter's Guide*. Cambridge, MA: JLA Publications, 1992.

McQuown, Judith H., *Inc. Yourself: How To Profit By Setting Up Your Own Corporation.*, 6th ed. New York: Macmillan, 1988.

Melchinger, John H., *Developing Target Markets*. Southborough, MA: Educational Training Systems, n.d.

Nicholas, Ted, *How to Form Your Own Corporation Without a Lawyer for Under $50.00*. Wilmington, DE: Enterprise Publishing, 1981.

Olson, Nancy, *Starting a Mini-Business: A Guidebook for Seniors*. Sunnyvale, CA: Fair Oaks, 1988.

Perri, Colleen, *Entrepreneurial Women*. Kenosha, WI: Possibilities Publishing, 1987.

Phillips, Michael, and Salli Rasberry, *Marketing Without Advertising*. Laytonville, CA: In Business Bookshelf, 1986.

Pinson, Linda, and Jerry Jinnett, *Marketing: Researching and Reaching Your Target Market*. Fullerton, CA: Out of Your Mind, 1988.

Pinson, Linda, and Jerry Jinnett, *The Home-Based Entrepreneur*. Chicago: Dearborn, 1993.

Porter Henry, *Secrets of the Master Sellers*. New York: AMACOM, 1987.

Putman, Anthony O., *Marketing Your Services*. New York: John Wiley & Sons, 1990.

Rice, Frederick H., *Starting a Home Based Business*. Winoski, VT: University of Vermont, 1985.

Ries, Al, and Jack Trout, *Bottom-Up Marketing*. New York: McGraw-Hill, 1989.

Robbins, Anthony, *Awaken the Giant Within*. New York: Summit, 1991.

Withers, Jean, and Carol Vipperman, *Marketing Your Service*. Seattle: Self-Counsel, 1987.

Yoho, Dave, and Jeffrey P. Davidson, *How To Have a Good Year Every Year*. New York: Berkley, 1990.

Ziglar, Zig, *Zig Ziglar's Secrets of Closing the Sale*. Old Tappan, NJ: Fleming H. Revell, 1982.

388

Part-Time Travel Agent

More Resources For The Intrepid Traveler

As a service to our readers, we are pleased to be able to offer the following books for your consideration. All of the books listed are available at finer booksellers, or directly from The Intrepid Traveler. Complete instructions for ordering by mail will be found at the end of this section.

The Intrepid Traveler's Complete Desk Reference
By Sally Scanlon and Kelly Monaghan

Now that you have embarked on your exciting new lifestyle as a part-time, home-based travel agent, arm yourself with this indispensable reference work. *The Intrepid Traveler's Complete Desk Reference* will quickly allow you to become an old hand at making bookings and talking the language of the industry.

Among the invaluable job aids you will find in *The Intrepid Traveler's Complete Desk Reference* are:

- The three-letter locator codes of the world's airports that are used to make airline bookings. Look up the city name to get the airport code, or look up the code to find out which airport it identifies.
- The two-letter codes that identify the world's airlines, also used in bookings. In addition, you'll get the new three-letter airline codes the industry will be adopting.
- A much more extensive listing of supplier contact numbers than we had space for in this book.
- Visa requirements around the world.
- Time zones at a glance.
- Sources of FREE travel information, across the nation and around the world.
- A glossary of common (and obscure) travel industry terms, including hundreds of industry acronyms and the cryptic abbreviations used in CRS systems.
- And much, much more!

All the information you'll need to look like a pro. *The Intrepid Traveler's Complete Desk Reference* is one reference you'll use every day that your are in the travel agent business.

The Intrepid Traveler's Complete Desk Reference. Sally Scanlon and Kelly Monaghan. ©1994. $14.95.

❧   ❧   ❧

A Shopper's Guide To Outside Agent Opportunities
By Kelly Monaghan

There are a growing number of outfits offering you the chance to become a travel agent — overnight — and start reaping the many benefits available to the travel industry insider. But which one is right for you?

This Special Report, updated regularly, to keep on top of the ever-changing outside agent scene, provides straightforward, *unbiased* information about the current crop of offerings.

In this no-holds-barred Report, you will learn . . .
- How to evaluate an outside agent opportunity.
- What the glossy brochures *don't* tell you.
- How to find the best deals.
- The hard questions to ask before signing up with any company.
- Which companies charge *no sign-up fees whatsoever*. (And which ones charge the most)
- What you get from each company. And just as important, what you *don't* get.
- The truth about travel industry benefits and why many companies offering outside agent opportunities don't want to tell you about it.

Get past the hype and the salesmanship. Get the straight information from someone who's been there. This insider information — not available anywhere else — will save you weeks of time and let you narrow your search for an outside agent relationship that will work for you. It can also save you thousands of dollars in sign-up charges and annual fees.

A Shopper's Guide To Outside Agent Opportunities. **Kelly Monaghan. ©1994. $19.95.**

ℰ   ℰ   ℰ

Travel Agents: From Caravans & Clippers To The Concorde
Eric Freidheim

Long before Moses led his people to the Promised Land, people looked for aid and counsel in their travels. Now Eric Freidheim, editor-in-chief of *Travel Agent* magazine and a member of the Travel Hall of Fame, traces for the first time the development of a dynamic vocation and fills in the void in travel histories that has left untold the colorful and often dramatic story of how travel agents have helped build tourism into one of the largest global industries.

Here is the inside scoop on one of the world's most glamorous callings:
- Travel arrangements in Roman times.
- Counseling travelers from the Crusades to the Napoleonic era.
- Tour operators and travel agencies before Thomas Cook.
- How early American entrepreneurs developed the U.S. agency business.
- Rivalry between agents and guide book authors.
- How the first-ever pleasure cruise in America resulted in cannibalism.
- Travel scams of the nineteenth century.
- How women built the first major retail agency chain.
- The inside story on how ASTA, ARTA and other agency groups were formed.
- Where technology is taking the travel industry.

Here's what people have been saying about *Travel Agents: From Caravans & Clippers To The Concorde*:

"Fascinating! A true history of our industry."
    Earlene Causey, President
    American Society of Travel Agents (ASTA)

"Clear, well-written, and fun. Don't miss it!"
Stevan Troboff
Institute of Certified Travel Agents (ICTA)

Travel Agents: From Caravans & Clippers To The Concorde. **Eric Freidheim.**
©1994. $23.00 (hardcover)

❦   ❦   ❦

How To Get Paid $30,000 A Year To Travel (Without Selling Anything)
By Craig Chilton

Have you ever seen a Winnebago transported on the back of a truck? Or an ambulance? Or a hearse? A fire truck? Or a UPS truck? Chances are you never have.

Craig Chilton, author of *How To Get Paid $30,000 A Year To Travel (Without Selling Anything)*, will tell you why the delivery of recreational and specialty vehicles is America's greatest "sleeper" travel lifestyle. There are about 50,000 people throughout the USA and Canada who do this all the time, on a full-time or part-time basis, working for more than 1,000 manufacturers and transporter companies.

Here are some basic facts:

- In all states and provinces, all you need is an ordinary driver's license to deliver RVs. (Larger, specialty vehicles require a chauffeur's license.)
- All companies provide full insurance coverage for vehicle and their drivers.
- All vehicles are new, so they're covered by manufacturer's warranty in case of breakdown.
- Companies pay all road expenses and return transportation, apart from earnings. (Earnings normally are based on the number of miles driven per trip.)
- This lifestyle is nothing like trucking. No freight. Very few regulations. It's like getting paid to drive one's own car.
- College students (18 and over) are needed during the summer months to supplement the regular work force. They typically earn $8,000 to $12,000 during that season.
- Thirty percent of those living this lifestyle are retired people over age 65 who never worry about a "fixed income." (There's no upper age limit. As long as a person is a safe driver, he's in demand, due to his experience and maturity.)

Craig Chilton has appeared on more than 500 talk shows to inform the public about this profitable and fun lifestyle. *How To Get Paid $30,000 A Year To Travel (Without Selling Anything)* reveals Craig's system for maximizing this exciting lifestyle and lists more than 3,000 potential employers throughout the United States, Canada, Europe and Australia!

Who hasn't dreamed of getting paid to travel? Now you can find out how. A complete career system for just $24.95

How To Get Paid $30,000 A Year To Travel (Without Selling Anything). **Craig Chilton. ©1991. $24.95.**

The Insiders Guide To Air Courier Bargains:
How To Travel World-Wide For Next To Nothing
By Kelly Monaghan

How would you like to fly from New York to Paris for $199, round-trip? Or from Miami to Madrid for $99. Or from L.A. to Tokyo for free?

Sound impossible? It's not!

Every day, hundreds of people take off to exotic ports of call as air couriers. This sitting next to them on the plane have no idea of their "secret mission." They certainly don't know that the courier beside them paid only a fraction of the lowest available fare. In fact, the courier might even be flying **for free!**

An air courier is someone who accompanies time-sensitive cargo shipped as passengers' baggage on regularly scheduled airlines. Sometimes these people are employees of air freight companies. Most of the time, they are "freelancers," ordinary people — like you! — who perform a valuable service for the air freight company in exchange for a deep, deep discount on their round-trip air fare.

Being an air courier requires no training, no advanced degrees, no special knowledge of the air freight business. **Anyone can be an air courier.** All it takes is a yen for low-cost travel, a taste for adventure, and the right insider contacts — contacts that *The Insiders Guide To Air Courier Bargains* provides in abundance.

Who should be an air courier?

Being an air courier is not for everybody. You have to travel alone. (The book reveals exceptions to this rule and other strategies for bringing a friend along.) You will be limited to taking carry-on baggage only. (There are exceptions to this rule, too!) You must be flexible about departure dates and length of stay (usually a minimum of a week or a maximum of a month). Die hard couriers are even willing to be flexible about the destination to which they travel.

In exchange, you get the lowest imaginable fares. It's even possible, following the suggestions in *The Insiders Guide* to **fly absolutely free!**

Are you cut out to be an air courier? You might be if you are . . .

- *A student.* Or anyone else with time on their hands and not a lot of money. Students and other young people have a natural desire to see the world and the flexible schedules to take advantage of low-cost airline travel.

- *A senior citizen or retiree.* The 'golden years' no longer mean a rocking chair on a quiet porch. Today's active seniors are sought after by courier companies. Their reputation for promptness and reliability makes them especially desirable. Why not stretch those retirement dollars and indulge your taste for world travel?

- *A freelancer.* If you work on a freelance basis, we don't have to tell you how difficult it is to plan vacations. Just when you hope to get away, a big project comes in. The air courier option actually works in favor of the freelancer. The shorter the notice, the cheaper the fare. You can finish a project one day and fly out the next using the strategies revealed in *The Insiders Guide.*

- *A teacher.* If the new tax rules made you think you couldn't afford to travel abroad to hone your skills, think again.

- *An entrepreneur.* Like the freelancer, the entrepreneur cannot plan vacations months in advance. But entrepreneurs often want to explore overseas markets or scope out potential offshore suppliers and keep costs down. Many importers find air courier travel a dollar-saving strategy for exploring new opportunities or keeping in touch with existing contacts.

- *An enthusiast.* Are you a bicyclist who's dreamed of seeing the Tour de France? An opera buff who wants to visit La Scala? An arm-chair archaeologist who will never see Machu Picchu? Feel free to dream big dreams when you travel as an air courier.
- *Ready for a change.* Air courier bargains are designed for the solo traveler. Are you ready for a change of pace? Is it high time you got away, by yourself, to relax or think things over? A week alone on a foreign beach can work wonders!
- *A smart shopper.* Even if you don't have to pinch pennies, air courier travel can expand your travel horizons. After all the $500 (or more!) you save on air fare can pay for that luxury hotel you've always wanted to stay in but thought you could never afford! Or the same amount of money you budgeted for a weekend getaway could take you to Europe!
- *Adventurous.* Let's face it, "beating the system" is fun! Picking up the phone and saying, "I'm available. What's the next flight out?" can bring the kind of thrills that well-planned vacations never offer.

Here's what people have been saying about *The Insiders Guide To Air Courier Bargains* —

"An extraordinary value! The definitive book on the subject."
     Arthur Frommer

"There have been a number of books published on courier travel, but there is only one that's worth the money. That's *The Insiders Guide To Air Courier Bargains.*"
     The Shoestring Traveler newsletter

"As it is every taxpayer's obligation to research and pay the minimum amount of taxes legally required, it is every traveler's DUTY to read this book."
     Sandia Review of Books

"Everything you need to know."
     Travel & Leisure

"If you've ever dreamed of seeing the world but thought you could never afford to do it, this is the book for you!"
     Worldwide Investment News

"Had it not been for your book, I would never have known about getting on the list for further discounts or free travel. Thanks!"
     Fran P., Concord, CA

The Insiders Guide To Air Courier Bargains: How To Travel World-Wide For Next To Nothing, 1994 edition. Kelly Monaghan. ©1994. 240 pages. $14.95.

Note: This book is updated annually. If you have a copy of *The Insiders Guide To Air Courier Bargains* and it doesn't have this year's date on the cover, *you have an old edition!* Order your up-to-date edition today.

How To Get A Job With A Cruise Line
By Mary Fallon Miller

WANTED! Adults of all ages, backgrounds, skills, and talents. To fill broad range of positions in the booming cruise line industry. Successful applicants will enjoy adventure, travel, romance, and a steady paycheck!

If you have ever dreamed of running away to work on the Love Boat, you need this book. Mary Miller gives you the Insider's Advantage to getting hired. It's like having a relative in the cruise business.

How To Get A Job With A Cruise Line tells you precisely to whom, how, when, and where to apply. This book will save you hundreds of dollars, hours of wasted time, and endless frustration. Filled with insider's tips from successful people who are living the dream of working on cruise ships.

Here are just a few of the questions answered by this ground-breaking book:
* How do I get hired by a cruise line?
* How can I use my current skills?
* What are the different jobs like?
* What exciting places can I travel to?

If you want to work on the Love Boat (and who doesn't?), this book will give you the winning edge you need to beat the competition for those dream jobs!

The all-new, completely revised third edition contains the latest tips, techniques, policies, and contacts to make your cruise line job search a snap.

"Thanks! It's about time someone took the trouble to get the correct information to the public."

   Cheryl B. Clahr
   Director of Personnel, American Hawaiian Cruises

How To Get A Job With A Cruise Line, third edition. Mary F. Miller. ©1994. $14.95.

The Insider's Guide To Cruise Discounts
By Captain Bill Miller

ATTENTION! Couples, single travelers, honeymooners, wheelchair travelers, jetsetters: If you want to cruise aboard the best ships and play the lowest price — YOU NEED THIS BOOK!

Learn all the secrets you need to:
* Cruise on the best ships at the lowest prices.
* Get celebrity treatment on your next cruise.
* Buy travel at below wholesale prices.
* Qualify for deep, deep, last-minute discounts.
* Convince a reluctant spouse to cruise free.
* Cruise free!

The Insider's Guide To Cruise Discounts. Cpt. Bill Miller. ©1991. $12.95.

The Vacation Home Exchange and Hospitality Guide
By John Kimbrough

Discover a new world of affordable vacation travel! Say good-bye to over-priced, inadequate hotels by swapping homes with like-minded people throughout the world. John Kimbrough gives you a complete guides to . . .
- Vacation home exchanges — cost-free, with car swap.
- Hospitality exchanges — free or low-cost lodging, often with meals included.
- Bed-and-breakfast exchanges — at a fraction of the usual cost.

This is the most current listing of the many exchange clubs in the U.S., Canada, England, and around the world. You will learn . . .
- What each club has to offer and where.
- Which clubs are right for you.
- Each club's strengths and weaknesses.
- How to find the exchange you want.
- The easy way to go about making an exchange.

"Go for it! We have stayed in a 300-year-old fieldstone cottage in the Cotswolds, a remodeled manor house in Essex, an ultra-modern apartment in Bonn, and a comfortable chalet in Switzerland."
      D.B., Sacramento, CA.

The Vacation Home Exchange and Hospitality Guide. John Kimbrough. ©1991. $14.95.

❦   ❦   ❦

Special Reports from The Intrepid Traveler
The Intrepid Traveler releases a regular series of Special Reports containing, up-to-date, hard-to-get information about a variety of travel topics.

Consolidators: Air Travel's Bargain Basement
By Kelly Monaghan
In this Special Report, Kelly Monaghan unlocks the secrets of the world of "consolidators" and "bucket shops" — travel specialists who buy large blocks of seats from the airlines at deep discounts and then pass those savings on to you. The Report lists scores of consolidators across the U.S., both those who deal directly with the public and those you can work with through your travel agent.
      Learn how to . . .
- How to get "super-saver" fares, even when the "super-saver" deadline has passed!
- Find the consolidators that specialize in destinations to which you want to fly.
- Book by phone and receive your tickets in the mail.
- Protect yourself when dealing with consolidators.

Consolidators: Air Travel's Bargain Basement. Kelly Monaghan. ©1994. $4.00.

A Backstage Guide To New York's Theater Scene
By Kelly Monaghan

In this Special Report, former actor Kelly Monaghan brings an insider's perspective to the greatest theater town on earth. You'll learn how to . . .

- Get discount tickets — the day of performance or weeks ahead.
- Avoid the long lines at those half-price booths.
- Get tickets for "sold out" shows.
- Look like an insider and get backstage.
- Pick the best shows for celebrity spotting.
- Get a complete (and delicious!) dinner in the high-priced theater district for under $5.00!

A Backstage Guide To New York's Theater Scene. **Kelly Monaghan. ©1993. $4.00.**

❦   ❦   ❦

How to get books listed in the section

All of the books listed in this section are available directly from The Intrepid Traveler. It's easy to order. Here's how.

First, select the books you want and total their prices. New York State residents must add 8% tax to this amount. Next, figure the shipping and handling costs. For regular postage (Special 4th Class Book Rate) in the United States only, add $3.00 for the first book and $.50 for each additional book ordered. Add $.50 for each $4.00 Special Report ordered. For UPS delivery, add $4.00 for the first book and $1.00 for each additional book ordered. Remember that UPS can deliver only to street addresses (no Post Office boxes) in the continental United States. For foreign delivery, compute the regular postage, then add 10% of the cost of the books.

We can accept the following forms of payment: Checks drawn on a U.S. bank, U.S. money orders, and international postal money orders (for overseas orders). Foreign money orders (other than international postal money orders) *cannot* be accepted. Make your checks payable to "The Intrepid Traveler" and send to:

The Intrepid Traveler
P.O. Box 438
New York, NY 10034